BEARERS OF MEANING

BEARERS

"I have wished in this book to imitate the ancient writers of Comedy, some of whom when putting on a play sent on a messenger first, who explained in a few words what it would be about. Hence, having in this volume to deal with the five manners of building—that is, Tuscan, Doric, Ionic, Corinthian, and Composite—I decided that in the beginning would be seen the figures of each type that has to be discussed . . . to show a general rule at a single glance."
—*Serlio, Book IV*

Toscana
parti
.VI.

Proportione
quadrata

Dorica
parti
.VII.

Proportione
diagonea

Ionica
parti
.VIII.

Proportione
sesqui
altera

Corintha
parti
IX

Proportione
superbipartiens
tertias,

Composi
ta
parti
.X.

Proportione
dupla

OF MEANING

◆

The Classical
Orders in Antiquity,
the Middle Ages, and
the Renaissance

◆

JOHN ONIANS

◆

*. . . se non come determinatore,
almeno come motore . . .*

Francesco di Giorgio

PRINCETON UNIVERSITY PRESS ◆ PRINCETON, NEW JERSEY

Copyright © 1988 by Princeton University Press
Published by Princeton University Press,
41 William Street, Princeton, New Jersey 08540
In the United Kingdom: Princeton University Press,
Oxford

This book has been composed in Linotron Sabon

Clothbound editions of Princeton University Press books
are printed on acid-free paper, and binding materials
are chosen for strength and durability. Paperbacks,
although satisfactory for personal collections, are not
usually suitable for library rebinding

Printed in the United States of America
by Princeton University Press,
Princeton, New Jersey

*Library of Congress
Cataloging-in-Publication Data*
Onians, John, 1942–
Bearers of Meaning.
Bibliography: p.
Includes index.
1. Architecture—Orders. I. Title.
NA2815.O55 1988 729'.326 88–25510
ISBN 0–691–04043–5
ISBN 0–691–00219–3

First Princeton Paperback printing, 1990

10 9 8 7 6 5 4 3
10 9 8 7 6 5 4 3 2 1, pbk.

COLUMNAE MILLE
AEDES UNA
ELISABETHAE
DEDICATA

Contents

❖

Illustrations

✧

Acknowledgements

◆

Considering the importance of the Classical orders in the history of architecture and the substance of the theoretical writings about them, it is remarkable how little attention has been devoted to either. Many of the issues discussed here have never been treated extensively before. Those scholars who have directly addressed them stand out the more for their isolation, and their contributions have been a source of continuous inspiration. Most influential was Ernst Gombrich, who guided and encouraged the dissertation which was the first stage of this enquiry. He has lifted many veils, and his study of Giulio Romano fifty years ago at once revealed the mask-like character of the Renaissance façade and the complexity of the mind behind it. Also important were two others associated at some time with the Warburg Institute, Erwin Panofsky and Rudolf Wittkower. Their interpretations of Gothic and Renaissance architecture proved to be landmarks in the relation of style to intellectual context. Others were more directly forerunners in the present research. Erik Forssmann wrote two books which first demonstrated the richness of the history of the orders. John Summerson showed how the same subject could be handled more broadly and elegantly. Friedrich Deichmann started to decipher the colonnades of Early Christian churches. Alste Horn-Oncken revealed the mysteries of Vitruvian *decor*. Henry Millon demonstrated the value of the frequently fruitless attempt to relate theory to practice by his neat proof that it works for Francesco di Giorgio. James Ackerman revealed the tensions between *ars* and *scientia* not only for the builders of Milan Cathedral, but for Michelangelo and Palladio too. John Shearman, among his many other contributions, greatly enlarged the subject of Renaissance architecture by his studies of Raphael. More recently other scholars have done important work which contributes to the present study, particularly Howard Burns, Christoph Frommel, George Hersey, Volker Hoffmann, Joseph Rykwert, and Christof Thoenes. These have also shaped its development by their comments and criticisms—as have many others, chief among them my colleagues and students at the University of East Anglia.

Much of the research published here would have been impossible without travel grants from the University of East Anglia, and earlier from the Central Research Fund of London University and the Leverhulme Foundation. Preparation of the photographs would have been much less easy and enjoyable without the expert assistance of Michael Brandon-Jones. The drawings, an essential feature of this presentation, are the product of a long and rewarding collaboration with Don Johnson. The composition and editing of the text depended on the swiftness and accuracy of the typing of Joan Awbery and the word processing of Carole Leonard. Above all, I remember that the manuscript would not have come to Princeton if it had not been for the generous interest of the late Christine Ivusic, nor would it have improved so much in passage through the press without the alert editing of Eric Van Tassel.

Besides this material help, hospitality and essential backing have been provided by many institutions over the years since the project was first inspired by the twin muses of the Courtauld and Warburg Institutes. These include Syracuse University, the Kunsthistorisch Instituut of Amsterdam University, the Arizona Center for Medieval and Renaissance Studies and the University of Northern Arizona at Flagstaff, Mount Holyoke College, and the University of California at Los Angeles. The opportunity to bring the book to completion at the Center for Advanced Study in the Visual Arts in the National Gallery, Washington, surrounded by the many columns of that capital's buildings, provided me with the valuable reassurance that the Classical orders mean as much in the modern United States as they did in ancient Athens.

Beyond acknowledgement is all I owe to my father, Richard Broxton Onians, to my mother, Rosalind Lathbury, and to my family. With my wife, Elisabeth de Bièvre, I have walked and talked the length of this colonnade. Much of the life in this book is hers. Our two children, Isabelle and Charles, were often ahead of both of us in exploring behind columns.

Norwich, August 1985

BEARERS OF MEANING

Introduction

◆

BUILDINGS are as useful to our minds as they are to our bodies. Indeed, those elements which have the most important physical roles are also often the most important psychologically. This is why the posts, pillars, and columns which have assured people in many cultures of their buildings' structural stability have been just as critical in resolving other uncertainties and anxieties. This is also why we should not think of the Classical orders primarily as elegant solutions to a problem of structural design.

Before they were commended as Classical and before they were defined with legal precision as orders, the columns, capitals, and mouldings which we know as Tuscan, Doric, Ionic, Corinthian, and Composite were a material means of expression for communities, groups and individuals. Between their first appearance in ancient Greece and their eventual codification in Renaissance Italy, these forms were striking features of the buildings in which people in Western Europe formulated and developed their relationships to the gods, to each other, and to themselves; and it was often through their use that these relationships were articulated. The purpose of this study is to explore how this was done. In doing so it seeks to contribute to an understanding of the role of architecture in the formation of European culture and the European mind.

This book, then, is a history of these columnar forms before they became the Classical orders in the pages of Vignola's *Rule of the Five Orders* (1562). It thus concentrates not on the issues of their description and definition which so much occupied Vignola and most of his successors, but on the problems of how and why they were used in buildings and how and why they were discussed in texts. It is a history of the orders as forms, and it deals with their identification only when that is necessary to find out how they were thought about. It is a history which relies on two principal approaches: first, recording how the forms were employed, establishing patterns of usage, and suggesting reasons for those patterns; and, second, providing an account of what was said about the forms in texts, exploring the background to those observations, and analysing the intellectual framework in which they were developed. As far as possible, the two approaches are related in order to obtain a broad view of architecture as a field of both built practice and written theory. The relation between practice and theory is a persistent theme of the enquiry and has a particular importance because there are few (if any) fields of human activity for which the parallel records are so rich.

This does not mean that it is easy to relate buildings and texts. Even describing buildings is difficult, as there is rarely evidence that a particular form was called by a particular name. Indeed, throughout the book when names are used to identify forms this is done for convenience and should not be taken to imply that that was how the forms were named at the time. Even such distinct forms as capitals were probably more often referred to as "one of those" or perhaps "a simple one" or "a leafy one" than as Doric or Corinthian and so on. How they were in fact identified we can never know, since few records survive—whether in building contracts, letters, histories, or other documents—which make any reference to the forms here discussed. To judge by the general absence of any references to the orders in two thousand years of such literature, their choice was rarely the subject either of discussion or of formal agreement.

In this, architecture, like most fields of human action, will have been a realm in which actions—or for that matter reactions—were the result of complex thought processes, but thought processes which were neither formulated nor expressed in words. This will have been especially true of the actions of craftsmen and the reactions of most users of buildings; but it is also likely to have been true of the more educated architects and patrons. Even when it is argued in the following chapters that a particular use fitted the requirements of a patron or the expectations of a group of users, there should be no automatic presumption that the patron's or users' wishes had been communicated verbally. Successful architects and craftsmen, like successful employees and servants in general, succeed precisely by being able to internalize the requirements and expectations of their superiors. Since their experience of and response to architecture was basically the same as that of patrons and users, they could adjust their designs relying on this shared visual experience. Knowing in themselves how people normally responded to the design and placing of particular forms, they could also anticipate likely responses to changes in those features.

Since the notion of a shared visual experience is essential for explaining why there appears to have been so little need for the verbal discussion of choices which were so important, some attempt must be made to reconstruct it. This can best be done by reference to what can be inferred about the underlying mechanisms governing response to the visual environment. Whatever are the operations of the mind associated with vision, they must be such as would enable man and his ancestors better to survive, both in relation to the world as a hunter/gatherer and in relation to his own species as a social being. Those people will have been most likely to transmit their genes whose eyes were best adapted to survival in those two critical contexts.

Fundamental to survival in both would be an ability to process visual stimuli in such a way that significant variations in the environment would be immediately noted. This will have been true whether the person was a hunter looking for tracks, a gatherer looking for ripe fruit, or someone in a social context watching for a threatening or inviting gesture or expression. The mechanisms which enabled one of our ancestors to respond appropriately must have related to his or her typical experience of the world just as those characteristic of other animals related to theirs. As society developed and ornaments and clothing became important in the formulation of human relationships, the same mechanisms would have been involved. Or, rather, ornaments and clothes became important elements in the organization of social relationships precisely because the mechanisms of visual experience tended to predis-

pose people to see variations in such features as possibly critical for their welfare or survival. The same will have applied to architecture and the other visual arts as they emerged. Their power must have been founded on their tendency to trigger the same mechanisms. Not that all the arts will have worked in the same way. Architecture, for example, because of the similarity of built spaces to those found in woods and forests, would tend to evoke a response from the mechanisms most associated with movement through such environments. Indeed, buildings may well have preserved an assimilation to "arboreal" space precisely because the brain would react most readily to significant variations if that were so. Trees and woods have always had a special importance as at once the best source of food and the favorite haunt of enemies. The existence of an innate alertness to that natural context would help to explain the persistence of features such as tree-like columns and columnar shafts and the tendency to concentrate significant variation of ornament on areas such as capitals which occupied a position similar to that of the most significant features at the tops of tree trunks. The fact that a column was also man-like would have encouraged a similar persistence of the form and a similar concentration of significant variation in the head-like capital, where the eye would tend to be most alert to changes of expression. Since all people would inherit the same mechanisms, the same tendency to react to such variation in tree-like or man-like forms, the visual experience of all would be similar.

The shared experience of existing buildings would only reinforce and give further focus to such shared genetic predispositions. The situation with architecture would be similar to that with gesture and facial expression. Experiments with both animals and humans suggest that neurons in the cortex of the brain are genetically programmed to react to dangerous and important shapes, movements, and changes of colour—a sensitivity that may atrophy if never stimulated by such visual experiences, or may become increasingly sensitive if frequently triggered. The existence of a similarly variable relationship between stimulus and response in the context of architecture would explain one of the main conclusions of this book: that people at earlier periods appear to have been far more alert to the variations of architectural form discussed here than we are now. In the same way, a correspondence between reactions to variation of capital, etc. and reactions to variations of facial expression and gesture would prepare us for the observations in the final chapter that such variations in architecture were read as indices of variation of status and morality, character and emotion. For those are precisely the attributes which we are most used to expressing and finding expressed through modification of body and face.

One consequence of considering the visual experience of the architectural features described in the following chapters in this way is that it becomes even more important to treat the question of the reasons for their choice with considerable tact. If the reasons for such choices are like the reasons for our bodily gestures and facial expressions, this would help to explain why they were not verbally formulated and articulated. The reasons for those variations in our deportment are rarely expressed, chiefly because they communicate directly in their own terms. Our communication with each other visually is a self-sufficient activity parallel to verbal communication and with distinct advantages which are inherent in the more instinctive character both of the initial action and of the response to it. We feel we know the reasons for gestures and expressions without thinking about them. Our sense of what is going on is based only on genetic predispositions strengthened by previous experience of similar actions in similar contexts.

The reasons for the choice and placing of architectural forms to be presented here should be understood in the same way. They are based, like a hunter's expertise, above all on the author's accumulated experience of similar choices and placings in similar contexts. They should thus not be too readily accepted; but neither should they be rejected until the reader has built up a comparable experience. Since the reasons proposed for each individual building have been arrived at not just by analysing it internally but by comparing it with many others, the reader too will be well advised to go through the entire account before coming to conclusions about them. Ideally, indeed, readers should not make up their minds until they have visited the buildings themselves, where alone the forms can be fully experienced. For, in the end, the discussion of the use of the orders in practice seeks not to establish a

canon of knowledge but to reactivate now-dormant response mechanisms.

The parallel discussion of written theory raises quite different issues. While a study of practice presents us with the material results of actions unaccompanied by verbal reasons for them, a study of texts presents us with elaborate sets of verbal reasons and no physical actions. If the mechanisms involved in the generation of and response to the actions of practice are likely to relate to propensities which can be traced directly back to our animal origins, those involved in the generation of and response to verbal theory are as likely to be ones which emerged only in the last stages of our intellectual development. The latter are also likely to have tended to override the former. The experience of the environment would become less alert as architecture increasingly replaced nature in normal experience and as innate faculties were suppressed and overlaid by formal education. Those faculties involved in the response to theory, on the other hand, can only have become stronger as that same education fostered rational and self-conscious argument. The background to the formulation of and response to written theory is different from that which lies behind the formulation of and response to built practice and is often actually hostile to it. The power of architectural theory is greatest when it can replace the instinctive response with another. In this the relation between practice and theory in architecture is much like that in many other fields: from the most rudimentary situation where we offer someone a verbal excuse for some action they do not like to political propaganda on the large scale, the function of words is often precisely to persuade people that their spontaneous reaction is incorrect and that the real reason for what is happening to them is something other than that which they might naturally suppose. The recognition by governments and parents of the power of words to achieve this is a chief reason for their promotion of education and literacy.

A similar recognition led the architects discussed here to go to the trouble of writing so extensively on the subject. All were trying to demonstrate to potential patrons and especially to contemporary rulers that whatever the prevailing reactions to architectural forms might be they could be exploited and modified. From the time the orders were first given names which carried particular associations in ancient Greece there was a continuous attempt to replace the meaning inherent in forms, or rather naturally evoked by them, with meanings attached by words. Effectively, what theorists proposed to patrons was that the power of buildings to affect those who saw and used them could be brought under their control and used directly for their benefit. They did this by first identifying the values with which the patrons wanted to associate themselves publicly and then demonstrating that architecture could be made to embody or express them. Since the only patrons who would be worth addressing in written treatises were those who were educated enough to want to be thought so, the values exploited by all the writers were usually intellectually respectable ones already disseminated in more widely accepted texts from such fields as philosophy or theology, rhetoric or music. Each successive writer tried to offer a system of values which was more attractive to the patron or patrons he was addressing than any system already available.

The tradition of treatise writing thus develops largely independently of architectural practice, as each writer relates his formulations not to what happened in real buildings but to notions current in other forms of literature. Subsequently this separation of theory from practice was preserved as a result of the ultimately negative response of many patrons and their architects who sensed that however attractive were the ideas presented by the writers they had little to do with the reality of the way buildings affected those who saw and used them. Their own reactions must often have given the lie to the claims of theorists.

The generally cool response of Augustus to the first theorist, Vitruvius, was to be often repeated later. It was only in the Christian Middle Ages, with writers such as Hrabanus Maurus who were themselves patrons and were able to directly satisfy the need for a

new theoretical context for church building, that theory began to have a substantial impact on what happened in practice. Even at the Renaissance the influence of written theory is marginal until the sixteenth century. It was then at last, when education became an essential attribute of the powerful, that Serlio's treatise was able to seriously affect taste and shape responses to architecture first in Venice and then in Europe as a whole. Such was the power of the written word over the new educated elite that, for them at least, meanings which had earlier been sensed almost instinctively on the basis of experience could now be replaced by ones learned from texts.

This book, then, ends in sixteenth-century Italy, where the relation between theory and practice can be studied most fully and where the forms whose transformations and uses we have pursued finally become the orders. In a sense it ends where it should begin. For this is an account of the Classical orders only up to the time when they were recognized as such. The story of what happened afterwards and elsewhere is long and fascinating and is left for others to write. Nor is the account presented here anything like complete in itself. There are thousands of other buildings and many texts which must one day be taken into account. Some inconsistencies in the pattern of material dealt with are due to the hazards of the chase, as some texts or buildings seemed to give up their secrets sooner than others. Some omissions are deliberate, such as the decision to leave largely aside the vast body of Renaissance architectural drawings and the substantial number of editions of Vitruvius. Both of these categories of material, important in themselves, would have added further complexity to an already difficult subject. By concentrating on a limited series of buildings and a limited series of treatises, this work should make it easier for others to refine and expand what is only a partial and preliminary enquiry.

1. Lion Gate, Mycenae, fourteenth century B.C.

6

I

Classical Greece

◆

I saw the cornice
of the house collapsing, then the whole lofty roof
thrown to earth from its high posts.
One column alone was left . . .
of my ancestral home, and from its capital golden hair
streamed, and it took on a human voice. . . .
                                                    Now
thus I read my dream.
Dead is Orestes . . .
since the columns of a house are sons.
—Euripides, *Iphigeneia in Tauris*, lines 47–57

IPHIGENEIA'S dream, that the imminent destruction of a column representing her brother, Orestes, presaged the ruin of her ancestral house, hints at anxieties which have survived the centuries. For many people during the last two thousand years the passing of the standards represented ultimately by the Greek male and the Greek column would announce the collapse of Western culture. It is because Classical architecture seems literally to embody critical values that it has maintained its authority for most of that period. When we gaze on the columns of the Parthenon, built during Euripides' lifetime, we naturally see them as representing values and institutions on which our world is founded (Fig. 2). Euripides and his contemporaries probably already saw them in the same way. Indeed, Iphigeneia's dream may well have been inspired by his own feelings on visiting, or hearing about, the remains of her "ancestral house" at Mycenae, where a lone column carved above the portal was all that was left of a once great civilization (Fig. 1).

Marching orders

When Euripides and other Greek writers saw men as columns they did so because a colonnade had many of the properties they looked for in those on whom the safety of both home and state depended. The strength, erectness, and disciplined regularity of a row of columns were the qualities they most sought in the ranks of the army. The Greeks may well have dreamt of a phalanx which held together like a temple. The Euripidean image thus tells us how the Greeks viewed their youth. It also tells us how they viewed their buildings. If columns so clearly evoked the disciplined immovability which they looked for in their soldiers, it was as desirable that columns should follow a pattern of excellence as that the young men in the army should do the same. The emergence in the early sixth century B.C. of the two ways of building which we know as the Doric and Ionic orders implies the recognition of two such patterns. Indeed, what is true of many products of Greek civilization—epic and lyric poetry, history and philosophy, painting and sculpture—that they rapidly became paradigmatic first within Greece and then within Europe as a whole, is above all true of Greek architecture. Many factors contributed to the development of this feature within Greek culture generally, but in the case of architecture it was consistently reinforced by the recognition of the almost talismanic property of the column.

The exceptional standardization of Greek architecture cannot be over-emphasized. More than any earlier peoples the Greeks took care that all buildings of comparable status put up within a particular region should have similar plans, elevations, details, and even dimensions. Other cultures, in Egypt, Mesopotamia, Syria, and Asia Minor, had used similar architectural forms, and plan-types and column-types may show similarities within particular traditions; but in general their bases, capitals, and shafts as well as their ground plans were varied to suit the character of the deity, the nature of the site, and the taste of the patron. Even within a

2. Parthenon, Athens, 447–431 B.C.

single structure different columnar forms were often used. In the Greek world, which stretched over a vast area from Asia Minor to Italy and from Macedonia to North Africa, such variations were drastically reduced. For four hundred years from 600 to 200 B.C. the most important buildings—temples—had a similar plan consisting of a rectangular room surrounded by a row of tapered fluted columns. The principal distinction between buildings was only that between the two sets of forms which we now call Doric and Ionic. The former was used chiefly in Mainland Greece and the Western colonies, and the latter in the East, on the coast of Asia Minor, and on the Aegean islands (Figs. 3 and 4). Within an individual temple of either type all columns and capitals were usually exactly the same.

The reasons for this tendency to reduce temples to a stereotype are complex, but one is apparently very simple. A principal feature of Greek temples from the earliest times, particularly of Doric ones, is their incorporation of a hundred-foot measure. Many of the shrines of the eighth and seventh centuries which were still built of wood and mud brick were exactly a hundred

3. Temple of Apollo, Corinth, c.540 B.C.

feet long, for example those at Samos, Isthmia, Eretria, Olympia, and Thermon. The same measure appears in the temple of Hera at Olympia (Fig. 5) when it was rebuilt more robustly about 600 B.C., and in most of the early stone temples such as those of Artemis at Corcyra (c.590–580 B.C.), Apollo at Syracuse (c.565 B.C.), Apollo at Corinth (Fig. 3) and Hera at Paestum (both of around 540 B.C.), and it is still prominent in the greatest buildings of the following century such as the temple of Zeus at Olympia (c.470 B.C.) and the Parthenon at Athens (447–432 B.C.). The important change is only that the hundred-foot measure becomes embodied in ever smaller parts of the temple as the buildings as a whole become larger and larger. The importance of the measurement is borne out by the fact that a number of temples were actually known as *hek-atompeda* or hundred-foot buildings. This term perhaps suggests the reason for the number's importance, since already in Homer the most magnificent sacrifices were called "hecatombs" (that is, "of a hundred oxen"). If one hundred was the perfect number for a sacrifice, it could also be seen as the perfect number for a temple, which was also an offering to the deity. It is certainly the number rather than the measure which is important, since other temples incorporate the measure not of a hundred Dorian feet but of a hundred Ionian ells.

The persistence of the measure need not have been associated with a persistence of proportions and carved details, but it is. If we take a series of early stone temples again, the temples of Hera at Olympia, of Artemis at Corcyra, of Apollo at Syracuse, of Olympian Zeus

4. Temple of Artemis, Ephesus, mid-sixth century B.C.
(after Krischen)

and in those of later centuries to get progressively larger. There are also many minor refinements of proportions, adjustments in the spacing or size of corner columns, modifications to the profile and situation of mouldings and to the placing of relief sculpture in pediments and metopes; and these subtleties were to increase and become the glory of Greek architects. Otherwise individuality and inventiveness are conspicuously lacking; and this in spite of the fact that the buildings were constructed over a very wide area in a wide variety of religious, social, political, and economic contexts, in old cities in Greece and new colonies in the West, for tyrannies and oligarchies, in old cult centres and on new sites. In seeking to understand both the repetitiveness of the basic design of such temples and the consistency with which it is improved, we may turn to two features of the life of Mainland Greece and its Western colonies which stand out at this time as providing parallel cases. One is the concentration on trade in high-quality standardized products. Among the best examples are the vase forms for which Corinth was famous, with each individual *aryballos* or *hydria* resembling all others in its class. This stereotyping must have been stimulated by the pressures of international trade which meant that a buyer in Italy, for example, not being able to visit the workshop of the potter in Corinth, would simply ask for "more of those pots which went so well last year." The progressive modifications introduced all the time would result from the competition between suppliers as each tried to make his version of the object more attractive either in ornament or price without destroying its essential character. The area of popularity of the temple type matches that of Corinthian trade, and the wealthy tyrants and oligarchs seem to have ordered "one of those" just as they might have done with a pot. The builders, like the potters, did their best to satisfy their clients, keeping to the basic type while improving the details.

Another world in which repetition and improvement were both crucial was that of athletic competitions, the main form of communal cultural activity among the so-called Dorian peoples who formed the dominant classes in most of Mainland Greece and the Western colonies. At the Panhellenic meetings at Olympia every four years these Dorians came together to reaffirm that superiority in the athletic aspects of military training

at the same site (c.555 B.C.), of Apollo at Corinth (Fig. 3), and of Hera at Paestum (both of about 540 B.C.) all have similar proportions—6 × 16 columns, 8 × 17, 6 × 17, 6 × 17, 6 × 15, 9 × 18—and similar overall dimensions—19 × 50 metres, 23 × 49 m, 22 × 55 m, 22 × 62 m, 21 × 54 m, and 25 × 54 m. More remarkable still, they all use the same forms, the same upward tapering columns with concave flutes, the same capitals with a round echinus and a square abacus above, and the same entablature with a plain architrave below and a frieze above decorated with triglyphs and metopes, the whole crowned with a cornice which in most cases will have had the same mouldings. Never before had so much effort gone into making so many such similar structures. Variations are small, although there is a general tendency in the buildings listed above

which had initially enabled them to overrun the peninsula when they invaded from the North. In the games they displayed their excellence by competing in the execution of identical feats, running six hundred feet, jumping, and so on. By performing such an identical feat marginally faster or better than his rivals a young man could acquire greater fame than by any other act. Excellence, in other words, for the Dorian community was associated with the repetition of identical acts. There was no prize for inventing a new game. The establishment of the Doric temple type seems to depend on the influence of the temple of Hera at Olympia itself, and the people who commissioned the works were also often the same as those who attended the Olympic games: it is thus not surprising if they too sought excellence in the execution of an identical feat, treating the construction of a slightly longer hundred-foot temple as an equivalent to running the six-hundred-foot race a little faster.

The remarkable repetitiveness in overall scheme combined with a concentration on the modification of details which is an essential element in the emergence of stone architecture in Greece and its Western dependencies can thus be related to two features of life in the same area at the same period. In the other main region of the Greek world, the Aegean islands and the coast of Asia Minor, where the so-called Ionians were the dominant group or race, neither feature was so pronounced. Markets were more sophisticated and so there was less trade in stereotypes, while the softer urban way of life meant that athletic contests, such as the Olympic games, were a less appropriate focus of communal activity. Still, both features were present, and the first two large stone temples built in the area correspond to one another to a high degree. The first of these large temples was dedicated to Hera on the island of Samos around 570–560 B.C. and was built in limestone on a stylobate of about 52 × 95 m. Little has survived, but it probably had 8 columns on the front and 21 on the flanks, with a second complete row of columns inside that. We know much more of the temple of Artemis built soon afterwards (about 560–550 B.C.) at Ephesus on the Asiatic coast (Fig. 4). This was also dipteral (that is, with two rows of columns), again with 8 × 21 columns on the outside. Apart from its being slightly larger, at 55 × 115 m, the main new element was the use of marble throughout, a feature

found in most later Ionic shrines. As at Samos there were rich bases, and the capitals, which must also have been anticipated at Samos, had the cushion form with two curling volutes which later became the hallmark of the Ionic order. Around 530 B.C. the temple on Samos was burnt, and the tyrant Polycrates immediately began its successor. This was bigger again, at c.59 × c.115 m, with double or dipteral colonnades, 8 on the front and 24 on the flanks. Also about the same period the temple of Apollo at Didyma was rebuilt on a similar plan. These are the only large stone temples from the mid-sixth century in the eastern Aegean with extensive remains, apart from an isolated largely Doric example at Assos and some much smaller and poorer structures with leaf capitals from the area of ancient Aeolis. As a series they illustrate precisely the same repetition of type and progressive increase in dimensions which we found in the Doric West, and it is possible that the series started with the rebuilding of the temple of Hera on Samos as a deliberate response to the rising influence of the same divinity's shrine at Olympia. In both cases what was involved was the transformation of an existing relatively simple largely wooden building into a magnificent stone one.

Another important building type which illustrates the factors affecting the development of Greek architecture is the treasury. If the temple provided a vehicle for competition in each separate city, the treasury provided a means for bringing architectural competition back to the cult centres themselves. The rows of treasuries which were erected at Olympia and Delphi in the sixth and fifth centuries enabled individual cities to display the dedications and trophies which were the emblems of the wealth and success of their citizens. They were a particularly important form of expression for those cities which were too small to have a grand temple, or too remote for it to be well known if it existed. Olympia and Delphi, as the two most popular cult centres for all Greeks, provided the best sites for such monuments, while the fact that Olympia was a predominantly Dorian centre and Delphi the mainland centre where the Eastern Greeks were most at home encouraged different cities to concentrate on one type or the other, following regional loyalties. At Olympia (Fig. 5) all of the monotonous shrines or treasuries which are identifiable and of sixth-century date were constructed either by cities of the Greek Mainland,

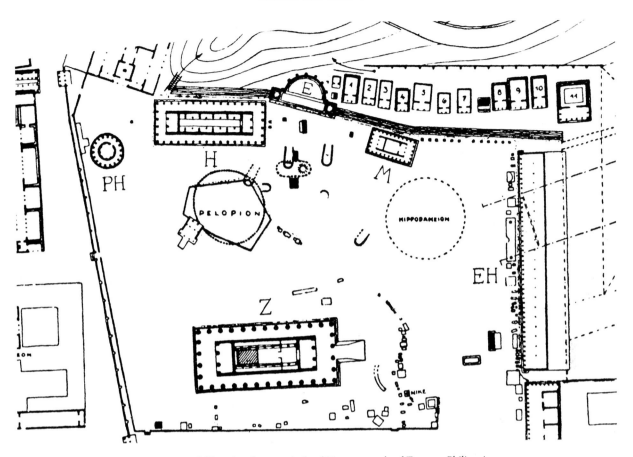

5. Sanctuary of Olympia, plan: H temple of Hera, Z temple of Zeus, PH Philippeion,
ST stadium, 1–11 Treasuries (after Dinsmoor)

such as Megara near Corinth, or by the Western colonies founded by such cities—the only exceptions being Cyrene in North Africa (still from the same cultural sphere) and the Megarian colony Byzantium on the Bosphorus. All employ elements found in the other Mainland and Western buildings, and the Treasury of Megara of about 510 B.C. is a good example of the full vocabulary. All these cities were Dorian, and it is clear that Olympia in the Dorian Peloponnese served as a focus for their loyalties and for architectural competition between them. Mainland cities also built treasuries at Delphi, but often they were communities either not so closely identified with the Dorian invaders, such as Sicyon, or actually opposed to them, such as Athens, traditionally the only major state in the peninsula not to have been overrun. Still, whatever their racial asso-

ciations they always used the local way of building, that is Doric, which was the order of the main temples at Delphi too. The only Ionian feature of the Treasury of Athens (c.510 B.C.) and the fronts of the temple of Apollo, paid for by the Athenian family of the Alcmaeonids, was the extensive use of marble which had strong Eastern associations; though the Eastern connections of late-sixth-century Attic patronage were more clearly visible in the contemporary plan to build a vast temple of Olympian Zeus at Athens itself, almost certainly using Ionian forms. Other treasuries at Delphi were more clearly Eastern in character (Fig. 6). Those of Cnidos and Siphnos, two communities in the southwest Aegean, of the mid- to late sixth century, make extensive use of the rich marble mouldings of the temples at Samos and Ephesus, although they substitute fe-

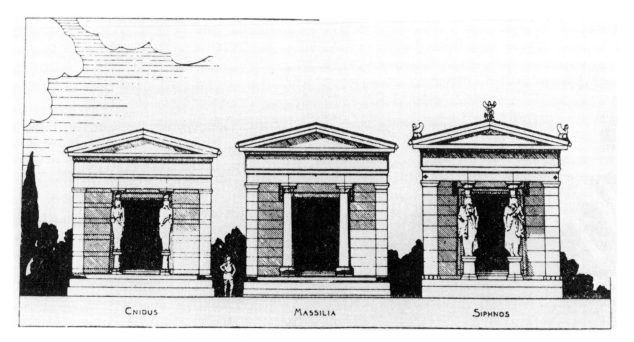

6. Treasuries at Delphi, all sixth century B.C. From left to right: Treasury of Cnidos,
Treasury of Massilia, and Treasury of Siphnos (after Dinsmoor)

male figures for columns with volute capitals. Two others with similar mouldings also indicate general Eastern loyalties, and the palm-leaf capitals of their columns probably are intended to assert an even more local pride. One is thought to be the Treasury of Clazomenae, halfway up the coast of Asia Minor, and the other that of Massilia (Marseilles), a colony of Phocaea, one of Clazomenae's neighbours (Figs. 6 and 15a). Both relate to the leaf capitals from the earlier sixth-century temples from the same area, ancient Aeolis. The only large monument at Delphi which used the true Ionic volute capital was the large marble column erected by the Aegean city of Naxos around 550 B.C.; but the general East Greek interest in the sanctuary is indisputable.

Architectural forms in the Greek world of the sixth century thus had primarily regional associations. The fact that the treasury of the Dorian colony Cnidos used what we call Ionic forms while that of the Athenians, who were racially more closely linked with the Ionians, used Doric ones shows that they had not yet acquired

the specifically racial identifications which their later names imply. This does not mean that the forms were still politically innocuous. They could already be used to assert ancestral loyalties as in the Massiliot Treasury. Moreover, the development of Olympia as a focus of an assertively Doric political unity enabled people to recognize the use of one set of forms rather than the

7. Capital from Throne of Apollo, Amyclae, later
sixth century B.C. (after Koldewey)

other as fundamentally divisive. Perhaps in acknowledgement of the dangers this implied, when the shrine of Apollo at Amyclae near Sparta was given a new and magnificent form in the latter half of the sixth century the architect Bathycles from Magnesia in Asia Minor invented capitals which cleverly combined the Western echinus with the Eastern volute, as if to symbolize Apollo's role as a unifying force in the Greek world (Fig. 7).

The fifth and fourth centuries: racial associations

The events which gave new and more precise significance to the two ways of building just described were the two great conflicts which dominated fifth-century Greece. The wars, first between Greece and Persia and then between Sparta and Athens, forced many Greeks to take sides as they had never done before, to formulate opinions that would justify their actions, and to analyze the causes underlying the conflicts in which they were involved. This whole process is perceptively documented by the writings of Herodotus and Thucydides. Among the fruits of this new self-consciousness are the insights into human behaviour which emerge first in the dramas of Aeschylus, Sophocles, Euripides, and Aristophanes, and then in the more abstract formulations of the dialogues of Plato. Plato's main concern was to establish the principles governing human behaviour and to provide guidance in the choice of actions. The problem of choice was essentially the same whether you were taking sides in the Persian wars or picking your pleasures in an Athenian street. It was also the same if you were deciding which way to build. But what gave architecture its particular importance in the new situation of conflict and choice was the way regional architectural habits became linked with political realities. When Persia pushed to the shores of the Aegean it was the Eastern Greeks, builders of marble temples with pretty volute capitals, who quickly surrendered to them, while it was the Greeks of the Mainland and the West, with their simpler limestone structures and austere disc capitals, who were in a position to resist. When Athens tried to build up a power base as the protector of the Eastern Greeks against the Persian enemy and provoked the Spartans to enter the field against her at the head of a Mainland and chiefly Do-

rian alliance, it became increasingly necessary for her citizens to reinforce their natural ancestral bond with their Eastern Ionian kin. In this divided world, while the majority of the Greeks still followed local conventions, the Athenians at least were faced with a delicate and even dangerous choice.

The first sign of a conscious change of architectural preference on the part of the Athenians is their erection of an Ionic stoa or portico at Delphi, in commemoration of a naval victory which has usually been connected with the campaign to liberate the Ionian cities after the battle of Salamis in 480 B.C. The earlier Athenian dedication at Delphi, the treasury probably built thirty years earlier, had still been Doric, although in marble. The use of Ionic for the stoa should probably be seen less as a proclamation of Athenian alienation from her Mainland neighbours than as a commemoration of the resurgence of Eastern Greece as a result of the victory of a combined Athenian and Ionian fleet over the Persians. Another Athenian gesture of friendship with the Eastern Greeks was the erection of a temple to Athena at Sunium, perhaps around 460 B.C. Placed on the easternmost tip of Attica, this structure, surrounded by Ionic columns on only its two seaward sides, was well calculated above all to make arriving Ionians feel at home. Otherwise Doric continued as the main order employed for Athenian buildings throughout the next fifty years, in buildings as diverse as the Hall of the Mysteries at Eleusis, the shrine of Nemesis at Rhamnous, the Theseum, the Stoa of Zeus in the Agora, and the two great structures on the Acropolis: the Parthenon (447–432 B.C.) and the Propylaea (438–432 B.C.). The Athenians had strong reasons for wishing to associate themselves primarily with Mainland culture. The contrast between the Ionians' surrender to the Persians and the Mainland Greeks' victory over them had greatly strengthened the self-confidence of all who lived in the peninsula itself. They now found themselves looking down on those Eastern neighbours who had, in the sixth century, been manifestly their superiors in wealth and intellectual vitality. Indeed, Herodotus, who although an Eastern Greek himself came from a Dorian city, could form the opinion that the Ionians were not even really Greeks[1] and could portray both the Athenians and the Ionians proper as ashamed of the Ionian name.[2] Small wonder, then, if the Athenians continued to favour the Mainland tradition.

Still, it was the Aegean Greeks who financed the Athenian empire by their payments of contributions for the maintenance of a fleet nominally intended to protect them from the Persians, and when the treasury of this confederacy was moved from Delos to the Acropolis in 454 B.C. and was used to rebuild its monuments, it was politic that the Ionians' tradition should also be acknowledged. This was particularly true in the case of the rear chamber of the Parthenon, which was probably always intended to house the confederacy's revenue, and it is virtually certain that its roof was supported on four Ionic columns. There can hardly have been structural reasons for the choice, since superimposed Doric columns would have served just as well, as they did in the main chamber. Ionic columns were also used for the inner colonnade of the otherwise Doric Propylaea, which was paid for out of the same funds. Other buildings—the Stoa Poikile, the Stoa of Zeus, the temple at Rhamnous, and the Theseum—incorporated Ionian features, but it was the Parthenon and the Propylaea that made the most assertive combination of Eastern and Western forms.

Indeed, both structures were central to Pericles' building programme, and it is tempting to see their combination of Doric and Ionic features as a direct expression of his Panhellenic ambitions, which were cultural as well as political.[3] These ambitions are most fully presented to us in the Funeral Oration which Thucydides puts into the Athenian leader's mouth in 430 B.C. at the outset of the Peloponnesian War which was to destroy his dreams. Athens, Pericles says, is a "school for the whole of Greece,"[4] and one of the main reasons for this is that, while the Spartans "pursue a manly character through their education by laborious training from the time they are young, ... we [the Athenians] pass our lives in a relaxed way and yet are no less ready to face equal dangers."[5] The same point about the Athenians combining opposed qualities is made in the famous claim that the Athenians "love beauty without extravagance and love wisdom but without softness."[6] This is a thinly veiled assertion that the Athenians have an interest in luxury and philosophy—the two things for which the Ionian cities were most famous—yet can still match the physical and moral capacities for which the Dorians were renowned. The correlation between the Periclean speech and the Periclean buildings makes it highly likely that

the two orders had by now acquired their names. It also makes it likely that the use of Doric for exteriors and Ionic for interiors was an appropriate expression of the ways of life of the two races, the one fond of manly exercise in the open and the other given to a gentler and more feminine indoor life. Both Thucydides and Aristophanes show how the confrontation between the Spartans and Athenians led to history being viewed increasingly in terms of a conflict between two racial communities with different attributes. Thucydides tells how the Dorians conquered the Peloponnese and sent out colonists to Sicily and Italy, while Athens colonized Ionia and most of the islands.[7] He also has the ambassador of Athens to Syracuse referring to the Athenians thus: "we who are Ionians, when considered with regard to the Peloponnesians who are Dorians ..."[8] The emphasis on the manly character of the Spartans is constant, and several remarks in Aristophanes make it clear that the Ionians were often thought of as effeminate.[9] Thucydides shows too how their manners of dress were thought to express the same opposition: the Athenians and the Ionians were the first to stop wearing armour and to adopt a luxurious way of life with delicate linen robes, while the Spartans not only adopted a much more restrained style of dress with little distinction between rich and poor, but also stripped naked for athletic training.[10] For the Athenian historian the oppositon between the cultures of Dorians and Ionians was fundamental and the Peloponnesian War its inevitable result, with the two aspects of the Greek personality, the physical and the intellectual, matched in an unequal contest. The Funeral Oration commemorates the end of Pericles' short-lived vision that the two could be united at Athens. The combination of the two orders in Periclean monuments, like his foundation of the Panhellenic colony of Thurii in southern Italy, reflects the aspirations of that brief period.

Pericles, still hoping that Athens might unite rather than divide the Greeks, was careful to balance the two orders. But after his death (429 B.C.), with the intensification of the Peloponnesian War the Athenians found themselves increasingly dependent on their Ionian allies. This led to a new public acknowledgement of their links with those peoples. Erechtheus, King of Attica, was claimed to have been grandfather of Ion, the ancestor of the Ionians, and Euripides wrote the play *Ion* to draw attention to this fact, while a new Ionic temple,

8 (at right). Erechtheum, Athens, 421–405 B.C.

9. Temple of Apollo Epikourios, Bassae, later
fifth century B.C. (after Krischen)

the Erechtheum (after 421–406 B.C.), was begun on the Acropolis (Fig. 8). Its site, once occupied by the palace of the Mycenean kings, had long contained shrines dedicated to different members of the royal house. The decision to build a magnificent new temple thus drew attention to Athens as the original centre of resistance to the Dorians, and since Erechtheus, the common ancestor of both Athenians and Ionians, figured prominently in its dedication, the temple also served as a monument to Attic-Ionian unity. The symbolic importance of the Erechtheum is confirmed by the tradition which always denied entry to it to Dorians.

Perhaps one last tribute to Pericles' hopes of Panhellenic unity was the isolated temple of Apollo at Bassae in the Peloponnese (Fig. 9). Possibly erected after the Plague of 429 B.C., which had carried off the great leader, it may have been designed by his favourite architect, Ictinus. Certainly it combined Doric and Ionic in an even more striking way than the latter's Parthenon. Its Doric exterior was balanced by an equally rich series of Ionic columns on the interior of the cella itself. In this it not only takes up the Periclean idea; it also makes an exactly similar appeal for unity to that made by the architect of the neighbouring shrine of Amyclaean Apollo a hundred years earlier. Now, however, the hope that Doric and Ionic could be fused has been replaced by an awareness that all that can be hoped for is peaceful co-existence.

Corinthian: a new life

The origins of the third Greek columnar form which by the time of Vitruvius would come to be recognized as an independent type—the Corinthian—is much more obscure, as indeed is the reason for its name. The first known capital, with a tall bell decorated with acanthus leaves and four volute forms at the corners, was one found by the excavators of the temple of Apollo at Bassae at the end of the cella next to the statue (Fig. 9). The capital itself was destroyed almost immediately, in mysterious circumstances, but it has been thought that it belonged to the central of the three terminal columns, and that similar capitals may have been used for the two flanking ones as well. Subsequently it was to reappear in slightly variant forms on the interior orders of the Great Tholos at Delphi of c.400 B.C., the temple of Athena Alea at Tegea of c.360 B.C., the Tholos of Epidarus of c.350 B.C., and the temple of Zeus at Nemea of about twenty years later. Its open forms suggest an origin in metalwork, and Callimachus, who is credited with its invention by Vitruvius, also made a bronze chimney in the form of a palm tree for the Erechtheum. Moreover, its similarity to the capital of the column shown supporting the statue of Nike in Phidias' Athena Parthenos and its use on a much-enlarged marble reproduction of a bronze offering table in the Choragic Monument of Lysicrates (after 334 B.C.) both imply a link with the decorative arts. Perhaps the strongest evidence for an origin in bronzeworking is the name Corinthian, for the Hellenistic texts which probably refer to the Corinthian capital call it *korinthiourgēs* ("of Corinthian workmanship"), a term normally applied to the bronze statues and furnishings for which that city was famous.

This, however, does not explain the form's emergence. Vitruvius' story was that Callimachus was inspired to invent the capital having seen an acanthus plant growing up through a basket on a girl's tomb, and it has recently been pointed out by Rykwert that the acanthus is indeed a plant associated with tombs in comtemporary vase paintings, and that many of the buildings listed above, especially Bassae and the two *tholoi*, can be seen to be connected with life and death.[11] It is true too that acanthus decorations figure prominently on a fourth-century Attic war memorial and were used on the funeral car of Alexander the

Great (323 B.C.),[12] while Corinthian capitals are found on a magnificent fourth-century tomb at Belevi in Asia Minor. It may also be noted that in a period when false etymologies were both popular and respectable, as Plato shows, the name acanthus may have been understood not so much as "point-flower" (*akē-anthos*) but as "healing flower" (*akein*, "to heal"). This would explain its first appearance in a temple specifically dedicated to Apollo the Healer and its exceptional popularity at the shrine of Asclepius the Healer at Epidaurus, where it is found in at least four major fourth-century structures, a number equalling its use at all other sites (Fig. 10). Since the associations of life/death and healing can be seen as cognate, both may have influenced the capital's invention and establishment. In a similar way, in the great fifth-century monument at Delphi the acanthus is associated with the Thyades, devotees of Dionysus, god of renewal.[13] Given the existence of this group of associations it is easy to understand why an acanthus capital is found particularly frequently both in buildings generally connected with life and death, such as Bassae and the *tholoi* at Delphi and Epidaurus, and in a structure connected with Dionysus, such as the Choragic monument of Lysicrates, designed to support a tripod won as a prize for a performance at the Dionysiac festival.

The other main feature of the early use of the Corinthian capital is its use exclusively for interiors (Fig. 10). The Monument of Lysicrates is no exception, since it is not a building at all but an enlarged offertory table. Otherwise the acanthus capital is always at first applied to the interiors of Doric buildings. That it is not used on exteriors is likely to be because it originated as a form of interior decoration, but its use on interiors can probably be understood in a more positive way. We have already suggested that it may have been thought natural to apply Ionic to interiors because of its inherent refinement and its association with the effeminate Ionians. The simple austerity of Doric on the other hand was associated with exteriors because the manly Dorian virtues were normally displayed outdoors, in battle and in athletic contests. In Antiquity the male was generally connected with the outdoors and the female with the indoor life, as is evident from the convention which the Greeks inherited from the Egyptians of representing men as brown-skinned and women as white. Once the different associations of the

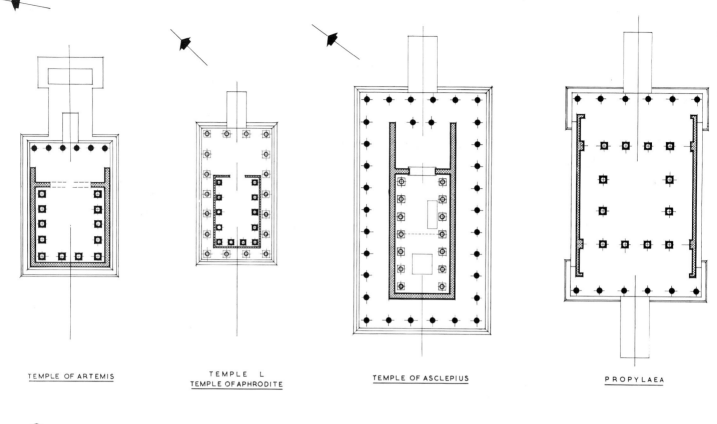

TEMPLE OF ARTEMIS

TEMPLE L
TEMPLE OF APHRODITE

TEMPLE OF ASCLEPIUS

PROPYLAEA

 — DORIC

— IONIC

— CORINTHIAN

10. Sanctuary of Epidaurus, plans of buildings of the fourth century B.C.,
showing arrangements of orders. From left to right: temple of Artemis;
temple L (Aphrodite); temple of Asclepius; Propylaea

interior and the exterior had been recognized and had been given architectural expression by the Athenians, it must have been an easy step for the Dorians to wish to make the same distinction without introducing the alien Ionian element and so to adopt the pretty new acanthus capital, free of racial overtones, as suited to their purpose. The use of Corinthian for the interiors of a whole series of Peloponnesian buildings would thus correspond to the Athenians' use of Ionic. This correspondence may also explain the establishment of the epithet "Corinthian." Corinth was the Dorian city which, above all others, was identified (in the same way as Ionia) with urban values, trade, craftsmanship, sensual luxury, and femininity—"Corinthian girl" being an accepted term for prostitute. Corinthian thus seems

to have become recognized as a rich interior order in which, essentially, an acanthus capital replaced the typically Ionic volute form, while the Ionic base form, fluted shaft, and entablature—being much less emphatically identified with racial qualities—were retained. It is, indeed, a general rule that from now on capital forms become increasingly important for the differentiation of the orders, and that all the other elements of the complete building systems which Doric and Ionic originally constituted are differentiated less and less clearly.

The first monument in which Corinthian is combined with Ionic alone is the Philippeion, a round structure at Olympia begun by Philip of Macedon after his victory at the battle of Chaeronaea (338 B.C.),

11. Philippeion, Olympia, c.330 B.C. (cf. Fig. 5, PH) (after Dörpfeld)

which established his dominance in the Greek peninsula (Fig. 11). As a circular monument, evoking the earlier *tholoi* with their underworld associations, and housing statues of the Macedonian royal family, it was evidently a dynastic memorial. It shares with earlier *tholoi* an inner Corinthian order, here in the form of half-columns. The outer ring, however, is no longer Doric but Ionic. This innovation may just reflect the choice of an Ionian architect, but if the above characterization of Ionic and Corinthian is correct, it is more likely to be intended as an assertive statement on the part of Philip that, far from being a half-barbarian, less civilized than the Greeks he conquered, he was more civilized—certainly more so than the Dorians. Besides combining the two most refined architectural forms,

Ionic from East Greece and Corinthian from the Mainland, the Philippeion also significantly combined for the first time the Attic Ionic frieze and Eastern Ionic dentils within the Ionic entablature. The combination not only of the two most refined orders but also of the two most refined frieze decorations presented Philip as someone who identified himself with the least barbaric elements of the Greek tradition, and someone more genuinely Panhellenic than any of the true Greeks. He thus effectively countered the Greek view of him as a crude savage, and by erecting such an elegant structure at the great centre of Greek national life he even returned the compliment.

The situation of the building made it eminently susceptible to such an interpretation. Built opposite the

Pelopion, shrine of the eponymous ancient ruler of the Peloponnese (which had recently acquired a grand Doric portico), and adjoining the long row of Doric treasuries, it emphatically affirmed Philip's claim to have begun a new period with new values (Fig. 5). Since his son Alexander, who completed the structure, was exceptionally well educated, having been taught by Aristotle, the claim was not an unrealistic one; and Alexander's civilizing mission throughout the East, with urbanization as the key to its policy, proved the justice of his ambitions. When Alexander himself died, his funeral car also combined Ionic and Corinthian elements in its canopy supported by four Ionic columns decorated by acanthus stalks.[14]

Alexander's death in 323 B.C. left the entire eastern Mediterranean in Greek hands. By then Doric and Ionic, which had started off just as regional forms, and Corinthian, which probably began as a form associated with death, immortality, and healing, had acquired secondary and even tertiary associations. Thus Doric and Ionic had first been given specific racial associations and subsequently, as the Dorian and Ionian groupings came increasingly to be identified with particular characteristics and values, they took these on too. Doric came to be the order of the outdoors and of physical simplicity, and Ionic the order of the indoors and intellectual refinement. Corinthian, for the Dorians at least, had also come to represent interior refinement, and to judge by the Philippeion, it was thought to be if anything more emblematic of these qualities.

II

The Hellenistic world and the Roman Republic

❖

Different classes and different activities

ALEXANDER'S conquest of a large part of Asia and of Egypt dramatically enlarged the area in which the forms of Greek architecture could be found. It also brought a sudden increase in the wealth of at least the ruling and commercial classes of the Hellenistic world, which produced a permanent shift of architectural patronage from the religious to the secular sphere. Both factors led to an enormous increase in the number of buildings using Doric, Ionic, and Corinthian forms. At the same time, the confusion resulting from the greatly increased mobility of both architects and patrons and the greater likelihood of purely random factors influencing the choice of forms made it much more difficult to establish patterns of usage. By the time Greek forms were taken over by the Romans in the second and first centuries, they had become even more isolated from their cultural context, and the way they were used depended even more on the whim of the patron or the origin of the architect.

The overall picture, however, is fairly distinct. Doric declines in importance: it is used less and less for major temples and becomes typically the order of minor buildings such as the stoas which increasingly border the agoras of Hellenistic cities and the courts of gymnasia and private houses. Ionic, on the other hand, appears in a whole series of enormous and opulent late-fourth-century temples in Asia Minor—Athena Polias at Priene, Apollo at Didyma, and Artemis at Sardis—and notable later structures at Sminthe in the Troad, Magnesia on the Maeander, and Teos. In stoas it is found almost exclusively on the upper and inner colonnades, while Doric is confined to the more common and accessible lower and outer ones.[1] This consolidation of the relative importance of the orders is only reinforced by the economic decline of Mainland Greece and the rise of Ionian fortunes after centuries of Persian domination. Nevertheless it is counterbalanced by a limited spread of Doric across the Aegean for some sacred structures. A striking example is the Hieron on Samothrace, built in the third century and actually replacing an Ionic structure. Another is the temple of Athena at Pergamum, also probably of the third century, when the use of Doric is in contrast to the earlier Ionic temple of a similar dedication at Priene farther down the coast. These buildings may represent isolated assertions of the essential dominance of Doric as the only true Greek order, in the same spirit as Plato's opinion that Dorian was the only truly Greek musical mode.[2] The rulers of Pergamum, at least, were well known for their desire to revive and renew earlier Greek artistic traditions as a matter of state propaganda. Corinthian continues as primarily an interior order, as in the Arsinoeion of Samothrace of the early third century, where it is combined with a Doric exterior. It also slowly emerges to greater prominence, being used for a great fourth-century mausoleum at Belevi near Miletus, perhaps for its funerary associations, and finally achieving the highest status with its application to one of the largest Greek temples, that of Zeus Olympius at Athens, begun in 175 B.C. (Fig. 12).

The use of a single column-type in an individual building can never tell us as much about attitudes to the orders as those cases where two or three types are used together. In these we can infer reasons why one

12. Temple of Zeus Olympius, Athens, begun 175 B.C.

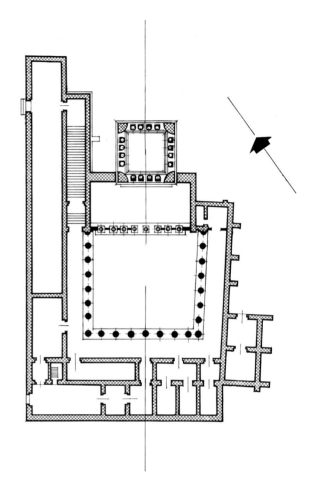

order may be employed in one part of a building and a different order in another part. When patterns of usage recur, we can establish a currency of architectural values. The buildings mentioned so far have been chiefly single-function, and so almost the only secure values we have been able to establish are those which distinguish interiors from exteriors.[3] By the second century, on the other hand, elaborate architectural forms were applied to a whole series of multiple-function structures, making it possible to establish values of a more complex kind (Fig. 13). Typical are the gymnasia at Priene and Miletus. At Priene the Lower Gymnasium has a large court for athletic exercises surrounded by Doric columns. Behind these on the north side is an interior row of Ionic columns leading into the lecture room or *ephēbeion*, which has windows framed in the Corinthian order. At Miletus only three sides of the court are Doric, but the entrance propylon on the south and the whole north side are Ionic; the *ephēbeion*, also on the north side, has even more Corinthian features than at Priene. Also at Miletus, the Bouleuterion or council house of about 170 B.C. has a somewhat simi-

lar arrangement, but here both the entrance propylon and a shrine in the middle of the court are Corinthian; the court itself is Doric, as is the wall decoration both inside and outside the council house itself, but the columns which support its roof are Ionic. In this case the propylon is apparently a prelude to the shrine, a structure which appears to be Roman in its surviving form but which probably replaced a Hellenistic predecessor. Another Corinthian shrine which in its present form is a Roman refurbishing of a Hellenistic structure is the cult room of the Heroön at Pergamum, a building which otherwise repeats the arrangement of the gymnasia at Priene and Miletus, being entered from an

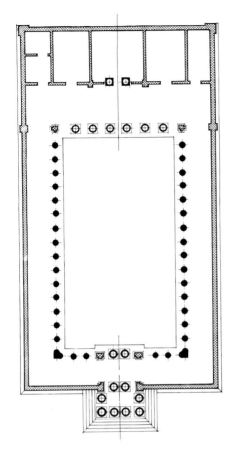

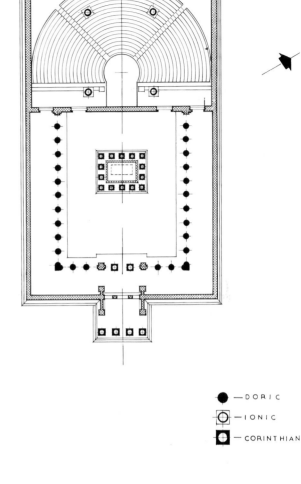

13. Plans of buildings of the second century B.C., showing arrangements of orders. From left to right: Heroön, Pergamum; Gymnasium, Miletus; Bouleuterion, Miletus

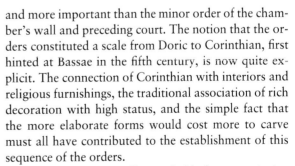

● — DORIC
⊕ — IONIC
▣ — CORINTHIAN

Ionic portico which is itself preceded by a Doric court (Fig. 13).

These monuments provide enough variety and at the same time enough consistency to enable us to establish certain principles. The most important rooms, whether shrines or lecture rooms, which often also served as cult places, are Corinthian. The least important areas, the open courts, are Doric. Ionic occupies an intermediate role; this is most obvious when it appears on one side of an otherwise Doric court as an introduction to a Corinthian room and also when, in the Bouleuterion at Miletus, it is used as the main order of the council chamber itself, which is less important than the shrine and more important than the minor order of the chamber's wall and preceding court. The notion that the orders constituted a scale from Doric to Corinthian, first hinted at Bassae in the fifth century, is now quite explicit. The connection of Corinthian with interiors and religious furnishings, the traditional association of rich decoration with high status, and the simple fact that the more elaborate forms would cost more to carve must all have contributed to the establishment of this sequence of the orders.

These buildings are all remarkable for a new insistence on the importance of differentiation. Earlier, such differentiation was normally exploited in buildings for gods and kings where differences of status could be enormous and critical, not in buildings such as gymnasia where the range in the status of those who used them, or in their activities, would be relatively small. The new architectural differentiation within these Hellenistic buildings reflects the general comtemporary fascination with differences of a much more subtle character than the traditional broad horizons of rank. These are most clearly developed in the writings of Aristotle, but are manifest at all levels of Hellenistic art and literature. Many of them originate in the opposition between Spartans and Athenians, such as the difference between those people who concentrated on the use of the body and those who concentrated on the use of the brain, or the difference between a fondness for outdoor and one for indoor activities. Others are more the fruit of intellectual analysis, such as Aristotle's observation in the *Politics* that within the citizen body there are three classes of people, the *euporoi* (people with ample resources), the *mesoi* (middling people), and the *aporoi* (people lacking in resources).[4] A realization that people and their activities could be differentiated in all these different ways, along with the observation that there were different types of oratory appropriate to different contexts and different types of music for different moods, reflected a new understanding of the varied order of the world. The harmony of society was seen to be based on a balance between polarities—between people who were poor and people who were rich, people who used their bodies and people who used their heads, people who worked outside and people who worked inside. The same co-existence of differences was seen to be necessary to the harmony of the individual, who should develop both his body and his mind. It was this last interest in the different functions of the human male which led to the institutional importance of the gymnasium as a combination of exercise ground and lecture hall. As it came to be recognized that wealth, intellectual pursuits, and indoor activity often went together just as did poverty, manual labour, and outdoor life, the richer forms of Corinthian could appropriately be used in the lecture rooms and the poorer forms of Doric for the exercise courts, while Ionic could serve to smooth the transition. Then too, since increasing value attached to the first three associations—wealth, intellect, and the in-

doors—Corinthian became increasingly linked with higher absolute status, as in the cult buildings of the Heroön at Pergamum and the Bouleuterion of Miletus, where its use parallels that in the great temple of Zeus at Athens. The importance of the differentiation of architectural environments within a single complex is a direct reflection of current attitudes to the necessary divisions both within society and within the individual.

The other main building type in which a similar architectural differentiation is found at the same period of the second century is the stoa. In the grandest two-storey stoas with two colonnades in each storey, most notably in the Stoa of Attalus at Athens, the traditional combination of a Doric outer order with an Ionic inner one is extended on the upper floor by having a more refined Ionic order in the front and a new type of capital with tall-leaf decoration behind. This produces a progressive increase in richness from fluted Doric to unfluted Ionic below, to fluted Ionic, and finally to unfluted shaft with elaborate leaf capital above. Since there are enough earlier examples of Doric behind Doric and Doric above Doric to prove that this particular combination was not necessitated either aesthetically or structurally, as has often been suggested, it would seem probable that the series is intended to articulate the progressive change from a very public outside space below to a more private upper space above and behind. The further an order is from the public space, both horizontally and vertically, the more ornate it is. We do not know exactly what went on on the upper floors of stoas, but it is likely to have been business of a more private and exclusive character than that carried on below. Vitruvius, describing the similar upper galleries of Roman basilicas, emphasizes the need to conceal those above from those in the open space below.[5] All this would confirm what we might have inferred from the other types of buildings, that Greeks were increasingly coming to acknowledge the "exclusive" (and hence superior) associations of interiors when compared with the more "common" and accessible exteriors. In a wide range of Hellenistic buildings, from cult buildings to gymnasia to stoas, movement through a building was apparently seen as a movement from lower to higher activities accompanied by a continuous crescendo of architectural ornament.

14. Sanctuary of Athena, Pergamum: section of stoa,
late third century B.C. (after Conze)

Local traditions, local values

There was not, however, uniform agreement on the relative status of different activities. The Dorians were naturally reluctant to surrender their ancient values. There is thus almost a manifesto attaching to the character of the boat constructed by Hiero II, King of Dorian Syracuse, in the later third century.[6] The boat was surrounded on the outside with *atlantes*, that is giant male figures like those used earlier on the Doric Olympieum at Acragas, bearing an entablature decorated with triglyphs. The forms were emphatically Dorian and were directly identifiable with the heroic past when the Sicilian Greeks had defeated the Carthaginians. A poem inscribed on the boat told how the giants had made it to sail the paths of heaven, while large letters on the prow acclaimed its builder as "Hiero the Dorian." The inclusion of a gymnasium in the interior along with the use of giants on the exterior would fit with virile Dorian interests, as also would the mosaic floors showing scenes from the *Iliad*. The notion that the boat functioned as a manifesto is confirmed by its being sent as a gift to Ptolemy IV of Alexandria. Not only were the Ptolemies lovers of indoor pursuits both intellectual and sensual, but Ptolemy also had a great river boat—in effect a floating palace—designed to accommodate such pursuits.[7] Instead of a gymnasium it had a symposium or drinking room, and with its scented cedar woodwork, its gold, and its varied marbles, it formed the greatest possible contrast to Hiero's vessel. The only Greek order mentioned in the surviving description is Corinthian, which was used for the columns of the main room or *oikos*. The Corinthian interior thus matched Ptolemy's values as closely as the Doric exterior of the Syracusan boat did those of Hiero. One boat may well have been intended as a comment on the other, but we do not know which came first. The next most important room on Ptolemy's boat was built, according to the text, "in the Egyptian manner"—that is, with columns whose capitals were shaped like rose blossoms and decorated with lotus flowers and palm blooms. Perhaps the similarity between the Corinthian capital with its tall and highly ornamented bell shape and ancient Egyptian forms encouraged the juxtaposition of the two types as emblems at once of the diversity and the unity of the two cultures. Certainly the use of ancient Egyptian forms must have been as much intended to assert a claim to the inheritance of earlier local tradition as was the row of *atlantes* on Hiero's vessel.

A similar and even more artificial revival of local forms is also found in Pergamene monuments. The tall leaf capitals referred to earlier found in stoas at Pergamum and Athens, both of which were Pergamene royal commissions, are clearly adapted from the leaf forms associated with the same area three hundred years earlier, as in the Treasury of Massilia (Fig. 15). There is even a possibility that the capital type was specifically recognized as Aeolic, since Aeolis was the ancient name of the region. If so it would have been particularly ap-

propriate to introduce the capital in the stoa of the Athena sanctuary at Pergamum, which also housed the famous Pergamene library (Fig. 14). If its capitals were thought of as Doric, Ionic, and Aeolic, they would have neatly epitomized the three basic dialects of the Greek literature which were stored inside, thus expressing the Pergamene rulers' inheritance of the Greek tradition in its entirety. Whether or not this was so, the site of the portico with a library behind and trophy reliefs in front was a suitable place to combine refined interior columns and more austere outer ones: the "Aeolic" leaf capitals would have shown a respect for indoor, the plain Doric for outdoor, activities. Like the Athenians, the Pergamenes could claim that their patroness Athena herself had a taste for both intellectual and military pursuits. Just as the Athenians could claim to combine the qualities of contemporary Dorians and Ionians, so the rulers of Pergamum could seek to combine those claimed by the rulers of Syracuse and Alexandria. The rulers of all three Hellenistic cities could use architecture, and particularly the choice of column and capital, to assert links with ancient traditions.

The Roman Republic: from ignorance to anarchy

Among the Greek communities of southern Italy the sense of such traditions had never been very strong. Colonies there might be Dorian, Ionian, or Aeolian. Pericles' Thurii was intentionally Panhellenic. Populations tended to become mixed, and so did architectural forms. In Etruria to the north, the confusion was even greater, with Greek capital types being supplemented by those of Levantine origin. Rome, situated between the two cultural areas, was destined to be enriched by both, especially after she achieved total dominance in the third century B.C.; though in general early Etruscan influences were replaced by more powerful Greek ones. Thus the temple of Jupiter on the Capitol probably originally employed the simple timber forms with plain round capitals which Vitruvius was to call Tuscan, but the stone temples which survive from Rome and the surrounding areas from before 80 B.C. can be recognized as Doric, Ionic, or Corinthian. Only rarely in this period is there an obvious reason why one order rather than another was chosen. One example is the Basilica

15. Aeolic capitals from: left (a) the Treasury of Massilia, Delphi (cf. Fig. 6); right (b) the Stoa of Athena, Pergamum (after Coulton)

16. Basilica, Pompeii, interior, c.120 B.C.

at Pompeii of c.120 B.C. (Fig. 16). There the main hall was supported on giant Ionic columns with a smaller order of Ionic half-columns in the surrounding aisle. These, however, changed to Corinthian full columns at one end, where a two-storey pedimented portico marked an elevated tribunal. The Corinthian order, the free-standing columns, and the pediment all assert the distinction between the lofty activity of the administra-

tion of justice and the commercial business which would fill the rest of the space. Both sets of forms contrast with the exterior of the slightly later amphitheatre in the same city (Fig. 17). This was surrounded by a row of plain arches supported on rectangular piers, and was built of rubble-faced concrete instead of the basilica's stuccoed brick. The Romans were already taking up and extending the principles of differentia-

17. Amphitheatre, Pompeii, c.80 B.C.

tion found in the Hellenistic world. Sulla's conquest of Greece in 86 B.C. only encouraged this development, and it was an awareness of current Greek values which made Sulla himself want to replace the primitive timber columns of the temple of Jupiter on the Capitoline, the most important of the Roman world, with marble Corinthian shafts from the temple of Zeus Olympius at Athens (Fig. 12).[8] The same awareness also influenced

his lieutenant Catulus when he constructed a new Tabularium or Record Office close by. The surviving floor of this structure employs Doric half-columns of tufa and travertine, attached to a massive concrete-vaulted arcade (Fig. 46).

These buildings apply Hellenistic principles of differentiation, but they do so much more thoroughly than their Greek models. The greater richness of the Roman structural vocabulary which exploited piers and arches as readily as columns and entablatures enabled the contrast between elegance and strength to be made much more forcibly. From now on the opposition between slender column and massive square pier, often with attached half-column, would be as decisive for the definition of relative status as the different column-types had been for the Greeks. A scale of structural forms from strong to weak was now added alongside the scale of ornament from simple to rich. It had always been possible to regard the stumpier Doric forms as stronger than the more attenuated Ionic and Corinthian, but the new range of structural forms made the distinction fundamental. At the same time yet another range of alternatives was introduced—that of materials. In Greece the ready availability of marble and, failing that, of fine limestone had meant that monumental buildings were generally built of materials which were similar in appearance or structural properties. In Italy on the other hand, the simplest material, rough concrete, contrasted dramatically in all its properties with the most refined, polished marble, while between these poles came grey tufa and white but still coarse travertine. Even in marble alone, by the time of Augustus there was an increasingly wide range available, from plain white from Carrara to imported varieties which might be both figured and coloured. Since the materials at the top of the scale were both the most expensive and the strongest, it was inevitable that they should be used for the highest-status buildings, especially temples, and for those parts of buildings where concentrated strength was most important, the columns and entablatures. In the same way, those materials at the bottom of the scale could most naturally be used for structures or parts of structures where strength could be achieved by massive construction and where cost was a limiting factor, as in the podia and walls of temples and most characteristically the piers, arches, and vaults of utilitarian secular buildings. If desired, the poorer materials could also be faced with stucco or marble to combine economy with elegance. Buildings of the first century B.C. could thus be as clearly differentiated by their materials as by their structural forms or their orders. Often the three scales were combined under the pressures of cost, structural necessity, and convention. Many first-century B.C. secular arcades have an attached order of Doric, with

18. Temple of Fortuna Virilis (travertine) and round temple by the Tiber (marble), Rome, late second and early first century B.C.

perhaps Ionic above, made out of concrete, tufa, or travertine, while the colonnades of temples were increasingly Corinthian and of marble (Figs. 18 and 19).

This, however, is only an overall pattern, and in the years following Sulla it is the disorder and arbitrariness of architectural practice which is the most striking feature. Architecture mirrored political events as one

31

19. Theatre of Marcellus (travertine) and Temple of Apollo Sosianus
(marble), Rome, both late first century B.C.

leader after another sought to establish his authority. Backed by money and military power, individuals could indulge their wildest fantasies and go to any lengths to impress their rivals and the Roman populace with their architectural achievements. The result was an ever-increasing range of architectural types and ar-chitectural forms, as Pompey, Caesar, and Anthony all rose and fell without establishing clear traditions. This was the disordered world that Augustus found after his victory over Anthony at the Battle of Actium in 31 B.C., and this was the world he was to weld into the Roman empire.

III

Vitruvius

◆

The first "theory" of architecture

IT WAS in this world, where rules were either unknown or ignored and where the orders could be mixed or modified at the whim of patron and architect, that Marcus Vitruvius Pollio, an aging and not very successful architect who served under Julius Caesar in Spain, pondered and eventually published his *Ten Books on Architecture (De architectura libri decem).*[1] *Architectura* had already been ranked as a discipline equal to medicine by Cicero,[2] and Varro had given expression to the new status of the art in his one-volume treatment of the subject.[3] But it was Vitruvius who composed the first study of architecture which in its scale and systematic comprehensiveness matched the elaborate texts which had already brought consistency and order to the better-recognized arts such as music or rhetoric. In the Greek world, writings on architecture had been restricted to commentaries on individual temples, such as that of Theodorus on the temple of Artemis at Ephesus, and handbooks on individual orders such as that of Silenus on Doric symmetries.[4] The greater importance that the art had already acquired in Rome, as evidenced by its treatment in Varro as one of the nine "disciplines," is a reflection of its critical role in the service of politicians and generals. Since the third century architectural expenditure had been a primary means of winning electoral support and also a virtual obligation on triumphant generals as a means of returning to the city some part of their spoils. Architecture had thus become at Rome almost as important an art for a politician to exploit as rhetoric. Consequently it called out for serious treatment in much the same way as rhetoric had done in fifth- and fourth-century Greece, where it had become one of the first arts to receive a theoretical exposition.

By giving architecture an ordered intellectual foundation, Vitruvius set out both to ennoble it as an art and to reform it in practice. As he says at the end of his dedication to Augustus: "in these volumes I have expounded all the rational principles [*rationes*] of the discipline" (I, pref.). He goes on to talk about the science (*scientia*) of the architect and to claim that his work stems not only from the practice of building (*fabrica*) but also from theoretical reasoning (*ratiocinatio*) (I, 1, 1). The application of the latter, he says, means using shrewdness and reasoning (*ratio*) to enable you to describe and explain your work. His claim that architecture is a *disciplina* based on the *scientia* of the architect and on his application of *ratio* is backed up by the demonstration that the architect must have a knowledge of subjects that were already established as systematic disciplines, such as writing, drawing, geometry, history, philosophy, music, medicine, law, and astronomy. This, he says, is not as difficult as it sounds because, although each subject is different in its practical method (*opus*), their theoretical basis (*ratio*) is common to all; even a moderate knowledge of the latter is sufficient to enable a person to judge and test work in any of these areas. Hence his treatise should be of service not just to those involved in building but to all wise and sensible persons.

Ratio and the orders

Vitruvius wanted to raise architecture to the level of *scientia* or "knowledge," and the best way to achieve this was by showing that it was a fundamentally mathematical art. Thus Vitruvius begins his account of temples in Books III and IV, the most important section of the treatise, with a general statement of the mathematical principles of architectural design. Temples should be laid out according to a system of proportion using a fixed *modulus*, or "little measure." "For without commensurability [*symmetria*] and proportion [*proportio*] no temple can have a rational design [*ratio compositionis*]; that is, it must use an exact system, corresponding to that seen in the limbs of a well-shaped human being" (III, 1, 1). Nature has laid out the human body so that all its parts can be measured by using the others. The face, for example, is the length of the palm, and both are a tenth of the height of the whole body, while the foot is a sixth of the same overall height, the cubit or lower arm a quarter, and so on. These are the proportions that ancient painters and sculptors have relied upon. "In the same way the members of temples should have an appropriate response of commensurability between the whole structure and the individual parts" (III, 1, 3). It is essential that a temple should have a numerical relationship among its parts so that it may have the same perfection of layout as the human body. Vitruvius is here referring to the proportional schemes of sculptors, such as that of Polyclitus in the fifth century and of Lysippus in the fourth; and since temples did indeed acquire increasingly proportional designs at just this period, it was easy for him to relate the two developments. Plato too had been concerned with mysteries of numerical relationships (III, 1, 5); thus, mathematics could be seen to be of even more fundamental importance. This leads Vitruvius to present the plans and elevations of temples basically in terms of mathematical proportions, which was easy, since it was in such terms that Greek architects must have described their buildings in their commentaries. The tradition of writing on Ionic buildings was the strongest, and so it is with Ionic that Vitruvius begins. Throughout, column spacing, column height, base height, capital height, and the divisions of the entablature are given in terms of column diameters, the module by which all parts of the building can be measured. The actual forms of mouldings, capitals, etc. are also given, but never in such detail that they could be reconstructed simply by following the text. Only the mathematical relationships are complete and self-explanatory.

Vitruvius was probably the first person to combine the separate accounts of the different columnar forms in order to establish a consistent set of alternatives. The same attempt to give new coherence to a disparate group of inherited traditions is seen in his discussion of their origins. As with the treatment of the forms, the need for such a discussion is stated in terms of a need for the application of rational principles. At 1, 1, 5, he stressed that an architect should know history in order to be able to explain the *ratio* behind the ornaments he used. Accordingly, in the same way that Aristotle in the *Poetics* had given accounts of the origins of tragedy and comedy, Vitruvius (IV, 1, 3–10) gives accounts of the origins of the orders. Dorus, King of the Peloponnese, quite by chance built a temple of Juno (Hera) in a form that later was called Doric. This name was in fact first used by the Ionians when they built a temple to Apollo following the pattern that they had seen in the Peloponnese. Not knowing the proper proportions, and wondering what *ratio* to follow in making the columns both strong and good-looking, they made the bottom diameter a sixth of the height, imitating the relationship between the length of a man's foot and his height. Later when they wanted to build a temple to Diana in another form they modelled their columns on the slender female body, using a proportion of one to eight; at the same time they gave the columns bases like shoes, put volutes on the capitals which corresponded to curls of hair, and fluted the shafts in imitation of the folds of matronly robes. This order came to be called Ionic. At a later stage when their taste was more refined they made the proportions taller: one to seven for Doric and one to nine for Ionic.

This account contains elements from various traditions. The association of Dorians with Hera and Ionians with Apollo, for example, seems to recall the tribal associations of Olympia and Delphi noted earlier. But most elements of the story seem to reflect the situation of the late fifth and early fourth centuries during which the theory of the two orders was developed. Not only does it employ the version of the mythical origins of the Ionians found in Euripides' *Ion*, but the proportions given for the original Doric and Ionic would be inappropriate at any other time. Doric had, with a few exceptions, begun as stumpy and had arrived at a proportion of around 1:6 only in buildings such as the early-fourth-century temple of Athena at Tegea; while Ionic was usually over 1:9, but in important temples before and after 400 B.C. it hovers around 1:8, being about 1:7.75 on the temple of Athena Nike (430s B.C.) and 1:8.75 on the temple of Athena at Priene (c.350 B.C.). In general the concentration on the diverse racial origins of the orders seems to reflect precisely the preoccupation with racial divisions that developed in the Peloponnesian War. Another preoccupation of the period was with mathematical proportions, as manifested in the late-fifth-century *canon* of human proportions of Polyclitus and in many passages of Plato. Indeed, a precise parallel to the thought here is found in Plato's *Timaeus*,[5] where the divine *tektainomenos*, or architect of the universe, designs the world in his own image, and his children, the gods, make men and women after the same model. Plato's divine architect thinks like the Ionians in the Vitruvian myth. The Greeks had brought the myth to a high level of development, and Plato still employed the technique. A myth usually consists of an accretion of fantasy around a kernel of truth, and this one is no exception. Although Doric and Ionic columns can never have been adapted from the forms of man and woman, it was nevertheless true that the Dorians, as warrior-invaders, tended to worship male deities, while the Ionians, who were involved in peaceful wealth-creation, tended to worship females, often with fertility associations. As a result, most of the major Doric temples were dedicated to male gods and the major Ionic temples to female ones. The later-fifth-century prejudice that the Dorians were strong and manly and the Ionians weak and effeminate only encouraged the development of a theory that their architectures expressed the same sexual opposition. The only modification to this original explanation of the two main orders is the remark about the proportions of the two orders becoming more slender. This addition, which is indeed tacked on at the end, must have become necessary in the Hellenistic period when a taste developed for increasingly thinner columns.

The account of the origin of Corinthian must also be a Hellenistic addition. It is quite separate from the joint explanation of Doric and Ionic, and we would not expect such an explanation to become necessary until the order was fully accepted. The inventor of the myth clearly wanted to match the elaborate explanation of Ionic, and, just as other Hellenistic writers tried to match and surpass their Classical models, so did he with his eye for detail and fondness for sentiment. Vitruvius says at the outset that Corinthian in its even greater slenderness and prettiness imitates the form of a young girl, and he goes on to tell how the fifth-cen-

tury sculptor Callimachus invented the capital after seeing by chance an acanthus plant growing up round a basket placed on the tomb of a Corinthian maiden (IV, 1, 8–10). The story is as pretty as the capital, an "artificial" myth whose only historical elements are probably the reference to Callimachus and the funerary associations.

With this bouquet of Hellenistic sensibility Vitruvius closes his account of three columnar forms copied from three distinct physical types. At IV, 1, 12 he does admit that there are other types of capitals, but notes that all must be reduced to the general proportions of the main three and classed under the same names: Corinthian, Pulvinate (cushion-shaped, i.e. Ionic), and Doric. The various tall leaf capitals should presumably be seen as types of Corinthian, the different low volute capitals as types of Ionic, and those decorated only with simple mouldings as types of Doric. Even the Tuscan elements which are dealt with at IV, 7 in the context of "Tuscan dispositions" were probably intended to be thought of as belonging in the category with Doric, having capitals of similar profile and both capitals and columns of the same proportions. However varied their origins, the series of the orders is presented as closed.

The myths had concentrated on the explanation only of capital types and the proportions of columns; they failed to provide *rationes* for the entablatures. Vitruvius himself was aware of this and goes on immediately at IV, 2, 1 to declare that, as he has just discussed the *origines* of columns, it is not inappropriate for him *isdem rationibus*, "on the same principle," to deal with the *principia* and *origines* of their ornaments. The principle which leads him to discuss the origins of entablatures may be the same which led him to discuss those of columns, but the approach to the problem is quite different, because it depends on a considerably more sophisticated intellectual tradition. Myths had been invented simply to provide *an* explanation, and this meant that little attention was paid to their consistency either with historical fact or with each other. But from the fifth century onwards, competition and the increasing sophistication of their audiences sharpened the judgement of those who were expected to provide explanations of phenomena whether natural or architectural. These pressures demanded that they show that what they could offer was not *an* explanation but *the* explanation, one that could rank as knowledge (*epi-*

stēmē). Aristotle showed how one way to come closer to knowledge was to analyse the causes of anything: formal, material, motive, and final. Vitruvius' explanation of the forms of entablatures reflects the new standards of scientific enquiry which had become current in the Hellenistic period. He carefully describes the elements of a wooden roof and explains how each functions. He then claims that when the first stone temples were built they imitated the forms of their wooden models, so that triglyphs, for example, were the ends of beams and mutules those of rafters. He thus analyses aspects of the formal and material causes of entablatures. He also demonstrates his ability to arrive at *the* explanation in his study of the triglyph. Some people, he says, have claimed that triglyphs are windows. But triglyphs occur all the way round temples, even at the corners where windows would be structurally impossible; so that explanation must be wrong. What Vitruvius does is advance an hypothesis, test it, and refute it. The fact that he attributes the erroneous hypothesis to others shows that here, as in the case of the explanation of columns, he is only summing up the work of earlier writers, in this case presumably Greeks of the third or second century. He must be indebted to the same sources when he goes on to show how this new rigorously analytical approach can be used to establish standards of architectural criticism. For if Ionic and Doric entablatures derive from wooden models, and if the dentils of the one and the mutules of the other both represent rafters, then dentils and mutules cannot be used together in the same entablature. This criticism is evidently intended to restrain the licence of Late Hellenistic and Early Roman architecture and strikes a note of restrictive discipline that is recurrent in the *Ten Books* and is often revived in later architectural theory. Just as the older myth-making tradition provided, in the story of the genesis of Corinthian, a model for the use of the imagination by later architects, so the newer logical tradition provided a criterion for the later repression of deviation or invention.

The roots of the scientific thought on which these paragraphs are based lay in the Greek need to establish the principles that governed the organization of the natural world (Gr. *physis*, Lat. *natura*). It is accordingly by reference to nature that Vitruvius formulates an important general critical principle: "thus they thought that that which cannot happen in truth [sc. in

a wooden roof] could have no *ratio* in a representation [i.e. the stone entablature]. For all things which had a fixed appropriateness [*proprietas*] and which were derived from the true habits of *natura* they used for the perfection of their work, and they approved of those things whose explanations were shown in their discussions to have a *ratio* of truth" (IV, 2, 5–6). The primitive wooden structure represents "nature," which is always bound by certain rules. The stone building which derives from it has to reproduce the natural situation. The principle is of wide application and underlies Vitruvius' criticism of the contemporary painted architecture of so-called Third Style wall decorations. As part of a wider critique of fantasy paintings he attacks the painted representation of "reeds supporting roofs or pediments piled on candlesticks," because such things "do not exist, cannot come into being, and have never been" (VII, 5, 4). In order to demonstrate the danger of being associated with such a style he also tells the story of how the inhabitants of Tralles were in danger of making a laughing stock of themselves by having scenery designed in such an arbitrary way until they were brought to their senses by a local mathematician (VII, 5, 5). Vitruvius and his Greek sources believed that nature had to be obeyed in art because scientific enquiry had shown that natural reality was bound by rules, and art had also to be founded on rules in order to achieve the status of science. To disobey those rules was to be both stupid and immoral.

Decor and *decorum*

The importance of theories of natural order for the development of theories of architecture is revealed in yet another passage where Doric, Ionic, and Corinthian are discussed. Near the beginning of the first book Vitruvius tells how the temples to different gods should be in different orders.

Temples to Minerva, Mars, and Hercules will be Doric; for to these gods, on account of their manliness [*virtus*] it is appropriate [*decet*] that buildings are put up which are without delicate ornaments. Temples to Venus, Flora, Proserpina, Fountains, and Nymphs will seem to have suitable characteristics [*proprietates*] if they are built in the Corinthian order; for works in honour of these soft and gentle goddesses will have their decorative appropriateness [*decor*] enhanced if they are more slender and prettily ornamented with leaves and volutes. Temples to Juno, Diana, Father Bacchus, and similar deities will follow the correct principle of intermediate decoration [*ratio mediocritatis*] if they are Ionic, because a definition of the appropriate character of their temples will derive from a balance between the severe manner of Doric and the softness of Corinthian. (I, 2, 5)

As in IV, 2, 6, the argument is again based on an understanding of the essential—the natural—character of architectural forms; here, however, the key idea is not just *proprietas* but *decor*. Indeed, the whole passage is an elucidation of *decor*, one of the abstract notions of which architecture is said to consist: *ordinatio* (Gr. *taxis*), "organization"; *dispositio* (Gr. *diathesis*), "arrangement"; *eurhythmia*, "beauty"; *symmetria*, "proportion"; *decor*, "principle of appropriateness"; and *distributio* (Gr. *oikonomia*), "distribution" (I, 2, I). *Decor* is described rather loosely as "the correct appearance of a work using approved elements and backed by authority" (I, 2, 5). This authority derives from either *statio* (Gr. *thematismos*), "prescription," *consuetudo*, "custom," or *natura*, "nature." The rules about the use of the orders are introduced to provide an illustration of the first type. An example of *decor* deriving from "custom," on the other hand, is the use of an elegant vestibule as the prelude to a magnificent interior; a low and unworthy vestibule would be quite inappropriate just as it would be wrong to put an Ionic dentil in a Doric entablature. "Natural" *decor* consists in putting temples to gods of health in healthy spots and ensuring that each part of a house gets its correct lighting, with bedrooms and libraries, for example, getting theirs from the east. *Decor*, is, thus, generally the principle of appropriate appearance, one which would have been more familiar to the Romans under the name of *decorum*, both terms sharing the same root as the impersonal verb *decet*, "it is fitting." Cicero had dealt at length with both ethical and rhetorical *decorum*, a term which was a suitable adjectival translation of the Greek *to prepon*, "that which is fitting." *Decor* on the other hand had, before Vitruvius, meant visual beauty generally (as it still does at VI, 2, 5). Vitruvius apparently uses it for *decorum* here only because he wants a word to fit easily in the series of abstract nouns listed above.

Decor (or rather *decorum*) is, then, a Greek idea,[6] formulated as a means of ensuring that people followed the pattern of nature. It had a central place in Aristotle's *Ethics* and in his *Rhetoric*. Later it had been taken up enthusiastically by the Stoics, who asserted that man should "live according to nature," which meant doing *to kathēkon*, "that which belongs to you," or in other words *to prepon*. The second-century B.C. Stoic Panaitios had turned this notion into the basis of a whole theory of ethics, and his ideas had been transmitted to Rome by Cicero in his *De officiis* (*On Duties*), which attempted to prescribe for each class of people (men, women, rich, poor, etc.) what was natural and fitting to do. The Stoics and other lovers of order had elevated this principle to counter the Epicurean argument that since all was governed by *tychē*, "chance," there was no need to set rules for human behaviour. Certainly we seem to hear echoes of Stoic criticism of the Epicureans in Vitruvius' attack on the random fantasies of the so-called Third Style paintings which disregard natural order. It would, however, be wrong to see *decorum* always as an ethical and Stoic term. It had a much more realistic place in the literature of the arts, especially of rhetoric and music, being justified by the argument that if the style of a speech or a piece of music was not consistent with its subject it would simply lose expressive effect and not work so well. Not that it is ever detached from its ethical foundation: thus Cicero in the *Orator* says "As in life so in rhetoric, nothing is more difficult than to judge what is appropriate [*quid deceat*]. The Greeks call this *to prepon* and we *decorum*. . . . Ignorance of this leads to many errors, not only in life but often in poems and orations too."[7] Vitruvius was well aware of Cicero's work on rhetoric.

So much for the general origin of the idea of *decorum*; but what of the more specific sources of Vitruvius' theory of *decorum* in architecture? The remarks on "natural" *decorum* point to the origins of the idea in natural philosophy, particularly physics and biology. But the talk of matching a rich vestibule to a rich interior is more reminiscent of the general remarks on architectural *decorum* found in Aristotle's *Ethics* and Cicero's *De officiis*, where it was insisted that rich and important people should live in impressive houses. The theory of the application of the orders, however, seems to have most in common with rhetoric. First, although Vitruvius uses other words where we use "order" (e.g. *mos, ratio, opus, consituta*, etc.) the term that recurs most frequently is *genus*, which meant originally "race" but which had come by assimilation with the Greek *genos* to be used for "class," "sort," "kind," etc.

With the latter sense it was regularly used for "types" or "styles" of speech. Cicero's statement in the *De oratore* that there are three types of oratory, "one which is full and round [*plena, teres*], another which is fine and strong at the same time [*tenuis, non sine viribus*], and a third which partakes of both types [*particeps utriusque generis*] which has an admirably intermediate quality [*mediocritas*],"[8] provides a close model for Vitruvius' classification of Doric and Corinthian as extremes of "severity" and "softness," with Ionic embodying *mediocritas* in between. Unlike Vitruvius, Cicero was not referring there to named styles, but he refers to the famous three named styles of oratory at *Orator* 8, and Quintilian was later to give a full account of them in the *Institutiones oratoriae*; Attic, originating in cultivated Athens, is compressed and coherent; Asiatic also matches its audience, being inflated and empty; the third, Rhodian, is intermediate, consisting of a mixture of the other two.[9] This classification had probably become established in the Late Hellenistic period, and although in rhetoric it was Rhodian, the last style to develop, which was intermediate, while in architecture the latest, Corinthian, was one of the extremes, the classification would have provided a useful model for Vitruvius in his ambition to do for architecture what Cicero had done for rhetoric. The theory that Attic, Asiatic, and Rhodian each developed to suit the character of the local audience naturally invited comparisons with the way Doric, Ionic, and Corinthian were also seen to reflect local characteristics.

Vitruvius thus found it easy to relate the two arts, and what he says about matching the *genera* to differing architectural contexts, which is almost certainly his own addition to architectural theory, reveals most clearly his debt to rhetoric. Adjectival descriptions of rhetorical *genera* had long been established as the basis of a theory of *decorum*, in order to enable a speaker to identify a suitable style. There is no evidence that this had ever been done for architecture. Vitruvius had to invent some adjectival characterizations before he could match style to subject, as Cicero had done at *Orator* 70: "a refined [*subtile*] style for demonstrations, a moderate [*modicum*] style for speeches designed to please, and a vehement [*vehemens*] style for persuasion." What Vitruvius did was to apply to the architectural *genera* the same sort of epithets that had been applied to rhetorical *genera*, carefully choosing those

(severe, soft, manly, womanly, etc.) that readily suggested the architectural context to which they would be appropriate—that is, the temples of either tough masculine deities or soft feminine ones. Hitherto the vocabulary of architectural description has been limited to the definition of visual effect (as by words such as "shining"), of value (by words such as "rich"), or of degree of finish (by words such as "polished"). Beginning with Vitruvius the description, and so also the perception of architecture, could exploit a new range of metaphorical experience: words such as "severe" and "soft" introduced to architecture sensual, emotive, and even moral connotations which had previously only been applied to other arts such as sculpture and music.

Indeed, the similarity of Vitruvius' stylistic vocabulary to that already applied to sculpture and music suggests that, although the general matrix of three styles derives from rhetoric, he was also influenced by writings on the other arts. We know from Cicero's analogies between rhetorical and sculptural style that an established view of the development of Greek sculpture saw it as starting out "hard" and becoming progressively "softer."[10] Since for Vitruvius Doric was the first style and Corinthian the latest he seems to apply to architecture not only the vocabulary of sculpture but also its historical model. Sculptural criticism might naturally have interested Vitruvius because sculpture was the closest of the arts to architecture. Musical theory, on the other hand, was an appropriate source not only because it was the most highly developed art theory of Antiquity, but also because it dealt with music in terms of a set of "modes" which were closely analogous to the architectural *genera*. The modes were differentiated from each other absolutely in mathematical terms, that is by being based on different sets of notes, just as the *genera* were distinguished by the different proportions of their elements. Also the modes, like the *genera*, took their names from racial groups of the Aegean world: Dorian, Phrygian, Lydian, etc. In fact the only one of the main musical modes whose name corresponded with that of an order was the Dorian, and this had from Plato onwards always been characterized as *andreios* ("manly, courageous")—that is, possessing the same quality as the Latin *virtus* which Vitruvius associates with Doric.[11] The whole classification of the musical modes employed such sexual-moral categories, while the moral overtones in the characterization of the Doric order are unique, as if in recognition of its comparability to the similarly named mode. Each of the arts had successively undergone a major stage of theoretical development, rhetoric and music in the fifth and fourth centuries, painting and sculpture in the fourth and third. Each had been enriched by the influence of the other. Now architecture took its place in the process.

In spite of the variety of its sources, this theory of the application of the *genera* to sacred structures is remarkably simple and coherent. It does not, however, provide any guide to the choice of columns in houses or public buildings, although Vitruvius was certainly interested in formulating rules for the *decor* of secular buildings in other ways. This deficiency must reflect the difficulty he had in expanding the theory. It seems that he never got beyond the initial statement of it. He makes no attempt to refer to temples which conform to the rule later in the treatise, and his classification of temple doors at IV, 6, I does not correspond to that of columniations: "The *genera* of doorways are these: Doric, Ionic, and Attic." He gives no guide to the choice of *genus* either here or in his account of house design, where he simply notes that Doric doors should have Doric proportions and Ionic doors Ionic proportions, and that these should be the same as in temples. When he does make specific recommendations for the use of the orders, as in the passage on stoas, he simply records usage: the outer colonnade should be Doric, and if there are interior columns they should be one-fifth higher than the outer ones and should be either Ionic or Corinthian. In only one case does he attempt to expand the original theory of columnar *decor*. Discussing the colonnaded courts that were often placed behind theatres, he says: "But their columns will not have the same ratios and proportions as I recorded for sacred structures; for in the temples of the gods columns should have *gravitas* [heaviness, seriousness], but in porticoes and public works they should be distinguished by their *subtilitas* [thinness, refinement]" (V, 9, 3). He goes on to make clear that he is referring to their proportionate slenderness, suggesting heights of 7½ diameters for Doric and 9½ for Ionic and Corinthian instead of the lower 7 and 9 for temples. Thus, although he does not show how the familiar scale of the orders can be applied to individual buildings, he does demonstrate how the whole scale could be transposed and made suitable to secular work in general. Since in practice Greek architects had actually often used stockier

columns in stoas than in temples,[12] he must again be inventing a rule of his own, and again the principle is apparently derived from rhetorical theory. Heaviness and lightness were metaphors regularly used to describe styles appropriate to "serious" and "light" subjects. Vitruvius noticed that the opposition between "religious" and "secular" was similar in character to the rhetorical polarity and decided that accordingly their respective columns should be literally "heavier" or "lighter" in proportion.

The moral framework

One implication of Vitruvius' remarks on proportions is that columns which are shorter and thicker have a greater dignity than more slender ones. This implies that Doric must be the most dignified of the three orders, and it is notable that, in the initial passage on *decor*, the *virtus* which is attributed to Doric can also be seen as marking it out as morally superior to the others. *Virtus* and *gravitas* were closely connected in the predominantly Stoic moral teachings of Cicero, especially as revealed in the *De officiis*. However tentatively, Vitruvius is establishing principles of architectural aesthetics which relate clearly to contemporary moral attitudes. Yet what is most striking about these principles is that they completely reverse those implied in contemporary practice. While he found himself calling short, thick forms nobler than taller, thinner ones and attributed to Doric a moral excellence of *virtus* which Corinthian could not claim, Hellenistic architects and their Roman imitators showed a clear preference for taller forms, especially Corinthian, in all major buildings. Clearly it was more important for his theory to seem morally right than for it to reflect contemporary realities. In this it started a tradition which has continued to this century. Vitruvius, like later writers, knew that if his book was to meet with the approval of the educated audience for which it was intended, it was more important that it respond to their professed values than that it mirror contemporary architectural practice.

His interest in architectural morality in general and the idea of *decorum* in particular thus has to be related directly to the context in which he was writing in the early years of Augustus' rule. It is to the emperor himself that the book is directed, and the idea of *decorum* already underlies its dedication (I, pref.). There he repeatedly refers to Augustus' desire to have buildings which match the size of his achievement and the scale of his deeds. The idea that a great man, ruler of a great country, should build great buildings springs from the same interest in "appropriateness" as the theory of *decor*. Specifically it is an expression of the principle of *megaloprepeia* (appropriateness in great things) which had been elaborated by Aristotle as the principle that should govern the expenditure of great men[13] and which, translated into *magnificentia*, had received its most recent formulation in Cicero's *De officiis*. The latter book, Cicero's last word on ethics, had been particularly concerned with appropriateness of behaviour, and it seems fairly certain that it was an attempt to present an alternative to the free-for-all of the Late Republic, when people paid more attention to what they were able to do than to what was their natural duty (*officium*). Although Augustus (as Octavian) may well have abetted Cicero's subsequent murder, once he achieved his goal of supreme and unchallenged power he too was anxious to replace licence with order, to persuade each person to take his place in a stable society. Literature became a major vehicle of persuasion. Virgil in the *Georgics* used the bees as a model community where each member performed his appropriate task, and in the *Aeneid* presented a hero whose only interest had been to do what he was called to do as leader. Another hireling poet, Horace, in the *Epistle* which is better known as the *Ars poetica* argued the importance of appropriate behaviour for poets, both in their own actions and in their poetry. His attack on unnatural and inappropriate modern poetry is exactly parallel to Vitruvius' contemporary attack on unnatural and inappropriate wall paintings; the parallel in vocabulary and principle with Vitruvius' architectural criticism is equally striking. All these works completed in the twenty years after Actium (31 B.C.) communicate the same mood. The authors are all the more convincing because they must genuinely have shared their ruler's desire for a return to a more ordered world and must also have felt that the licence found in poetry, painting, and architecture was closely connected with the political and moral malaise of the Late Republic. It is a sense of this connection which must partly explain their heavy dependence on ethical principles in the formulation of artistic theory. This dependence was, how-

ever, reinforced by a conviction that if the Greeks were their superiors in art, they were the Greeks' betters in morality, and that their contribution to the development of art theory should be in the moral sphere. Just as Augustus had punished Anthony, the undecorous Hellenizer, so they should reprove flagrant misbehaviour in the arts. Hence *decor*, with its moral roots, receives much the most expansive treatment among the elements of architecture. Virgil had contrasted the Greeks' gift for artistic accuracy and finish with the Romans' care in the enforcement of a moral code involving the appropriate treatment of the humble and the proud. Vitruvius combines Greek and Roman qualities by adding the moral *decor* to the more technical *ordinatio*, *dispositio*, *eurhythmia*, etc. and by, besides giving elaborate details of the mathematical basis of the orders, also insisting that they follow the *mores naturae*, "habits of nature."

For all its shortcomings Vitruvius' treatise achieves what it sets out to do, to elevate architecture to the level of a discipline or science. It showed that its practice involved an exact attention to rules and that those rules were essentially the same as those recognized as governing not only other arts but human behaviour and indeed the whole natural world. Nowhere is this more apparent than in the passages dealing with the orders, and indeed the theory of the orders can be seen to constitute the strongest and most fully worked out part of the treatise. Yet all this is achieved at enormous cost. Most strikingly the whole theory of *decor*, which he developed in order to demonstrate the relationship between architecture and the traditionally respected fields of music, rhetoric, and ethics, bears almost no relation to the realities of contemporary or earlier architecture. Vitruvius' need to develop a theory which would above all match the level of the literary theories of other activities meant that it was to them and not to actual practice that he adjusted his ideas. This may seem a weakness to us when we turn to Vitruvius for enlightenment on ancient architecture, but it was eventually to be the source of the book's greatest influence. When Renaissance patrons, scholars, and architects looked at the *Ten Books* entirely afresh, it was precisely the acceptability of his ideas to men already familiar with the ancient writings on ethics and rhetoric which guaranteed the work's success.

IV

The Roman Empire

❖

The irrelevance of theory

IF VITRUVIUS' theory of architecture owed little to earlier practice, it also had little influence on the future. It is true that under Augustus there arose a new purism and accuracy in the interpretation of the Greek orders, but there was no adoption of Vitruvius' rules. No one applied his principle of matching orders to temples, and the major temples to male deities such as Mars Ultor erected directly by Augustus are not Doric, as Vitruvius would have wished, but elegant Corinthian (Fig. 27). If it was the emperor's policy to favour the promulgation of such ideas it was not his practice to follow them. There is no evidence either that Vitruvius' recommendation of thinner forms for minor secular buildings was taken up. Contemporary structures continued to reflect the reverse scale of values. The only area in which this Vitruvian recommendation may have found a response is in the increase in the use of pilasters. Just as the engaged column represented a literal reduction in bulk from the free-standing form, so the flat rectangular pilaster represented a reduction again. Rarely used in the Greek world, it now became extremely popular especially as a "light" form appropriate to "slighter" contexts. Thus on the Arch of Augustus small Doric pilasters flank the main arch with its large Corinthian half-columns. In a wider context the pilaster is also associated with plain Doric forms on two floors on the amphitheatres at Pola and Verona (Fig. 20), while the higher-status Theatre of Marcellus in Rome has Doric and Ionic half-columns (Fig. 19, p. 32). The thin pilaster thus came to be opposed to the column in much the same way as the large rectangular pier. The one form was inferior because it was so light, the other because it was so crude. The range of architectural expression available to the Roman architect was once again increased.

The range was at its greatest in the Early Empire, when all the orders were still current and Doric and Ionic were still used for less important buildings. Within a century, however, variation of order—the principal means of architectural differentiation in the Greek world—had lost its importance as Corinthian became almost universal. Many buildings actually had their orders changed, while others which would once have been given Doric and Ionic forms received Corinthian from the start. At Pompeii and Herculaneum, for example, after the earthquake of A.D. 63 many Doric and Ionic capitals received Corinthian trappings in stucco. In Rome the temple of the deified Augustus can be seen from representations on coins to have been originally built by Tiberius with Ionic capitals, perhaps (as was probably also the case with the Ionic temple of Augustus' adoptive father, Julius Caesar) so as not to seem to challenge the genuine Olympians; but by the mid-second century after rebuildings by Domitian and Antonius Pius it is shown as Corinthian.[1] In the early first century Doric and Corinthian were still used to indicate difference of status within individual structures or groups of buildings. The magnificent aqueducts built and restored by Claudius in 43–54 still have Doric arches where they span minor roads, with Corinthian reserved for the great double arch of the Aqua Claudia spanning the Via Labicana and the Via Praenestina (Fig. 28). Within a few decades, though, virtually all arches were to use Corinthian and related forms. Typically the Porta dei Leoni at Verona, which had originally been built (probably under Augustus) with a Doric order, was replaced by a much more elaborate structure using Corinthian variants. The expansion of Corinthian at the expense of the simpler orders

20. Amphitheatre, Verona, first century A.D.

is equally well illustrated by the exteriors of amphitheatres. In the first-century examples of Nîmes, Verona, and Pola, Doric details are found on both lower and upper storeys, giving the buildings a simple strength which well matches their function as arenas for physical contests (Fig. 20). By the time of the Amphitheatrum Castrense (c.220) in Rome or the contemporary amphitheatre of El Djem (Fig. 33, p. 56) in North Africa, Corinthian and Corinthian derivatives are used throughout. Doric and even Ionic had by this time largely vanished, while the increasing importance of the amphitheatre in public life made it less appropriate to mark it out as a low-status building type. By the third century it is as if any building worthy of a Roman citizen is also worthy of the Corinthian order.

An Italian order

The spread of Corinthian made it more difficult to differentiate buildings by the use of the orders, but, as if in response to this, a large number of variations on the basic form were introduced using different leaf types and replacing the volutes with human and animal figures which might be particularly appropriate to the building's function. Such variations had already begun to appear in the Hellenistic period, and Vitruvius had acknowledged their existence at IV, 1. One of these variations, however, seems to have acquired a status quite different from the others, and that is the form called (since the Renaissance) Composite. Essentially it is a standard Corinthian capital with the upper part re-

21. Arch of Titus, Rome, late first century

placed by a combination of echinus and corner volutes. Ancestors of this form are found already in the third and second centuries in southern Italy and Etruria, as in the "Temple of Peace" at Paestum, c.100 B.C., and the slightly earlier "Tomb of Ildebranda" at Sovana, but the earliest examples of the fully developed form still *in situ* are probably all of the later first century A.D. Most famous are those on the Arch of Titus, erected in the 70s (Fig. 21). Another set adorns the courtyard of the Domus Flavia, the palace of Titus' brother Domitian on the Palatine. Simplified specimens discovered in the Colosseum seem to come from the colonnade which was erected round the top of the seating there at the same date or soon after (Fig. 24). Other contemporary ones are found on the rebuilt Porta dei Leoni at Verona. Its insistent appearance in these and later monuments convinced Renaissance authorities that it was a genuine new order in spite of the fact that it was not referred to by their revered Vitruvius. Alberti's identification of it as a deliberately invented "Italic" form is particularly suggestive, since it implies that he saw it as an Italian rival to the Greek orders.[2] The capital type does indeed have a distinctively Italian, rather than Greek, ancestry, and recent opinion argues that it was introduced by Augustan architects.[3] At no time would it have been more natural that an Italic, Latin, or Roman order should be developed than under Augustus when national pride was strengthened by Horace's *Satires*, a supposedly traditional Italian literary form, by Virgil's *Aeneid*, a Latin rival to the Greek epic with

43

22. Atrium Vestae, Rome, late first century

Italia as a new promised land, and by the construction of a separate Latin library to match the Greek one in the precinct of Apollo Palatinus. It is true that no Augustan building using the Composite order survives, although a magnificent set of probably Augustan capitals is preserved in the fourth-century S. Costanza (Fig. 36, p. 61). But a relief in Florence, which has been identified as representing the temple of Vesta in its Augustan form, shows it with capitals which are Composite in their combination of leaves and volutes. Capitals of similar type are also found in Hadrianic and later buildings of the Atrium Vestae and so were clearly associated with the cult (Fig. 22). The shrine of Vesta was one of the most sacred sites in Rome. In it was housed the *palladium*, the sacred image brought from Troy and religiously guarded by the Romans as a *pignus imperii* (assurance of their dominion).[4] There too burned the fire whose extinction would mean the destruction of the city. Arguably no other shrine was so closely identified with Rome's fate, and it would thus have

been a highly appropriate place to introduce a "Roman" order.

At the Renaissance this capital came to be called Composite, and it is likely that its "mixed" nature is important for its meaning. Both the Vesta and the S. Costanza capitals can be understood as combinations of the Greek orders; the latter type in particular, which became standard, can be seen as a fusion of Doric echinus, Ionic volutes, and Corinthian leaves. The Romans always prided themselves on taking the best features of Greek culture and combining them in their own way to make something superior, and the combination of the orders would be a perfect demonstration of this in architecture. What this might have meant to a Roman as the culmination of a biological development is indicated by Vitruvius' commentary on the way the Corinthian capital can be combined with either Doric or Ionic entablatures: "And so out of the two *genera* is created [*procreatum*] a third by the introduction of a new capital."[5] This remark is even more appropriate to the new capital and even suggests how some younger contemporary of Vitruvius might have sought to please his ruler by inventing a national capital which could be seen as the pinnacle of architectural evolution.

Such self-conscious inventions do not always catch on immediately, as we saw with Vitruvius' theories, but a new bout of nationalism in Vespasian's reign revived interest in the form. Moreover, its revival under the Flavian dynasty confirms our identification of it as distinctively Roman and Italic. Vespasian and his sons Titus and Domitian, for whom the Colosseum, the Arch of Titus, and the Domus Flavia were erected, were all anxious to re-establish links with Italian tradition after the reign of the Graecophile Nero, and especially to bring back the spirit of Augustus. Also, the use of the order on the Arch of Titus, a use repeated in later arches commemorating Roman victories, is consistent with the association of the order with the dominance of Rome and is difficult to explain in any other way. Finally, its use on the Colosseum may be particularly instructive (Fig. 23). As it stands, the outside has three storeys of half-columns one above the other, Doric, Ionic, and Corinthian, with a crowning storey of Corinthian pilasters. Inside there are the remains of an upper interior colonnade of marble and/or granite columns crowned by Composite and Corinthian capi-

44

23. Colosseum, Rome, after A.D. 72

24. Colosseum, Rome: capital from upper interior portico

tals. There was also, originally at least, one triumphal-type arch surmounted by a *quadriga* and with Composite capitals at the entrance on the main axis, as can be seen in the representation from the Tomb of Haterii. The upper interior colonnade was perhaps originally entirely Composite too, since only the Composite capitals from this position have the simplified forms used throughout the building (Fig. 24). The Colosseum always had some of the character of a triumphal monument. The men and animals used in the games there were often the prizes of triumphant generals, and the games themselves were ritual re-enactments of Rome's humiliation of the nations of the world. As a setting for

this ritual the arrangement of the orders was especially appropriate. The gamut of inferior foreign orders was used for the relatively low-status travertine exterior, while "Roman" Composite is reserved for the emperor's entrance and the interior where emperor and populace would sit. It is worth pointing out that the series of the orders on the outside rising from Doric to Corinthian, although often wrongly referred to nowadays as canonical, was perhaps never otherwise used in Rome. Only one other certain example of it has ever been found: the Sebasteion or Caesareum at Aphrodisias in Asia Minor, erected under Claudius.[6] A quite explicit commemoration of Roman imperial domina-

25. Capitolium, Sufetula (Sbeitla), mid-second century:
rear view of three temples

tion, being adorned with reliefs such as that showing Claudius as victor over Britain, this monument confirms the triumphal associations of such a series. Aphrodisias is not far from Pergamum, which offered the closest Greek prototype for such a triumphal combination in the Stoa of Athena with its Doric, Ionic, and Aeolic orders (Fig. 14, p. 27). The Pergamene re-invention of the Aeolic capital may indeed have provided the most direct inspiration for the invention of an Italic form. The Stoa was as much a triumphal monument as the Colosseum. Both were decorated with the armour of conquered peoples, and the books of the different Greek tribes imprisoned in the adjoining library

for the benefit of the Pergamene population were only a more discreet emblem of power than the people and animals from throughout the world gathered in the Colosseum for the pleasure of the citizens of Rome. What is distinctively Roman is the creation of a new form by the arrogantly imaginative fusion of elements which the Greeks had regarded as biologically separate.

Alberti, then, was probably right in his interpretation of the Composite capital. First developed as an Italic or Roman *genus* under Augustus, it achieved full recognition under the Flavians. Like most artificial creations it never seriously challenged the firmly estab-

lished Corinthian, but its continued use in the great series of triumphal arches, from that of Titus at Rome to
those of Trajan at Beneventum and of Septimus Severus at Rome again, suggests that architects working
directly for the emperor were well aware of its meaning. If it was not introduced as self-consciously as has
been argued here, it is hard to see how it alone of all
the many Corinthian variants should have maintained
a clear identity for a thousand years and been consistently recognized for most of that period as superior to
Corinthian. The Capitolium at Sufetula in modern
Tunisia, of the mid-second century, is a good example
both of its national associations and of its superiority
over Corinthian (Fig. 25). In the triple temple which, in
its imitation of the shrine of the Capitoline triad in
Rome, was a prominent symbol of Roman rule, the order of the central cella dedicated to Jupiter is Composite, while the two flanking ones for Juno and Minerva
are Corinthian. The primacy of the central cella is also
stressed by its having half-columns along its flanks in
contrast to the pilasters of the other two. From its initial function as an expression of Roman superiority
over the Greeks, Composite came to be seen as a symbol of domination over the empire as a whole.

The triumph over nature

The Capitolium at Sufetula is also characterized by
another feature. The three temples and the forum in
front of them are approached through a grand gateway
decorated with Corinthian half-columns (Fig. 26).
These shafts and those on the outside of the rear wall
of the temple are all left with a covering of rough masonry. It is as if all the orders on the outside of the complex are unfinished compared to those within it. The
device is not new. It recalls the Forum of Augustus at
Rome, whose marble refinements were surrounded by
a high tufa wall with a roughly handled exterior (Fig.
27). One function of the wall was to keep out fires;
however, it may also have had an expressive purpose,
emphasizing the difference between pre-Augustan
Rome and the transformation of the city under the emperor. Augustus is said to have boasted that he found
Rome brick and left it marble.[7] He might also have
claimed to have found it tufa and left it marble. Any
visitor to Rome would have gone straight to the new
forum to see what the new ruler could achieve, and the

26. Capitolium, Sufetula (Sbeitla): entrance arch

emphatic enclosure wall ensured that the contrast between the old city and the new was as dramatic as possible. The Capitolium at Sufetula may have been designed with a similar expressive goal in view. The city
is one of the farthest inland of the great cities of Roman
Africa and thus one of the closest to the frontier between the empire and barbarism. With its unusual triple temple employing the Composite order, the enclosed rectangle represented Rome more directly than
any other such complex. With its main entrance towards the south it seems also specifically designed to
impress those approaching from the wild desert beyond the *limes*. The effect of the contrast between the

rough shafts outside and the smooth ones within is well calculated to make the visitor feel that he has moved from a tough and unrefined world to one that is ordered and elegant. It is as well placed and designed to illustrate the benefits of the Roman empire in general as Augustus' forum was to illustrate the benefits of his government. The wall of the Forum of Augustus in a sense marked a frontier in time, that of the Sufetula Capitolium a frontier in space. In both cases the frontier is between order and disorder, though the disorder is of civil war in one case and of barbaric nature in the other. By using the same forms, outside as if in their natural state and inside refined by art, the designer of the Sufetula complex effectively showed that the key to Roman civilization was the taming and refinement of nature to produce a better world.

The Romans were always conscious that the luxury of their life depended on the exploitation of land and water,[8] and they constantly reminded themselves of the natural origin of their possessions and pleasures. Catullus addressed his boat as a pine tree from Mt Pelium; a polished slab of African marble might be called a piece of Numidian mountain; a new aqueduct could be called the New Anio after the stream which supplied it. The emperor who built the Anio Novus and who in general showed the greatest interest in controlling nature was Claudius (41–54). Besides building and restoring a number of aqueducts, he gave the port of Ostia improved protection from the sea and developed new facilities there for the import of grain; he built canals to free Rome from floods and dug a massive tunnel to drain the Fucine lake; his power over water he above all demonstrated by crossing the Channel and bringing Britain into the empire, a feat which he commemorated as the conquest of Ocean in the inscription on his triumphal arch in Rome, which was appropriately also an arch of one of his aqueducts. This distinctive interest in the subjugation of nature for the benefit of Rome was perhaps also responsible for the unparalleled popularity of unfinished masonry in buildings associated with him. Superb examples are the arches of the Aqua Claudia now called the Porta Maggiore (Fig. 28); two great corn stores, the Porticus Iunonia Frumentaria at Rome and a portico adjoining the new harbour at Ostia; and finally the substructures of the temple of Claudius on the Caelian hill (Fig. 29). These works all exploit variations of rough and uncut masonry as do no

27. Arch into Forum of Augustus with temple of Mars Ultor, Rome, late first century B.C.

other ancient buildings. Most expressive are the columns of the Porta Maggiore: their Corinthian capitals are still lacking the final carving of details, and their shafts are entirely composed of similar capitals in an even rougher preliminary state. The viewer is reminded that he is looking at stone in transition from a rough unhewn condition in the quarry to a possible ultimate refinement under the sculptor's chisel. The two arches of the aqueduct which spanned the Via Praenestina and

28. Porta Maggiore, Rome, mid-first century A.D.

29. Temple of Divus Claudius, Rome, third quarter
of first century: basement

the Via Labicana at the point where they met must always have marked the division between country and city, a natural place to meditate on such a transition. The water above, on its way from mountain spring to city baths, was in the same transitional state as the travertine columns. Also in a transitional state was the corn stored in the warehouses at Ostia and Rome, on its way from some distant field to an urban bakery. Aqueducts and granary both housed raw materials in transit, and the material of which they were made was appropriately left in a state of transformation. It was

Claudius who presided over all these examples of the subjugation of nature for the benefit of the Roman citizenry, and the basement of the temple which he received as his reward provided the most brilliant commemoration of such subjugation. Halfway between the natural tufa of the Caelian and the polished marble of the Corinthian temple, the Doric pilasters with their alternating bands of raw and smooth travertine suitably recalled the lifework on which the status of the god above was founded. No emperor was more closely associated with the unfinished and the transformed than

Claudius, whose mother called him an "unfinished monster" and whose deification was satirized by Seneca as an *Apocolocyntosis* or Pumpkinification.

When the Romans thought of nature tamed for their pleasure they thought not only of water in their baths and bread in their homes but of games in the circus, and perhaps for this reason among the most conspicuous examples of such unfinished masonry outside Rome are amphitheatres such as that at Aosta with its bands of shaggy stone and those of Pola and Verona (Fig. 20) all of the first century. Water in an aqueduct, grain in a granary, and wild men and beasts in the amphitheatre all represent natural materials in an intermediate state, as do untrimmed stones.

Perhaps because of its slightly repellent quality, which would have become even more apparent as polished marble became more widely available, really rough masonry was exploited at Rome only for a brief period. Masonry which was left smooth but without the final detailing proved more acceptable in similar contexts. The capitals of the Porta Maggiore which were left in this state had perhaps been anticipated in the similar capitals of the Horrea Agrippiana, a granary near the Forum, built at the earliest under Augustus.[9] But the most famous example of such a treatment is the Colosseum (Figs. 23 and 24). Not only do its Corinthian capitals also have plain uncarved leaves, but the complicated spiral of the Ionic volute is reduced to a simple disc. The striking contrast with the refined finish of the Theatre of Marcellus (Fig. 19, p. 32), built earlier of the same materials, draws attention to the different function of the later building in the same way as does the rustication of the amphitheatres of Pola and Verona (Fig. 20). The two types of lack of finish are both applied to the same types of building.

Finding your way through the Roman empire

When the hero of Petronius' *Satyricon* found himself drunk and tired on the streets of Cumae in the mid-first century he was glad to find that his young companion had marked the columns and piers of the town with chalk so that they could readily find their way to their lodgings.[10] As the number of columns in the cities of the empire rapidly increased, their role as landmarks must have become correspondingly important, and distinctions of colour, surface treatment, and material

must have become more and more telling. The passerby may have paid as much attention to such variations in columns within the city as he did to the information on the columnar milestones outside it. It was thus a happy chance that the Roman builders had an ever wider choice of column shafts to use in new and ever larger constructions. Besides, as more and more capitals were Corinthian, shaft variation also became a more significant index of status. For both these reasons, great interest attaches to the way the new range of marble and granite columns came to be used during the second and third centuries. Two large architectural enterprises where this use can be well studied are the Markets and Forum of Trajan of about 110 and Hadrian's Pantheon of fifteen years later.

In Trajan's Forum and in the adjoining market areas also constructed by him, the older means of differentiation are still exploited (Fig. 30). To the west of the Forum, adjoining the earlier Forum of Julius Caesar, a commercial portico called the Basilica Argentaria was built as an arcade supported on tall square piers of rusticated travertine and peperino, continuing the Claudian treatment in a lighter mode. On the east side, against the Quirinal hill, a much more ambitious scheme of shopping streets was constructed, the so-called Markets, rising in terraces from a hemicycle decorated with a row of Doric pilasters made of brick but with travertine mouldings. Both areas were thus marked out as of lower status than the great Forum itself. This was divided into two areas by the enormous Basilica Ulpia: to the north a small court containing Trajan's Column was flanked by Greek and Latin libraries; to the south a much larger court with hemicycles in its sides terminated in a curved wall with, at its centre, a monumental portal. In this grand sequence of spaces there was only one Doric column, Trajan's column itself, 100 feet high, with a Doric base and capital but with its flutes covered by the spiral frieze recording the martial emperor's Dacian campaigns. The pedestal was decorated with the trophies of war and crowned by swags of laurel, and the victor's laurel also covered the mouldings of the column's base. The rich Doric order appears aptly chosen to match the *virtus* of Trajan the soldier in a rare example of true Vitruvian *decor*. It may seem surprising to use for such a monument an order which had come to possess such lowly associations, but the use of marble and the rich egg-and-dart

30. Forum of Trajan, Rome, early second century:
Trajan's Column and columns of court

carving of the echinus of the capital made clear that this was no ordinary Doric. Little is known of the decoration of the adjoining libraries, but they seem to have had an inner elevation of two orders of Corinthian columns of Numidian and Phrygian marble, creating a colourful architecture of interior refinement in contrast to the column outside—a contrast similar to that between the lecture room and the palaestra of a Hellenistic gymnasium. The great Basilica itself had two encircling Corinthian colonnades, the outer of Italian cipollino, the inner of grey Egyptian granite (the inner columns clearly predominate by their greater size,

richer colour, and exotic provenance). The large court on the south of the Basilica was surrounded with fluted Corinthian columns of Phrygian marble, while the exedrae on either side had central niches flanked by Corinthian columns of grey granite. The magnificent curved wall at the opposite end was faced with freestanding Composite columns framing an arched entrance, the whole surmounted by an array of sculpture with trophies flanking a six-horse chariot group. Apollodorus, the architect of the whole, seems to have assumed that movement from north to south was as important as that in the other direction, if not more so.

The reverse axis now seems the main one chiefly because under Hadrian a great temple was erected to Trajan, largely blocking the northern approach. If, on the other hand, we visualize the complex as originally completed it is likely that its purpose was at least partly to extend the existing Fora towards the north, so that they could be more directly approached from the great Via Lata, always the main entrance to the city for people coming from northern Italy. A worthy approach to the centre of empire had always been lacking. Viewed in this way the great Column would have served as an excellent marker attracting the visitor's attention just off the axis of the Via Lata. After passing this Doric emblem of the emperor's manly strength and the libraries, emblems of his love of wisdom, the visitor would then traverse the Corinthian spaces of the closed Basilica dedicated to commerce and law and the open Forum to find himself before the magnificent Composite triumphal façade; through this he would pass to the Forum of Augustus, the Forum Transitorium, and the Forum Romanum itself. Just as the whole Trajanic complex was paid for by the booty of the Dacian wars, so the honorific arch could be seen as the final reward for the victories recorded on the Column. The progression also aptly expressed the historic achievement of the Romans as they had moved from austere strength and virtue to the enjoyment of wealth and luxury.

The Pantheon (c.118–c.128) is a simpler unit and is much better preserved, but even within its relatively compact arrangement of portico and rotunda there is considerable colouristic differentiation, which emerges all the more clearly since the order is Corinthian throughout.[11] The outer row of columns in the portico is of grey granite; the inner ones are pink. The sense of movement increases with the contrast between the white marble pilasters outside the main door and the dark Phrygian marble ones inside and with the richer colouristic changes of the interior. Thus the small pilasters of the upper order were originally of red porphyry, a hard igneous rock another stage deeper in tone and colour than the inner colonnade of the portico, while the main order below consists of an alternation of Phrygian and Numidian marble. The latter are so employed that the darker Phrygian is used for the main axis (that is, the entrance niche and the apse opposite) as well as for the cross axis (that is, the two opposed apses on either side of the rotunda), while Numidian is

used for the minor rectangular recesses arranged in a diagonal X pattern in relation to the upright cross of the main axis. The main apse opposite the entrance is given overall predominance by having more elaborately fluted columns which do not bear an entablature, as do those in all the other recesses, but stand free in front of the rotunda wall. This emphasis on the main axis from the entrance is reinforced by the use of triangular pediments on the aediculae which flank this axis on either side of the entrance and the main apse, in contrast to the segmental pediments on the aediculae adjoining the apses of the cross axis. The column shafts of some of these aediculae have been changed, but it is almost certain that the triangular-pedimented ones originally had shafts of fluted Numidian marble, while the other ones were originally of porphyry.[12] If so the contrast between the aedicules of the minor and major axes is between unfluted igneous materials and fluted true marbles—that is, the same contrast as that between portico and interior and between upper and lower orders too. The overall pattern is clear. The colour and finish of column shafts play an important part in the organization of the building. They describe and control axes of movement and vision. A Roman visitor to the Pantheon must have been much more alert to such modulations than his modern equivalent, who will probably only be left with a generalized impression of opulence. But then, for the second-century Roman finding his way through a city which was becoming increasingly like a labyrinth of colonnades, every significant change in the shafts which he passed must have helped to bring order to his experience.

A new visual alertness to columns as a means of communication probably also explains other developments in their use at the same period. One of the most striking of these is the placing of richer orders under simpler ones, and not over them as had been usual previously. Good examples of this are the Porta dei Leoni at Verona, which is probably after A.D. 65, and second-century structures such as the façade of the Library of Celsus at Ephesus c.135 (Fig. 31) or the Market Gate at Miletus c.160. In all of these Composite is found below Corinthian, although buildings such as the Sufetula Capitolium make it clear that it was considered the superior order. There is thus a complete inversion of the pattern found in virtually all earlier structures, whether Hellenistic stoas or Roman theatres and am-

31. Library of Celsus, Ephesus, c.135: façade

phitheatres, where the superior order was placed on top. There is no obvious reason for this startling departure from precedent, but a study of the elements which are common to these three buildings may help us to arrive at an explanation. All three reflect the new interest in ostentatious display. In the Porta dei Leoni a traditional simple Doric gate was replaced by a very elaborate façade a few feet in front using much richer forms. The Porta dei Leoni as it now survives is the inner face of a gate which may well have had an equally elaborate exterior, like the Porta dei Borsari in the same town. If so, both gates are likely to have been intended to provide Verona with a much more impressive façade to greet arriving travellers. The façade of the Library of Celsus is equally clearly intended as an advertisement for the library, the family of Celsus, and the

32. Theatre, Sabratha: *scaena*, late second century

33. Amphitheatre, Thysdrus (El Djem), third century

richest appearance. It is difficult to explain this reversal except as a consequence of a new visual awareness, a consciousness that the first visual experience of a city or a building is decisive in affecting our estimate of it. At the same time a similar consciousness of the importance of initial visual impact could justify putting the richest elements of a façade at the bottom where they would be most visible, instead of at the top where visually their effect would be lost. Thus the associated tendencies to emphasize both the first part of a building and the lowest part of such a first element can be seen to stem directly from a new concern for visual effect. The interest in giving a good impression which these and many other such buildings reveal can also be related to the parallel interest in the exploitation of laudatory rhetoric as a means of publicity and propaganda. A façade could easily make a building or a city seem greater than it was, just as a panegyric could a man.

If the use of a richer lower order does indeed reflect a concentration on the "grand entrance," then we should expect that in cases where superposed orders are found unconnected with such entrances the old rule of placing the richer above would prevail. This is indeed so. In a number of theatres of the late first and second centuries the *scaena* was apparently decorated with Ionic below and Corinthian above, as at Ephesus, Gerash, Miletus, and Aspendus. It is in the nature of a theatre scene that it is experienced as a two-dimensional screen by the spectator and is never approached by him. Yet these scenes are not without interest, for they too show how the developing visual awareness made it possible to use the orders to focus the spectator's attention. At both Ephesus and Miletus, for example, the pairs of columns that stood at either end of the lower order were not Ionic but Corinthian. This exceptional introduction of a variation of column type into a row of columns of the same size can only have been intended to provide a visual emphasis to the termination of the series. Taken together the Roman theatres of the late first, second, and third centuries display innumerable variations. Besides the examples with Ionic still below Corinthian—hardly surprising in the Greek East, where most surviving specimens are situated—others, such as Lepcis Magna of the mid-second century, are Corinthian on both levels but with the lower clearly predominant in size and richness. In the

city. The two-storey colonnade framing three doors below and three windows above, with the upper and lower entablatures projecting and receding in a dramatic alternating pattern, introduces a new ostentation to the exterior of a secular building. The exterior was apparently more elaborate than the interior, which had only Corinthian capitals. The Market Gate at Miletus with its similar arrangement is another case where a structure which traditionally would have been quite simple was given a new elaboration. What all three buildings show is that a new importance was attached to entrances. Until this time entries of all types, city-gates, propylaea, etc., had usually been simpler, or at least no more elaborate, than the buildings to which they led. Now the entrances themselves present the

34 (at right). Basilica, Lepcis Magna,
dedicated 216: interior of apse

56

slightly later three-storey *scaena* at Sabratha a more complex design combines a greater emphasis on the lower colonnade in terms of scale with a new emphasis on the middle tier in terms of fluting (Fig. 32). This emphasis on the middle storey is repeated in the exterior of the third-century amphitheatre at El Djem (Thysdrus) in Tunisia, where Corinthian is found top and bottom with Composite between (Fig. 33). Probably the purpose of this type of arrangement is to achieve the same effect vertically as we found in the scene at Ephesus horizontally. There a richer order was placed at either end of a series to provide a strong termination; at Sabratha and Thysdrus a richer order is placed between two simpler ones to provide a strong centre. The idea of emphasizing the centre is also found in a horizontal series in the third-century basilica at Lepcis, where a pair of giant Corinthian columns stand at the centre of the apses at each end of the building where the emperor's representative might sit, clearly dominating the two smaller superposed Ionic orders on either side (Fig. 34). The traditional colonnade with columns

of virtually identical size, material, and order was becoming broken up to provide an emphasis sometimes on the ends and sometimes on the centre. Similar principles could be applied vertically too. The importance of such variations was that they brought order to the movements of the eye over a two-dimensional surface such as a *scaena*, just as they brought order to the movement of the visitor in a three-dimensional space such as a forum. In the case of the variation of the columns and capitals in the apse of the basilica at Lepcis, the effect is to focus both eye- and body-motion.

Earlier the Greeks and Romans had tended to see colonnades as consistent wholes whose beauty resided in their perfect regularity. Now the spectator was expected to scan a building and to look for features, especially in the columnar organization, which would articulate it. This expectation was one aspect of the developing visual awareness of the first centuries A.D., and it must have been stimulated by the need to discern an order in the chaos of columns which most cities of the Roman Empire would have presented.

Early Christianity

◆

The triumph of Christ

Constantine's victory over Maxentius at the Milvian Bridge in 312 brought with it the victory of Christianity. Having fought and won under the sign of the Cross, the emperor went on to reward the religion of Christ with protection and support. By the mid-fourth century churches were rising everywhere. Though not derived from temples, they gave columnar forms as prominent a place inside as pagan shrines had given them outside. Often, indeed, earlier temples were stripped to provide the colonnades for the new basilicas and, as with Sulla's stripping of the Athenian Olympieum for the benefit of the Roman Capitol, there is more than a hint of triumph in such plunder. This was certainly the case with the supposed transfer of columns from the Temple of the Unconquered Sun in Rome to Haghia Sophia in Constantinople.[1] Even more explicitly triumphal was the transfer of Composite, emblem of Roman superiority, to the new religion.

This transfer is heralded in the remarkable rejection of the order on Constantine's own triumphal arch, the first for two hundred and fifty years not to use the triumphal Roman form, and confirmed by its repeated use in Christian monuments later in his reign. Few of Constantine's own buildings survive, but St Peter's is known through Renaissance drawings (Fig. 35; cf. Fig. 139, p. 245). From these it appears that while the fountain in the atrium was surrounded by Ionic columns and those in the nave seem to have been chiefly Corinthian, the twelve that closed the ends of the four aisles and the transepts were probably all Composite. Composite too were the six spiral-vine columns around the tomb of Saint Peter in front of the apse. The triumphal

significance of this area was asserted in the mosaic inscription on the arch separating nave and transept: QUOD DUCE TE MUNDUS SURREXIT AD ASTRA TRIUMPHANS HANC CONSTANTINUS VICTOR TIBI CONDIDIT AULAM ("Because with You as leader the world has risen triumphant to the stars, the victorious Constantine has established for You this hall"). With its inscriptions, its arch shape, its mosaic decoration showing the standard circled by the victor's laurel, and its Composite capitals, the east end of St Peter's recalled many features of earlier triumphal arches, and we know that its diaphragm arch was called a "triumphal arch" at least in the Carolingian period.[2] The arch of Constantine was probably dedicated in 315/16, and St Peter's was perhaps planned around 320. It is as if Constantine, in gratitude for Christ's aid at the Milvian Bridge, decided to surrender the order to Him. The victory was Christ's, not the emperor's.

Once transferred to Christ, Composite became the emblem of a greater victory, victory over death, and it is to this victory that the mosaic inscription alludes. Composite was thus particularly appropriate in funerary monuments such as the transept of St Peter's itself, and it naturally became the order of other mausolea and sarcophagi. Many fourth-century sarcophagi employ the same triumphal imagery as the arch of St Peter's, and those which have columns use Composite capitals, as does the great mausoleum of Constantia, the emperor's daughter (now S. Costanza), c.337–350 (Fig. 36). If, as has been suggested, some of these funerary monuments represent the Heavenly Jerusalem in which the saved will live forever, Composite may also be thought of as the order of that city. The transfer of the order from Rome to Jerusalem would follow the transfer from emperor to Christ.

35. Transept of Old St Peter's, Rome, 320s: drawing by
Maarten van Heemskerck, National Museum, Stockholm

Colonnade and liturgy

St Peter's represents a contrast with earlier religious buildings not just in the prominence it accords to Composite. Another new feature, one it shares with many early churches, is its exploitation of a sequence of orders, Ionic in the atrium, predominantly Corinthian in the nave, and Composite in the transept—a sequence which was further elaborated by the use of several different types of shaft and capital even within the nave colonnade. The variation of capital and shaft are as typical of Christian churches as monotonous repetition had been of pagan temples, as Deichmann observed.[3]

The reasons for the change lie in the difference of religious experience. Every step taken in a Christian church, every passage in the liturgy, potentially involved psychological transformations and the dramatic realization of some bold metaphor such as rebirth or salvation. From the moment of decision to enter the portal to the experience of baptism and the eucharist, the worshipper was in constant movement and transformation. The distance from the squalor of the street outside to a vision of Heaven in the apse might be only a few yards, and the architect and decorator had to work hard to make that journey convincing. In many ways this short walk was much more demanding than

36. S. Costanza, Rome, c.337–350: interior

the journey from the city gate to the forum with its temple, and the architecture and decoration reflected this. Just as the acceptance of the Christian faith involved the surrender of rational standards, just as the experience of worship was spiritual rather than intellectual, so the rational principles of regularity and order that had earlier governed colonnade design were left behind as different orders, materials, and ornaments were combined in the naves of the new churches and even in the compact interiors of baptisteries.

At St Peter's the relation between the sequence of the orders and the sequence of religious experience is fairly easy to establish, since the orders are concentrated in different areas. Thus the simplest order, Ionic, is associated with the forecourt, where the worshipper would take water from the fountain in allusion to his first entry into the Church through baptism; Corinthian is found in the nave, where he would offer prayers; and Composite is found above all around the tomb and altar, where he would witness the eucharist, token of fi-

61

37. Lateran Baptistery, Rome, c.435: interior

nal salvation and victory over death. In later buildings the sequence may be more compressed. One example is the Lateran Baptistery, which provides a virtual epitome of St Peter's (Figs. 37 and 38). Originally founded by Constantine, who himself endowed it with eight porphyry columns, it acquired its present form under Pope Sixtus III (432–40). Although restored and rebuilt during the sixteenth and seventeenth centuries, it must preserve the original arrangement of the orders, since the present mixture cannot postdate the Middle Ages. There is perhaps already a promise of transformation in the grand portico, where two Composite columns stand between flanking Corinthian pilasters. More strikingly, on the inside the eight columns around the baptismal basin support capitals of three different types. The two pairs of capitals on the north-

south entrance axis are Ionic, the pair to the east are Corinthian, and the pair to the west are Composite. This bizarre grouping of capital types in a small ring of supports can be understood only in terms of the remarkable drama of baptism as entry into the Church. Having been attracted by the magnificent entrance, the catechumen found himself on the minor Ionic axis; then in the course of the baptismal rite he is likely to have turned first to the east and then to the west. Since the adjoining Lateran basilica was, like other early churches, laid out with its entrance to the east and altar to the west, the arrangement of the Baptistery columns was perfectly calculated to prepare the baptized for the liturgical experience to which he could look forward. The strongest evidence for the correspondence between the arrangement of the orders and a liturgical sequence

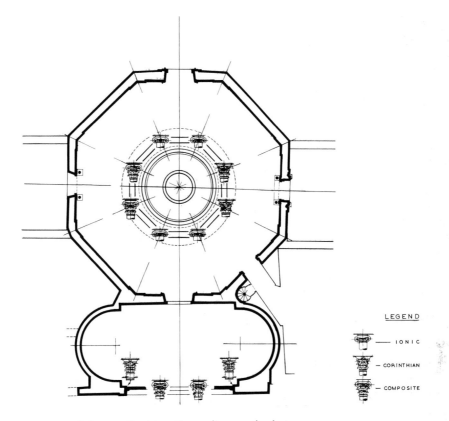

38. Lateran Baptistery, Rome: diagram of orders

is the series of verses which Sixtus had carved on the entablature sections between the columns.[4] The first of these, opposite the entrance, explains what happens "here": "Here is born from gentle seed a people destined for the heavens, a people whom the spirit brings out of the fertile waters." After this allusive description of the projected advantages of becoming a Christian, a series of other verses point out different aspects of baptism until, at the west, the text sums up what the rite has achieved: "You who *have been* reborn in this fountain hope for the Kingdom of Heaven; those who have been born only once cannot attain the happy life!" The message carried by the two Composite capitals looks forward to entry into Heaven just as the Composite columns of the porch invite entry into the Church.

Many other churches in Rome provide evidence for the use of columns in the Early Christian period, but the two most striking examples are the two galleried basilicas of S. Lorenzo fuori le mura (579–590) (Figs. 39 and 40) and S. Agnese (625–638) (Figs. 41 and 42). At S. Lorenzo the church as built by Pope Pelagius had at ground level five columns on either side of the nave and two carrying an architrave across it at its entrance. All are of fluted Phrygian marble, but while the rest are true Corinthian, the two next to the arch of the apse have volutes carried by victories with trophies carved in between. At gallery level the two columns over the entrance are of green granite with contemporary Corinthian capitals, while all the others are fluted Phrygian and bear re-used Corinthian capitals, except for the two nearest to the apse which are again different, being Composite. The startling use of military "victory" cap-

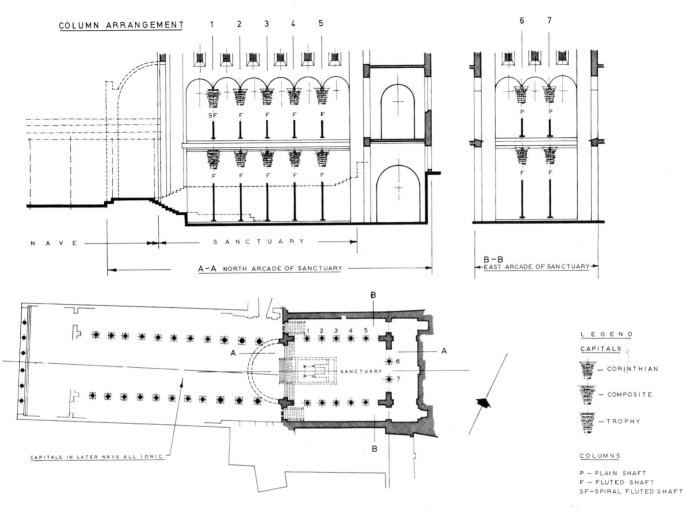

40. S. Lorenzo fuori le mura, Rome: diagram of orders

itals below and Composite above for the columns adjoining the arch of the apse helps to reinforce the suggestion both that that order was deliberately introduced into churches as an emblem of Christ triumphant and that it was used to give specifically triumphal associations to the arch. The contemporary mosaic inscription on the arch refers directly to Saint Lawrence's martyrdom, the moment when he too as soldier of Christ triumphed over death. The change of order also draws attention to the importance of the altar area in the early Church, both as the site of the transformation of the eucharist and as the place where the worshipper might often have a vision of paradise in

the apse or on the arch itself. At S. Lorenzo, this columnar articulation is further accompanied by a build-up to the change of capital in the arrangement of entablature blocks (robbed from several different buildings) to form a crescendo of ornament along the nave.

At S. Agnese forty years later, the situation is similar but more complicated (Figs. 41 and 42). At ground level the colonnades on either side of the nave are again chiefly Corinthian, but now it is the last *two* capitals on each side by the triumphal arch which are Composite. Composite too are the capitals carrying the gallery over the nave at the entrance. The shafts are extremely varied as well, with light granite columns supporting

39 (at left). S. Lorenzo fuori le mura, Rome, 579–590: interior

41. S. Agnese fuori le mura, Rome, 625–638: interior

the Composite at the entrance, a mixture of light-col-
oured fluted and unfluted marble columns carrying the
Corinthian up the nave, and red marble emphasizing
the distinction of the final four Composite columniations. It is worth noting that the Composite specimens
here are much simpler than the Corinthian, thus making it clear that it was indeed the absolute associations

of the form rather than its generically greater richness
which motivated its introduction. In the gallery, as at
S. Lorenzo, the two columns over the entrance are
again distinguished from the rest, in this case by having
spiral flutes and Ionic capitals. The others vary both in
shaft and capital, the first two on either side from the
entrance having spiral flutes and Composite capitals,

66

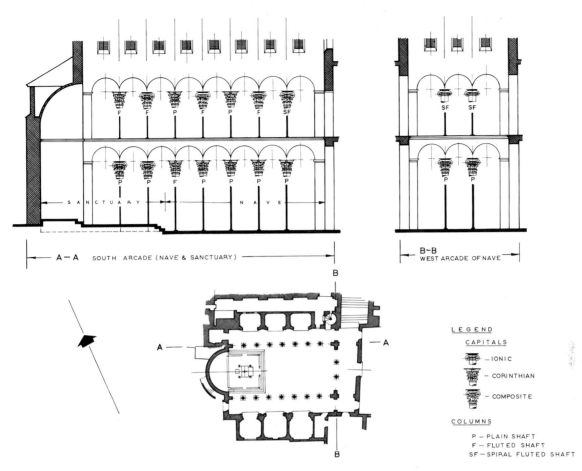

42. S. Agnese fuori le mura, Rome: diagram of orders

followed by a rhythmic pattern of fluted and unfluted shafts bearing a varying series of capitals running Corinthian (Composite on the right), Composite, Corinthian, Composite, Corinthian, Composite, Corinthian, though the differences of order are hard to perceive. In spite of this irregular variation in the gallery the overall organization again emerges clearly. As in the Lateran Baptistery the first order met is the same as the last, with lower-status ones in between. This emphasizes the importance of both door and altar. More clearly than at S. Lorenzo, the gallery is inferior in status to the floor of the church, having Ionic instead of Composite

at the entrance and Corinthian instead of Composite as the last order before the altar. This inferiority is appropriate to the gallery as the *matroneum*, an area occupied by women, and, as we shall see, this came to be asserted even more clearly in the Greek East.

In view of the clearly greater status of Corinthian and Composite it may seem surprising that S. Maria Maggiore (c.432–440), alone among the great basilicas, employed neither of these orders but used Ionic throughout. Since the church was one of the calculated achievements of Sixtus III, who also rebuilt the Lateran Baptistery where the orders were so carefully chosen, the selection of Ionic demands to be taken seriously. Probably the explanation lies in the delicate role Sixtus wished S. Maria Maggiore to play in Early Christian Rome. Founded and decorated by him as the first church in the city to honour the Virgin, it was inspired by the theology of the Council of Ephesus (431), which had endowed Christ's mother with a new dignity as Mother of God. Apart from a few minor martyrs women had not received much respect within the Church as yet, and this grand building, being based on contentious theology, can hardly have been guaranteed a welcome. Accordingly Sixtus seems to have calculated it to imitate, but not to equal, the three great basilicas of the Lateran, St Peter, and St Paul. It approaches them closely in length, but both in its order and in its single rather than double aisle it would have manifested a suitable modesty. The choice of Ionic here thus reflects the same tact as that which led Augustus to use that order for the temple of the Deified Julius.

Another case where an unusual order requires an explanation is S. Pietro in Vincoli, which has re-used Doric columns of Greek marble in the nave. The church was perhaps given its present form by the Empress Eudoxia, who also presented it with Saint Peter's chains just after 450. Doric had virtually ceased to be used as early as the Late Empire, and it had never found a place in the standard Early Christian Ionic-Corinthian-Composite scale; so an explanation for its use here (if the possibility of random choice is excluded) must be sought farther back. As Vitruvius was perhaps the only person to have formulated a separate rule for the use of Doric, it is not unreasonable to look to him for guidance. His recommendation of Doric for temples to gods with emphatically manly characteristics would certainly be applicable here, as the church was specifically built to house the chains which had bound the most robust of the saints and there was thus no other church in Rome with such associations of virile strength. It may seem strained to suggest that builders at this time may have referred to Vitruvius, who was never popular. Yet if Krautheimer is right to talk of a "Renaissance" at this time and of a return to Classical precision after the sloppiness of the fourth and earlier fifth centuries, such a reference would be quite appropriate.[5] The exceptional use of fluted Greek Doric justifies such a specific interpretation, just as in the case of Trajan's Column.

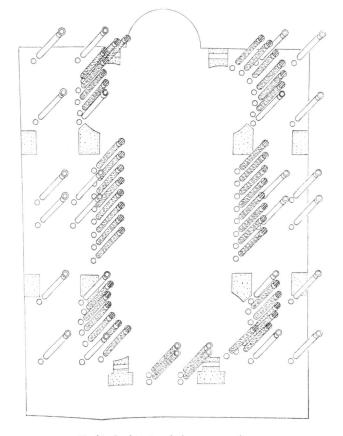

43. Haghia Sophia, Istanbul, 532–537: diagram of orders at gallery level (shaded tops of columns indicate Composite capitals, open circles indicate Ionic) (after Deichmann)

Composite had never been as popular outside Rome as it was in the capital, and Ionic had instead served much more frequently as an alternative to Corinthian, especially in the East, where Greek traditions were most persistent. It is thus by the use of Ionic and Corinthian that the builders of the Early Christian churches outside Rome marked off major and minor areas. At Tigzirt in Algeria, for example, the basilica of c.450 has Ionic columns along the nave and larger Corinthian ones at the triumphal arch. There was an upper order too along the nave, but that was probably Ionic, as in Justinian's church of St John at Ephesus, where both levels of the church were in that order. The use of galleries was very prevalent in the East, where they seem often to have been occupied by women, and in the majority of cases they are Ionic, just as the main order below is usually Corinthian. In the fifth century this is true of Nea Anchialos, Basilica A, and of both the Acheiropoietos and St Demetrius at Thessalonica. Ionic is also found above both Corinthian and Composite, though in this case just attached to the wall surface, in the Orthodox Baptistery at Ravenna c.450. Subsequently, when Byzantine architects developed their own forms out of Corinthian and Composite these were again used to set off the main order of the ground floor from Ionic galleries, as in Justinian's SS. Sergius and Bacchus (pre 536). In a more complicated scheme at Haghia Sophia (532–537), Ionic is used for the minor outer colonnade of the gallery behind an inner Composite row along the nave, for the single gallery colonnade at the west, and apparently also for the destroyed atrium portico (Fig. 43). Both entrance and gallery were thus marked off as less important than the main central space. In the slightly earlier Constantinopolitan church of St John Studios, too, Ionic may well have been used for both atrium and gallery, providing a similar contrast with the Composite-derived main order of the nave. Certainly at S. Apollinare in Classe at Ravenna, of the 530s, a Byzantinizing form of Composite along the nave is preceded by Ionic in both the narthex portico and the west window. More unusual is S. Vitale at Ravenna, of the same date around 530 but built as a deliberate expression of the new ascendancy of the Eastern Emperor Justinian on Italian soil (Fig. 44). Here the contrast is not between inferior Ionic and superior Corinthian or Composite, but between a relatively inferior Composite and a superior Byzantine cushion form. Composite is found in the narthex and in the galleries of the octagon, while it is the new Byzantine type which is used for the ground floor of the octagon and for both ground floor and galleries of the sanctuary. This example demonstrates—as we might have expected from the way the new Byzantine capitals swept away the old Classical forms, particularly in court circles—that they were thought of as definitely superior, even to Composite. Indeed, one of the cleverest ways of asserting the predominance of the emperor in Byzantium over Rome was to demote Composite capitals from their position near the altar and replace them with a new Greek form. The Greeks had never had any reason to welcome the Composite order,

44. S. Vitale, Ravenna, c.530:
capital in sanctuary

which expressed Roman dominance by arrogantly compressing the Greek forms, and the order had never been widely used in the Eastern Mediterranean. In their own churches they could accept it as above all a Christian order, but when it came to a church such as S. Vitale, which was as much a political as a religious monument, the national associations of the order were treated as more important.

Whether in the East or the West, columns were used with a new dramatic expressiveness. The reason is not simply that the Christian liturgy was more dramatic than that of most of its pagan predecessors. The use of architecture was only one aspect of a much broader attempt to control and influence the worshipper through his eyes and ears. Christians looked and listened with a new alertness. Hymns, sermons, and inscriptions elaborated on the connections between space and liturgy. Saint Ambrose in the late fourth century composed an inscription for a baptistery drawing attention to the meaning of its eight corners, eight being associated with the eighth day of the new Creation and Christ's Resurrection on the eighth day of the Passion.[6] Many writers saw entry into the Church as equivalent to entry into the Kingdom of Heaven, and the apse behind the triumphal arch was the place where Heaven might increasingly be represented. For those who could read neither church fathers nor inscriptions, paintings and mosaics provided, as Gregory the Great pointed out, a silent literature. If in this world pictures became the bibles of the poor, colonnades may be said to have become their liturgical commentaries.

Christian columns

All this may help us to understand why architects chose one column-type rather than another, but it does not explain the fascination with columns in the first place. Columns had long been a measure of wealth and status from the time when they were taxed in the Late Republic, and the mass production of monolithic columns of standard dimensions in the empire had ensured that they were readily usable as *spolia* when architects working for both pagan and Christian clients in the fourth and fifth centuries began to plunder earlier structures. Nevertheless, in the century before Constantine columns were increasingly rejected as supports for major buildings and were often reduced to a small-scale decorative role on structures consisting essentially of massive walls and piers bearing heavy concrete vaults. This was true even of building types which had traditionally given the greatest prominence to the column as a support—for example, temples such as that of Venus and Rome, or basilicas such as that of Maxentius, both of the early fourth century. Against this background it is surprising that the new vocabulary is avoided in all the great early churches, which instead restore the column to its place as a critical structural support and, indeed, make greater demands on its strength and stability than ever before.

A principal reason for this tendency emerges from a comparison of major Early Christian monuments with the architectural imagery of the New Testament. In *Galatians* 2, 9, the apostles James, Cephas (i.e. Peter), and John are called "columns." This idea can in turn be related to *Ephesians* 2, 20, where the church is said to be "built" on the foundations of the apostles, and to *Revelation* 21, 14, where the wall of the Heavenly Jerusalem contains twelve foundations each marked with the name of one of the apostles. These last two texts in particular seem to have captured the imagination of Constantine, the chief inaugurator of Christian architecture. Already in a speech at the Council of Nicaea

(325) he visualized the Church as a façade of twelve marble columns bearing a pediment.[7] Subsequently, in the wave of building which followed the Council, he erected groups of twelve columns or pedestals round the most important churches in the four religious and political centres of the empire. Eusebius explicitly tells us that the circular structure built over Christ's tomb in Jerusalem was decorated with twelve columns representing the twelve apostles,[8] and around Constantine's own tomb in the church of the Holy Apostles in Constantinople there were twelve pedestals, each inscribed with an apostle's name.[9] At St Peter's in Rome the emperor also erected twelve columns round the tomb of the prince of the apostles, two in each transept and two at the end of each of the four aisles—the very columns mentioned earlier as bearing Composite capitals. Although there is no text to confirm their meaning, their placing is so unusual, and their grouping is so similar to that round the other two great tombs, that it is hard to avoid the same identification. A circular group of twelve columns also figured prominently in the basilica at Constantine's northern capital, Trier. Each group is in a sense a representation of the Church and looks forward to the Heavenly Jerusalem. Nowhere was this more appropriate than at the Holy Sepulchre of Christ himself, on whom first and foremost the Church was based and who, as the Lamb, would stand at the centre of the Heavenly City. Christ had looked forward to a Church literally "built" on Peter, the rock, and it was on Constantine, who saw himself as the thirteenth disciple, that the final foundation of a worldly Church was to depend. Constantine amply fulfilled his vision at Nicaea. At Jerusalem, Rome, and Constantinople the groups of twelve column/foundations were erected around the tombs of the three successive inaugurators of the Christian Church.

Under Constantine and his successors the same imagery was taken up and developed in related contexts. In S. Costanza, the mausoleum of Constantine's daughter, twelve pairs of columns were grouped around her tomb closely paralleling the arrangement at her father's. The dome, its drum pierced by twelve windows, apparently was decorated with a representation of the Heavenly Jerusalem. Through the transparency and at the same time the looseness of the symbolism, the building can be endowed with meaning without challenging the authority of its models. Equally low-

45. Sarcophagus of Junius Bassus, died 358, St Peter's, Rome

key is the sarcophagus of the *praefectus urbis* Junius Bassus (died 358) now under St Peter's (Fig. 45). The two registers of scenes on its front are suggestively separated by twelve composite columns in two rows. More explicit is the Mausoleum of the Gothic Emperor Theodoric at Ravenna (c.520), which has twelve curious projections on the dome. These can best be understood as an intentional analogy to the twelve piers around the tomb of his model, Constantine; indeed, a misunderstanding of such an intention may well be revealed in the names that were later inscribed on them, those of the four evangelists and eight of the apostles. In all these examples the number twelve seems to have been chosen deliberately, and the same may have been true of the twelve columns that marked off the sanctuary in Justinian's new Haghia Sophia.[10] In other cases surviving texts which give similar interpretations may not demonstrate any intention on the part of the builder, but they do confirm the currency of the iden-

tification of columns with people, and especially with apostles. Thus in a Syriac hymn describing the Justinianic cathedral at Edessa the columns of the outer courts are said to represent the Tribes of Israel that surrounded the Tabernacle, while the group of eleven columns which supports the ambo is seen to represent the eleven apostles who were present in the upper room at Jerusalem (*Acts* 1, 13), and the ten columns which adorn the choir are said to represent the ten apostles who fled at the Crucifixion.[11]

Apart from these Christian examples of the identification of columns with figures, there is one pagan shrine which may imitate Christian practice. When Vettius Agorius Praetextatus, a notoriously pagan successor to Junius Bassus as urban prefect, rebuilt the Porticus Deorum Consentium in the Forum in 367, he adorned its front with twelve columns which do not correspond to the Flavian architecture behind (Fig. 46). The shrine had traditionally contained twelve famous

46. Porticus Deorum Consentium, Rome, 367 (foreground),
with Tabularium, 78 B.C. (above and behind)

quered Sun in Rome for his new Haghia Sophia in Constantinople.[13] Both pagans and Christians were preoc-
cupied with metaphors of victory and triumph.

Apart from the possible case of the twelve columns
of the Porticus, there is little evidence that pagans ever
saw columns as substitutes for more naturalistic representations of sacred figures. In Christianity, on the
other hand, such a substitution of abstract symbols in
place of statues might well have been seen as a subtle
way of getting the benefits of a permanent image without incurring the charge of idolatry: columns were
safely aniconic. Silver figures of Christ and the twelve
apostles and of four angels were given by Constantine
to the Lateran,[14] but it is noteworthy that for St Peter's,
where an identification of columns with apostles was
proposed, no such gifts are recorded and indeed the
Liber pontificalis, which lists the gifts, mentions the offering of columns to St Peter's at exactly the same point
where the offering of statues was mentioned in the Lateran.[15] This may well confirm that columns were
thought of as a safe substitute. Certainly the two most
frequent groupings of columns in the eastern parts of
early churches are fours for ciboria and twelves farther
from the altar, echoing the disposition of the figures in
the Lateran.

The texts quoted above give some idea of the peculiar importance of columns for Early Christian architects, but another document gives a hint of yet another
reason for their popularity in churches of the period.
Paulinus of Nola has left several letters and poems describing the buildings which he either erected or restored around Nola in the early fifth century. In one of
these he deals with the construction of a baptistery and
goes on to meditate on what he can learn from its design. As part of this meditation he hopes that "Christ
Himself may erect in us *columns* and remove the *piers*
which block our souls and that He may thus create
wide access to our senses; so that He may Himself walk
in them, just as Wisdom was wont to place her healing
steps in the five porticoes of Solomon, and so heal our
bodies by His touch and our hearts by His teaching."[16]
The columns that Christ will erect in us are contrasted
with the old-fashioned piers that at present block up
our souls and prevent His passage there; if our soul is
supported on columns it will be as open as the porticoes of Solomon's Temple. Evidently Paulinus is thinking of Christ as light, enlightenment. For the replace-

statues of the Olympian gods, and the columns may
well be intended to represent these in the same way that
twelve columns represented the apostles in so many
contemporary churches. The fact that capitals with trophy decorations were sought out from some earlier
building for this late witness to paganism suggests that
there was even an attempt to allude to a final victory of
the religion of the Olympians over that of the apostles.
Such a gesture would match the spirit of the pagan Emperor Julian the Apostate, who had died only three
years earlier with the words "You have conquered, O
Galilaean" on his lips.[12] It also seems to have provoked
the final celebration of Christ's victory when Justinian
removed columns from the Temple of the Uncon-

ment of piers by columns hardly makes walking any easier; it only diminishes the perceived bulk of impervious material, and the reference to our "senses" would be more appropriate in the context of enlightenment too. The importance of light in Early Christian architecture is manifest in almost every account of churches of the period, and it has long been realized that gold, marble, glass mosaics, and windows were all exploited for their ability either to admit or to reflect light. The preference for columns over piers apparently could carry the same associations. Paulinus clearly intends his remarks to be most applicable to an entrance portico, and one of the odd features of fifth-century churches in particular is the prevalence of triple- or quintuple-arched entries supported on columns, replacing the doors separated by piers of masonry which had been an earlier norm.[17] Another new feature of the period are rows of windows separated by columns or colonnettes, particularly at east and west ends. In both these cases the replacement of piers by columns is closely linked to the introduction of more light and a greater openness.

In the Early Christian period the column took on an unprecedented importance. For the Greeks it had been one element of a building system. For the Romans it was a major ornament and frequently a key to architectural organization. But in the churches of the fourth and fifth centuries, unencumbered by the entablatures, pediments, and wall mouldings with which it had been associated by the Greeks, and increasingly free from the competition of alternative forms of support which had deprived it of its authority in the Roman period, it took on a dominant role in terms of both structure and decoration.

VI

The column in the Christian Middle Ages

◆

The encyclopaedic tradition: from natural properties to mystical significance

THE WRITERS and builders of the Early Christian period thought of themselves as giving the first intellectual and architectural expression to a new religion. By the early ninth century, when Charlemagne refounded the Roman Empire in the West and embarked on an extensive building programme, he and those who helped him knew that they were looking back, trying to gather up lost threads and re-establish institutions, both political and religious, which had become very weak. A typical figure in this movement was Hrabanus Maurus, author of the *De universo*, the first great Christian encyclopaedia, which was to be one of the intellectual foundations of the Middle Ages.[1] The work was written in the 840s, after Hrabanus had retired as abbot of Fulda and before he was appointed archbishop of Mainz. In his preface addressed to Charlemagne's son, Louis the Pious, he describes his work as consisting of "remarks on the nature of things and on the properties of words, and also on the mystic signification of things." This effectively sums up Hrabanus' relation to the encyclopaedic tradition. At its head stood the *Natural History* of Pliny the Elder, which dealt with "the nature of things." This had been followed by the *Etymologies* of Isidore of Seville, which elaborated on Pliny by also talking about "the properties of words." Hrabanus' intention was to go one step further by discussing "the mystic significance of things." His was to be the first encyclopaedia which discussed the material universe in terms of a Christian interpretation. It was to incorporate the material of his predecessors and go beyond them.

The way in which Hrabanus epitomizes the development from the Classical to the Medieval world can be understood by comparing his passage on columns with those of his predecessors. Pliny, writing about A.D. 70, a century after Vitruvius, provides the basic text.[2] In a few lines in Book XXXVI he summarizes knowledge of the orders in a way which indicates already an advance on the earlier writer. Thus he states that there are four *genera*: "those whose lower diameter is a sixth of their height are called Doric; those whose lower diameter is a ninth, Ionic; those where it is a seventh, Tuscan; while Corinthian columns have the same properties as Ionic, only, in that their capitals are one diameter high, they look taller. . . . Besides these types of columns there is another called Attic with four equal sides."[3] Tuscan is now for the first time treated on a par with the Greek orders, and a square Attic form is introduced, though without achieving the status of a *genus*. Isidore, Archbishop of Seville, wrote his *Etymologies* around 623.[4] He gives two almost identical discussions of columns, in Book XV "De partibus aedificiorum," and Book XIX, "De constructione." Whether as a result of his own efforts or those of an intermediate source, his formulation is much neater and more coherent than Pliny's: "There are four *genera* of round [columns]: Doric, Ionic, Tuscan, and Corinthian; and these differ from each other in diameter and height. The fifth *genus* of columns is called Attic, and these have four or more angles with equal sides."[5] There are thus now five equal *genera*, four round and one angular. For the first time, the round *genera* are said to differ in height as well as in proportions; and, also for the first time, the possibility of polygonal columns is introduced. Since it is unlikely that

Isidore would have known such columns, he may refer to them only in order to give his text greater comprehensiveness. More closely related to contemporary practice is his own etymological discussion of columnar forms: "Bases are the supports of columns which rise from the foundations and carry the weight of the building above. *Bases* is the name of a very strong stone in Syrian speech. Columns, which are so called because of their length and roundness, support the weight of the whole structure ... Capitals have that name because they are the heads [*capita*] of columns [*columnae*], just as the head comes above the neck [*collum*]. *Epistolia* [sic for *epistylia*] are put above the capitals; it is Greek and means 'put above.' "6 The anthropomorphic interpretation of columns, which had been of only incidental importance for Vitruvius, now becomes predominant and can probably be related to the new Christian tendency to see columns as representing figures, as discussed in the last chapter. In the same way the statement that columns "support the whole weight of the structure" hardly applies to Classical architecture, where they carry only entablatures, but exactly sums up the role of columns in the colonnade of a church, where they support a large sheet of walling which in turn carries the roof.

It is perhaps because he felt that Isidore's text related so well to Christian architecture that Hrabanus repeated it word for word before embarking on his own more explicitly Christian interpretation of columns in terms of "mystical significance":

The bases, however, can be mystically understood as the books of the divine Testaments on which rests all the doctrine of the holy preachers. For the columns are the apostles and the teachers of the Gospel. These persons were prefigured in the two columns which we read that Hiram put up when building the Temple of the Lord, as is written in the book of *Kings* and *Paralipomenon*, that is: Hiram completed the whole work of the king in the house of God, that is, two columns and the epistyles and the capitals, and something like netting which covered the capitals above the epistyles (II *Par.* 4). These are the columns about which Paul says: James, Cephas, and John, who seemed to be columns, gave Barnabas and me the right hand of friendship so that we should go among the Gentiles and they among the Jews (*Gal.* 2). By which words he seems to expound the mystery of the material columns, both what they apparently represented and why there were two. For they stand for the apostles and all the spiritual doctors, raised up toward the heavens and strong in

faith and works and meditation. And they are two because by their preaching they introduce both Gentiles and Circumcised into the Church; for the columns stood in the portico before the doors of the Temple, and they provided a wonderful decoration for its entrance by their ornaments and beauty. For the door of the Temple is the Lord: because no one comes to the Father except through Him (*John* 14); and as He says elsewhere: I am the door and anyone who enters through Me will be saved (*John* 10). Because the columns clearly stand at either side of the door, with the help of the text they show the entry of the Kingdom of Heaven to both peoples. The tops of the columns, that is the highest parts of them, are the minds of the teachers of the faithful, by whose thoughts dedicated to God all their works and words are guided, just as the limbs are guided by the head. But the two capitals which are placed on these tops of the columns are the two Testaments, by the meditation on the observance of which the holy doctors are ruled, both in their whole mind and their body. Whence it is right that each capital was five cubits high, for the account of the law of Moses is contained within five books. Also the whole sequence of the Old Testament is embraced in five periods. And indeed the New Testament preaches nothing more than what Moses and the prophets had taught us that it would contain. Further, the likenesses of chains and nets on the capitals are the variety of the spiritual virtues among the saints, about which it is sung to the Lord in the Psalm: The queen stood at your right hand in a golden garment, clothed in the variety of many charms (*Ps.* 44); or certainly the multiple interweaving of chains and the expanse of netting suggests the varied character of the elect, who not only adhere to the words of the holy preachers, faithfully listening and obeying, but also, like the nets and chains placed on the capitals of the columns, offer a spectacle of miraculous interconnection for all who look at them.7

In this shifting exposition Hrabanus weaves a complex web of ideas. The mystic meaning of bases, columns, and capitals is developed by reference to Iachin and Boaz, the columns of the Temple, and to Saint Paul's column analogy. If Hrabanus can see columns as apostles and teachers of the Gospel, it is because that identification is prefigured in Solomon's twin columns. Since the Temple also prefigures both the Church and the Kingdom of Heaven, the two columns standing at either side of the portal also represent the double mission to Jews and Gentiles, who will enter through Christ the door. This anthropomorphic interpretation is extended by seeing both bases and capitals as the Testaments, the bases because they are the basis on which holy figures rely, and the capitals because it is by the Testaments that they are ruled as by their heads. The separate elements are not new. The idea that the Old Testament mystically prefigures Christ's coming and the rise of Christianity was already developed in the New Testament itself. The Temple of Solomon had been taken as a model for the Christian Church since the time of Constantine.[8] Even the equation of the two columns to the twin communities of Jews and Gentiles had been made a century earlier by Bede.[9] What transforms Hrabanus' thought is the integration of these ideas with the anthropomorphic and numerological interpretations of real columns current in the Early Christian period, to create what is a general theoretical interpretation of columnar elements in Christian terms. If we look at buildings with his eyes, any base can mystically signify a Testament and any column an apostle or teacher of the Gospel, while a structure modelled on Solomon's Temple could be liable to much more specific readings.

This would be an abstract exercise if it were not possible to show that major contemporary buildings were viewed in just such a way. Indeed, in a number of cases an interest in mystic significance is explicitly associated, just as in Hrabanus' text, with the imitation of Old Testament models. This is particularly true of a number of buildings directly connected with Charlemagne and his court. In this context the imitation of Old Testament models is part of a general attempt to authenticate the Frankish monarchy by assimilating the leaders of the Christian Franks to those of the ancient Jews, but the imitation is charged with a mystical as well as a political significance. The assimilation of the Carolingian world to that of the Old Testament affects both buildings and people. Einhard, the emperor's biographer and an enthusiastic student and patron of the arts, was identified with Bezaleel, the famous craftsman who worked for Moses;[10] and Odo of Metz, architect of the palace chapel at Aachen, was identified with Solomon's architect, Hiram of Tyre. The chapel itself was called "Temple of the most wise Solomon" by Alcuin,[11] while Notger even claimed that it was built "after the model of the most wise Solomon."[12]

If Charlemagne could be thought of as Solomon, Odo as Hiram, and the chapel as the Temple, then it is at least possible that the chapel embodied actual features of the building in Jerusalem (Fig. 47). In one respect this is certain. The emperor's throne raised on six steps is an explicit reconstruction of that of Solomon (1 Kings 10, 9).[13] The throne as the seat of wise judgement was particularly important as an attribute of kingship. On either side of the six steps there also stood two free-standing columns, recalling the Salomonic pair Iachin and Boaz, which were so important for Hrabanus.[14] Since each of these columns housed a relic of an apostle, Peter and Jude, they would also have had a function of mystical representation such as he favoured; they may even have been also intended to represent the two worlds of Jews and Gentiles. There is evidence that a similar mystical interpretation lay behind the design of the whole building. The contemporary writer Sedulius Scotus observed that the rule of the just king is supported on the eight columns of the virtues; the king's *aula* cannot be stable without them.[15] The chapel was referred to as an *aula* in its dedicatory inscription, and Charlemagne, seated on the throne of the wise Solomon in the first-floor gallery, was himself directly supported by the eight piers of the octagon. As we shall see, columns and piers were frequently assimilated at this period. Sedulius reinterprets the proverb attributed to Solomon—"Wisdom hath builded her house, she hath hewn out her seven pillars" (*Proverbs* 9, 1)—so that it is literally applicable to the new Solomon.

This anticipation of Hrabanus' thought might be seen as depending only on an isolated identification of Charlemagne with Solomon, were it not that other major churches of the period show the same concern both with the art of the Old Testament and with mystic interpretations. The chapel of the Saviour erected at Germigny des Près ca. 806 by Theodulf, Bishop of Orléans, is decorated with stucco reliefs of palms, etc., in imitation of the reliefs in Solomon's Temple, and its apse mosaic shows the Ark of the Covenant (Fig. 48). It has also been shown that the latter representation relies on a misinterpretation of the biblical text found in the *Libri Carolini*, according to which the Ark of Moses was decorated with just two cherubim, to which two more were added by Solomon—a dualism representing, like the two columns, the opposition between Jews and Gentiles.[16] Another feature of the building are the small columns set into the walls. Eight, two in each wall, carry the responds of the arches springing from the central piers; four more carry the chancel arch, two on either side; twelve are set into the apse itself. The

47. Palace chapel, Aachen, 792: interior

48. Chapel of the Saviour, Germigny des Près, ca. 806: interior

eight larger columns invite comparison with the eight "virtue" supports at Aachen or with the eight "beatitude" columns referred to in other texts at Fulda and Regensburg. Groupings of twelve and four had been found earlier representing apostles and evangelists, and, as we shall see, other contemporary and later buildings seem to use them too with the same intent.

Another major centrally planned church was put up by a prominent member of Charles' court, Angilbert, at Centula in northern France. As part of a whole new monastic complex containing several churches it was less appropriate for it to have Salomonic connections than for the two preceding examples, which were both palace chapels. It was, however, dedicated to the Virgin like the Aachen chapel, and as Angilbert himself tells us it was erected with the help of the emperor. It thus fits into the same world of court patronage as Theodulf's building. This makes it all the more interesting that the layout of the monastery was clearly intended to embody a *mystica significatio* of the sort that Hrabanus favoured. For Angilbert also tells us that as the Trinity is the basis of the Christian faith he decided on a plan including three churches;[17] while a twelfth-century account of Centula shows that trinitarian symbolism was carried much further, with the three churches being laid out round a triangular court, the whole complex being served by three hundred monks, and the main church having three altars covered by three canopies from which hung three crowns; there were also thirty reliquaries and three lecterns.[18] Equally important was the number twelve. As Angilbert tells us, twelve bishops attended the dedication; and in the church of the Virgin itself there were twelve altars, each dedicated to an apostle, as well as that dedicated to the Virgin.[19] Excavation has shown that the church was itself dodecagonal;[20] so here too Angilbert was careful to make the architecture itself symbolic. The idea of a church exploiting the number twelve is not new, but the interest in architectural symbolism is manifestly more dominant here in the whole group of buildings than anywhere before. Two monasteries of the same period also had similar layouts. Corbie is said to have had three main churches "in which the confession of the Trinity could find unified expression,"[21] and, imitating this, Corvey in Germany is said to have revealed the same divine mystery in its triangular plan.[22]

A similar interest is revealed in the church of Aniane,

farther south in France, which was built by Benedict, the Church reformer, after 779. In this case Benedict's biographer states clearly that it was his intention to express the *personalitas trinitatis* by placing a triple structure under the main altar.[23] The biographer also documents Benedict's interest in the religious art of the ancient Jews. The altar itself was modelled on that of Moses; there was a seven-branched candlestick following the pattern of that made for Moses by Bezaleel, and the lamps before the altar were put together with Salomonic wisdom. Concluding, Benedict's biographer tells how the monastery's furniture adds up. Seven altars, seven candelabra, and seven lamps all allude to the sevenfold gift of the Holy Spirit.[24] Benedict thus again combined the two ranges of interest that were found in contemporary Carolingian buildings and which recur intertwined in Hrabanus Maurus.

Given the early date of Benedict's work, he may have been a key figure in encouraging what emerges as a distinctively Carolingian approach to architecture. This is confirmed by his role under Louis the Pious, who succeeded Charlemagne in 814. Louis summoned him immediately in 815, and by 817 he was apparently established at a new monastery at Inda, near Aachen, and charged with a mission of monastic reform. King and abbot became closely linked. Louis apparently encouraged an identification of Frankish and Israelite monarchy even more than had Charles. At Ingelheim, one of his favourite residences, he commissioned two cycles of paintings.[25] One, in the palace hall, consisted of two series of secular rulers, on one side running up to Alexander the Great and on the other continuing up to Charlemagne himself. The other, in a church, consisted of two more conventional series, the one of Old Testament and the other of New Testament scenes; but the remarkable element was that the last scene of the Old Testament was Solomon with his Temple. It is difficult to understand this exceptional choice unless he saw Solomon the Temple-builder as Charlemagne's spiritual prototype, just as he saw Alexander as his secular model. It was as Solomon that Louis himself was addressed by the pope who came to crown him at Rheims in 816. When he built a chapel in his palace at Diedenhofen it was made to follow the model of Aachen, and if we are right about the Salomonic associations of that building they would be equally important here.

We know nothing of Benedict's new monastery at

49. St Michael, Fulda, 820–822: column in crypt

Inda except that Louis provided thirty monks for it, probably manifesting the same trinitarian interests as Angilbert. But we do know of works of building and decoration which were done soon afterwards at Fulda, an abbey which would have been under Benedict's supervision. Under Eigil (820–822), a centralized chapel of St Michael (Figs. 49 and 50) was put up, apparently in the tradition of the palace chapel at Aachen and with three altars.[26] The writer of the *Life of Eigil* provides the building with an elaborate interpretation. The single column of the crypt is Christ, and the eight columns of the main rotunda are the beatitudes, which are suitable supports for the dome, at the centre of which is placed the keystone, representing God; the circular plan stands for infinity, the hope of eternal life, and the eternal kingdom of the blessed. This commentary on the building is likely to have been inspired by some memory of an original programme. The imagery is certainly close to that associated with Angilbert and Benedict. Indeed, the idea of the eight columns as beatitudes is very similar to Sedulius Scotus' notion of the eight virtues supporting the king's *aula*, a suggestion which is borne out by another text which interprets the eight columns of a ciborium in Regensburg as either virtues or beatitudes.[27] Fulda is linked to contemporary practice not only by the use of architectural symbolism. After 822 the main church was equipped with a shrine

50. St Michael, Fulda: interior

like the Ark of Moses, decorated with cherubim and a bronze candelabrum.[28] The similarity with the furnishings of Aniane is so striking that it must depend on Benedict's inspiration. But what is most important for us is that the monk who wrote the inscriptions for the chapel of St Michael and the abbot who later commissioned the furnishings was none other than Hrabanus Maurus, who later elaborated similar ideas in his encyclopaedia. Hrabanus' interest in symbolism, and particularly in the significance attaching to the use of Mosaic and Salomonic features, was thus a fulfilment of the programme of Benedict and of the politico-religious ambitions of Charles and Louis. The *De universo*, although written under Louis' successor after 844, represents the fruits of a life spent at the centre of the Carolingian religious revival. Its value as a document for the theory of architecture is greatly enhanced by its connection with the world of Charlemagne, Louis the Pious, and Benedict of Aniane. It is under the influence of these figures that the foundations were laid for the specifically Western tradition of Medieval religious architecture and decoration.

Irminsul and Christussäule

Most of the Carolingian interpretations of the meaning of columns have antecedents in earlier Christian texts, but one does not. This is the identification of the single column at Fulda with Christ. It could just represent a simple extension of the existing habit of columnar interpretation, but the fact that the identification is isolated here and that it hardly recurred later suggests that some special circumstance prevailed at this time and in this region. One possibly influential circumstance was the destruction of the Irminsul shrine at Eresburg by Charlemagne in 772. This Irminsul was a tall wooden tree-trunk, "a universal column, supporting everything," according to a slightly later account, and it was an object of enormous veneration.[29] There are enough examples of the continuity of pagan and Christian traditions to make it quite possible for someone, possibly Hrabanus himself, to have been inspired by the Irminsul to erect the single column at Fulda, "out of which the whole building grows."[30] Such a single column in a crypt is unique and thus in any case demands a specific explanation. This transference from the pagan world would be similar to the Christian in-

troduction of the ciborium supported on four columns, which almost certainly derives from Middle Eastern shrines in which the heavens were shown supported by four columns following traditional opinion.[31] Fulda was only about sixty miles from the great shrine at Eresburg, and the early worshippers at the Christian sanctuary will often have been the children of those who had adored the Irminsul.

Another centre in the same region is Quedlinburg, where in the crypt of St Wigbert (c.930) can be found another unusual single column that may also represent Christ (Fig. 51). Behind the altar a row of five supports separates the main crypt from the ambulatory. Two pairs of round columns flank a square pillar that is distinguished not only by its angularity, but is also elevated on a higher base and has a more elaborate capital decorated with volutes. A central column in this position is extremely rare, and to have such variation within a row of shafts with four similar and one different is almost unheard of. Christ surrounded by the four evangelists, usually represented by their symbols, is a recurrent element in Christian iconography, and although the explicit identification of columns with evangelists has not yet been noted it would be a natural extension of the identification with apostles and teachers of the Gospel. Moreover, apostle columns were most frequent in such a situation grouped round an altar. An almost identical group of four columns on either side of a larger pier is found in the cloister of St Pantaleon at Cologne, which is perhaps of exactly the same date (Fig. 52). An additional peculiarity there is that the pier is placed in the middle of an entrance, perhaps that of the chapter house. Such an unusual arrangement calls for an explanation, and this may again be provided by Hrabanus Maurus: "For the door of the Temple is the Lord: because no one comes to the Father except through Him (*John* 14); and as He says elsewhere: I am the door, and anyone who enters through Me shall be saved." Hrabanus also quotes *Psalm* 20, "the Lord watches over our going out and our coming in," which may be even more appropriate here.[32] Christ, the column, stands in the middle of Christ, the door.

Both Quedlinburg and St Pantaleon were closely connected with the imperial house. Otto I's daughter, Matilda, was abbess of Quedlinburg, and it was Otto's brother, Bruno, Bishop of Cologne, who built St Pan-

51. St Wigbert, Quedlinburg, crypt, c.930

taleon. The imperial family was Saxon in origin, and another later church in Saxony provides useful additional evidence for the interpretation of piers and columns. St Michael's at Hildesheim was founded by Bishop Bernward, and a monk was called from St Pantaleon in 996 to be its first abbot (Figs. 53 and 54). The church which was built in the ensuing thirty years still largely survives. Unusually, its main façade toward the town was the south wall of the nave (Fig. 53). This was pierced by doors at either end, and had at its centre a rectangular pier made out of large blocks of sandstone unlike the rest of the structure. Extending from each side of this pier was a row of six smaller piers on lower bases. Since this peculiar arrangement does not recur on the north side, it is tempting once again to see the central pier as representing Christ, with the twelve smaller piers this time representing the apostles. As the church was consciously planned by Bernward as his tomb, with its internal arrangements adapted from the Holy Sepulchre at Jerusalem, which featured apostle columns so prominently, it is not inappropriate to find twelve apostle supports here.[33] The placing of the Christ pier is odd but should probably be understood as an expression of Hrabanus' text, in which Christ as *lapis angularis* is said to have united into a beautiful solidity the two people, Jews and Gentiles, who come

52. St Pantaleon, Cologne, cloister, c.930

53. St Michael, Hildesheim, 1001–33: entrance façade
(after Beseler and Roggenkamp)

towards him from opposite directions. Christ, the "cornerstone," unites the two walls coming from left and right as he had (in a different way) united the two side walls in the Quedlinburg crypt. Bernward was certainly obsessed with the significance of columnar supports. Only two of the twelve columns which adorned the nave still have their original capitals, but these are inscribed with the names of saints, who in this way virtually support the church. Given the general reference to the Holy Sepulchre it would be surprising if these columns were not also intended to recall the twelve apostles (Fig. 54). If so the interior of the church would have expressed the same symbolism as the exterior.

And, as if to complete this pattern, behind the altar to the east Bernward erected a magnificent bronze column which is always identified as the Christ column (*Christussäule*).[34] Hildesheim thus provides a documented example of a Christ column, as does Fulda. It also enables us to confirm our hypothesis that the idea of the Christ column is adapted from the Irminsul. In front of the altar of St Michael stood another column, always called the Irminsäule.[35] Another Irminsäule was also later erected in the town's cathedral, and legend had it that the Irminsul itself had been brought to Hildesheim by Louis the Pious.[36] There can be no doubt that the placing in St Michael of the Irminsäule to the

54. St Michael, Hildesheim: interior

west and the Christussäule to the east was intended to illustrate that Christ had directly replaced the Irminsul as the focus of religious devotion. Apparently even in the eleventh century the victory of Christ over paganism could not be taken for granted. Hildesheim demonstrates the connection between the Irminsul and the Christ column, and in fact Fulda, Quedlinburg, Cologne, and Hildesheim are all approximately on the perimeter of a circle round the site of the Irminsul. It is as if the imperial family, rulers of Saxony, went out of their way to provide new centres of Christian column-worship east, west, south and north of the old Saxon religious centre in order to wean their people from their

primitive faith. In doing so they were probably still fighting the same battle which the Romans had earlier fought using Jupiter columns.[37]

Angular pier and round column

At Hildesheim Christ was apparently represented both by a column and a pier. But at Quedlinburg and St Pantaleon he was represented by a pier in preference to a column; something which is surprising in view of the consistently higher status of the column earlier. Two factors may have brought about a re-evaluation of the rectangular support. One could have been an identification of the pier with the "cornerstone" (*lapis angularis*) to which Christ is assimilated at *Ephesians* 2, 20. The meaning of this expression was always obscure, with "cornerstone," "coping-stone," "keystone," and "angular stone" all being adopted at different times. The last interpretation would be quite reasonable at a time when scholarship was at a low ebb. Quedlinburg could thus be seen as a more literal demonstration of the architectural symbolism found at Fulda. The interpretation of the single column in the crypt there as Christ was certainly based on the *Ephesians* text: "And [ye] are built upon the foundation of the apostles and prophets, Jesus Christ himself being the chief corner stone; in whom all the building fitly framed together groweth unto an holy temple in the Lord." The monks of Quedlinburg may well have felt that by putting an angular rather than a round stone in the middle of the crypt they had made the "mystic signification" of the building even more explicit.

There is, however, a more general reason why the square pier may at this period have come to acquire a higher status than the cylindrical column: its superior strength. It is already apparent in the *Ephesians* text that if the prophets, the apostles, and Christ are to be the foundation of anything they must above all be strong, and Clement, recognizing this, had gone on to describe the apostles as the "greatest columns," referring particularly to the strength of Saint Peter and Saint Paul in bearing their hardships.[38] It was also precisely the property of strength which Hrabanus had chosen to emphasize with reference to columns. Speaking of those round Moses' Tabernacle, which he says represent the teachers of the Gospel, he tells how they demonstrate *robur* (strength) and *firmitas* (firmness);[39] and, discussing columns in general, he says they represent the apostles and doctors who are "strong in faith and works and contemplation."[40] In this situation, where it was above all the strength of a column which gave it its *mystica significatio*, the traditionally thick square form was obviously a better expression of its essence than the traditionally thin cylindrical one. At other periods the distinction in meaning between *columna* and *pila* might have been an obstacle to this, but, given that the encyclopaedists from Pliny onwards all talked of the existence of square columns, and that Latin usage had lost its precision, this was no longer a problem.

This did not mean that piers were automatically preferable to columns: traditional values could not so

easily be dispensed with. Thus Charlemagne at Aachen may have needed eight strong piers as virtues in the foundations of his *aula* because his rule could not be stable without them; but he also needed a multitude of marble columns higher up because they were the paramount attributes of wealth and authority. The problem was that the qualities of the two forms were contradictory. The pier could best express its property of strength if it was large and simple, while it was precisely the slenderness and richness of the column—and especially of its highest form, the Corinthian—which had previously guaranteed its status. One way to deal with this contradiction was to combine both value systems. This is apparently what was done at Quedlinburg, where the most important "column" has both the richest capital and the strongest shaft. The other was to employ both forms together, as at Aachen. The contradiction was especially violent in the Carolingian world because the true cylindrical column also carried potent historical associations with the world of imperial Rome, while the pier in its simple strength also carried general associations of religious morality. It was not easy for Charlemagne to be both Caesar and Solomon. It was even harder to combine both pagan and Judaeo-Christian values. Still, since it was an interest in Solomon and Judaeo-Christian values which inspired Hrabanus, it was these above all which were transmitted to the following centuries.

From Romanesque piers to Gothic columns

During the tenth and eleventh centuries it was possible for builders either to go on using columns, following the great tradition which led back to the Early Christian basilicas in Rome, as did important figures in Italy such as Desiderius at Monte Cassino, or else to enthusiastically adopt the new architecture of massive piers, as did the Ottonian rulers in structures such as the cathedral of Speyer, built above the imperial mausoleum after 1030 (Fig. 69, p. 108). Sometimes the two forms could be combined, as in the classic alternation of column and pier found at Gernrode (961) and in many later buildings. But it was the pier which was much the most popular support for buildings large and small. This was especially true in Germany, where the plain square pier soon established itself, and in France, where a more complex form with attached shafts was developed in a series of great eleventh-century churches. It is possible to see the development of the pier as simply reflecting a combination of an interest in Roman forms and structural needs. But it is striking that many of the buildings where it first appears have no vaults to support, and the notion that contemporary architects suddenly felt a need to copy Roman aqueducts rather than temples seems rather perverse. If instead we turn to Hrabanus Maurus and the buildings which directly reflect his ideas, an explanation can be provided which has substantial textual support. The Carolingian court in whose environment he worked was the fountainhead of most subsequent artistic developments, and his encyclopaedia was the most up-to-date and respected account of Christian knowledge, circulated in many copies. His insistence on strength as the most important property of the column in a Christian context may well have persuaded some builders to prefer the pier to the true column.

The pier had powerful advocates in the Romanesque period, but it is not surprising that the tide eventually turned in favour of the more established form. Apart from anything else the inherent difficulty of seeing a pier as a type of column would have become greater and greater with the resurgence of Latin scholarship in the eleventh and twelfth centuries. The first conscious rejection of the pier in favour of the column thus comes in the later eleventh century and is recorded in a chronicle describing the reconstruction of the abbey of St Trond, in present-day Belgium. Abbot Adelhard (1055–82), we are told, rebuilt "the nave of the monastery although it was not at all ruinous and, throwing down the extremely strong piers [*eversis fortissimis pilariis*], put up in their place columns which were impressive to look at [*spectabilibus columpnis*]."[41] As we are later told that there were twelve of these columns and that the main altar was dedicated to the twelve apostles, it is virtually certain that the main reason for the unnecessary expenditure was the desire to accurately embody the apostolic symbolism. The chronicle also tells us that Adelhard's building fulfilled the demands of the *doctores* that the church should be laid out *ad staturam humani corporis*, with the sanctuary as the head and so on. The abbot's enthusiasm for symbolism was clearly strong. The remarkable element in the light of our earlier observations is that his interest in symbolism apparently provokes the destruction of just those strong rectangular forms which had been so

recently endowed with authority. The clue to the reversion to the traditional preference for the round form lies probably in the new accuracy and precision of the architectural vocabulary. For the chronicle correctly identifies the rectangular form as a pier, that is as an absolutely distinct form from the column and one which had never been charged with meaning. The correct use of language required the change of form.

Particular interest attaches to what happened at St Trond because the rejection of the pier in favour of the column is as much a central feature of architectural development in the subsequent Gothic period as it is in the Early Christian world. Most significant, an exactly similar concern for symbolism inspired Abbot Suger in his reconstruction of the east end of St Denis, arguably the first Gothic building (Fig. 55).[42] In his *De consecratione* of 1144 he describes the two rows of columns round the apse:

The inner ones, expressing the number of the twelve apostles, and the same number in the outer aisle, signifying the prophets, all rose up to support the lofty structure, which is, as the apostle says, spiritually edifying: "Already," he says, "you are not guests and strangers; but you are fellow citizens of the saints and servants of God, built upon the foundations of the apostles and the prophets with Jesus Christ as your crowning cornerstone, he who joins both walls and in whom the whole edifice, whether spiritual or material, grows to become a temple dedicated to the Lord."[43]

This quotation, incorporating a modified version of *Ephesians* 2, 19–21, makes it clear that Suger was anxious to make the allegory as precise as possible. As there is no parallel for the double row of columns, still less for two rows of supports both of the same number with the outer made clearly "minor" in diameter, and as all these features are deliberately explained in the text, it is hard to believe that the obsession with columnar symbolism was not a major factor in determining the architectural vocabulary. If we are right, then this obsession would also affect the design of the upper parts of the building. For if Suger was concerned to employ forms that would be clearly recognizable as Classical *columnae* (and he tells us that he even considered importing ancient ones from Italy), this would automatically make it necessary to construct upper parts of a lighter structure than anything known previously; with two rows of such flimsy supports this was doubly

55. Abbey church, St Denis, choir, 1140

desirable. Structurally the new design element which had the most decisive effect was the extension of the hemicycle of columns, popular earlier, into an extended U shape running back to the crossing, so as to allow the number to be increased to twelve. This meant that the downward and lateral thrust of the high walls and vaults, which were now essential for a building of the importance of St Denis, were no longer carried on piers. They thus needed to be reduced and their weight concentrated more precisely. At the same time Suger's parallel interest in light symbolism, following the teachings of the Pseudo-Dionysius and of Hrabanus too, would encourage a similar development.[44] The reduction of the mass of the wall was naturally accompanied by the enlargement of the windows. The need for symbolic columns and the need for symbolic light were two decisive influences on the emergence of Gothic. One is reminded of how the replacement of piers by columns to bring in more divine light was also a feature of Paulinus' church at Nola seven hundred years earlier.

The apparent association between the use of columns and the formation of the Gothic architectural style continues in the great cathedrals of the following decades. At Notre Dame of Paris in 1163, and at Laon around the same date, columns are even found all along the naves as well as in the choirs, the integrity of their forms being preserved by arresting the vaulting shafts at their capitals. At Sens columns are paired in order to give them greater strength; they also still alternate with piers, which were indeed always necessary to provide support at the crossing. In none of these buildings does any significance attach to the number of the columns, and it is notable that the two great twelfth-century interpreters of architectural symbolism, Honorius of Autun and Sicardus, see columns not only as apostles but as bishops, who of course could not be counted.[45] In the great cathedrals of the next generation—Chartres after 1194, Bourges after 1202, Rheims after 1211, Amiens after 1220, and Beauvais after 1247—round, or occasionally polygonal, columns are again used throughout, though a number of colonnettes or shafts are added to provide a greater continuity from elements above the capital. Only from the mid-thirteenth century does the compound pier, in the characteristically complex Gothic form, return as the normal support. The period of popularity of the structurally weak column thus corresponds precisely with the period when symbolism most interested ecclesiastical writers from Honorius of Autun, about 1100, to Durandus of Mende, about 1260.[46] It also appears most prominently in the very churches where the major structural advances were being made. In the end its replacement by the structurally more appropriate pier comes at exactly the time when architects were beginning to assert themselves and achieve a greater independence from their patrons.[47]

In some of the buildings of this period columns may still represent specific individuals. The six pairs of columns behind the main altar at Coutances and at Le Mans may well continue the traditional notion of having the twelve apostles in a similar position. Certainly at about the same time at Valenciennes Jacques de Guise had twelve foundations put down for twelve columns "in honour and reverence of the new city of Jerusalem and the twelve apostles."[48] The same explicit symbolism is found in a much more important building, the Sainte Chapelle in Paris (1243–48), where all but four of the slender supports between the windows were adorned with the figures of apostles holding cross medallions (Fig. 56). The entire edifice is thus seen literally to be raised up on the twelve apostles as if in fulfilment of the texts of *Ephesians* 2, 20 and *Revelation* 21, 14. It may not be an accident that the introduction of figures to make the symbolism explicit occurs at exactly the time when the column fades out and when the symbolism could thus no longer be read from the form itself. The area where the idea of using sculpture to make the symbolism explicit was most enthusiastically taken up was in Germany. At Cologne, masons from the Sainte Chapelle began the new cathedral in 1248 and applied to the choir piers statues of the twelve apostles, of Gabriel, and of the Annunciate Virgin. Later at Cologne other figures were applied to the piers of transept and nave as they were completed, and the same practice was followed elsewhere, notably at Xanten, Naumburg, and Aachen. In Italy S. Maria Novella in Florence (1279) was as important for the spread of Gothic as was Cologne Cathedral in Germany, and there too paintings of the apostles were once attached to the church's twelve piers (Fig. 74, p. 118). Once again, the number of supports and the attached figures turned the material building into a representation of the Church and a transcendental prefiguration of the Heavenly City.

Besides church interiors, the other area where columnar symbolism was concentrated was church portals. Already in the lost late-eleventh-century North Portal of Santiago de Compostela decorative shafts may have concealed a mystery,[49] for we are told that there were twelve of them, with another in the centre surmounted by a figure of Christ. Column-figures themselves first appeared at St Denis, probably mostly representing the precursors of Christ. The sudden emergence of large, almost free-standing statues in this context could well be explained by a desire to give visual expression to the anthropomorphic columnar symbolism employed by Suger in the interior. Since the inscription on the portal referred to Christ as the "true door,"[50] it would have been highly appropriate to have his ancestors preceding it making a parallel with the columns of the outer courts at Edessa, which were said to represent the Tribes of Israel.[51] The precursors would be *outside* the door just as the prophets were *outside* the apostles around the altar. Hrabanus had introduced the notion of columnar symbolism by discussing the columns which stood at the door of Solomon's Temple. He had even implied that the columns of the portico of the Temple represented the Old Testament patriarchs and prophets who preceded the Incarnation,[52] shortly before he talked of Christ as "the door."[53] Suger may thus have derived his juxtaposition of anthropomorphic columns and the "true door" directly from Hrabanus. Once introduced, the column-

56. Sainte Chapelle, Paris, 1246–48: interior

figures are found in exactly the same series of buildings as the columns forming arcade supports. In the West Portals of Chartes they are again precursors of Christ, but on the later Portail Royal patriarchs, prophets, and apostles figure prominently, as they do on the façade of Notre Dame at Paris and at Rheims and Amiens. After the mid-thirteenth century figures are still found at portals, but no longer clearly attached to columns, which vanish from façades at the same time as they do from interiors.

The fascination with columns, as both structural and decorative elements, which is associated with the birth of Gothic architecture and sculpture can thus be seen as the culmination of a tradition of Christian exegesis which had found its most articulate exponent in Hrabanus Maurus, whose encyclopaedia had achieved an enormous authority, and whose enthusiasm for *mystica significatio* struck a chord in a whole generation of scholars and churchmen. The only other explanation for the fondness for columns would be a respect for it as an Antique form. But this seems excluded by the very nature of the shift from Romanesque to Gothic, involving as it did the rejection of a Classical vocabulary. There is, moreover, a convenient parallel with the Early Christian period, where also the rejection of the structurally sound pier in favour of the column seems to depend partly on mystical interpretations of architecture, though never carried as far as in Gothic buildings. The interest in the symbolism of light which has been often shown to be a characteristic of the first Gothic edifices was also found in Early Christian churches, and the Pseudo-Dionysius who inspired Suger was an Early Christian writer. Indeed, in spite of the differences between the two types of architecture, chief of which is the Gothic demand for vaulting, they share many features—their height, their large windows, the thinness of their walls, and their enthusiasm for the column—and all these features can be related to a common interest in the mystical significance of the church. In the later period, when Christianity provided not just spiritual succour, as in the Early Christian era, but a real intellectual backbone for contemporary culture, such an interpretation had a much greater influence. In the twelfth century the idea of columnar symbolism, which had originated a thousand years earlier just as an inspiring metaphor, has a direct impact on architectural technology and even leads to the revival of life-size statuary.

When Hrabanus dealt with the mystic significance of architecture in his encyclopaedia he showed how all the elements of a building—columns, doors, windows, and so on—not only could be but actually were charged with meaning. In a sense he provided a coherent theory for Medieval architecture. He was not the single cause of subsequent developments, but his ideas, presented in textbook form, can be seen as triggering changes which had important catalytic effects. Without his reference to square columns and the importance of strength it is hard to explain the sudden popularity of the pier, a form which had been available since Early Christianity but which had been consistently rejected in favour of the true column. Once the pier had been introduced for symbolic reasons in the eighth and ninth centuries it made possible the development in the eleventh century of stone vaulting such as had been unknown in the Christian West. When more accurate scholarship in the twelfth century prevented the term "column" from any longer being applied to a square form, it was probably also Hrabanus' text which led builders from Suger onwards to abandon piers and return to columns. Since by now great buildings could no longer be conceived of without vaults, this change led in turn to a drastic transformation of the upper parts of churches to enable their weight to be carried on much slenderer supports. At the same time, in a parallel development, his statement not that the apostles can be *represented* by columns, as the Early Christians had thought, but that the columns "*are* apostles and teachers of the Gospel" led first to groupings of columns which took account of this and eventually to the addition of statues to the surfaces of those columns in order to make the identification literally clear. There is thus a symmetry between the Early Christian period, when the ban on life-size Classical statues led to their replacement by safe aniconic columns, and the Gothic period, when the life-size statue re-emerged out of the column, as the Christian world recovered its confidence after the millennium. Hrabanus was not alone in bringing about these innovations, but his *De universo* was in a sense, as he said of the Testaments, the base on which later ideas were founded.

VII

The orders in the Christian Middle Ages

✦

The *renovatio* of the orders

THE THEORIES behind the renewal of Carolingian architecture are more ancient Jewish than ancient Greek or Roman, yet, as is well known, in practice it was the forms of pagan and Christian buildings that were revived.[1] Charlemagne was an emperor as well as a king, and the equestrian statue and the triumphal arch were as important as the Salomonic throne or the Temple. He searched Italy for Classical columns and capitals, and S. Vitale is a more tangible source for his palace chapel than the buildings of ancient Israel. At the same time Einhard and his circle seem to have shown as much interest in Vitruvius as in the Old Testament and to have begun a serious study of the text,[2] though this was probably more part of a general revival of interest in Classical literature than an aspect of the architectural revival. Certainly the revival of the orders seems to depend more on earlier practice than on earlier theory.

The magnificent building in the monastery of Lorsch which was probably erected as a royal council chamber around 790 has robust Composite half-columns on the ground floor, while the capitals of the shorter fluted pilasters above are Ionic (Fig. 57). Although it is not impossible that this use of a minor Ionic form over a major Composite one represents a continuous tradition, it is most likely that we see here a revival of Early Christian usage such as could have been found in the Orthodox baptistery at Ravenna. At Lorsch it is difficult to tell whether the designer really thought of Ionic as inferior, but this does seem to be the case in Eigil's St Michael rotunda at Fulda, where the single column of the basement which is still in place is primitive Ionic,

while the columns of the chapel above seem, from the surviving evidence, to have been opulently Corinthian and Composite (Figs. 49 and 50). It would be interesting to know if the "E." whom Einhard refers to as having made an ivory casket illustrating the use of columns by the ancients was indeed the abbot of Fulda, as has been suggested.[3] In spite of the barbarization of the Ionic form, the building seems clearly to attach itself to the earlier tradition by which Ionic was used to mark off minor areas. Another use of Ionic for a minor area, but one which presumably depends on a quite different source from those considered so far, is found in the Ottonian church at Gernrode (founded 961). Here the capitals of the nave galleries are marked out as Ionic by the tiny balusters added to the basic trapezoidal block, while the capitals of the main order are of Corinthian derivation. This usage can only be connected with that found in such Byzantine basilicas as St Demetrius at Thessalonica, which makes it quite certain that the church was erected following Eastern models, perhaps due to the influence of the Empress Theophanou, daughter of the Byzantine emperor, who was an early patroness. Equally Byzantine is the use of more correct Ionic in the rear upper parts of the west end of Essen Cathedral (early eleventh century), with which the imperial house was also closely linked. The placing of Ionic behind and above Corinthian corresponds to the placing of Ionic in the rear of the galleries of Haghia Sophia, the church of the Eastern emperor (Fig. 43, p. 68).

A late-tenth-century set of illustrations bound into a manuscript at Sélestat shows clearly characterized Ionic and, more surprisingly, Doric capitals, as well as Ionic and Corinthian bases (Fig. 58).[4] The pages are

57. Abbey gatehouse, Lorsch, c.790

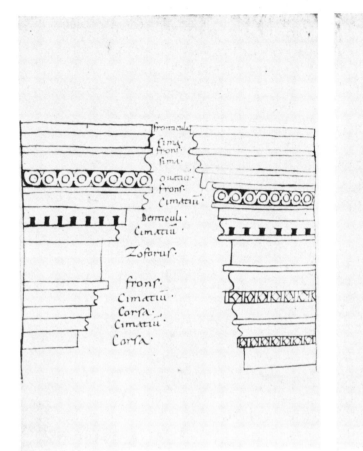

58. Sélestat, Bibl. Mun., MS 1153 bis, fols. 35ᵛ and 36ʳ, c.900

bound up with Vitruvian and other excerpts, perhaps from the ninth century. An Eastern origin for some of this material is suggested by a Renaissance manuscript, now in Florence, with illustrations which are clearly descended from the same original, but with the identification of Doric and Ionic given in Greek letters.[5] As the Ionic capital is also more correctly represented there, the Florence manuscript may well be closer to the archetype. Further evidence that the Sélestat manuscript is connected in some way with a Greek tradition is found in the use of Greek letters in the heading to the transcription of Vitruvius' rules for human proportions. This transcription, although dated by Wirth some decades earlier than the capital illustrations, may well derive from the same source, which could be an

illustrated and abbreviated Vitruvius of Byzantine origin. Artistic contacts between the Byzantine empire and the Ottonian world of the later tenth century are well documented. In architecture Gernrode and Essen are clear examples, and in 1017 the chapel of St Bartholomew at Paderborn was constructed *per operarios Graecos*.[6] Curiously enough, the latter building includes, among other clearly Eastern features, a set of capitals attached to the walls which look suspiciously as if they may derive from a Doric tradition. This tradition is, as with Gernrode's Ionic, admittedly not the same one as that represented by the manuscript; however, literary traditions are often parallel to, but independent of, practical ones.

After about 1000 it becomes increasingly difficult to

59. S. Prassede, Rome, Chapel of S. Zeno, c.820: above (a) portal; at right (b) interior

talk of the use of the Classical orders north of the Alps, though the foliate capitals of both Romanesque and Gothic architects represent a clear continuation of the Corinthian tradition. In Italy, however, the orders become more rather than less important with the recovery of economic and political life and they continue to be used with great care into the Gothic period.

Italy: clergy and laity

In Rome it is possible to talk essentially of a continuity of the Early Christian tradition. This is apparent, for example, in the most striking church to survive from the Carolingian period, S. Prassede, rebuilt by Pope Paschal I about 820. The most clearly organized part of the structure is the chapel of S. Zeno (Fig. 59).

The chapel is entered through a portal flanked by two black basalt columns with Ionic capitals. Inside, the cross vault is carried at the corners by four more columns. The two towards the entrance are grey granite with ordinary Corinthian capitals, while the two nearest the altar are two taller shafts of black basalt again, but with capitals decorated with pointed lotus leaves. The use of black shafts thus focuses attention both on the entry and on the altar, while the sequence of capitals, from Ionic to Corinthian to the taller type with lotus leaf, gives a strong sense of progression. There is some doubt about the use of orders in the nave, since the six free-standing columns along each side of the nave have Corinthian capitals later remodelled with inverted volutes. But it is possible that there was always a contrast with those at either end, three of which are

normal Corinthian and the fourth Composite. Certainly such a marking of the ends of a colonnade, which had its antecedents in the *scaena* architecture of the Roman Empire and in the portico of the Lateran Baptistery, was to become a prominent feature of many churches rebuilt at the time of the revival of the papacy in the twelfth century. At S. Maria in Trastevere (c.1130) the two rows of Ionic and Corinthian capitals terminate at either end in a Composite pilaster, while at the nearby S. Crisogono (c.1130) the uniform Ionic series is stopped by Composite pilasters near the door and Corinthian near the altar. In neither case does the arrangement seem intended as an expression of status or function. Instead, this is conveyed at S. Maria in Trastevere by the introduction of Corinthian capitals on the first and third columns at the altar end of the

nave colonnade, where it would have flanked the choir enclosure,[7] and both there and at S. Crisogono by the use of Corinthian columns to support the triumphal arch. In both churches these columns are dark granite in contrast to the lighter grey granite columns of the nave. Rather, the purpose of the change of order at either end seems purely aesthetic, to create an effective termination to the series; and this is confirmed by the use of a similar device in the almost contemporary porticoes of SS. Giovanni e Paolo and S. Cecilia, in both of which a line of Ionic columns is stopped by a pair of Corinthian capitals, on columns at the former church (Fig. 60) and pilasters at the latter.

Another feature of S. Prassede which links Early Christian to later practice is the use of Ionic for the portal of the Chapel of S. Zeno. St Peter's in the fourth

60. SS. Giovanni e Paolo, Rome: portico, c.1130

century already had a broad Ionic portico, but in the twelfth and thirteenth centuries porches of varying size were added to a large number of Roman churches, and these are virtually all Ionic, sometimes combined with Corinthian. S. Prassede itself acquired one consisting of two columns carrying an arch, and similar structures are found at S. Maria in Cosmedin, at S. Clemente, and at St Peter's itself. Other churches had broader porticoes. Those at SS. Giovanni e Paolo and S. Cecilia have already been referred to, but even more magnificent is the thirteenth-century one in front of S. Lorenzo fuori le mura. The use of Ionic for porches can be seen as an enthusiastic extension of Early Christian usage. The popularity of Ionic for interiors at the same period is more difficult to understand. The Ionic naves of S. Cri-

sogono and S. Maria in Trastevere have already been described, with Corinthian and Composite capitals marking either end. A similar arrangement is found at S. Saba (rebuilt c.1205), but with different Ionic capitals marking either end on one side and Corinthian and Composite marking the ends on the other. Paschal II's S. Clemente of c.1108 uses Ionic throughout, and Ionic is also used for the large nave added to S. Lorenzo fuori le mura c.1220 (Fig. 40, p. 65). Finally, at the Aracoeli built for the Franciscans after 1250, where the choir enclosure stretched far back up the nave, the small remaining public space inside the west door is marked by two pairs of Ionic capitals, with a third pair of Corinthian ones signalling the beginning of the more private area to the east where Corinthian and Compos-

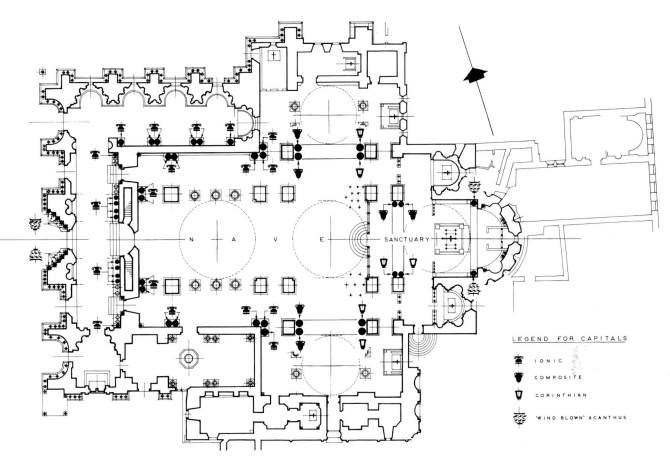

LEGEND FOR CAPITALS

IONIC

COMPOSITE

CORINTHIAN

'WIND BLOWN' ACANTHUS

61. St Mark's, Venice, after 1063: diagram of orders

ite specimens are freely mixed. In all these cases Ionic is associated with the more secular areas of the church, nave as opposed to sanctuary, congregational space as opposed to priestly space.

In Early Christian churches a subtler modulation from Corinthian to Composite was used to express the liturgical significance for all of movement through the church. Now the more abrupt contrast between Ionic and Corinthian is used to mark an absolute distinction between laity and clergy. The new importance of this distinction is likely to be due to the increasing strains between the two groups which developed throughout Europe in the eleventh and twelfth centuries. The most striking of these was the contest between pope and emperor focusing on legal prerogatives and on the right to make particular appointments. These strains provoked many ecclesiastics to write asserting the absolute separation of laity and clergy.[8] A typical example is the statement by Humbert, a Burgundian cardinal in Rome around 1060, that just as clergy and laity are recognized as separated in place and function within the walls of basilicas, so they should also be outside.[9] The use of the orders in Roman churches over the next two hundred years perfectly illustrates that text. The differentiation of Ionic and Corinthian areas inside the church is not the only element in this. The frequent addition of a prominent Ionic porch outside along with the use of Ionic for the nave effectively reduced the difference between the secular world outside and the secular area inside. Where previously the separation between the secular and the sacred had been at the church door, now it was moved to somewhere halfway along the church. At the same time, the new status of the priestly area to the east was emphasized by the construction of elaborate ciboria supported on dark porphyry columns with Corinthian and Composite capitals, in bold contrast to the grey granite usual in Ionic naves.

Outside Rome, fewer Early Christian churches survived to provide examples for the ambitious new buildings which arose with the rapid economic recovery after 1000. This was particularly true in Tuscany, in the cities of the lower Arno valley. Without a strong local tradition, builders there needed to look farther afield for models, and that meant not only to Rome but to the cities of the Byzantine East, with which strong trading links existed and where artistic activity, unlike at Rome, was still very vigorous. The tendency to look to the East was even stronger at Venice, on the other side of the Italian peninsula. As a result two of the greatest undertakings of the eleventh century, the cathedral at Pisa and the church of S. Marco at Venice, both begun around 1063, reveal a strong influence from the Byzantine world.

This is clearest in S. Marco, which was certainly designed and built by Greek masters after the model of the now-destroyed Justinianic church of the Holy Apostles in Constantinople (Fig. 61). It is thus not surprising that the arrangement of the orders in the building shows a close dependence on Justinianic practice as still visible in Haghia Sophia. The capitals of the church's 600-odd columns, which have all been catalogued by Deichmann,[10] lend themselves to complex interpretations. But for our purposes two features of the use of the orders are most important. One is that Ionic is used consistently on the inner wall of the narthex and the outer west, south, and north walls of the nave, giving it an inferior position compared to the richer leaf forms of the façade and the rest of the interior. As Deichmann says, the scheme relates to the use of Ionic in the rear of the galleries at Haghia Sophia.[11] The other feature is more remarkable: this is the differentiation of the capitals of the columns supporting the three arches spanning the choir and the two transepts. In each case the capitals are Corinthian on one side of the arch and Composite on the other, an asymmetrical arrangement which is the more striking because these

capitals, which carry the only arches spanning the principal spaces, are some of the most prominent in the building. It might be thought from this alternation that both capital types are of equal status. However, while in the choir both orders are equidistant from the altar, with Composite to the left and Corinthian to the right, in the transept the capitals are so placed that on both sides it is Corinthian which is to the east towards the altar and Composite which is on the west towards the entrance.

The cathedral at Pisa was also designed by a Greek, Buscheto, and it too was modelled, though less directly, on a Byzantine building, St Demetrius at Thessalonica. As at S. Marco, there are a large number of columns and the interpretation is complicated by the length of time the church took to complete.[12] Still, some significant patterns do emerge. Ionic appears only in the dwarf orders of the inner and outer galleries, and even there it is mixed with the Corinthian and Composite capitals which predominate throughout the building. This idea of Ionic as a minor gallery order probably comes directly from St Demetrius. In the main colonnades of nave and transepts, Corinthian and Composite are mixed in a largely haphazard way; in the choir, on the other hand, it is a low Corinthian alone which is found. As at S. Marco, then, Corinthian seems to be treated as a relatively superior order. However, the most striking connection with the Venetian church is the prominence given to asymmetrical pairs of Corinthian and Composite capitals. Much the grandest of these is the pair (now replaced by copies) carved for the great west door in the mid-twelfth century, with Composite on the left and Corinthian on the right (Fig. 62). Smaller and less prominent examples are also found on the exterior of the southern apse, the first part of the building seen by most visitors, where balancing pairs are found in both the lower and upper orders. Later a similar balancing pair was placed in the upper colonnade of the baptistery, immediately over the door. Such pairs were evidently an important feature, chiefly associated with doorways.

An attempt to explain the function of such an asymmetrical pairing might take account of three points. First, it may be of Byzantine origin. Secondly, it seems to be associated with buildings where, unusually, Corinthian is treated as superior to Composite, creating a series Ionic-Composite-Corinthian. Thirdly, it is asso-

62. Pisa Cathedral, west door, twelfth century

ciated with areas of transition, transition from the world into the church and transition from nave to choir. The first two points may be connected. Greek architects at Byzantium might have had good reason to resent the lofty status accorded to the "Italic" or "Roman" Composite above their own native Greek orders. Especially during the reign of Justinian, when a last brave attempt was made to bring Italy firmly under the control of the Greek emperor, a symbolic downgrading of Latin Composite beneath Greek Corinthian could have been an effective way of giving architectural expression to the emperor's ambitions. We have already suggested that the use of Byzantine capitals for the sanctuary of S. Vitale may have been motivated by exactly such considerations. Nor was it difficult to find a justification for inserting Composite between Ionic and Corinthian. Instead of seeing its mixed forms as an expression of triumphal combination, architects could as easily have seen it as a form in transition, an Ionic capital in the process of becoming a Corinthian one. In the Early Christian world, where the changes of capitals in the Lateran Baptistery were intended to mirror the inner transformation of a catechumen entering the Church, the idea of one capital growing into another by a process of metamorphosis would seem completely natural. We may never know if this is really what hap-

63. S. Frediano, Lucca, after 1112: interior from baptistery

pened. But, if it did, it might have led to the use of an Ionic-Composite-Corinthian series in Justinian's Holy Apostles, where it would have been available to inspire the architects of S. Marco. Certainly, seen in these terms, the use of the orders in the latter church becomes relatively clear. Ionic is used for the outer areas of the nave, Composite for the western or people's side of the transept, and Corinthian for the eastern side where the priests served as intermediaries with God. The arches which rose on one side from Composite capitals and came down on the other on Corinthian ones well expressed how the worshipper, who came from an Ionic outside narthex, was, as he stood in the nave, in a situation of potential transformation from a worldly to a spiritual state.

The closest we can come to confirming this hypothetical reconstruction is through a study of another major church of the period, S. Frediano at Lucca (Figs. 63 and 64). Though not the cathedral, S. Frediano was the chief church of Lucca, in rather the same way as S. Marco was in Venice, housing as it did the city's baptistery. It must thus have been expressly intended to rival the baptismal churches of Lucca's competitors, Pisa and Venice, when it was begun in 1112. Fortunately, however, its reduced size and small number of columns make its analysis much easier, and what emerges is that

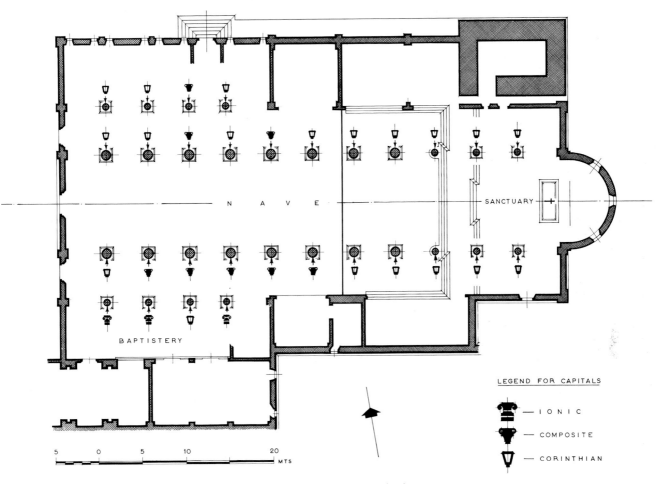

64. S. Frediano, Lucca: diagram of orders

it uses all the principles found at Venice and Pisa, only much more firmly and clearly. As a result there is here no doubt that Corinthian is the most important order, since it is used for the five pairs of columns in the choir area east of the pulpit. (The easternmost of these pairs derives a further emphasis from an additional laurel-wreath decoration.) The nave, on the other hand, is chiefly Composite. Yet what is especially revealing is that the Composite nave is clearly only a transition from an even lower-status Ionic. Thus Ionic is used prominently for the gallery of the façade, and also for the colonnade leading to the baptistery in the south aisle immediately inside the façade.[13] The outside

world and the baptistery naturally have the lowest-status order and the altar area the highest, while the nave is an area of transition, halfway between the world of man and that of God. This interpretation is further strengthened by the use of Corinthian capitals for the colonnade leading to the chapel of the Holy Cross, which balances the baptistery at the west end of the north aisle. That chapel, like the choir area and unlike the baptistery, is fully appropriated to the divine. The "transitional" nature of Composite evidently is important, and, in order to emphasize this property, Corinthian is mixed with Composite in the nave, with the last pair of columns before the step up to the choir being Composite on one side and Corinthian on the other. The orders are also slightly mixed in the colonnades leading to the baptistery and the chapel of the Holy Cross. In that leading to the baptistery, one Corinthian column is incorporated into the Ionic series as if in promise of the spiritual state to come. There is some difficulty in interpreting the colonnade on the other side of the church, since its easternmost bay now leads to a side door and it is just possible that this arrangement was intended from the first. It is, however, more likely that there was originally no door and the colonnade led only to the chapel of the Holy Cross. In this case the interruption of the series of four Corinthian columns by a Composite one can be seen effectively to draw attention to the colonnade's function as a gate between the worldly nave and the consecrated chapel. Not only, then, is the nave thought of as a general transition zone between the world and God, but the colonnades to the side chapels are treated as barriers marking analogous transitions in a more precise way. Finally, most important for our present enquiry into the function of asymmetrical pairs of Corinthian and Composite capitals, the combining of Corinthian with Ionic in one columnar screen and of Composite with Corinthian in the other can be regarded as precisely equivalent to the mixing of pairs in gateways.

An awareness of the significance of such zones of transition led builders to balance the Composite capital, itself an emblem of transition, with the Corinthian form to which it looked forward. The worshipper entering the main door of Pisa Cathedral was made conscious of his own incomplete state by the capital on his left, and by the one on the right he was made aware of the possibility of fulfilment. As he stood in the nave, surrounded by an irregular mixture of Composite and Corinthian, he would have the same feeling, and when he approached the altar, where one form of Corinthian alone could be seen, he would feel that fulfilment could be there achieved only by the priests.

One further confirmation that the many Composite-Corinthian pairs found in Italy around 1100 were all liable to be read in the same way, and that Composite was always thought of as inferior, is the recurrence of Composite on the left and Corinthian on the right. This is true, for instance, of the choir of S. Marco, the main door and lower order of the south apse at Pisa, the Pisa baptistery, and the window at nearby Segromigno

Monte. It is also true of the naves of S. Bartolommeo and S. Maria Forisportam at Lucca, in each of which the right arcade is completely Corinthian, while the left is interrupted by one or two Composite capitals. The left was often thought of as inferior to the right, and in the liturgy it was also associated with the earlier of two events; thus, the Gospel was read from the left and the Epistle from the right. Moreover, since the Gospel concerned Christ and the Jews, and the Epistle Paul and the Gentiles, there was a tendency to associate the left with Judaism and the Old Testament and the right with Christianity and the New. These same ideas had made it easy for Iachin and Boaz, the two columns on either side of the door of Solomon's Temple, to be associated with Peter and Paul, Jews and Gentiles, and Old and New Testaments; and, although the patristic texts which make the identification do not say which was left and which was right, it will have been natural for the left-right opposition to be transferred to them. It is against this background that, also around 1100, at S. Ambrogio, Milan (a church comparable in status to Pisa Cathedral, S. Marco, and S. Frediano), two pairs of columns can be read as clearly embodying this Jewish-Christian polarity. Inside at the east end of the aisles there are two free-standing columns bearing the symbols of salvation of the Old and New Testaments: that on the left Moses' Brazen Serpent, and that on the right the Cross. At the west door, too, the main shafts at either side are carved in relief with an analogous pair of symbols: a rod (that of Moses and/or Aaron) on the left, and the Cross again on the right. The inspiration must come from the patristic interpretation of Solomon's columns. Two columns actually inscribed "Iachin" and "Boaz" were built into the portal of Würzburg Cathedral soon afterwards.[14]

The relation between asymmetrical pairings in twelfth-century churches and the tradition of patristic interpretation is well documented by contemporary writers. Hugh of St Victor (died around 1141) sees the two walls of the church as representing both Jews-Gentiles and laity-clergy, and he explicitly identifies the laity with the left side and the clergy with the right.[15] Just as the Jews in the Old Testament received only half of God's message and the Gentiles the whole of it, so the laity is in an incomplete and the clergy in a fulfilled spiritual state. He thus adapts the traditional opposition of Old and New Testaments to the contemporary opposition between laity and clergy. Those who paired the "incomplete" Composite with the "complete" Corinthian did the same. Hugh's text is particularly helpful in explaining not just the pairing at portals, where the patristic interpretation of the columns of Solomon's Temple provides a model, but also the use of asymmetrical pairs on transverse arches. The importance of such arches is precisely that they join the two walls of the church, just as Christ the *lapis angularis* joined the two communities of Jews and Gentiles. The arch across the choir of S. Marco supported by asymmetrical capitals was significantly the only one to link both sides of the church. It appropriately stressed the need for the two separate communities, laity and clergy, to be united.

The appositeness of Hugh's text can be judged by applying it to another Tuscan church, S. Miniato at Florence (Figs. 65 and 66). Begun by Bishop Hildebrand after 1018, it probably acquired its present form chiefly in the twelfth and early thirteenth centuries. Its lavish decoration of Antique and Medieval capitals exploits the opposition between Composite and Corinthian in a highly structured way. Composite is consistently associated with less holy areas and Corinthian with more holy ones. In the nave, the four free-standing columns nearer the door have Composite capitals and the four closer to the nave-altar Corinthian, while an epitome of this scheme is found both in the raised sanctuary, where the front pair is Composite and the rear Corinthian, and below in the crypt, where before the altar the two to the west are Composite and the two to the east are Corinthian. Corinthian is decisively associated with the more holy or priestly parts of nave, sanctuary, and crypt. The arrangement of the piers is more complex. Each pier has four capitals, three low down continuing the main arcade and carrying an arch across the aisle, and one high up carrying a transverse arch across the nave. Of the twelve low capitals, those on the western pair in the nave are all Composite, those on the eastern pair are Corinthian on the left and Composite on the right. Those higher up, carrying the transverse arches, are arranged chiastically: Composite and Corinthian left and right on the western piers, and Corinthian and Composite the opposite way round on the eastern ones. Finally, we are left with the capitals of the half-columns that terminate the arcades at either end of the church; those to the west are both Composite,

while those to the east are again an asymmetrical pair, Corinthian to the left and Composite to the right. The church thus combines a sequential change of order from west to east, from lay to clergy areas, with asymmetrical pairings around the longitudinal axis. The new element is that it is clearly not possible simply to regard the left side of the church as representing the laity and the right side the clergy, since the pairs are arranged in an X pattern. Even this, however, turns out to be explicable in terms of Hugh's writings. In the rite of dedication of a church, he points out, the priest makes a diagonal cross in the middle of the building by drawing two lines in ashes from the left-hand side at the east end to the right side at the west, and from the right side at the east to the left side at the west. These lines, he explains, run from one side to the other because "faith began with the Jews and later went over to the Gentiles."[16] The same idea is developed by his contemporary Honorius of Autun, who says that the two lines actually *represent* the Jews and the Gentiles; if they had continued straight they would both have persisted in error, but as it is they are saved by coming together in Christ, the cornerstone.[17] The X-shaped pairing of the high capitals in the middle of S. Miniato directly recalls the dedication rite binding the two sides together in an X pattern. In this it is much more effective than the cross-shaped arrangements of discs found at the centre of the Cosmati floors of contemporary Roman churches, which have also been explained as recalling the dedication ritual.[18] There the configuration refers to the diagonal cross but brings out nothing of its meaning. At S. Miniato, on the other hand, if the first asymmetrical pair toward the west, Composite on the left and Corinthian on the right, is taken to represent a laity side and a clergy side (in the standard left-right opposition), the reversing of that arrangement in the next pair expresses their having met in the cross of Christ and so having exchanged sides. The relation produced by that reversal, with Corinthian on the left and Composite on the right in the eastern transverse arch, is carried through in the responds of the choir arcades, flanking the altar. The centre of the diagonal cross joining the two nave arches is, appropriately, the nave-altar, the place where laity and clergy do indeed meet in Christ. Equally appropriately, the configuration results in a scheme whereby Corinthian is on the favoured right-hand side for the human visitor as he

65. S. Miniato, Florence, eleventh century and later: interior

enters the church, yet it is also on the right from God's point of view at the high altar. The close connection of the arrangement of capitals to the liturgy and commentaries on the liturgy suggests the direct involvement of priests in detailed design decisions. Once constructed, the building could itself be read as a wordless commentary; though that meaning could also, if desired, be explicated in sermons.

S. Miniato, a popular monastic church, is a natural place to find a controlled expression of recent thought on the relations between the laity and the clergy. It is also especially natural in Tuscany to find so many churches which comment more loosely on the same relationship. Matilda (1046–1115), Countess of Tuscany, sought during her life to liberate her territories from the domination of the German emperor and, when she died in 1115, by leaving them to the Church in Rome she implicitly acknowledged the superiority of clerical over lay authority. She also gave the Tuscan cities reason to join her in that acknowledgement, since a dependence on the weak pope guaranteed their autonomy as submission to the strong emperor could not.

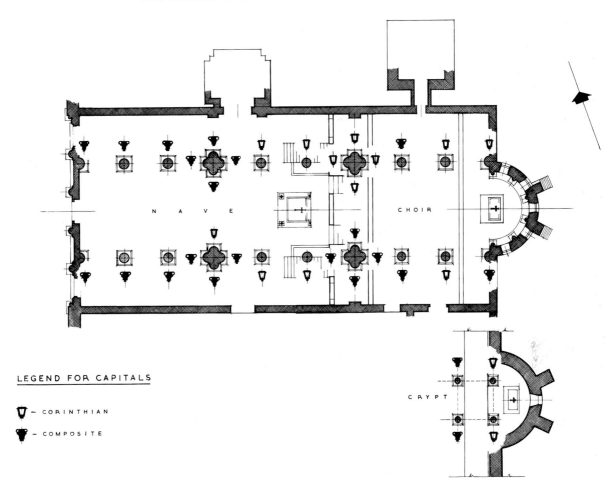

66. S. Miniato, Florence: diagram of orders

Even the lay communities of the Arno Valley had sound political reasons for elevating clerical at the expense of secular authority.

Although the principles applied in all the buildings just discussed are similar, there is no need for them to have been common knowledge. Each building could be understood on the basis of an internal analysis. The only requirement is that the worshipper be alert to change within the building and particularly to change in the capitals, the one area where sculptural elaboration was concentrated. He might know what sort of changes and meanings to expect, but a particular change in one building might have a quite different meaning in another. A striking demonstration of this is the reversal of status in the relationship between Composite and Corinthian in a whole set of contemporary buildings just down the hill from S. Miniato, in Florence itself. In these it is Composite which is the perfect form and Corinthian the imperfect. They thus exploit the idea of an Ionic-Corinthian-Composite series such as was used in Early Christian Rome, rather than the Ionic-Composite-Corinthian series for which a Byzan-

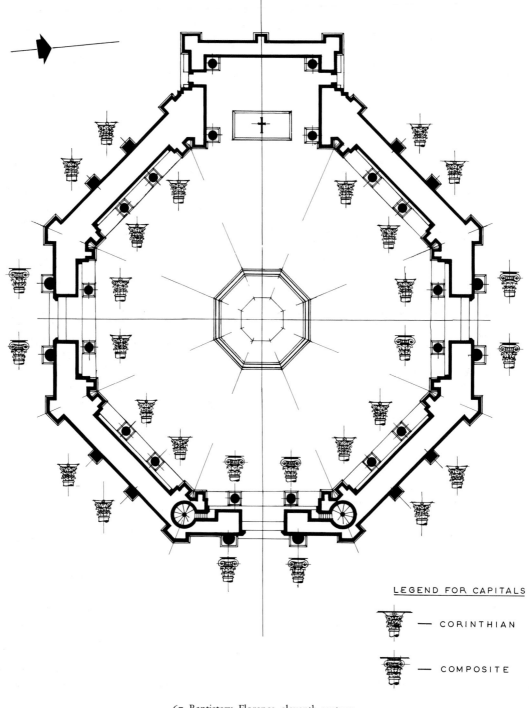

LEGEND FOR CAPITALS

— CORINTHIAN

— COMPOSITE

67. Baptistery, Florence, eleventh century
and later: diagram of orders

68. Baptistery, Florence: south façade

tine origin has been proposed. The best example is the great octagonal Baptistery, which, like S. Miniato, was probably begun in the eleventh century and largely completed in the twelfth (Figs. 67 and 68). In the interior the gallery has unfluted Ionic colonnettes, following Byzantine practice, though here they are flanked by much bigger fluted Corinthian pilasters (Fig. 78a, p. 134). Below, larger Corinthian pilasters flank recesses in seven of the sides, and between these are pairs of large Corinthian columns of grey granite—except at the north door, where Corinthian is balanced by Composite, and at the east door leading to the cathedral, where both are Composite, the left one being plain granite and the right one fluted marble. Composite is thus clearly used for the most important forms in the most important area, Ionic for the least important forms in the least important area, and Corinthian for the intermediate areas and forms. The idea of varying the orders at ground-floor level can be traced back to the Lateran Baptistery.

More remarkable is the exterior, which has an extraordinarily complicated articulation in green and white marble. The attic at the top, with its framing of fluted Corinthian pilasters, is almost certainly later. Below, on the seven sides whose decoration is preserved, intricate patterns are created by the variation of capital type (Corinthian or Composite), shaft type (round plain, round with spiral flutes, octagonal, or square)

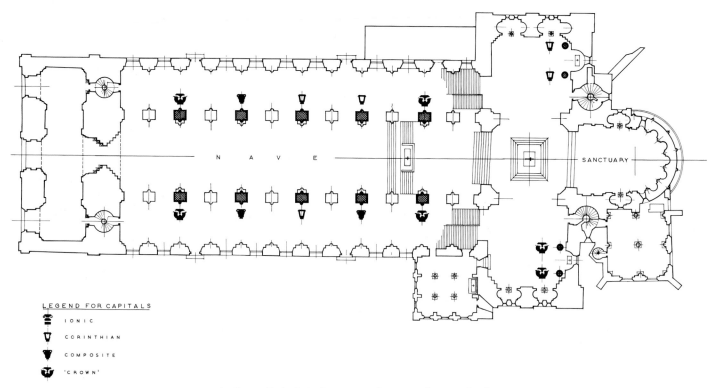

LEGEND FOR CAPITALS

IONIC

CORINTHIAN

COMPOSITE

'CROWN'

69. Speyer Cathedral, after 1030 and c. 1100: diagram of orders

and pediment type (segmental or triangular). The basic articulation is given by two attached orders one above the other, Composite on the cardinal faces containing the doors, and Corinthian on the intermediate faces. These minor faces are also distinguished by having rectangular rather than round shafts on the ground floor. More elaborate is the arrangement of the orders on the window frames above, three to each side. Only the three pairs to the east are all Composite; on all other sides only the central pair is Composite, the other two being Corinthian. But this simple differentiation is expanded by the variation of the shafts. Of the three types—round with spiral flutes, round unfluted, and rectangular pilasters—only the three pairs to the east are all both round and spiral-fluted. Those above the north and south doors (Fig. 68) have round spiral-fluted shafts on the central window and pilasters on the sides; those on the minor intermediate faces have round unfluted shafts in the centre and pilasters on the sides. The architect has thus used a complicated nota-

tion to distinguish the face with the main door from the faces with lesser doors, and these three faces together from the minor intermediate ones. To do this he exploits not only a hierarchy of the orders but a hierarchy of shaft forms, in a more precise way than had been done since Antiquity. The remarkable regularity with which the scheme is applied—with only one deviation, that is the use of Ionic instead of Composite on the central window of the southwest face—is evidence of a new rigour in the control of the execution as well. Both the precision and the regularity could be achieved only through a quite new type of intellectual discipline. There can be little doubt that the architect was trying to recover not only the formal vocabulary of the Ancient world—which is used with much greater conviction on this building than any other—but also its essential rationality and order. The reason for this exceptional display of rationality and Antique refinement may emerge from a study of one last Romanesque building, in distant Germany.

Speyer: the emperor gets his own back

Only one building north of the Alps rivals the Tuscan ones in its careful use of the orders: this is Speyer Cathedral (Figs. 69 and 70). Begun in its present form by Conrad II in 1030, to house the tombs of the German kings and emperors, the church owes much of its decoration to the Emperor Henry IV (1050–1106). As part of his programme of improvement, capitals were added to lofty engaged shafts along the nave, and great columnar aedicules were added to the east wall of the transepts. All the capitals were carefully cut and carefully placed. In the nave the five capitals on each side are organized in east-west symmetry centred on the middle shafts of the north and south walls. The central pair of capitals is Corinthian, the two pairs east and west of these are Composite (except the one to the east on the north side, which is Corinthian), and the last pairs at either end of the nave have an individual form of leaf decoration with curious drill holes. In the transepts the southern aedicule has capitals of this last form (Fig. 70), while the northern one has Corinthian. With the help of the Italian parallels an interpretation can be attempted. Given that the last pair of capitals towards the altar is always the most important when variation occurs, the unusual leaf form with drilled holes which occupies that position must be the most highly esteemed. The Composite capitals which come next would then be lower in status, and the least important type would be the Corinthian. No Italian building provides a parallel for the progressive rise in status towards the west as well as towards the east, but this can be directly related to the unique double-ended character of Speyer and other German churches, in which the traditional eastern apse containing the altar was balanced at the other end of the nave by an apse or gallery for the imperial throne. Speyer with its western gallery thus had a focus at the west almost as important as that at the east, and the arrangement of the capitals running outwards from the central shaft took account of this. The capitals even articulate the difference in status between the two ends of the nave. The two capitals at the west, although of similar type to those at the east, are notably poorer in detail with shallower carving and less piercing of the surface. God and emperor are both of the ruler class, but God's authority is higher. It is less easy to be sure about the reasons for the choice of cap-

70. Speyer Cathedral: aedicule in S. transept, c.1100

itals in the transept aedicules, but a reference to Italian practice suggests at least one possibility. Since the capitals in the north transept are of the lowest type (Corinthian), and those in the south (with the pierced leaves) are of the highest (Fig. 70), the poorest and richest forms are balanced about the church's axis to left and right, exactly as we found in Italy with Composite and Corinthian when Composite was the lower and Corinthian the higher. The arrangement would then correspond to that of the capitals bearing the transverse arch across the choir of S. Marco, which occupied a similar position near the altar.

There remains the question of how the most important form, that placed at either end of the nave and in the south transept, came to be given a position of superiority above both Composite and Corinthian. There are earlier parallels for a new "order" being given a higher status than an existing form. The new Composite was exalted above Corinthian in Roman times, and Byzantine forms were in turn given a higher status than Composite, as in S. Vitale. In both cases the motive was state policy: the Romans wanted to demonstrate their superiority over the Greeks, and in turn the Byzantine emperor wanted to assert his dominance over Italy. The new capital at Speyer may have been intended, in a similar way, to show that the new master of Italy was the German emperor, and its peculiar design is compatible with such an interpretation. One of its distinguishing features is that the unusual leaf forms which mark its corners and the middle of its sides do not stay separated at the bottom of the capital, but all rise from a single band which runs uninterrupted above the top of the column shaft. In this they closely resemble the leaf forms which spring from the circlets of Medieval crowns. Simple versions of such crowns were found in the imperial graves under the choir of Speyer, including that of Henry IV himself, in whose reign the capital was created.[19] An origin in the world of metalwork would certainly help to explain the strange pierced patterns running along the edges of the leaf forms, which recall the bands of jewels or rivets characteristic of precious metal objects. The crown was the prime visual attribute of the ruler and, as such, was placed not only on the heads of real kings but on images of Christ and God as well. It was thus highly appropriate that the crown capital should be found at the east end of the nave, near God's altar, as well as at the west, near the emperor's seat. Henry was obsessed with asserting his rule over Italy, and his crowning by the pope in 1084 had been the symbol of his success in that endeavour. No more potent emblem could be found for his new "imperial" capital.[20]

It has long been recognized that the rich leaf carving of all the Speyer capitals finds a contemporary parallel only in Italy and was probably the work of Italian sculptors. It is now clear that the placing of the capitals to express both political ambitions and liturgical organization must likewise be Italian, for Henry's work at Speyer can be understood only as an adaptation of the forms and principles being developed in eleventh-century Tuscany. He had reason enough to imitate Tuscan practice. It was in Tuscany that his Italian ambitions met their strongest resistance. Under the protection of the Countess Matilda, the cities of the Arno Valley fought hard against his invading army, turning instead to the pope as their ultimate suzerain. It was Matilda's policy which set the stage for the later opposition between the rival factions of Guelphs, loyal to the pope, and Ghibellines, loyal to the emperor—an opposition which was to polarize civic life in Tuscany for the next three centuries. Since the overlordship of the pope was only nominal, the Guelph movement was essentially one of local nationalism resisting foreign domination. In his Italian campaigns Henry could not fail to be impressed by the magnificence of the churches of the cities he sought to conquer. Encamped outside Florence, he could have admired the rising S. Miniato, and when he took Lucca and Pisa he will have seen many other rich buildings, all surpassed by Pisa Cathedral to whose construction Matilda lavishly contributed and where her mother was buried. His sense of cultural inferiority can only have been reinforced by the nationalistic literature which sprang up in the wake of his invasion. Typical were the writings of Rangerius, Bishop of Lucca. In a poem of c.1095 he launched an extended attack on the "Frankish and Teutonic kings and peoples who join together in a criminal and sacrilegious conspiracy."[21] His sharpest darts he aimed at Henry himself, "the king who, being a Teuton, snarls that he can do anything [*frendens sibi cuncta licere*]."[22] His central theme is the opposition between German and Italian culture. To the "Teutonic rage," "a savage race," is opposed the innocence of the "Tuscan flock" and the virtue of the "strong and magnificent men of Italy."[23] The Germans' speech, characteristically, is "hardly human . . . and frightens even by its sound."[24] The outcome is inevitable when the "Teutons, a hard race but stupid, governed more by impulse than by reason," are defeated by the "just lash" of the "Tuscans." Stung by such taunts, Henry may well have felt that if he claimed to rule Italy he could hardly strengthen his claim better than by bringing some Italian order and refinement to the imperial church. The Italian mason served the emperor well who showed him not only how to adorn his church with capitals which were the very emblems of Italian civilization, but how to even trump the Italian forms with his own. Italian visitors to Speyer, when confronted with its highly organized scheme of capitals, must have found it less easy to accuse the emperor of being a "barbarian" governed more by impulse than reason.

Rangerius' poem does more than help us to understand why Henry should have transformed Speyer so soon after it was built. It also helps us to understand the general revival of Classical forms in eleventh- and twelfth-century Tuscany. The churches built at this period in the area between Florence and Pisa have a richness of materials and a purity of vocabulary which sets them apart from other Romanesque churches, both elsewhere in Italy and throughout Europe. As Rangerius shows, under Countess Matilda's rule the Tuscans developed a unique national consciousness. This led them to value their common traditions and, when faced with the threat of invasion from Germany, to concentrate on those features of their culture which reminded them of the time when Italy had been the victor over the northern barbarians. Nothing was more evocative of Italian superiority than the marble colonnade with its ancient capitals. Rangerius, indeed, refers with

pride to the new cathedral of S. Martino at Lucca, with its magnificent twin colonnades, as emblematic of Tuscan virtue.[25] Finally, Rangerius also indicates how natural it was that the architecture of churches in Lucca and elsewhere should be used to comment directly on the relation between church and state. Not only was the church of S. Frediano the setting for one of the most important debates described in the poem between the representatives of pope and emperor, but all the new churches of the area illustrated how "clergy and people, like a mind united with a body, strove to sanctify their streets."[26] If the bishop of Lucca could think like this just before 1100 it is not surprising that when S. Frediano was rebuilt the year after he died, in 1112, its colonnades commented directly on all the same issues. Rangerius' ambitious poem is closely connected in subject with the equally ambitious churches. It is also connected in style. Both attempt a new Latinity. The Romanness of the new churches bespeaks the same desire to establish a cultural distance from the North as that revealed in Rangerius' criticism of the intrusion of French into the Italian language. Rangerius well understood the advantage of such visual statements over verbal ones. As the pope is made to say after a display of overweening conduct from the emperor's side: "Brothers, you have before your eyes what we are telling you about. There is no need to prove it in a long discussion."[27]

VIII

The crisis of architecture: Medieval and Renaissance

◆

Architecture and Christian morality

IT IS POSSIBLE to see the persistent interest in symbolism which is evident in Christian architecture from the fourth to the fourteenth centuries as nothing more than an expression of new sensibilities and attitudes which were fostered by the new religion. There is, however, another factor which may have had considerable force in encouraging this interest. This is the fundamentally negative status of architecture in a strict system of Christian morality.[1] To build for any purpose implied an inappropriate faith in the permanence of material things in this world and was easily seen as an expression of personal vainglory. To endow one's building with a symbolic meaning, on the other hand, provided it with a certain justification as a witness to a higher truth. A row of columns represented worthless worldly display, but as a group of twelve supports standing for the twelve apostles, foundations of the Church, they could acquire immediate spiritual value.

The extent to which architecture was anathematized by Christianity has seldom been appreciated by historians. In the first book of the Bible, man's desire to build already brings on him a divine judgement. The inhabitants of Babel set out to build a city and a tower, as they say, to make themselves a name. God saw the arrogance of it and put a stop to their building by confounding their language. Subsequent attempts at building fared even worse. As Christ says in *Luke*, 17, 28–29: "in the days of Lot, they did eat, they drank, they bought, they sold, they planted, they builded; but the same day that Lot went out of Sodom it rained fire and brimstone from heaven, and destroyed them all." After

that the righteous gave it up, and from Abraham onwards they preferred to live in tents. Even the Lord himself had no permanent house. The only permanent buildings in the Bible to receive divine approval are those put up by Solomon, and even then strict conditions are attached. Solomon was allowed to build a Temple and a palace only because he was a man of peace unlike his father, David (1 *Chronicles* 28, 3), and because he chose the gift of wisdom and walked with the Lord. Within a few generations all the conditions had been broken, and God brought the inevitable destruction on both structures. Jerusalem fared hardly better than the Cities of the Plain. Christ offered no encouragement to build, either: "lay not up for yourselves treasures upon earth (*Matthew* 6, 19). The only building he believed in was metaphorical: ". . . thou art Peter, and upon this rock I will build my church" (*Matthew* 16, 18). It is this metaphorical language which Saint Paul takes up when he calls James, Peter, and John "columns" (*Galatians* 2, 9). Real buildings receive the same treatment in the last book of the Bible as in the first. "Alas, alas, that great city Babylon, that mighty city! for in one hour is thy judgement come!" (*Revelation* 18, 10). Nothing is more emblematic of the replacement of man's dominion by Christ's than the destruction of Babylon, whose prosperity was built on trade and industry, and the coming of the Heavenly Jerusalem, whose main feature is its wall with its twelve foundations and twelve gates, and which does not even have a Temple: "And I saw no temple therein: for the Lord God Almighty and the Lamb are the temple of it" (*Revelation* 21, 22).

The scriptures are clear: building is bad; even erecting a house for God is difficult to justify. It is hardly surprising against this background that, from the beginning under Constantine, churches were continuously compared with, and made to correspond to, the Heavenly Jerusalem and were described in the metaphorical language of Christ and Saint Paul. It is equally easy to understand why the builders who above all put excessive energies into one building and by so doing in a sense created three new styles—Justinian with Haghia Sophia, Charlemagne at Aachen, and Suger with St Denis—all sought to present themselves as successors to Solomon, the one individual who received divine approval for great expenditure on construction.

The need to justify architecture in this way was kept alive by a constant stream of criticism from those who regarded themselves as the custodians of essential Christian standards. Thus, already before Justinian, Paulinus' elaboration of symbolism both in inscriptions and commentaries can be seen as a response to Jerome's earlier letter to him reminding him that "the true temple of Christ is the believer's soul; adorn this, clothe it, offer gifts to it, welcome Christ to it. What use are walls blazing with jewels when Christ in His poor is in danger of perishing from hunger?"[2] What better response to Jerome's assertion that his soul is the true temple, and his sneers elsewhere about "columns of glowing marble,"[3] than Paulinus' argument that the replacement of piers by columns at the entrance to his church is a reminder to the Christian to open his soul to Christ? Such criticism only strengthened with the economic growth after 1000, and the intensification of architectural symbolism which seems to underlie the creation of Gothic can be seen in part as a consequence of this.[4] Saint Bernard talked derisively of "the vast height of your churches, their immoderate length, their superfluous breadth."[5] Suger was an obvious target for his criticism, and when Bernard asked "what does this gold in the sanctuary?" the abbot of St Denis was able to provide a response in the language of Pseudo-Dionysian mysticism, explaining how the precious material matched the spirits of the saints "radiant as the sun."[6] It can be no accident that Paulinus and Suger, who have left us the most elaborate symbolic interpretations of churches to survive from the Middle Ages, were each exposed to the criticism of the severest Christian moralists.

Gothic versus Classical

The response to the moral criticism of architecture was not limited to purely verbal defence. If we are right to suggest that some of the most important features of the Gothic style inaugurated by Suger—the use of the true column as a structural support, the enlargement of windows, and the development of column figures—derive from the abbot's desire to make the symbolism manifest, then moral pressures can be seen to be decisive influences on the creation of the new architectural language. The importance of these moral pressures which particularly affected architecture would explain the fact (which has often puzzled art historians) that the emergence of a Gothic style in building anticipates by decades the development of so-called Gothic sculpture and painting, and that when they do emerge it is clearly in a role of subservience to architecture. Once it is realized that the new style is the product neither of general social, economic, or intellectual changes nor of a natural development, but rather of the impact of moral pressures on architecture at a time when economic recovery produced an unparalleled expansion of that dangerous art, then the artistic innovations of the twelfth and thirteenth centuries become more easily understood.

It is especially significant that the moral pressures were strongest at the very period and in the very region in which Gothic was invented. The Gothic cathedrals of the Île de France were erected against a background of vehement hostility on the part of leading churchmen of the School of Paris. Petrus Cantor (died 1197) wrote against architectural excess (*Contra superfluitatem aedificiorum*), ridiculing his contemporaries for their madness in building richly worked structures for transient sinners when the Old Testament figures, who lived much longer, dwelt in tents; modern builders, with their taste for lofty edifices, were more like the giants who built the tower of Babel.[7] Alexander Neckam (died 1217) in his *De naturis rerum* introduced his chapter on buildings in a similar vein: "The extent of human affectation is shown in part by the expenditures dedicated to pleasure which an empty boastful pride consumes and squanders in the superfluous magnificence of buildings."[8] The entire chapter of what is basically a scientific encyclopaedia treats architecture not as an art but as a vice. Responding to this continuous assault, builders tried increasingly to transform their churches from massive monuments into miraculous otherworldly symbols. The ultimate expression of this approach was the Sainte Chapelle erected by Saint Louis in 1246–48 (Fig. 56, p. 89). Consisting as it did, once past the entrance bay, of nothing but twelve slender supports, each with an attached apostle statue carrying a cross emblem, framing enormous jewelled windows, it represented the final reduction of the church to a miraculous prefiguration of the Heavenly City, its foundations marked by twelve crosses, the one divinely approved building which would last forever. It thus completed the development of an acceptable symbolic architecture begun by Suger. Recognized as such, it provided the model for thousands of churches throughout Europe. Cologne Cathedral showed triumphantly how the same approach could be applied to the biggest structures and established the style in Germany. S. Maria Novella in Florence—which is supported on twelve piers, each decorated (at least at the time of its dedication) with twelve images of the apostles—did the same for Italy.

One way to defend architecture against its critics was to create a new style which distanced itself from earthly materialism and evoked the Heavenly Jerusalem. Another and exactly contemporary response was to take direct account of the strictures of the moralists and to build churches which were low, lacked towers, had little or no carved decoration, and used flimsy timber roofs instead of massive vaults. This was the approach of the Cistercians (founded by Saint Bernard in the twelfth century) and of the friars such as the Franciscans, Dominicans, and Augustinians (founded in the thirteenth), most of whose churches, especially in the early years, consciously expressed humility, simplicity, and impermanence in different ways.

The contrast between these two solutions to the moral problem of architecture has already been illustrated in the confrontation between Suger and Saint Bernard. It could also be illustrated in many places throughout Europe in the ensuing two hundred years, and early-fourteenth-century Padua provides a particularly enlightening example. There the financier Enrico Scrovegni set about building a magnificent palace and chapel inside the ruins of the Roman arena, which he had acquired in 1300. This he did within a stone's

throw of the appropriately low and simple wooden-roofed church recently erected by the Augustinian friars. The confrontation of values was too abrupt, and on 9 January 1305 the friars tried to have his scheme reduced, claiming that "there ought to be not a huge church in the arena, but a small one, with one altar in the manner of an oratory and not with many altars; and further it should be without bells and without a bell tower. . . ."[9] There is certainly a measure of simple jealousy in their complaint, but the overt argument is presented as a moral one: "He should not have built a large church there, with the many other things which have been made there more for pomp, vainglory, and wealth than for the praise, glory, and honour of God."[10] The appeal was unsuccessful, and Scrovegni completed the adornment of his chapel with the brilliant frescoes of Giotto. Nor did he allow the moral criticism to stand unanswered. An inscription on his tomb inside the chapel provided an eloquent justification:

This place, called the Arena by the ancients,
Becomes a noble altar to God, very much filled with divine
    majesty.
. . . places filled with evil are put to honest use.
Behold, this which was the home of heathens, constructed
    by a great multitude,
Has been demolished with great wrath
And is now miraculously abandoned.
. . .
Divine virtue replaced the profane vices,
The heavenly joys which are superior replaced earthly
    ones.[11]

The text cleverly exploits traditional Christian attitudes to architecture to show that the erection of the chapel in the ruins of the Roman area has a lofty symbolic meaning. The arena, like the tower of Babel, was constructed by a great multitude and, like the earthly Babylon, was destroyed by divine wrath. The new chapel, on the other hand, anticipates the coming of the new Jerusalem, with divine virtue replacing profane vices and heavenly joys replacing earthly ones. It was a further clever choice on the part of Scrovegni, or his advisers, to dedicate the chapel to the Annunciate Virgin. The transformation of the arena into a place of virtue could be seen to recall the much more fundamental transformation of the whole world at the moment of the Incarnation.

71. Giotto: Arena Chapel, Padua, c. 1305:
left (a) *Injustice*; right (b) *Justice*

72. Architectural settings after Giotto, Arena Chapel, Padua, c.1305.
From left to right: (a) *Nativity*; (b) *Last Supper*; (c) *Pentecost*

Certainly the theme of transformation evoked by both inscription and dedication can be seen to provide the key to an understanding of Giotto's use of architecture, a use which precisely confirms the recognition of Gothic as a new virtuous style anticipating heavenly architecture. Thus in the lowest band of decoration the profane vices mentioned in the inscription are placed on one side opposite divine virtues on the other, and the central figures in each series, *Injustice* on the left and *Justice* on the right, are both given expressive architectural frames (Fig. 71). Injustice is shown seated in a massive round arch, already riven with cracks. The falling keystone proves that the building is Roman not Romanesque, thus alluding directly to the arena demolished by divine wrath. Justice, on the other hand, is enthroned in an elegant Gothic niche made up of pointed and cusped arches recalling the style of the chapel. This contrast between Roman vice and Gothic virtue is also developed in the narrative scenes above, where the Temple of the errant Jews consistently has the heavy walls and piers and round arches of Romanesque architecture, while the buildings associated with Christ constitute a carefully modulated sequence rising to a Gothic climax (Figs. 72 and 73). The hut of the *Nativity* is twice shown as a rectangular structure of slender wooden posts. This becomes transformed in the *Last Supper* and the *Washing of the Feet* by the addition of delicate inlay and elaborate cusping, and finally emerges with a full panoply of Gothic colonnettes

and pointed and cusped arches in the *Pentecost* (Fig. 72). The structure is always of the same shape and viewed from the same angle, and its progressive transformation brilliantly illustrates the slow unveiling of the Christian message, until finally the apostles gathered together at Pentecost prepare to go out and bring it to the whole world. The gift of tongues which they then receive may well be understood as making up for the confusion of tongues which brought the Tower of Babel to a halt, serving as a sign of approval for the construction of a physical as well as a spiritual church. Although the arcade is not shown extended round the rear walls of the building, perhaps because of the visual complication this would produce, the arrangement of four bays on a long side and two on a short implies a structure with twelve supports. If completed in this way the building would even more clearly represent the Church supported by the twelve apostles who are shown as its sole occupants. The building echoes, in both forms and meaning, the Sainte Chapelle of fifty years earlier, where also twelve apostles are associated with twelve slender supports bearing pointed cusped arches. Gothic, then, is emphatically sanctioned as the architecture of the Christian Church. Moreover, its status relative to Romanesque and Byzantine forms is made explicit by the juxtaposition of *Pentecost* with the *Expulsion of the Money-Changers from the Temple* immediately above, where the Temple with its marble columns and horse statues is manifestly derived

73 (at right). Giotto: Arena Chapel, Padua, c.1305: above (a) *Expulsion of the Money-Changers from the Temple*; below (b) *Pentecost*

74. S. Maria Novella, Florence, after 1279: interior

from S. Marco in Venice (Fig. 73). While this is a sly dig by the moneylender Scrovegni at the merchants of the neighbouring city, it also indicates how strongly he felt that only Gothic architecture was safe from moral censure. Finally, the whole use of architecture in the frescoes can be seen to have one overriding goal, the construction of an irrefutably virtuous context for the chapel itself. It is as if the progressive transformation of the rectangular gabled *Nativity* hut into the Gothic room of *Pentecost*, is designed to lead on to the rectangular gabled Gothic chapel itself, whose arched corbeltable was self-consciously incorporated into the *Pentecost* scene. Scrovegni has used both inscription and painted decoration to good effect, and, confident that his architecture at least is blameless, he is shown over the entrance door proudly presenting his chapel at the Last Judgement. The implication is clear. For him at least the use of Gothic forms alone, symbolic as they were of the Christian Church, was enough to deflect the Almighty's wrath. Lying in his Gothic chapel even a usurer such as he could happily await the Last Trumpet, secure in the knowledge that his building had more in common with the Heavenly Jerusalem than with the earthly city of Babylon. Architecture in general might be damnable, but Gothic was the architecture of salvation.

The Arena Chapel confirms our suggestions that architecture in general was regarded as morally dangerous and that Gothic carried symbolic associations which constituted an indirect moral defence. Indeed, Giotto's use of architecture in the frescoes would lead one to believe that this last point was widely understood. Whether this is so or not, the frescoes must certainly have helped to broadcast the message, and it is tempting to see the spread of Gothic through Italy in the fourteenth century as accelerated by the propaganda for it in this most authoritative of monuments. Nowhere is this spread of Gothic more evident than in Venice where, from the Doge's Palace downwards, buildings were smothered in a welter of cusps, crockets, and pointed arches, and—most suggestive of all— even proud St Mark's was given Gothic trimmings as if in response to its mockery in the *Expulsion of the Money-Changers*.

The introduction of a Gothic vocabulary in fourteenth-century Venice is particularly striking in view of the confidence of the existing Byzantine tradition. The same is even more true of the earlier Gothic conquest of Florence, where a whole series of monuments continued into the thirteenth century testifying to the vigour of a Tuscan Romanesque style. Given the robustness and pride of this tradition, it is hard to see the construction of enormous Gothic monuments, especially S. Maria Novella (from 1279), S. Croce (from 1294), the Duomo (from 1299), and the Palazzo Vecchio (from 1299), as simply a reflection of changing fashion. If, on the other hand, Gothic was seen as the architectural expression of the Christian faith, and round arches and Classical forms were seen as morally tainted by pagan and Jewish associations, the change can be recognized as the result of compelling need. No people can have been more zealous in bringing this need to the attention of the citizens than the Dominican and Franciscan friars who were responsible for the construction of S. Maria Novella and S. Croce, and it is appropriately those churches which authoritatively introduce the new forms. The rejection by the friars of the existing architectural tradition is emblematic of their rejection of the prevalent worldly way of life. The adoption of the new style represents a reaffirmation of Christian values. The city first helped to finance the friars' own churches and then went on to rebuild its own institutions in the same mould.

The living Church

The architecture of S. Maria Novella, the earliest of the major Gothic monuments, may have been intended as an explicit architectural commentary on the reform movement (Figs. 74–76). A remarkable feature of the building is that while the eastern parts, which are the earliest executed, are entirely Gothic the last three bays of the nave towards the façade, which were built around 1300, revert to Romanesque in several features.[12] For example, the third bay from the entrance, beyond the pulpit, is almost square and so has almost semicircular arches; and many of the capitals are explicitly Classical in character (Fig. 74). The mixture of round and pointed arches and of Gothic and Classical capitals might at first sight seem to be due only to a combination of carelessness and conservatism. However, a detailed analysis of the scheme suggests that some calculated effect is intended. The third bay, with its rounded arches, also contains a large door in the

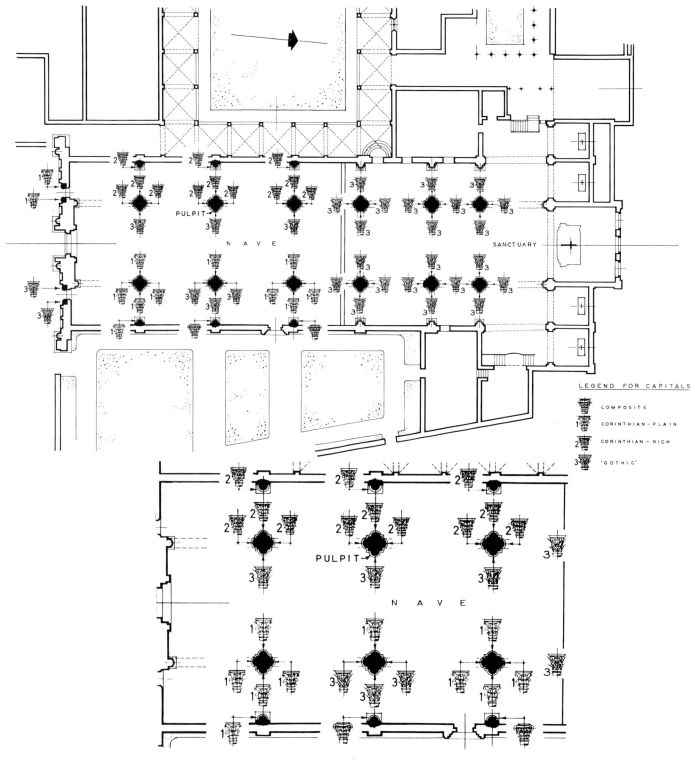

LEGEND FOR CAPITALS

COMPOSITE

1 CORINTHIAN – PLAIN

2 CORINTHIAN – RICH

3 'GOTHIC'

75. S. Maria Novella, Florence: diagram of orders,
with detail of nave

76. S. Maria Novella, Florence, three types of capital. From left to right:
(a) plain Corinthian; (b) rich Corinthian; (c) Gothic

right aisle wall, and the two capitals which support the vault on either side of this door are both Composite, unlike all others in the church. The greater width of that bay thus marks it as an important axis across the nave from that door. The rest of the scheme can be seen to be constructed regularly about that axis and the major axis of the nave. The key to the exploitation of both axes is asymmetrical balance. Thus, for anyone standing inside the aisle door between the two Composite capitals, the three capitals which he sees on each of the two piers in front of him are all Gothic on the left and all Corinthian of a plain uncarved type on the right (Figs. 75 and 76). In the same way, for anyone looking down the nave from the façade, the capitals supporting the first three bays of the main vault are also all Gothic on the left and uncarved Corinthian on the right. This regularity is continued in the aisles. In the left-hand aisle all the capitals supporting the vaults and arcade of the first three bays are again Corinthian, but this time with richly carved leaves. In the right aisle there is less possibility of regularity because of the interruption caused by the side door, but the majority of capitals are plain Corinthian. There are, then, three types of capitals—plain Corinthian, rich Corinthian, and Gothic—carefully arranged. The three types can easily be thought of as a series, running from plain Corinthian to rich Gothic; the carved Corinthian is transitional between the other two just as, earlier, Composite could

be thought of as transitional between Ionic and Corinthian.

Once this has been pointed out, further parallels with Romanesque usage suggest themselves. The asymmetrical balance between Corinthian and Gothic which confronts those who enter the church (whether from the main façade or from the side door) recalls the asymmetrical balance between Composite and Corinthian found earlier. The only difference is that it is now the Gothic form, not the Corinthian, which anticipates the decoration of the holier parts of the building around the altar. The mixture of capitals in the first three bays of S. Maria Novella marks the "transitional" character of that space, just as did such mixtures in Pisa Cathedral, S. Frediano in Lucca, and S. Miniato. It was entirely appropriate for those bays to be differentiated in this way, since they constituted the congregational part of the church, outside the screen which ran across the whole width of the building in the fourth bay. The citizen who came to the church to listen to a chastening sermon would have been made well aware, by the capitals he could see, that the full architecture of spirituality existed only beyond the screen. Inside the door but outside the screen, he was improving himself but was far from perfect. The notion of a transitional state in a transitional area was, indeed, far more clearly expressed than in the earlier churches we have examined. There, the changes from Ionic to Composite to Corinthian were quite abrupt. Here, the changes were gentle and organic, as the plain Corinthian capital acquired the more naturalistic detailing of rich Corinthian and finally burst into vigorous natural life with the Gothic form. The opposition between simple Corinthian and rich Gothic was stated at its strongest in the capitals of the nave vault. But the worshipper whose eyes strayed from the right aisle to the left aisle and thence to the left nave wall would be able to appreciate how one form could actually become the other. It is also possible that the remarkable variation of bay size, producing a range in arch forms from almost round-headed to pointed, Romanesque to Gothic, was also intended to show how transformation could be an organic process. For someone entering through the original main door in the side of the nave into the third bay, with its round arches, the experience of looking east along an arcade in which the arches became more and more pointed must have been both striking and disturbing.

The layout of the capitals in S. Maria Novella clearly owes something to that at S. Miniato and develops the same theme, the opposition between the worldly laity and the spiritual clergy. Even the new feature—the simple opposition between the two sets of capitals on either side of the nave supporting the vaults, Romanesque on one side and Gothic on the other—can be related to the interpretation proposed for the earlier church. The opposition makes much more clear the idea that a church is built with two walls, one the laity and the other the clergy. The only surprising element is that it is the left wall which represents the superior clergy and the left the inferior laity. This too, however, has a justification. The two previous churches on the site had had their entrances to the right and their altars to the left in terms of the present building, while the new monastic buildings were sited entirely to the left. Both factors made it more appropriate to associate the left with the clergy and the right with the laity.

This dramatic opposition between Romanesque and Gothic in the first great Gothic church of Florence is well designed to impress in a city so proud of its Romanesque tradition. It is as if the friars are warning the Florentines that, Christians though they may be, their spiritual life is far from complete. Gothic architecture represents a greater spiritual fulfilment. There can be little doubt where the friars got the unusual idea for building a Romanesque-Gothic transition into their church in the first place. When the Dominicans arrived in Florence they were given an existing eleventh-century church.[13] When they had already outgrown it in the early thirteenth century, they built a larger Gothic church alongside it. Both churches lie under the existing building with their axes across it, the first church under the nave and the second under the transept. The Romanesque and Gothic buildings thus corresponded in their relative positions to the Romanesque and Gothic parts of the present structure. It is likely that the Dominicans had already regarded their transfer from a borrowed Romanesque church to their own Gothic one as symbolic and now realized that they could exploit a similar symbolism in their final building. To this end they first of all incorporated some elements of their second church in the eastern parts of the third one, and then went on to recall the transverse axis and Romanesque character of their first church in the nave. This is certainly the reason for the construction of a large door in the left aisle. Moreover, since this door is carefully placed exactly on axis with the central bay of the friars' cloister on the other side of the church, the relation between nave area and cloister also directly recalls the relation between nave and choir in the two previous churches: this relation was the same as that between nave and choir on the new axis from the great west front. In terms of both axes, Gothic forms marked the direction in which the friars could be found. By placing the citizens of Florence in a Romanesque nave from which they could glimpse their own Gothic choir the Dominicans could be seen to be offering them a new vision and a new religious experience. By carefully arranging the capitals even in the Romanesque area they could also show how their new vision grew naturally out of the old and was even its natural fulfilment. By employing the language of capital variation, a language firmly established in Tuscany, they ensured that their message would be readily understood.

A study of the capitals of S. Maria Novella may help us to understand how Romanesque had come to be seen as a backward and incomplete style. But it can go farther and shed light on the meaning of Gothic itself. The contrast between Romanesque and Gothic capitals is not simply one between old forms which are tainted by a pagan materialism and new ones which are not; it is also a contrast between lifeless and living leaf forms.

Many of the Gothic capitals of S. Maria Novella, as of other contemporary buildings, are new precisely in their fleshiness, juiciness, and curving vitality, and even in an asymmetrical wind-blown effect. They are thus in stark contrast to the stiff and dry leaves of their Classical forebears. The new capital type may well be associated with the new endowment of church buildings with symbolic life, paralleling the transformation of stiff columns into fleshy statues in French cathedral portals. New physical life is given to dead Classical forms so that the dangerously materialistic church building can represent the live Church of Christ. In both cases the need to endow the building with spiritual meaning arose from the moral dilemma involved in being both a Christian and an earthly builder. A similar desire to vitalize the dead building led the Dominicans to give prominence to the lighting of candles held by the twelve apostles painted on the church's twelve piers. That act brought "light and life" to the whole Church.[14]

S. Maria Novella shows how the material church can become the spiritual Church, as plain Corinthian becomes rich Corinthian, which in turn becomes living Gothic, before our very eyes. Anyone who reached the east end with its cusped windows, its pointed arches, and its apparently growing capitals must have felt himself to be close to experiencing the "live" Church. Later on, the Dominicans of S. Maria Novella went even farther in trying to represent the Church. When Andrea di Bonaiuto decorated their chapter house, the "Spanish Chapel," after 1366 he painted on the left wall the Church Militant, with Dominicans as its active embodiment and a magnificent church covered in crockets and tracery as its material expression. The church is based on the rising Florence Cathedral and reminds us that the decision to rebuild the cathedral after 1299 may have been directly prompted by the way Gothic was shown as the fulfilled Christian style in S. Maria Novella a few years earlier. It was certainly a happy chance that the Romanesque Baptistery would relate to the Gothic cathedral standing before it in the same way that the first three bays of S. Maria Novella related to the rest of the building. Yet the image of the Church in the chapter house as far surpasses the cathedral in its Gothic attributes as the perfect Church surpasses all individual buildings. In general, if each Gothic church seems to try to surpass each earlier one in a way never seen before, it is because the style we call Gothic was an emblem of Christianity, and to be more Gothic was to be more Christian.

Architecture justified

Cusps and crockets may have served their purpose for a time, but they could not in the end sanctify architecture as a whole. Churches might prefigure the Heavenly Jerusalem, but secular buildings such as Scrovegni's house or the Palazzo Vecchio hardly could. As money accumulated in the coffers of the merchants of Western Europe and the temptation grew to perpetuate the status it conferred by the erection of buildings, and as similar strains developed in other parts of the Christian system, it became increasingly clear that a new Christian moral code had to be forged to replace that of the primitive Church. The group who felt most keenly the disparity between the ideal Christian life and the real human situation were the orders of friars working on the very interface between the spiritual and secular worlds, and it was the friars who were the leaders in the much-needed reform. Chief among those who provided the intellectual foundation for this restructuring of Christian attitudes was the Dominican Saint Thomas Aquinas (c.1225–74), whose great *Summa theologica* reviewed the whole of theology, including thought on vice and virtue. Among many modifications and clarifications of earlier positions was his fundamental reappraisal of the ethics of expenditure. This was based on his elevation of Aristotle to a place of authority rivalling that of the Christian fathers. The new position was expounded both in Aquinas' *Commentary on the Nicomachean Ethics of Aristotle* and in the *Summa* itself.[15]

Pagan moralists had often been turned to before. Petrus Cantor had called on Roman Republicans such as the Scipios, the Catos, and the Laelii as his witnesses against the corruption of art. Neckam had quoted Horace, and Saint Bernard Persius. Aquinas, however, did not merely turn to pagans for support for a Christian position; he also founded a new Christian position on pagan theory. The theory he used was that of appropriate behaviour summed up in the Greek *to prepon* and the Latin *decorum*, which has already been discussed in the context of Vitruvius; more specifically, he concentrated on the theory of *megaloprepeia*. Aristotle had used the term *megaloprepeia* (Latin *magnificentia*) at *Ethics* IV, 2 to describe the great expenditure which it is appropriate for great people to make for important things. "For the expenditures of the magnificent [*megaloprepēs*] man are both great and appropriate. So too will be his works, and thus his expenditure will be great and appropriate to his works." Going on to elaborate a hierarchy of great works, Aristotle argued that the greatest were those for the gods; second came those for the common good, and third those for the individual. Of those undertaken for the individual one of the best was the building of a house appropriate to a man's wealth; and, in general, expenditure on permanent things was to be preferred. Large-scale expenditure on building, whether for God, for the state, or even for oneself, was thus no longer damnable but desirable; for if the rich and powerful man did not spend money in this way he would be liable to the charge of meanness. The magnificence which had been spurned by Petrus Cantor in his *Summa* as a vice was now enthroned by Aquinas in his *Summa* as a virtue. Architecture, victim of attack since the Early Christian period, could at last find protection under the very mantle of Christian theology.

Thomas Aquinas was canonized in 1323, and from then on his teachings became a predominant influence on the later Middle Ages, especially in his native Italy. It was in Italy too that the crisis of architecture was greatest. The expansion of trade, production, and banking created enormous differences of wealth and status which, since the collapse of imperial authority, developed largely without the social validation provided in the north by the feudal system. The despots and merchants who competed for power and position thus had a remarkable degree of freedom to give expression to their ambitions, which increasingly received architectural expression as they sought through buildings to give permanence to their unstable positions. The "house" became as never before the emblem of permanent power and was marked as such by arms and inscriptions. At the same time, vigorous forces emerged to counter the new excesses. Besides the friars in their sermons, the city councils sought to impose restraint through the laws.[16] Façade design was liable to strict control, especially near town halls, which were thus allowed to assert themselves more decisively. In such a world the recovery of a code of architectural

expenditure, which originated with the philosopher Aristotle and also carried the authority of Christian theology, was timely indeed, especially for the new type of patron. If he could show that his building activities were consistent both with the ancient theory of social order and with recent Christian morality, he could free himself of major inhibitions. Moreover, if such a justification could be put on record he could ensure his reputation not only for the present but for the future too.

An early and explicit example of such a written justification is that provided for several members of the Visconti family by Galvano Fiamma. Having seized power in Milan in 1322, the Visconti rapidly set about a vast architectural campaign intended, like Augustus' programme in Rome thirteen centuries earlier, to guarantee the fortunes of a whole dynasty. This architectural activity, together with the family's other deeds, was then all carefully recorded in a work which has survived under the title *Opusculum de rebus gestis ab Azone, Luchino et Johanne Vicecomitibus*, apparently composed by Fiamma as the fourteenth book of a *Chronicle* of Milan.[17] Fiamma, born in that city in 1283, was a professor at Pavia and a noted teacher of Aristotle until he became secretary to Giovanni Visconti when the latter was elevated to archbishop in 1342. The unusually substantial chapters devoted to building works are presented in terms taken precisely from the tradition of Aristotle and Aquinas. Chapter 9, on the building operations of Giovanni, is headed *De magnificentiis Johannis Vicecomitis episcopi novariensis*. Those of Azo (ruled 1328–39) fill several more chapters. The first is entitled *De magnificentia aedificiorum* and contains an elaborate introduction:

Azo Visconti, considering that he had made peace with the Church and had freed himself of all his enemies, decided that he would make a glorious residence for himself. For the philosopher [the usual term for Aristotle] says in the fourth book of the *Ethics* that it is the work of the wealthy man to provide himself with a suitable [*decens*] house. For, as he says in the sixth book of the *Politics*, the populace is astonished when it sees spectacular houses. This being so, Aristotle thinks that the prince attains such power that he can no longer be attacked; at the same time, the prince gets a magnificent residence which is suited to the size of his household. Besides this, it is also desirable that the prince should put up magnificent and noble temples, because the philosopher says that admirable expenditure of the sort that a magnificent prince should make is that done for God. In view of all this, Azo Visconti began two magnificent works: one that concerned with divine worship, a wonderful chapel in honour of the Blessed Virgin, and the other a magnificent palace suitable as a residence.[18]

The following chapters describe the buildings as promised: the chapel with its marble decorations and paintings; the "round campanile of baked bricks decorated from top to bottom with marble colonnettes, a delight to look at";[19] the palace with its tower, aviary, and zoo.[20] After more chapters devoted to wars, Fiamma returns again to the problem of architecture in Chapter 23:

It is appropriate [decet] for the magnificent prince to make great expenditures for the whole community; for the philosopher in the Ethics says that property held in common is like that dedicated to the gods . . . Therefore, Azo Visconti, the lord of the city, whose responsibilities covered all fields, after attending to his own building works directed his magnificence to the public sector.[21]

This leads into a description of a new tower, new streets, "for the great ornament of the city and for the comfort [consolatio] of people travelling around," and underground drains.[22]

Fiamma implies throughout that Azo is actually guided by Aristotle, and the Visconti ruler thus emerges as a wise prince guided by a philosopher. But that guidance is apparent only in the accounts of architecture, and a careful reading shows that Aristotle is introduced simply to provide a justification for non-religious building both private and public. Azo's actions are thus justified in terms both of divine law and of pagan ethics. Deeds that might otherwise reveal a trust in transient things and expose the Visconti to the charge of the pursuit of vainglory were made to redound to the patron's credit.

Virtue and vainglory in the fifteenth century

Just as architecture was recovering its confidence in the first half of the fourteenth century, it received a setback which was both material and psychological. The ravages of the Black Death in the 1350s not only gravely disrupted the previous economic growth but also brought in its wake a wave of prophetic warnings of divine retribution. Thus, forty years after Fiamma's eulogy of Azo Visconti, Coluccio Salutati, one of the new group of Florentine humanists, pointed a con-

77. SS. Stephen and Lawrence, Castiglione Olona, after 1420: capital

temptuous finger at the vast but tottering palaces of his contemporaries, whose walls, already cracking like the arch of Giotto's Injustice, showed "that the world is a mirror of vanities [quod mundus sit speculum vanitatum]."[23] Only in the fifteenth century, and particularly after the return of the papacy from Avignon to Rome, did a new wave of confidence and wealth produce a new stimulus to patronage. Perhaps the first and most striking representative of the new wave was Cardinal Branda Castiglione. He was already seventy when he began the redevelopment of his home town, Castiglione Olona, north of Milan, in 1420, and he continued it till his death in 1443, erecting palaces for himself and his relations, a school, a collegiate church, and the chiesa di villa. It was probably Castiglione too who instigated a literary commentary on these projects, not in the form of a traditional chronicle but in the new humanist form of a letter.[24] The letter, written by Francisco Pizzolpasso, Bishop of Pavia, is dated 5 January 1432 and is addressed to Giovanni Cervantes, Cardinal of S. Pietro in Vincoli. The description of the church of St Stephen and St Lawrence is the most important part of the letter, and the most significant feature of the description is the characterization of the building as Doric (ad filum ut aiunt doricum).[25] This sudden reappearance of a Classical order which had virtually vanished in the Middle Ages is unlikely to represent the intention of the builders of the church, which has standard Lombard Gothic columns with leaf capitals—though their proportions are not far from being appropriate (Fig. 77). Rather, Pizzolpasso's description was probably based on Vitruvius, of whose text he owned a copy.[26] Inspired by the Vitruvian recommendation of Doric for temples to manly deities such as Mars and Hercules, he has chosen to refer to the order which he deems appropriate for two martyr saints of similarly manly character. The association between saints and pagan deities was the more natural since the church of S. Lorenzo in nearby Milan was supposed originally to have been a temple of Hercules. Vitruvius found the order appropriate for such figures because of their *virtus*, and Pizzolpasso praises the *virtus* of the building's exterior.[27] His interest in the relevant passage of the Roman writer was almost certainly excited by the reference to the general principle of *decor*, which allowed him to praise the Gothic church in terms appropriate to the theory of Aristotelian magnificence, essentially a theory of *decorum*. The same interest in a theory of architectural appropriateness appears in the final paragraphs of the letter, where the cardinal's constructions are claimed to represent the "man and virtue itself and the distinctive emblems of piety." As such they are an example to others to do the same. They are made for later generations and the glory of God. "What a difference there is, good Lord, between one type of glory and another!"[28] Presented in this way the architecture takes on a new function: it becomes an expression of its builder and his moral qualities. It is almost like a portrait, as Pizzolpasso implies when he says that later generations will be inspired by Castiglione's buildings just as the Scipios were inspired by the wax images of their ancestors. Something more is intended here than an identification of the *virtus* of the martyr saints with that of the cardinal, for both now find an expression in the *virtus* of the church itself. The letter ends, in a tone more appropriate to the pulpit than to the study, with a fervent call to imitate the *virtutis exempla* of Castiglione and join in a revival of building. Pizzolpasso goes far beyond simple justification, and he also goes beyond what would be required in a letter to a friend. He seems to wish to address a wider public. In fact we know that others read the letter beside Cardinal Cervantes; Pier Candido Decembrio certainly did, and Nicholas of Cusa probably did too.[29] The final draft was completed just before Pizzolpasso's departure for the Council of Basle, which had begun in 1432, and its public tone suggests that it was intended to be circulated there. If it was, it may well have played an impor-

tant part in the acceleration of the architectural Renaissance, for two churchmen at the council were later to rival and surpass Cardinal Castiglione. Nicholas V's vast scheme for rebuilding St Peter's, extending the Vatican, replanning the Borgo, and restoring Rome can only be compared to Castiglione's programme, and at its heart lay the new chapel of St Stephen and St Lawrence, recalling by its dedication the church at Olona. Pius II's construction of a church, a family palace, and other monuments at his birthplace of Corsignano—renamed Pienza so that its name, like that of the Lombard cardinal's birthplace, could commemorate the man—constitutes an even more precise imitation. Pizzolpasso's appeal—and he may only have been Castiglione's mouthpiece—seems to have found a worthy response. The letter may also have had the effect of encouraging the two popes to ensure that elaborate literary descriptions of their projects also survived them. Nicholas V made sure that his biographer Giannozzo Manetti wrote a full account of his scheme, which he had barely begun, and also that he built into it an argument of justification, which we must consider later. Pius left his own record in his *Commentaries*.

Justification had clearly been less of a problem for Pizzolpasso than for Fiamma, but the criticism of architectural expenditure was still rife later in the century. Not surprisingly the most celebrated builder of them all, Cosimo de' Medici, had the most elaborate defence. This was provided by a learned cleric, Timoteo Maffei, in a work probably written in the 1450s, professedly to refute the thesis that his "reputation for magnificence [*magnificentiae nomen*] . . . to a Christian reveals more vice than virtue."[30] All the old arguments are advanced on either side, and new and more specious ones invented, in a lengthy dialogue which aspires to close the issue. And, indeed, it is never treated so fully again, although it crops up in the work of figures such as Pontanus and Savonarola towards 1500.

The embarrassment of the Classical

The elaborate defence of Cosimo de' Medici shows that in spite of all that had been done to provide a justification for architectural activity it could still be as easily called a vice as a virtue. Whether, like Scrovegni, a builder used the approved forms of Christian Gothic; whether, like Azo Visconti, he followed the rules of magnificence by building for the public good; whether, like Castiglione, he presented his investment in architecture as a rejection of the pleasures of consumption and as a moral example to others—the shadow of Babel was always there. Indeed, for an Italian builder of the late fifteenth century the problem was greater than ever. If he built a house for himself and his family as his wealth and status might oblige him to, and if he marked it with his name or coat of arms to serve as a moral example like the builders of Antiquity, he might seem to invite the judgement of God precisely as had the inhabitants of Babel, who had set out to make a "name" for themselves. If, moreover, he rejected Gothic with its positive Christian associations in favour of a Classical vocabulary, he ran the additional risk of seeming to reject the entire Christian message. This is why many of the builders of the most explicitly Classical structures of the fifteenth century reveal considerable embarrassment along with their pride in the new forms, often providing either a formal or inscriptional antidote to the dangerous style. One example is the Medici church of S. Lorenzo (c.1420) in Florence, the first in Italy to reject Gothic. The new entablature, of Classical derivation, is decorated prominently with winged cherubs' heads. Never used in Antiquity, of course, the cherub was one of the safest forms of Christian decoration, having been the only live form used in Solomon's divinely authorized Temple. Its sudden reemergence is most easily understood as a way of demonstrating that although the structure abandoned the Christian Gothic style in favour of one tainted by paganism and materialism, it was still decisively attached to a tradition approved by God. S. Lorenzo was the first church to use generally Classical forms, and Sigismondo Malatesta's S. Francesco at Rimini was the first to use ones which were specifically Antique. The façade is closely adapted from the Arch of Augustus nearby, but it is significant that Alberti—or the executant architect, Matteo de' Pasti—has consciously rejected the Arch's Corinthian capitals in favour of a new Composite form with a winged cherub's head at the centre, and has also introduced winged cherubs into the entablature above. To those who might protest that the title *templum* on the foundation medal[31] referred to the pagan "temple," Sigismondo could claim that the temple he imitated was that of Jerusalem. There is the same balance of pagan pride and Christian modesty in the

façade inscription, the first to rival the dedication of an ancient temple. It begins pompously with Malatesta's name, as if to challenge the Almighty as a successor to the tower of Babel, yet it ends piously ANNO GRATIAE MCCCCL. An even grander Classical structure was the vast palace at Urbino built largely by Federigo di Montefeltro before his death in 1482. The long inscription round the central court insists that the building was erected unselfishly for his family and his descendants, and that Federigo embarked on its construction only after he had brought peace to the papal territories. In this the inscription echoes Fiamma's introduction of Azo's architectural activity and explicitly invites comparison of Federigo with Solomon the "man of peace." Smaller, and Classical in a different way, was the palace which Diomede Caraffa built about the same time in Naples. It was one of the first to use for its decoration prominent pieces of ancient sculpture. It too had an inscription, this time on its façade: IN HONOREM OPTIMI REGIS ET NOBILISSIMAE PATRIAE DIOMEDES CARAFFA COMES MATALONE MCCCCLXVI.[32] "For king and country. . . ." What better cause? No one could accuse him of vainglory, and his declaration that the building was for the public good established its respectability in the tradition of "magnificence."

The Italian city which in the later fifteenth century came closest to rivalling Rome with its marbles and its columns was Venice. But it was also the city where Gothic forms had been most securely established. The new Classical forms had thus to be well protected against charges of either paganism or vainglory. Pietro Lombardo's extravagant marble church of S. Maria dei Miracoli of 1481 has a large cross emblem in the centre of its façade, complete with four roundels intended to recall the usual position of the four evangelists, and similar groupings are found both to left and right and inside the church. More remarkably, other such patterns are found on the equally rich palace of Giovanni Dario of a few years later (1487). The large roundels surrounded with groups of four and twelve smaller ones can only be intended to emphasize the building's Christianity, with their references to the evangelists and apostles. Equally defensive is the inscription URBIS GENIO IOHANNES DARIUS: "[Dedicated by] Giovanni Dario to the spirit of the city." Like the Caraffa palace, it is erected for the public benefit and is thus an appropriate expenditure for a rich man. Mauro Coducci's

Palazzo Vendramin-Calergi (originally Loredan), c.1500, carries a different inscription at gondola height: NON NOBIS DOMINE/NON NOBIS, taken from the beginning of *Psalm* 115, "*Not unto us, O Lord, not unto us*, but unto Thy name give glory . . ." The palazzo, one of the richest ever put up in Venice, was apparently erected for God's glory and not that of its owners. The same message is carried by the smaller but even richer Palazzo Trevisan-Capello of about the same date. Among its sumptuous intarsias and reliefs appears the text SOLI DEO/HONOR ET GLORIA. This is taken from 1 *Timothy* 1, 17: "Now unto the King eternal, immortal, invisible, *the only wise God, be honour and glory* for ever and ever, amen." Again the inscription explicitly rejects any charge of personal vanity and serves as an antidote to the pagan ornament. The same is true of the contemporary Palazzo Malipiero at S. Maria Formosa. After the spectator has revelled in its richness, its Classical orders, and the row of profile heads like ancient coin types on the frieze, he is suddenly reminded by the IHS medallion in the very centre that he has misinterpreted the whole. The medallion virtually completes the Palazzo Loredan inscription: ". . . not unto us, but unto *Thy name* give glory. . . ." The name of Christ is literally there to receive its due tribute. It is worth emphasizing that these inscriptions are not here simply because the buildings are unusually grand or the patrons particularly religious. The Gothic Ca' d'Oro was richer and the Gothic Palazzo Foscari bigger than any. It can only be the Classical forms which require defending. Exactly the same situation was faced in Venice's rival, Genoa, on the other side of the peninsula. Here expenditure tended to be concentrated on extremely elaborate portals, and soon after the introduction of Classical forms for these, around 1450, the name of Christ, the IHS monogram, appears and is frequent until around 1500. Almost always it occurs between family arms or Antique busts, and sometimes it is combined with both, as in the case of two magnificent portals of Spinola and Doria palaces showing the triumph of those families. Always it is there to convey the message "not unto us but unto Thy name give glory." Saint Bernardino (1380–1444) had in his sermons explicitly told people to use the IHS monogram on their palaces instead of their own arms;[33] but it is remarkable that it is not until Classical elements appear that patrons seem to have taken his

recommendation really seriously. In Rome, unlike other cities, residences built by cardinals, with their plain walls and simple windows, were so much simpler than the ancient buildings with which they were surrounded that the question of justification was not so urgent as with the palaces of secular magnates. One of the most prominent of them, however, that of Domenico della Rovere (a nephew of Sixtus IV, during whose papacy he was created cardinal), bears on the lintels of its windows besides the prelate's name the motto SOLI DEO already noted on the Palazzo Trevisan.

Throughout Italy, then, when Classical forms were introduced in the second half of the fifteenth century they were accompanied by a new type of inscription which once again reminds us of the fundamental moral problem facing the Christian builder. The problem, which had been reduced over the preceding two centuries by the use of Gothic forms and by the use of literary justifications, was suddenly brought to the fore again by the revival of the tainted forms of the pagan world, forms whose negative associations for a Christian were confirmed in many contemporary paintings of the Nativity, where the simple stable is erected in the ruins of magnificent Classical structures.

Another way of getting round the problem of using Antique forms was to combine them with enough Gothic features to prevent them being thought pagan. This may be the explanation for the preservation of the Gothic windows of S. Francesco at Rimini, and it is probably in the same light that we should view the persistence of Gothic elements in other buildings, such as those by Michelozzo. Gothic was particularly favoured by the popes, who had perhaps the greatest reluctance to be seen to give up the official Church style. It is almost certainly in this way that we should understand the Gothic windows, with their elaborate tracery, used by Bernardo Rossellino in the east end of the church he built for Pius II at Pienza (1460–62), and by other architects in Sixtus IV's buildings in Rome (such as the Ospedale di S. Spirito and S. Maria della Pace, both of which use elaborate tracery forms for the octagons which are their holiest parts) and in the enormous new church at Loreto (c.1470–95). Sixtus' nephew Giuliano della Rovere even replaced the round-headed windows of S. Pietro in Vincoli with traceried Gothic ones.[34] In all these cases the use of Gothic is highly self-conscious, since other window types were readily available, and the forms used were even more Gothic than those found earlier. Apparently the older style continued to have an absolutely higher religious status than Classical forms, at least in some quarters, throughout the fifteenth century. Gothic could be completely supplanted by Classical forms only when they too could be seen to carry an equal and even greater moral conviction.

In the subsequent chapters the importance of moral pressures will frequently be apparent as theory after theory is generated to justify the use of Classical forms. The struggles of builders and writers to restore to them the irrefutable authority of which they had been robbed by the later Middle Ages constitute an heroic sequence of intellectual endeavour, as one analogy after another from more acceptable activities is pressed into service. If, in the end, the forms seem strong enough to stand on their own and finally sweep away the indigenous Gothic tradition of Northern Europe, it is because collectively these analogies build up such complexities of meaning that the forms themselves become more richly charged than even Gothic with its symbolism of the living Church. But the reason why they were resurrected at all from the tomb in which they had been so decisively laid around 1300 had little to do with morality and its pressures. It related to the rise of more basic needs, needs which, as so often, became adorned with moral justifications and explanations only in the subsequent process of acquiring respectability.

IX

The Tuscan Renaissance

◆

Brunelleschi as Dante

BRUNELLESCHI's rejection of Gothic in favour of a range of forms of ultimately Classical derivation was startling but consistent. In a series of major buildings—the Ospedale of the Innocenti, S. Lorenzo, the Barbadori Chapel in S. Felicita, the Pazzi Chapel, and S. Spirito, all erected in the years after 1419—he used pediments and entablatures, semicircular arches and domical vaults, fluted pilasters and cylindrical columns, and Ionic and Corinthian capitals to develop an ordered architecture of prismatic clarity. The usual explanation of the return to earlier forms is that it is simply one aspect of the revival of Antiquity, the Renaissance, which, it is argued, was the dominant force behind changes and innovations in literature and the arts in fifteenth-century Florence.[1] This view was already being presented by Filarete in 1464,[2] by Giovanni Rucellai in his *Zibaldone*,[3] and by Antonio Manetti in his life of Brunelleschi written around 1480,[4] and was finally given canonical authority by Vasari.[5] Manetti even gave it an historical foundation by claiming that Brunelleschi spent time in Rome with Donatello after losing the competition for the bronze doors of the Florence Baptistery in 1401; that he measured and drew ancient buildings there, learning to distinguish Ionic, Doric, Tuscan, Corinthian, and Attic; and that he subsequently used these forms in the appropriate places in his buildings.

There is, however, no evidence that any of this is true, and recent opinion agrees that the visit is probably Manetti's invention in order to give his hero authority in the terms of the 1480s. Recent opinion also agrees that hardly a single feature of Brunelleschi's buildings can be directly derived from an Antique source, and that most can be shown instead to depend on Romanesque example.[6] One might imagine that this would lead scholars to question the underlying assumption that Brunelleschi was an architect of the Antique revival. Some have sensibly suggested that he may have had political reasons for incorporating elements from a more recent local vocabulary.[7] But most disregard the problem, arguing that Brunelleschi must have mistaken the Baptistery, his most influential model, for a Roman temple and that he must have supposed other Romanesque structures, such as SS. Apostoli, were Carolingian and so Late Roman too.[8] The proponents of this view argue that there was a strong literary tradition, from the fourteenth-century chronicler Villani onwards, which described the Baptistery as either wholly or partly a Roman building, and that a similar tradition attributed the other buildings to Charlemagne.[9] Although it is true that the fourteenth- and fifteenth-century historians of Florence competed vigorously in the concoction of spurious links with ancient Rome,[10] there is hardly enough consistency between one author and another to convince us, in the absence of any firm evidence, that these stories (whose origin lay in a tradition of rhetorical invention more than of scientific enquiry) would have been generally accepted as the truth. Indeed, if Brunelleschi was really interested in reviving Antiquity, it is unlikely that these structures would have been his only models and that he would have shunned the hundreds of indisputable Roman monuments which were readily accessible in central Italy. Given the evidence, the notion that Brunelleschi wished to revive Roman architecture seems at best improbable and at worst absurd. The main reason for its persistence can only be the popularity of the idea that the revival of Antiquity was the dominant obsession of contemporary Florence.

This last idea is also highly questionable. The main

evidence for it is the enthusiastic search for ancient manuscripts by humanists such as Poggio Bracciolini, and the serious study and careful use of Classical Latin by authors such as Leonardo Bruni in his *Historia Florentini populi*. The group of people concerned with these activities was small, however, and their shared interest in the revival of correct Latin effectively isolated them from the majority of their contemporaries who lacked their learning. What is more, there were many who felt that the classicism of Bruni and others was fundamentally hostile to the Florentine tradition. Thus around 1420 Ser Domenico da Prato launched an attack on the likes of Bruni and Niccoli, arguing that their respect for the ancients would inevitably paralyse creative energy in contemporary Florence: "they will cripple their young listeners with their statements that 'it is impossible to do or say anything in a way that it has not been done or said better by the ancients.' "[11] Domenico repeatedly indicates that the Latin humanists' hostility to Dante is one of their greatest crimes. For him, achievement in contemporary Florence could only be based on the great tradition of poetry in the Tuscan *volgare*. Nor is his defence of the Tuscan language unusual. A few years earlier, perhaps around 1415, Cino Rinuccini had composed an *Invective Against Certain Slanderers of Dante, Petrarch and Boccaccio*, in which the recent generation of humanists were criticized for similar reasons.[12] A few years later, around 1425–26, Giovanni Gherardo da Prato, teacher of Dante at Florence University, presented a similar argument in his *Paradiso degli Alberti*. Giovanni's goal was simple: "to exalt our mother tongue as well as I know how and to ennoble it in the way it has already been ennobled by the three crowns of Florence,"[13] that is, the three great writers of the Trecento. His intention is stated even more explicitly by one of his speakers: to show "that the Florentine idiom is so polished [*rilimato*] and copious [*copioso*] that one can express, argue, and debate in it any abstract and profound thought with the most perfect lucidity."[14] There was thus a movement to revitalize Tuscan which was just as strong as that to revive Latin, and might just as easily have provided a frame of reference for Brunelleschi's stylistic innovation.

Indeed, a review of the evidence suggests that Brunelleschi is much more likely to have aligned himself with the former tendency than the latter. In 1415 a law was passed making the vulgar language compulsory for all legal contracts among members of the *arti*, and it will have been notaries such as the artist's father, Ser Brunellescho, and Ser Domenico da Prato who had to put the law into effect.[15] Giovanni da Prato, on the other hand, was an active adviser on the cathedral cupola project, and although he did not always see eye to eye with Brunelleschi, the two clearly knew each other well and exchanged sonnets—written, naturally, in the *volgare*.[16] Brunelleschi, then, was linked to the Tuscanists by milieu as he was not to the Latinists, who conspicuously never mention him in his lifetime.[17] There is much evidence for his interest in practising the vulgar tongue in both speech and writing, and none for his use of Latin. Moreover, one of his earliest biographers tells us that he particularly admired Dante.[18] Finally, nothing shows so clearly which side Brunelleschi was on in the contest between the two languages as Alberti's laborious translation of the *De pictura* into the *volgare* for his benefit—hardly a compliment if he was identified with the Latin humanists!

Perhaps, then, it is appropriate to dispense with the later myth, current from Manetti onwards, and look elsewhere for Brunelleschi's motivation in copying the Baptistery. An obvious possibility is that he saw it for what it was, a genuinely Tuscan building, and that he sought to use it as the basis for developing a truly Tuscan language of architecture. Admittedly, for him to consider the Baptistery as a Tuscan building would set him apart from the literary tradition which claimed that it was at least partly Roman in origin, an opinion shared even by such Tuscanists as Giovanni da Prato. But the Roman claim was based on political expedient and had as little scholarly basis as the spurious genealogies which also appear in contemporary historical works. There is no reason to believe that workers in the Opera del Duomo, a workshop which was essentially a continuation of that which had originally built the Baptistery, subscribed to the erroneous claim of the myth-makers—if they even knew of it. Then, too, the stylistic correspondence of the Baptistery with other monuments, many of them with dated inscriptions, such as S. Miniato, Pisa Cathedral, and the church at Empoli, was evidence which would perhaps carry more weight with a humble artisan than with a littérateur whose task was inflation and ornament. Again, there can be little doubt that Brunelleschi's connections were much closer with the Opera than with Chancery historians. There is also some indication that even those within the myth-making tradition had to work hard to demolish the correct view of the Baptistery. When Coluccio Salutati introduced his claim for the Roman character of the building by first denying that it was either Greek or Tuscan—*non graeco, non tusco more factum sed plane Romano*[19]—he cannot have meant *ancient* Greek or Etruscan. Both Greeks and Etruscans had faded out long before Florence had been founded by the Romans. *Graecus*, on the other hand, was regularly used by contemporaries to refer to Byzantine,[20] and *Tuscus* to refer to modern Tuscan.[21] Such a rhetorical assertion would normally be used as a convention for disposing of accepted views, and the two natural views of the Baptistery would be that it was the work either of Greeks, as were Pisa Cathedral and the Baptistery mosaics (which were Byzantine "Greek" in style, as Cennini said of Giotto's predecessors),[22] or of modern Tuscans, the inhabitants of Matilda's Tuscany. Salutati, far from proving the popularity of the "Roman" myth, implicitly admits that the Baptistery was more usually recognized for what it was, Byzantine and/or Tuscan.

Brunelleschi, then, was if anything more likely to see the Baptistery as Medieval Tuscan than to see it as Roman, and it is also more likely that he wanted to revive a Tuscan than a Latin tradition. Yet why, if he was concerned with a Tuscan architectural tradition as a counterpart to the literature of Dante, Petrarch, and Boccaccio, did he not base himself rather on the architecture with which they were associated in time, the Gothic style of the cathedral or of Orsanmichele? The answer must be that Gothic, whatever its positive spiritual associations, must always have been regarded as an alien style. For Burchard of Hall, writing in Germany around 1280, it had been *opus francigenum* ("Frankish work").[23] For Filarete around 1460, it was the architecture of "the people north of the Alps, the Germans and French."[24] For Manetti, Brunelleschi's biographer, the "German method of building . . . lasted down to . . . the age of Brunellescho."[25] The origins of Italian Gothic in France and Germany must always have been well known, and its specifically German associations can only have been reinforced in the first quarter of the fifteenth century by political and architectural events in Milan. There Gian Galeazzo Visconti made extensive use of French and German architects for the construc-

tion of the very Gothic cathedral after 1386 and, upon receiving the title of duke from the German emperor, set about expanding his imperially sanctioned power southwards, dying at the siege of Florence in 1402. Baron and others have shown that the threat from Milan, which continued under Filippo Maria Visconti, especially in the 1420s, had an important effect on Florentine politics, reviving fear of German imperial domination and encouraging the development of a Republican constitution as a defence.[26] Against this background the foreign, and especially German, associations of Gothic are likely to have taken on an importance they had not had earlier.

This same political climate which made it more likely that Gothic should be seen as an emblem of foreign domination also gave a new importance to the earlier monuments such as the Baptistery. Just as Gothic could be seen as linked to the Ghibelline or imperial party, so the Romanesque buildings could be seen as linked to the Guelph party which backed the pope against the emperor. As we saw in chapter VII, the Baptistery was erected in the period around 1100, when Florence had first achieved independence from the empire under the protection of Countess Matilda. Indeed, perhaps for this reason Villani among others already tells us in the fourteenth century that the Guelph party always used the Baptistery as a centre for their activities.[27] In spite of all the many transformations of the Ghibelline-Guelph opposition, the Guelphs had always seen themselves as guardians of Florentine autonomy and the national consciousness. In these circumstances, if Brunelleschi sought to do for Tuscan architecture what the "three crowns" had done for Tuscan literature, he had every reason both to reject the Gothic tradition and to return to the Romanesque. Apart from everything else the forms of a building such as the Baptistery could be seen to relate to the forms of ancient Roman architecture in exactly the same way that the *volgare* related to Latin—that is, as a less regular provincial vernacular compared to a lofty and regular archetype.

Brunelleschi's revitalization of Tuscan architecture can thus be seen to pursue precisely the same goals as the contemporary movement to revive the Tuscan language. The purpose of his activities was analogous to Giovanni Gherardo's aim of learning to use the "refined and copious" Florentine vernacular as an expressive instrument of "the most perfect lucidity." Refinement and lucidity have always been recognized as qualities which distinguish Brunelleschi's buildings from those of his predecessors, and it is even possible to see the coherent geometry of his groundplans and elevations as an equivalent to Giovanni's "abstract and profound thought." Alberti a little later also enunciated a programme for the reform of the Tuscan language which might as easily be applied to Brunelleschi's buildings. In the preface to the third book of the *Della famiglia*, a work which he composed around 1433 as a demonstration that the *volgare* could deal with the same range of ideas which Cicero had handled in the *De officiis*, Alberti expresses his confidence that "surely our language will become similar to the Latin idiom if only our learned men will make every effort to refine and polish it by their studies and labours."[28] Alberti's own efforts to refine the Tuscan dialect included the composition of the first vernacular grammar, in which it is argued that the *volgare* is just as tractable in terms of grammar as are Latin and Greek.[29] His elimination of irregularities in the written language and his pursuit of refinement and polish have their precise parallels in Brunelleschi's buildings of the 1420s and 1430s. We know from the anecdote in Billi's biography which quotes Brunelleschi's criticism of a builder for incorporating a "faulty" element from the Baptistery in the Innocenti Hospital, that he saw himself as refining and purifying the architectural vocabulary.[30] What sets Brunelleschi apart not only from his predecessors but also from his successors is the scrupulous consistency, with which he deploys, in a given building, a limited number of elements—columns and pilasters, entablatures and pediments—in regular geometrical relationships which recall the norms of Antiquity. Brunelleschi's buildings have always seemed to recall those of ancient Rome not because he was anxious to copy such monuments but because he was anxious, like Alberti with the Tuscan dialect, to improve a local and national style by endowing it with the qualities of regularity and order which so clearly characterized the Roman achievement. Alberti knew the rules of Classical Latin very well; so it was easy for him to adjust the usage of *volgare* accordingly. Brunelleschi may have got his sense of Classical order partly from his early education, partly from looking at those ancient buildings which were within his reach, and even partly by

looking at Vitruvius. His desire to assimilate Tuscan to Classical rules reflects his desire to rival the ancients, not to imitate them.

If Brunelleschi was indeed trying to derive from the Baptistery the ground rules for an improved Tuscan architecture, this might help to explain why his work immediately became a model for others. After he had extracted from the upper gallery of the Baptistery the motif of large Corinthian pilasters framing smaller Ionic columns, for use in the Barbadori Chapel in S. Felicita of c.1423 (Figs. 78a and 78b), the same motif is taken up in a remarkable way by two otherwise highly independent artists. Donatello's St Louis niche on Orsanmichele of c.1425, perhaps designed with Michelozzo's collaboration, and Masaccio's *Trinita* in S. Maria Novella of c.1426 (Figs. 78c and 78d) both use the same forms in the same relationship, a correspondence which is hard to parallel at any period in art. It is as if at this moment of Tuscan self-consciousness all were anxious to join in asserting the authority of the indigenous language of the Baptistery and readily took up Brunelleschi's lead. There is, indeed, a link in all these works with those arch-guardians of the Tuscan tradition, the Parte Guelfa: Brunelleschi's patron in the chapel, Barbadori, and Lensi, the most likely patron of the *Trinita*, were both members of that organization,[31] and the St Louis niche was the party's own commission. Nor should it be forgotten that the Parte Guelfa itself experienced something of a renaissance at this time, receiving new statutes in 1420 and commissioning a new palace—designed, naturally, by Brunelleschi—soon afterwards. There can of course be no certainty about whether these works of painting, sculpture, and architecture were indeed intended as part of a vernacular revival, just as there can be no certainty that the Parte Guelfa was a focus of such a movement in the arts. Still, it is interesting to note that the prominent inscription under the *Trinita* is emphatically vernacular in both language and lettering, although Latin was much more normal on such grand monuments. What is certain is that Brunelleschi, Donatello, and Masaccio all joined in copying the Baptistery in the very years, around 1425, when Florentine fortunes were at their lowest with defeat at the hands of the Visconti. If Giovanni da Prato and others exploited a revival of the Tuscan language as a means of rallying national sentiment in the same years, might the artists not

78. Above left (a) Baptistery, Florence, eleventh century and later, gallery; above right (b) Brunelleschi: Barbadori Chapel, S. Felicita, Florence, c.1423; facing page left (c) Donatello: Orsanmichele, c.1425, St Louis niche; right (d) Masaccio: *Trinita*, c.1426, S. Maria Novella, Florence (b and d after Battisti)

readily have joined in the patriotic movement? May not Donatello and Masaccio have answered Brunelleschi's call just as Domenico da Prato did that of Matteo di Meglio?[32]

There is no truly contemporary witness to tell us what Brunelleschi intended to achieve with his architecture, but the earliest testimonies we do have hardly support the view of him as a reviver of Antiquity. Alberti, as we saw, translated his work on painting from Latin into Italian to dedicate it to Brunelleschi, and he not only describes Brunelleschi's cupola of the Duomo as rivalling Antiquity but even suggests that he possessed skills unknown to the ancient world.[33] If anything, Alberti sounds as if he takes the side of Ser Domenico da Prato against the Latinists such as Bruni, who claimed that everything had been done and said better by the ancients. Another piece of evidence which may suggest that Brunelleschi was associated with a

Tuscan rather than a Latin revival is that when, in 1441, Alberti and his friends, in their enthusiasm for the *volgare* as a true rival to Latin, inaugurated the *certame coronario*, a literary competition in the vernacular, they chose the space under the cupola as the venue.[34] Since a contemporary source also tells us that the *certame* was specifically intended to cheer the Florentines when they were depressed by the continuous war with the Milanese, the contest can be understood, in the same way as the cupola, as a gesture designed to strengthen national pride against the threat of domination not only by Latin culture but also by German power. None of this evidence is conclusive, but all is more compatible with a view that Brunelleschi was a Tuscan rather than a Latin revivalist.

This explanation of Brunelleschi's architectural activity may help us to do more than understand his style. Although his relatively educated background may have

made him especially conscious of the political atmosphere and the movement to revive the *volgare* around 1420–26, other artists may have been aware of these factors too. We have already seen how he was joined by Masaccio and Donatello/Michelozzo in the revival of the architectural language of the Baptistery around 1425, and it is not impossible that the new interest of these artists in Tuscan works of a hundred or so years earlier in other mediums—the paintings of Giotto or the sculptures of Arnolfo di Cambio and Nicola Pisano—may have been inspired by the same revivalist spirit. It is certainly hard to see the return to an earlier tradition which is so manifest in these artists' works, especially in the 1420s, as connected with an interest in

the Antique. The association of this artistic revival with a brief period of national revivalism also helps to explain why the movement soon lost its unity when the particular crisis of confidence passed. After the 1430s "Tuscan" was less clearly opposed either to "German," as the Visconti threat faded, or to "Latin," as the language proved itself more and more an equal to its ancestor. As a result, an architect such as Michelozzo was able to combine Brunelleschi's basic language with both Gothic and Antique elements, something which Brunelleschi himself had largely avoided. Indeed, probably no one followed up Brunelleschi's precise analogy between Tuscan language and Tuscan art. Yet it is still useful to compare developments in the two fields; and, just as it is true that writers such as Alberti, Cristoforo Landino (1424–92), and Pietro Bembo (1470–1547) saw the best way of developing the Tuscan language as being to endow it with more and more of the properties of Classical Latin, so the story of the development of art and architecture over the next century is also the story of a greater and greater assimilation of Classical elements. When the influential Landino wrote that it was impossible to use the *volgare* well "if you have not first a true and perfect familiarity with Latin letters,"[35] he might have been providing the programme for his younger contemporary Giuliano da Sangallo, the first person to spend years in Rome drawing ancient monuments before returning to Florence to design buildings in a new and more Roman version of Brunelleschi's style. Such a Romanization of the Tuscan architectural vocabulary, like the Latinization of the *volgare*, considerably increased its acceptability outside Tuscany. The correspondence between the development of an "Italian" language and an "Italian" art—which as a conscious objective seems to begin with Brunelleschi—continues to be a relevant relationship for most of the Renaissance. The comparison of art and language enables us to accommodate the evidence of a growing interest in absorbing elements from the Antique without encouraging us to see that as a predominant or decisive element in the transformation of style. The history of Brunelleschi studies is an eloquent demonstration of how this last tendency has poisoned the study of Renaissance art at its very source.

Brunelleschi saw his task as essentially to purify and regularize the primitive Tuscan architecture which was best represented in the Baptistery. This affects his usage of the orders as well as his choice of forms. He shunned the combination of Corinthian and Composite, which must have struck him as highly irregular, especially as the two forms could even be found balancing each other in asymmetrical pairs. Presumably seeing Composite as no more than a bastard variant, he used Corinthian for all major forms throughout all his buildings, combining it always with either unfluted columns or fluted pilasters. The only other capital type he used was the Ionic, combined exclusively with an unfluted column or half-column. Always it is associated with minor forms. In the Barbadori Chapel small Ionic half-columns are framed by large Corinthian pilasters, in an arrangement which closely copies the gallery of the Baptistery. Elsewhere Ionic is the order of miniature columns bearing a horizontal element. In the Barbadori Chapel such Ionic colonnettes support the altar, while on the lantern of the Old Sacristy of S. Lorenzo and on the interior of the Duomo cupola they support balustrades. Since the last usage can only derive from such galleries as those of S. Frediano at Lucca, Pisa Cathedral, and the tower of Prato Cathedral, Brunelleschi's studies of Romanesque evidently took him well away from Florence. Brunelleschi, then, extracted two rules from earlier Tuscan monuments: Corinthian is for major forms; Ionic is for minor ones. He also corrected their irregularities: this meant suppressing both the Composite capital and the fluted column shaft which disturbed the uniform series of the Baptistery's ground-floor colonnade.

By extracting rules from the earlier buildings and purifying their language he brought a new consistency to columnar usage. Indeed, his insistence that columns of the same size in the same row should have identical shafts and capitals represented a return to a rule which had last been adhered to twelve centuries earlier. Brunelleschi purifies and in a sense "Latinizes" Tuscan usage in much the same way that Alberti Latinizes the Tuscan dialect in his contemporary grammar. Whether his knowledge of the importance of regularity in the ancient world stemmed from his educational background, from a study of Roman monuments, or from a familiarity with Vitruvius, its sole function is always to enable him to improve the Tuscan tradition. Antique usage itself is avoided just as are truly Antique forms.

Michelozzo: from the rules of grammar to the principles of expression

If Brunelleschi wanted others to use his language and apply his rules, his wish was fulfilled. The formal correspondences between the Barbadori Chapel and Masaccio's *Trinita* (c.1426) (Fig. 78d) have been alluded to above, and in the use of the orders the correspondence is exact—major Corinthian pilasters framing minor Ionic columns for the architecture, and Ionic colonnettes for the altar. More remarkable is the centre panel of the *Pisa Altarpiece* in the National Gallery, London (1426) (Fig. 79). This goes on to extend the principle to include Composite. Thus, while the smallest columns in the rear panel of the throne are Ionic,

79. Masaccio: *Pisa Altarpiece*, 1426, centre panel,
National Gallery, London

someone like Masaccio, who was less of an architectural purist than Brunelleschi, to see Composite as even more appropriate than Corinthian for the biggest forms, with Corinthian being suitable for columns of an intermediate size and Ionic for the smallest. Once the principle of varying the capital type according to the size of column had been established, it could easily be picked up, as happens in a monument of another type close in date to the *Pisa Altarpiece*. This is the Brancacci tomb in S. Angelo a Nilo, Naples, which was being executed in the joint studio of Michelozzo and Donatello, also at Pisa, in 1427 (Fig. 80).[36] It has a large order of full Composite columns below with a series of small Corinthian pilasters above, echoing the arrangement of Masaccio's throne. Donatello and/or Michelozzo felt, like Masaccio, that Brunelleschi's rules could be expanded.

The inclusion of Composite constituted a modification of Brunelleschi's restricted practice, though within the same framework. But the *Pisa Altarpiece* and the Brancacci tomb also introduce two further important innovations. The most striking of these is the regularization of superposition by putting Composite below and Corinthian above. Brunelleschi never seems to have dealt with this problem, and, if the façade of the Pazzi Chapel represents his design, he apparently favoured using the same order, Corinthian, both above and below. Nevertheless, the rule of placing Corinthian over Composite was probably extracted from the same Tuscan monuments used by Brunelleschi, since that arrangement is found both in the Baptistery interior (on the side towards the Duomo) and on the façade of S. Miniato. Placing the more important form below has the same advantage that was pointed out when we noted the feature earlier in the Roman period—that of keeping the major element closer to the eye. The same is true of the other innovation found only in the Brancacci tomb, the use of the full column below and the pilaster above. Again the major form is closer to the eye and the minor one farther away; and again this feature is likely to have been adapted from Romanesque practice, since the Baptistery interior has pilasters above full columns and S. Miniato's façade has pilasters above half-columns. The combination of these innovations in the Brancacci tomb represents, in a sense, a criticism of Brunelleschi in his reading of the earlier Tuscan monuments. His inference that only the relative

80. Michelozzo and Donatello: Brancacci tomb, 1426–28, S. Angelo a Nilo, Naples

the slightly bigger ones in pairs at the sides are Corinthian, and the largest ones, standing singly below, are Composite. Given the clear evidence on the relative status of Corinthian and Composite in the most important model, the Baptistery, it was quite natural for

81. Michelozzo: S. Marco, Florence,
after 1436: above (a) sacristy
detail; right (b) library detail

82. Michelozzo: S. Marco, Florence, small refectory, after 1436,
detail with Domenico Ghirlandaio's *Last Supper*

height of the columnar form was important for fixing its order meant that he could easily, as in the Cappella Barbadori, find himself in the position of juxtaposing a Corinthian pilaster and an Ionic half-column, although the half-column should naturally be regarded as the more important form. In the tomb this discrepancy is avoided, with the lower form being the more important in three ways: in capital, in height, and in relief (column vs. pilaster).

Whoever designed the architecture of the Brancacci tomb was evidently more sensitive to the expressive potential of architecture than was Brunelleschi, who was concerned in a rather schoolmasterly way to eradicate irregularities. Indeed, while the strength of Brunelleschi's reform was manifest in its consistency and its re-

finement, in fundamental ways it impoverished the architectural tradition. During the preceding thousand years architects had been able, by the variation of both capital and shaft, to carefully articulate the status and significance of different parts of a building. This capability was now precluded by Brunelleschi's rules. Even the one remaining variation between Corinthian and Ionic was of no expressive use, since it related only to difference in size of column, not a difference in importance. The Brancacci tomb represents a significant step beyond this. It acknowledges both that certain column types are more important than others and also that, at least in the vertical dimension, there are more and less important parts within a structure. Whether or not it was Michelozzo who introduced these principles in the tomb, it was certainly he who went on to recapture more of the lost ground and to show how the orders could once again be used to articulate much more significant gradations of status in a building.

The largest group of buildings laid out by Michelozzo was the Convent of S. Marco, erected by Cosimo de' Medici for the Dominicans from 1437 onwards (Figs. 81 and 82). The existing buildings on the site were greatly extended and, with the exception of the church, have survived almost unchanged. The most remarkable feature of the complex is that capital types are now used emphatically to differentiate status and function rather than just column-size. The apse of the church was carried on Corinthian pilasters, and the pilasters of the altar area of the sacristy were Corinthian too (Fig. 81a).[37] The main room of the sacristy, on the other hand, has a vault carried on low, simply moulded consoles. These same consoles are also used repeatedly throughout the living quarters of the monastery, and they can be related to similar simply moulded consoles which had already been used in the earlier Gothic conventual buildings (Fig. 82). Apparently intermediate between these two forms is Ionic, which is used for the more important parts of the monastery, the cloister and the library (Fig. 81b)—areas which had a major role in the devotional life of the monks. Variation of the degree of decoration according to the importance of the environment was already found in Gothic buildings; but Michelozzo's use of absolutely distinct forms, two of which are Classical in origin, can only be related to Romanesque practice. In a building such as Fiesole Cathedral, just up the hill from S. Domenico, S. Marco's mother house, he could see how Corinthian was used in the nave, Composite for the choir, and Ionic predominantly for the crypt. Fiesole Cathedral is, indeed, the only possible source for details such as the Ionic consoles (found there in the crypt wall). There and in other Romanesque buildings, he will have seen how the "Tuscan" forms so recently revived by Brunelleschi could be used in a more expressive way. For Michelozzo, however, the need to vary architectural details according to the context was more important than a purist Tuscan revival: hence his readiness to use the plain moulded console of Gothic origin. Still, in his later works Michelozzo avoided this form, and when he built the Chapel of the Novitiate at S. Croce (1445), of similar plan to the sacristy at S. Marco, he used Ionic

83. Michelozzo: Palazzo Medici, Florence, after 1446: court

consoles to mark off the main area of human activity from the more holy Corinthian altar space. The importance of Michelozzo's variation of the orders as an advance on Brunelleschi is well demonstrated by comparing his S. Croce chapel with the adjoining Chapter House or Pazzi Chapel (1443), which is Corinthian throughout, from its external loggia through its main congregational space to its altar area. The same com-

84. Palazzo Medici, Florence: chapel detail

Here too he carefully varied the orders. This is most clear in the court. The grand arcade at the bottom is carried on rich Composite capitals, the window colonnettes of the first floor have sub-Corinthian capitals with downturned leaves, and the gallery at the top is supported by Ionic colonnettes. This vertical arrangement of orders can be seen simply as a declining series, with Composite at the bottom, Ionic at the top, and a sub-Corinthian variant in the middle. But it should almost certainly be seen as also reflecting the relative importance of the parts, the grand arcaded *cortile* being the most important public space, where guests would be initially received, the first floor being more private, with the family's living rooms, and the top floor being the least important, containing bedrooms and minor offices. The most puzzling of the three orders is the one which I have here called sub-Corinthian. It is best understood as a re-creation of the first Corinthian capital as made by Callimachus in the Vitruvian story, with the downward-growing leaves recalling those pushed down by the tile on top of the offering basket on the maiden's tomb. Michelozzo thus seems to introduce it as an incomplete Corinthian form as if he wants to avoid the familiar developed type. The reason why he wanted to avoid true Corinthian in the secular parts of the palace is suggested by the restriction of that form to the chapel alone. Since he also uses Corinthian for all his other churches and altar areas, he appears to have thought of it as having peculiarly religious associations, in contradistinction to Ionic, sub-Corinthian, and Composite, which appear to be thought of as relatively secular. Sub-Corinthian and Ionic are thus used for the less important secular parts of the palace, and Composite for its most important secular area, the court (Fig. 83). True Corinthian is found only in the chapel (Fig. 84). A desire to associate Corinthian with the Christian religion would explain why Michelozzo went to the trouble of inventing or re-inventing his sub-Corinthian form. As a reconstruction of the original Corinthian capital created in pagan Greece, it could only be seen as worldly and pre-Christian. But the idea of making a distinction between secular and religious forms in the first place, and of using Composite to articulate this, must come from Michelozzo's penetrating researches into Tuscan Romanesque. He seems to have studied S. Miniato carefully enough to recognize that Composite and Corinthian are used to distinguish

parison between variety and uniformity can also be made between the Convent of S. Marco and the Innocenti Hospital nearby. Again the Innocenti Hospital is Corinthian both on its external portico and in its main cloister court. Ionic is introduced only in the second cloister of the Innocenti, built in 1437 after Brunelleschi had left the project. Admittedly the appearance of Ionic there and in the cloister of the Florentine Badia in the same year does suggest that Michelozzo may not have been alone in introducing it for conventual buildings, but his use of the order is much the most ambitious. Corinthian churches and Ionic cloisters became standard in Florence. Whether on this large scale or on the small scale of the S. Croce chapel, Corinthian was associated with God and Ionic with man.

Both S. Marco and the Novitiate Chapel at S. Croce were paid for by Cosimo de' Medici, and it was Michelozzo who built Cosimo's palace as well (now the Palazzo Medici-Riccardi) after 1446 (Figs. 83 and 84).

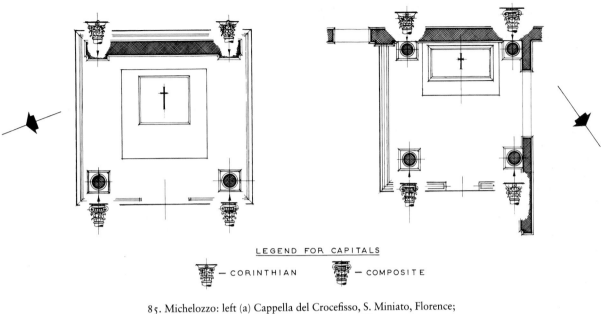

LEGEND FOR CAPITALS

— CORINTHIAN   — COMPOSITE

85. Michelozzo: left (a) Cappella del Crocefisso, S. Miniato, Florence;
right (b) Tempietto, Ss. Annunziata, Florence;
both c.1448: diagrams of orders

areas of the building, being associated with clergy and laity respectively.[38] By applying the same principle to the use of the orders in the Medici palace, he attached that building firmly to the Tuscan Medieval tradition. Many subsequent buildings apply the principle with the same implication. After the Palazzo Medici, the majority of palaces use Composite for the grand order of their courts, while in churches that form is generally shunned in favour of Corinthian.

Michelozzo's close study of S. Miniato is also apparent from his designs for the Cappella del Crocefisso commissioned for S. Miniato by Piero de' Medici and the shrine for Ss. Annunziata, both of 1448 (Fig. 85). Both contain a mixture of orders, and in both cases the mixture can be shown to be copied from S. Miniato. In the S. Miniato shrine, which surmounts the nave altar, the two rear pilasters are Corinthian and the front two columns Composite. This arrangement repeats that of the four columns of the raised choir behind and of those around the altar in the crypt below. The arrangement is also compatible with a secular/sacred opposition, the Composite pair at the front standing nearer the people and the Corinthian pair at the back nearer

the sanctuary. The layout of the capitals in the shrine just inside the door at Ss. Annunziata recalls S. Miniato in another way. It is again supported on two Corinthian and two Composite capitals, but this time they are arranged asymmetrically in an X pattern—exactly like the half-capitals supporting S. Miniato's transverse arches. Given the calculated use of the orders elsewhere, this is unlikely to be simply a formal reminiscence. One explanation would be simply that the shrine's position made it into a structure in which the sacred and the secular met or were combined: being at the beginning of the nave it was in a secular area, but being a shrine it was sacred. A more speculative interpretation would relate the arrangement to the theme of the painting which the shrine was designed to house, the Annunciation. The Annunciation is above all a moment when the human and the divine meet and mingle, when the sacred fuses with the secular. The mixture of capitals would thus reflect a similar idea to that which Panofsky traced in the mixture of Romanesque and Gothic in the almost contemporary *Friedsam Annunciation* (Fig. 86).[39] If this is correct, then a similar interpretation could be applied to Fra Angelico's contem-

86. *Friedsam Annunciation*, c.1440, Metropolitan Museum, New York

87. Fra Angelico: *Annunciation*, c.1440, S. Marco, Florence

porary *Annunciation* in the Convent of S. Marco, a short distance away (Fig. 87). There the Ionic cloister is strangely interrupted by an intrusion of Corinthian capitals in the area where the Virgin herself is placed. It is as if Fra Angelico, understanding and following the logic of Michelozzo's use of Ionic and Corinthian to mark off different areas within the whole complex, wanted to show that the relatively worldly Ionic building in which the Virgin lives must become Corinthian in the place and at the moment when the divine enters into her. Once again the closest parallels for such ideas of architectural transformation are to be found in the Medieval Tuscan tradition.

Michelozzo's remarkable study of Tuscan Romanesque gains an additional importance from the fact that all the buildings involved were put up under the direct or indirect patronage of the Medici. His extraction of the principles of Romanesque usage must owe much to their backing, as did Brunelleschi's revival of Romanesque forms earlier. The Medici are also likely to have realized the importance of Michelozzo's shift of emphasis from grammar to meaning. If there is any truth in the story that they rejected Brunelleschi's design for their palace in favour of Michelozzo's, they almost certainly did so partly because they realized that the greater expressiveness of his architecture was more useful to them than the greater discipline and lucidity of his rival. Michelozzo's language could communicate, as Brunelleschi's could not, their respect for tradition, their acknowledgement of social distinctions, and above all their acceptance of the dominance of the sacred over the secular. The greater expressive range of Michelozzo's architecture is chiefly due to his more open-minded study of Romanesque example, but it is also due to his readiness to look outside that narrow tradition and enrich it with both Gothic and Antique details. In this sense he provides the truest parallel to Dante, who had studied both Latin and French sources before attempting to rival them in *volgare*. Michelozzo may never himself have achieved such a successful integration as did the author of the *Divine Comedy*, but those who came after him, and were able to temper his expressive freedom with the rule of Brunelleschi, did.

Brunelleschi and Michelozzo were indeed Dante's heirs. The success of his Tuscan language was mirrored in that of their new Tuscan architecture, which was soon taken up throughout the peninsula—though not before facing several problems. What Brunelleschi had originated as a response to a particular crisis in Florence took on quite a different role in other cities. For one thing, whereas in Florence its integration in a local Christian tradition was sufficient to allay any qualms about the un-Christian connotations of a magnificent round-arched style, this was not true in other cities, where the viewer might be likelier to see a resemblance to the ubiquitous surviving Roman monuments than to more recent Romanesque ones. Thus, while the style enticed by its aura of national pride, sophistication and correctness—just as did the Tuscan literary language—it also evoked dangerously immoral associations. One response to this situation, already noticed in the last chapter, was the display of prominent inscriptions to neutralize the moral taint. But a more considered and less superficial response came from the pen of Leon Battista Alberti. As one of the people who had first welcomed the achievements of his fellow countrymen Brunelleschi, Donatello, Masaccio, Ghiberti, and Luca della Robbia, in his dedication of the *Della pittura* to Brunelleschi in 1436, and as an ardent enthusiast for both the literary and the artistic aspects of the Tuscan revival, Alberti had every reason to support the new movement. Also, as a Latin humanist he must have been anxious to strengthen the truly Antique elements in the new style and to remove any negative associations which might arise from their use. Finally, as someone who had become increasingly interested in architecture as an art, he had good cause to take up where the writers on *magnificentia* had left off and try to establish a new moral foundation for the art as a whole.

Alberti

◆

The debt to Vitruvius

The *Decem libri de re aedificatoria* is the first text after Vitruvius to take the art of architecture as its sole subject.[1] A complete draft was probably shown to Pope Nicholas V in 1452, but Alberti almost certainly continued to work on it until his death in 1472.[2] Earlier works by him from about 1432 make mention of buildings; and the *De pictura* of 1435, which contains material from Vitruvius, was also dedicated, in its Italian translation (1436), to Brunelleschi. By 1443 Alberti was advising Leonello d'Este on architectural matters, and he was involved more or less directly in building projects for the rest of his life. At the time he was writing his great treatise, around 1450, Alberti, the illegitimate son of a member of a prominent Florentine banking family, was widely respected both for his reinvigoration of Tuscan literature and for his knowledge of the ancient world. By his equal mastery of the *volgare* and of Classical Latin he was able to show that modern Italian culture was not inferior to that of Rome. His particular gift for taking ancient ideas and reworking them to take account of the contemporary situation is well demonstrated by his use of Vitruvius. The correspondences between the *De re aedificatoria* and the *De architectura* range from the tiniest details on the proportions of mouldings, and an overall identity in the number of books, up to the most fundamental aesthetic principles.[3] Yet all the correspondences only draw attention to the many new elements. Indeed, had Alberti just produced a paraphrase of Vitruvius, in the same language, he would have been wasting his time. His intention must instead have been to rewrite Vitruvius taking account of the changed context in which architecture found itself.

The debt to Hrabanus

The new context is apparent right from the beginning. Unlike the Roman writer, who began with a plea for patronage to a particular individual, Alberti begins his work with an expansive eulogy of architecture itself. Although he makes no direct reference to the problem of architecture and Christianity and takes all his evidence for the importance of architecture from the pre-Christian world, it is clear that he is dealing with an art whose legitimacy in his own time could not be taken for granted. There is no such encomium at the beginning of the *De pictura* or the *De statua*. The intention to use Vitruvius as a foundation and at the same time deliberately to modify him emerges first in Alberti's outline of the elements of architecture, where he replaces his predecessor's list of abstract nouns with a more concrete series: *regio, area, partitio, paries, tectum,* and *apertio* (I, 2). It is easy to understand why Alberti did not re-use Vitruvius' list: it was repetitious and confused, and it contained Greek words—a feature of Vitruvius which he found particularly distasteful. Alberti's list is both more complete and more closely related to specifically architectural problems. Thus, *regio* is the general siting of a building, *area* the outline arrangement of its plan, and *partitio* the subdivision of this. Having dealt with the foundations, he uses *paries* (wall) to embrace all the vertical elements and *tectum* (roof) the upper horizontal ones, with *apertio* (opening) finally including doors and windows. The logic of this scheme is Alberti's own, but the main feature distinguishing it from Vitruvius, the use of the concrete terms such as *paries*, shows the influence of the Medieval encyclopaedic tradition. Isidore had already divided his treatment of architecture into headings such as *de aditibus* (on entrances) and *de partibus aedificiorum* (on parts of buildings), and Hrabanus actually anticipates one of Alberti's headings with his chapter "De parietibus."[4]

The humanist's dependence on the Medieval rather than the Classical source at this crucial point in his work is important in itself. It shows that he was as much interested in correcting Antiquity in the light of the Middle Ages as he was in the reverse. It also alerts us to the possibility that some of his most characteristic opinions, opinions which have been thought of as either new or typically Antique in origin, may also derive from the Medieval tradition. When, for example, he gives prominence to polygonal plans in Book I, Chapter Eight, and recommends buildings with from six to twenty-four sides—types totally absent from Vitruvius—he must be taking his cue from Isidore, who (as quoted later by Hrabanus) had said that "the wall [*paries*] has that name because two are always equal [*pares*]. . . . For, whether a building is four- or six-sided, walls which face each other will always be equal. Otherwise the structure will be deformed."[5] The rare reference to the hexagon is particularly striking, and Alberti's insistence that "the sides should be so arranged that they are equal" repeats Isidore's thought almost precisely. Alberti's recommendation of the polygonal plan and his insistence that walls should be equal, which were to be so influential at the Renaissance,[6] apparently both rest upon Isidore's naive etymologizing, which derived *paries* from *pares*. It is equally interesting to note the source of one of Alberti's most celebrated notions, namely that "a row of columns is nothing more than a wall perforated and opened in different places" (I, 10). This idea, quite alien to Vitruvius, has been explained in terms of Alberti's understanding of Roman Imperial and Tuscan Romanesque architecture.[7] In fact his treatment of columns as the main element in his chapter on *paries* is exactly anticipated by Hrabanus, who had already dealt with *columnae* in his chapter "De parietibus." What lends particular piquancy to Alberti's following of Hrabanus in subsuming columns under walls is that Hrabanus' chapter title "De parietibus" only rests on a scribal error in the first place, for its contents are exactly the same as those which Isidore had put under the heading *de partibus aedificiorum*, and the chapter includes many features which have nothing to do with

walls. Presumably the intrusive "ie" was already present in the particular copy of the *Etymologiae* used by Hrabanus. Once the latter had perpetuated the error, it was easy for Alberti to see an intended significance in the association, and in his hands it provides the base for a coherent and influential theory.

Alberti's first list of the orders at I, 9—Doric, Ionic, Corinthian, Tuscan—probably also derives from the same source, for only Isidore and Hrabanus had listed the four types together in this way. Indeed, since Tuscan is not referred to as a separate order later on in the treatise, it is likely that Alberti mentions it carelessly here only because at the time he wrote this section he was particularly under the spell of Isidore/Hrabanus. Certainly the large number of correspondences with the Medieval tradition in the first book suggests that he wrote that section in a deliberate attempt to fuse the Medieval with the Vitruvian material, thus Christianizing the pagan author. He may have used both Isidore and Hrabanus, but everything from the former author was included in the latter, and the link from the latter's chapter "De parietibus" to Alberti's section on *paries*, which shows that he must have used the Carolingian source, means that he need not have known Isidore directly.

Further evidence for Alberti's interest in Medieval ideas is found in his application of anthropomorphism both to buildings as a whole and to columns in particular. When terms such as *membra* (members) or *frons* (forehead, front) had been applied to buildings by Classical writers, they had been not live metaphors but traditional descriptive terms. Alberti, on the other hand, brings the metaphors back to life, and this can only be inspired by the Medieval tradition of the anthropomorphic interpretation of church architecture. Talking of columns at IX, 7, he tells how they are taken "from the similitude of men," especially in their proportions. "Which is the same as what our own commentators on religious matters assert about Noah's Ark, that is that it is based on the human form." What this attitude means is seen in his rejection of Vitruvius' terms for the parts of a column: *summa columna* (top of the column), *entasis* (swelling), and *ima columna* (bottom of the column) become *caput* (head), *venter* (belly), and *planta* (sole of the foot). The Vitruvian terms are only incidentally related to the human body, while those of Alberti are consistently derived from it.

Already in 1400 the Milanese architects had made a liberal interpretation of such a metaphor, claiming that the relative proportions of the bases and capitals of the piers of their cathedral should be derived from the proportions of the human foot to the human head, "because the base of a column is also called a foot and the capital is also called a head."[8] Alberti, then, is only extending and giving authority to an earlier assimilation, which probably in turn goes back to Isidore's etymologizing: "capitals are so called because they are the heads of columns, just as the head comes above the neck [*collum*]."[9] Behind all these texts lies Vitruvius, but the important point is that Alberti follows the developed Medieval attitude rather than the tentative original idea in the ancient writer. He can only have been encouraged in his anthropomorphism by a familiarity with the notion of columns as apostles and the like, since his remarks on Noah's Ark reveal his interest in such Christian interpretations of architecture. Elsewhere he uses the expression *caput templi* (the head of the temple), which derives from the tradition represented by the St Trond Chronicle, Petrus Cantor, and Durandus, a tradition summed up by the last of these in the saying: "the disposition of the material church keeps to the pattern of the human body."[10]

Alberti's use of Medieval ideas leads to the placing of the Classical forms in quite a new context. He may well have derived his correct understanding of the ancient orders from his study both of Vitruvius and of Roman monuments, but his ideas on how they might be used in polygonal plans, how a colonnade might be assimilated to a wall, or how anthropomorphism might vitally enrich architectural vocabulary and theory derive just as decisively from the study of Medieval sources, and all involve either a modification or a rejection of Classical precedent. Even Alberti's choice of title, *De re aedificatoria*, links him more closely to a Medieval than a Classical tradition, since it rejects Vitruvius' heading *De architectura* and recalls instead the *De aedificiis* of the later encyclopaedists; although Alberti did have another reason for rejecting Vitruvius' term.

Latin language, Roman architecture, and the Italic order

"Unless I am mistaken the language of this book is both undeniably Latin and reasonably intelligible" (VI,

1). Alberti makes this claim at the beginning of the sixth book. With five books behind him and five still to go, he pauses to review the obstacles which had faced him in preparing his work. Later in the same book (VI, 13) he again refers to his intention to write in Latin and intelligibly. At one level these remarks are clearly intended to distance the author from Vitruvius, of whom Alberti remarked that he used a language which was "Greek for the Romans and Latin for the Greeks" and consequently could be understood by nobody. Certainly Alberti's rejection of such bastard Greek words as *architectura* and many other Greek technical terms such as *symmetria* or *entasis*, which he replaced by comprehensible Latin terms, fits with this policy.

Alberti's opinions on language form part of a broader nationalistic approach, as is apparent in the brief history of architecture which he also places at the beginning of the sixth book. In a summary we are told that the art of building first appeared in Asia, then flourished in Greece and "finally achieved maturity and perfection [*probatissima maturitas*]" in Italy (VI, 3). What he means, and more especially why, he uses the term *probatissima* to hint that the perfection is moral, is made clear in the following paragraphs. The architecture of Asiatic kings was characterized by great size and impressiveness; that of the Greeks, who were both poorer and wiser, was more refined and carefully planned; but the Romans, who came to wealth and power from modest and humble origins, constructed buildings that combined all qualities in moderation. They were disposed "to blend the grandeur of the greatest kings with their ancient frugality, so that neither did meanness prevent the attainment of functional sufficiency nor did attention to function alone make them parsimonious in expenditure. Within the limits of these considerations they did all they could think of to increase the delicacy and beauty of their buildings" (VI, 3). It is particularly the restraint of the Romans that Alberti would have us admire. The early Romans above all had this virtue. "The Italians, because of their natural frugality, decided for the first time that buildings should be like animals. For they noticed that those horses whose limbs seemed suited for particular functions usually proved most efficient for those same jobs. Hence they thought that beauty of form could never be separated from function and utility" (VI, 3). The same point is insisted on much later: "Among our forefathers I observe that the most careful and moderate of them took great delight in frugality and restraint, not only in their public and private dealings but also in building, and they thought that no luxury should be allowed to persist among the citizen body" (IX, I). Alberti makes it clear, however, that although luxury is not appropriate to the citizen, magnificence may certainly be appropriate to a city, especially to ancient Rome:

Because architecture had long been a guest in Italy and felt that she was eagerly studied there, she decided to do all she could to render the Roman Empire more admirable in its ornaments, just as all the other arts had done. So she gave herself to be thoroughly known and understood, thinking it a shame that the capital of the world and the glory of all nations should be equalled in her monuments by those whom she had surpassed in all other skills. (VI, 3)

The superiority of Roman architecture was a fitting complement to her superiority in other fields.

The third element in Alberti's nationalism is his treatment of the orders themselves. At first sight his virtual omission of the Tuscan column might seem to point in the opposite direction, but his argument is that the so-called Doric form was in fact probably in use in Etruria at least as early as in Greece (VI, 3 and VI, 6), an argument he supports with the rhetorical sneer "If we are to believe that the Greeks invented everything" (VI, 6). Alberti thus uses his observation of the similarity between Vitruvius' Tuscan and Doric to claim that the Italians were involved in the very beginning of the development of correct columnar forms. With even greater conviction he claimed that the Italians were also responsible for the ultimate fulfilment of this development, and in one of his boldest transformations of Vitruvius he recognized an order completely new to the literature, the Italic. This, our Composite, he saw as a deliberate creation by the Italians out of a combination of Ionic and Corinthian forms (VII, 6), and, as we have seen, he may not have been so far from the truth. For him the Italic is the last and the best of the orders, "which deservedly you may prefer" to the others (VII, 6).

What is most remarkable in Alberti's recognition of Italic as a form and his acknowledgement of its status is that he can hardly have been led to take either step from his study of Classical Roman buildings alone. In none of these could he have found decisive evidence either for the existence of Italic as a separate order or for its dominance over all other forms. The only structures which provided decisive evidence on both scores were the series of Christian churches from fourth-century Rome to thirteenth-century Tuscany where Composite could often be found as a separate form in the most favoured positions. Only the name, Italic, must have been derived from his studies of Roman buildings. Inferring from the silence of Vitruvius that the form was unknown to the Greeks, and finding it employed prominently on triumphal arches, he evidently came to realize that it was intended as a very symbol of Roman triumph, especially of Roman triumph over the Greeks whose two best capitals it combined.

He would, however, never have had the disposition to make this identification if nationalism had not already been an overriding influence on his thought. The fact that after him hardly anyone showed any interest in his Italic order suggests that its introduction by him was very definitely the product of pressures to which he was particularly exposed. It is likely that those pressures were the same as those which led Brunelleschi to create an architectural equivalent of the Tuscan dialect and Alberti himself to compose a grammar and inaugurate a rhetorical competition which would help to establish Tuscan as a genuinely Italian language. Alberti's explicit interest in a truly Italian revival is apparent as early as the 1430s when, in the *Della famiglia*, he complained how the national language had been corrupted because "Italy was occupied and ruled by various nations, Gauls, Goths, Vandals, Lombards and other such barbarians . . . and the people thus learnt this foreign language and that."[11] By the early 1450s, when he was writing the *De re aedificatoria*, consciousness of national unity was such that the principal states of the peninsula were even joined together into a formal Lega Italica. For Alberti the nomenclature "Italic" had a double advantage, as it enabled him to oppose not only ancient Italy to Greece but modern Italy to Germany and France.

Architecture moralized

So far we have seen two important ways in which Alberti sought to make an architecture based on Classical forms acceptable to his contemporaries: first, he based his theory on Christian as much as on pagan writers; second, he appealed to Italian nationalism. But his biggest problem was the moral vulnerability of architecture in general and of Classical architecture in particular, and to deal with this he had to embark on an even more substantial transformation of Vitruvius. The importance he accorded to morality is already apparent in his insistence on the moral superiority of Roman architecture over earlier traditions. Assertion, however, was not enough. He also needed to integrate morality into the very structure of his work and to show how it could govern the design of each individual building.

Faced with this need he turned, not surprisingly, to the general principle of appropriateness, *decorum*, which had already provided a guide to previous writers. As he says: "that which we should praise first in an architect is the ability to judge what is appropriate [*quid deceat*]" (IX, 10). Not surprisingly, too, he is most at pains to apply the principle to the morally more vulnerable secular buildings: "A *basilica* should not attempt to equal a *templum*. It should neither be raised on so high a podium, nor should its decoration have the seriousness [*gravitas*] required in a sacred structure" (VII, 14). The architecture of private buildings in general should be very restrained, but it may employ greater freedom in details. Yet, although they do not have to follow exactly the same rules as public buildings do, they should never become ugly or depraved. Public works must attend to *gravitas* and the letter of the law, but private ones may tend to *iocunditas* (gaiety). As an example, Alberti refers to the *festivissimus* (most festive) use of figures to support the door lintels of *triclinia* (dining rooms) and the use in garden porticoes of columns copied from tree-trunks (IX, 1). The opposition between *gravitas* and *festivitas* in the last passage is one that recurs. Townhouses should give an impression of *gravitas*, but villas may have the attractive quality of *festivitas* (IX, 2). Even within the townhouse, the portico and vestibule should tend to *gravitas*, but the inner rooms to *festivitas*. Whatever happens, in all environments, the qualities should never be mixed: *gravitas* and *maiestas* should be kept quite apart from *iocunditas* and *festivitas* (IX, 4). A similar opposition is seen in his assertion that temples to male gods should be decorated with *gravitas* and those to female with *venustas* (prettiness) (VIII, 3), which must be based on Vitruvius' recommendation of

Doric and Corinthian for tough and tender deities respectively.[12] Earlier Alberti himself had ascribed the quality of *festivitas* to Corinthian (VII, 6). Thus the masculine Doric and the feminine Corinthian embody the same contrast.

Alberti has a much clearer idea of how the principle of *decorum* can be applied than earlier writers such as Fiamma and Pizzolpasso, and much of this clarity stems from a consistent application of a fundamental opposition between two types of aesthetic qualities. Since this opposition is so important, it is essential to establish its source, and this turns out to be the most influential handbook on morality written in Classical Latin, Cicero's *De officiis* (On Duties). For there the assimilation of the opposition between aesthetic qualities to that between the sexes is already firmly articulated. As Cicero says: "there are two types of beauty. One is characterized by *venustas* and the other by *dignitas*. *Venustas* we should consider a feminine trait and *dignitas* masculine."[13] Like Alberti, Cicero is insistent that the two should not be mixed. That Alberti's two terms *gravitas* and *festivitas* are equivalent to Cicero's pair *dignitas* and *venustas*, and that Alberti knew this passage, is suggested by the fact that he uses one term from each pair for his own characterization of the masculine and the feminine: *gravitas* and *venustas*.

Elsewhere there is more evidence that Alberti was influenced by the *De officiis* in his treatment of architecture. Referring to the heights of podia he says: "The podium of a private house should not be more lofty [*superbior*] than is necessary to link it to the adjoining buildings" (IX, 2). This means more than just that the podium should match those of neighbours for visual reasons. The use of the word *superbus* (lofty or proud) and not *altus* (high) shows that the greater height would be tantamount to an arrogant claim to greater status. It is thus exactly an architectural expression of Cicero's declaration in the *De officiis* that "the private citizen ought rightly to live on terms of equality with his fellow citizens, being neither submissive nor superior [*neque summissum et abjectum neque se efferentem*]."[14] In a later passage, Alberti even seems to echo the construction of this sentence. He does not approve of the addition of fortifications to private houses, because these are appropriate to the castles of tyrants rather than to the houses of citizens living at peace in a well-ordered state: "they imply either fear or hostility [*aut conceptum metum aut paratum iniuriam significent*]" (IX, 4).

In one passage in the *De officiis*, Cicero himself deals with architecture. He discusses what is the proper sort of house. "The object [*finis*] of a house is to be useful, and the design should be made with that goal in mind, but at the same time attention should be given to comfort and dignity."[15] This is evidently the basis for Alberti's characterization of the whole of Roman architecture, which was quoted earlier: the Romans concentrated on the problem of utility but did what they could to create elegance and beauty. As in the previous instance, we note that Alberti uses different words to express a similar thought with a similar construction. This occurs also when Alberti takes Cicero's statement that "a man's dignity is to be enhanced by his house"[16] and expands it into: "Because we decorate our house as much to adorn our fatherland and family as for the sake of elegance, who will deny that such activity is the duty of a good man [*boni viri officium*]?" (IX, 1). Alberti here comes as near as he ever does to admitting his debt to this particular treatise of Cicero by his use of the word *officium*.

This last word also appears in another passage, where its use is even more significant. When Alberti says that the ancients realized that "different buildings should have different forms because they saw that they differed from each other in purpose and function [*fine et officio*]" (IX, 5), he is applying to buildings a word—*officium*—that had usually been reserved for men, and he goes on to use this application as the basis for formulating his theory that different buildings should have different decorative forms—in this case, Doric, Ionic, and Corinthian. He thus equates his architectural theory with the ethical theory of Cicero, who had argued that a man should vary his actions according to his circumstances or his role in life. Alberti's assimilation of architectural forms to human actions follows directly from his determination to show that buildings, like men, can be subject to the rules of morality.

Structure and ornament

Alberti's use of the ancient moral treatise affected the whole organization of his presentation of architecture. Thus, at the beginning of the sixth book he declares that he has dealt with the two parts of architecture that concern usefulness and strength (*ad usum apta* and *ad perpetuitatem firmissima*) and that it remains to treat of how grace and attractiveness (*gratia* and *amenitas*) are to be obtained. These two qualities, he proceeds to state, derive undeniably from beauty and ornament (*pulchritudo* and *ornamentum*), and these will be the subject of the remaining half of the work (VI, 1–2). With the exception of the last book, which deals with restoration and a few other odds and ends, the whole is thus divided into two equal parts, one concerned with functional aspects and the other with decorative. In fact, the two parts run parallel; so that, for example, in the first book columns are treated in terms of their function and their essential parts, while in the sixth book it is shown that they can be given different sorts of ornament. This division has no parallel in Vitruvius, who moves step by step from the elements of architecture to materials, to temples, to public buildings, and so on. No previous discussion of architecture had hinted at Alberti's separation between structure and decoration.

In the *De officiis*, however, Cicero introduces his second book with a preface reminding his son that in the first book he has shown how *officia* are derived from *honestas* (moral rectitude) and that he will now discuss the relation between *officia* and the material aspects of life, concentrating on the problem of what is useful and what not.[17] Indeed, of the three books of the *De officiis* the first deals with *honestas*, the second with *utilitas*, and the third with the problem of reconciling those two ideas. It is easy to see the connection in subject between the first five books of Alberti and the second book of Cicero. Both concentrate on the term *utilitas* as the heading under which to discuss functionalism, usefulness, expediency, and need. The connection between Cicero's *honestas* and Alberti's *pulchritudo* and *ornamentum* is at first less obvious. Yet Cicero himself explains the link in the *De officiis*:

And it is no mean manifestation of Nature and Reason that man is the only animal that has a feeling for order, for propriety [*quod deceat*], for moderation in word and deed. And so no other animal has a sense of beauty, loveliness, harmony in the visible world; and Nature and Reason, extending the analogy from the world of sensation to the world of the soul, find that beauty [*pulchritudo*], consistency, and order are far more to be maintained in thought and deed, and the same Nature and Reason are careful to do nothing in an improper or unmanly fashion, and in every thought and deed to do or think nothing capriciously.[18]

Honestas is the quality that the human soul approves in actions; it is the exact counterpart of the *pulchritudo* that the eye recognizes in outward appearances. In his treatment of a visual art, then, it was natural for Alberti to devote a section to the discussion of *pulchritudo* (aesthetic rectitude), matching Cicero's account of *honestas* (moral rectitude) in his study of morality.

Alberti makes one significant change in adapting the structure of the moral treatise to his own on architecture. He reverses the order of the two main sections. Cicero had treated *honestas* before *utilitas*, because it was obviously a criterion of higher importance in moral decisions. Architecture, however, as Alberti realized, was not an exactly analogous field. Indeed, it was Cicero who defined the difference for him when he noted that the prime object of a house was usefulness and that visual impressiveness was only a secondary consideration in its design. Since Alberti had taken over this idea and applied it not only to Roman architecture but to the whole subject of his book, it followed that he had to deal with the problem of usefulness first and beauty second. This scheme also conformed well with the fact that a building was usually finished structurally before its decoration was brought to completion.

The effect that Alberti's use of the *De officiis* had on the subsequent history of architecture and of architectural theory cannot be overemphasized. His division of his work and the whole treatment of his subject in terms of *utilitas* and *pulchritudo/ornamentum* gave the opposition between the two aspects of architecture enormous authority. Applying the Ciceronian dualism to architecture, Alberti formulated for the first time the opposition between structure and ornament. He himself did not see the opposition in its extreme form, since for him *pulchritudo* included proportions, which should be inherent in the structure. But, as the importance of proportion declined subsequently, the pertinent contrast became more and more that between the functional structure of a building and its decoration. The diffusion of this rational distinction from such an authoritative source as Alberti must have played an important part in creating a situation that was to obtain for four centuries, in which architecture could preserve the same structure while changing with increasing fre-

quency its clothing of decoration. Certainly it has only been a devotion to the same distinction that has allowed architects in the last hundred years to deny the need for any ornament at all and to concentrate on utilitarian considerations alone. Even if he would not have approved of quite such an extreme point of view, Alberti would certainly have recognized as his own many of the moral arguments used to support it. Before Alberti there was no hint of the separation between structure and ornament. For Vitruvius and other writers, a building had been an integrated whole from the finest carving on its surface to the unformed rubble of its core.

The orders as species

We have seen how Alberti was conscious of the Christian tradition of architectural writing as well as of the builders and writers of Antiquity. We have seen too how by his language and by his introduction of a new order he endeavoured to make his treatise essentially Italian/Roman, and how his theory of architectural morality reflected the same interest. What is the effect of this enriching of the Vitruvian tradition on his theory of columns? Like other architectural elements they are discussed twice, once in the first half of the treatise and once in the second: in the case of columns, the discussions are in Book I and Book VI. In the first passage Alberti makes an important statement: "columns have some features which make them different from each other; but here we will deal with what they have in common, because those pertain to the whole *genus*; the differences which mark the individual *species* we will deal with elsewhere in the appropriate place" (I, 10). The insistence that columns form a genus of supports, while the different orders are to be considered as species, is new and important. The theoretical nature of the statement recalls Cicero's observation in *De oratore*: "genus is that which unites two or more elements in a communion of similarity, while species is that in which they differ."[19] Cicero is here describing the need for the classification of cases in a chapter which discusses the general problem of organizing an art such as music, geometry, astrology, grammar, or (of course) rhetoric. To solve the problem of classification he says: "a system [*ars*] is therefore employed from outside, from some other sphere which is accepted by philosophers, a system which will tie together a loose and disorganized subject and impose on it a rational principle." The same point is made in the *Orator*:

Nor, indeed, are we able without the discipline of philosophers to perceive the genus and species of each thing, and by defining it to explain it and divide it into parts, to judge what parts are true and what parts false, to see what features are consistent and which inconsistent, and to distinguish ambiguities.[20]

Rhetoric had the most highly developed literature of all the *artes* in Antiquity. It was also of intense interest to humanists, particularly in Republican Florence. Alberti will have turned to Cicero's writings on the subject as naturally as to the *De officiis*. The general rules he found there provided excellent guidance for someone wanting to reorganize Vitruvius; besides, the distinction between genus and species could be seen as closely analogous to that between *utilitas* and *pulchritudo/ornamentum*. The structural function and common origin of columns was what united them into a genus, while it was the differences in their external ornaments that divided them into species.

The implications of this approach to columns are important. Vitruvius had employed the term *genus*, copying rhetorical usage rather than philosophical theory. For him an architectural genus was a type of columnar architecture associated with a particular race. He accepted the fundamental differences between their columnar elements, such as the absence of a base for the Doric order, as given facts. Alberti's decision, on the other hand, to see all columns as one genus meant that they had all to have the same set of members (I, 10). These are given as *arula* (pedestal), *basis* (base), column, and capital. In his desire to systematize the theory of the column, he saw not only the base as an essential element but even the pedestal—the latter being an element which had never figured previously in architectural literature, but which he had presumably observed in regular use on Roman monuments. The pedestal never became more than an optional extra, but the base, which admittedly had often been added to Doric by the Romans, now became an integral element of that order as it had always been of the others. Although Alberti when dealing with the orders does not actually call them species, failing in this as in other aspects to follow up his own theories, it is revealing that he could

talk of them in this way here. Instead of having the absolute and almost biological existence of a genus, the forms classified by the terms "Doric" etc. now took on a note of transience and inconstancy. Species or "visual appearance" referred to external attributes, not essential properties. This is a small but important step in the liberation of the architect from the tyranny of Greek architectural tradition.

Alberti's sense of freedom from this tradition as it was embodied in Vitruvius is already apparent in his invention of Italic and his identification of Tuscan with Doric. It is also manifest in his explanations of the origins of the Greek orders. At VII, 6 he tells how the capitals were developed. First came the Dorians, who introduced a form like a round dish under a square cover. Then came the Ionians, who did not like the bareness of the round dish and so put two pieces of bark hanging down either side. Finally the Corinthians took up Callimachus' idea of replacing the dish with a tall vase and decorating it with acanthus leaves. This account, though based on the Vitruvian myths, completely misses their point as providing separate *rationes* for each of three forms. It implies instead a continuous process of improvement of the basic form inspired by the pursuit of novelty (*rebus novis inveniendis*). Only his explanation of Italic, which comes immediately afterwards, has the spirit of the Vitruvian myths because, like them, it is required to explain an innovation. The Italians, he says, "added the refinement [*deliciae*] of Ionic to the gaiety [*festivitas*] of Corinthian and replaced the handles [*ansae*] with volutes." He seems to suggest that the Italians deliberately put together the two richest Greek capitals in order to surpass the Greeks as a nation. He certainly asserts that the new creation is preferable to the other forms. This is almost the only reference to Italic. Elsewhere when the orders are discussed only the Greek ones are mentioned, which shows how piecemeal was the composition of the *De re aedificatoria*.

Social values versus moral values

Alberti's clearest characterization of the three orders is at IX, 5. There he tells how our ancestors, seeing that nature was the best artist and noting that buildings differed in their functions (*fine et officiis plurimum differre*), decided to derive three styles (*figuras aedis or-*

nandae) from the three basic human types, the squat, the slender, and the intermediate. These styles they named after the people who had either favoured or invented them. "One was fuller [*plenius*], more suited to work and more permanent [*ad laboremque perennitatemque aptius*]; this they called Doric. Another was slender and extremely elegant [*lepidissimum*]; this they called Corinthian. The intermediate one, which shared both characters, they called Ionic." It has already been noticed that the observation that buildings differ in *finis* and *officium* is related to Alberti's interest in architectural morality. Comparing this passage to that in Vitruvius, it is now possible to see in more detail how a social model has replaced a rhetorical one. This is most apparent in the replacement of the term *severus* as the character of Doric, not just by another term from the field of rhetoric, *plenus*, but also by the expression *ad laborem aptus*, which clearly relates the order to the divisions of society. Doric is identified as the working class of architecture. Corinthian, by contrast, is credited with elegance—an upper-class attribute. Alberti's consistent interest in making analogies between architecture and humanity leads him to a new characterization of the orders, one that opens new possibilities for a theory which could match the different orders to buildings of different types. His characterizations also provided a theoretical basis for established practice, which throughout the Roman period and the Middle Ages had put the richer orders in the positions of higher status and the simpler ones in those of less importance.

Although he does not say so explicitly, his social theory of the orders must be based on the notion that working people are typically short and strong and simply dressed, while the members of the highest class are tall and slender and richly decorated. The same scale underlies his account of doorways. Pursuing his interest in consistency, he introduces for the first time three types of doors to go with the orders. He does this by replacing Vitruvius' Attic type with one called Corinthian, by giving them each elements of the appropriate columniations, and by endowing each with progressively larger dimensions (VII, 12). The Doric door not only is the smallest but is surmounted only by a simplified Doric entablature without metopes and triglyphs. The Ionic has a frieze more elaborate than usual in Ionic and two large volute consoles. The latter had already been mentioned by Vitruvius, but Alberti now deliberately describes them in language recalling his description of the Ionic capital. For Corinthian Alberti introduces a completely new door type, but one which he could have seen in Rome: this consists of a full pair of Corinthian columns complete with entablature, the whole surmounted by a pediment. The distinction in status among the three forms emerges particularly sharply because of the use of column and pediment for Corinthian alone. Only one chapter earlier Alberti had affirmed the distinctively ennobling character of the pediment: "They say that a pediment brings such dignity to a building that even Jupiter in his ethereal home needs a pediment to keep up appearances, although it never rains there" (VII, 11, based on Cicero *De oratore* 3, 46), while at VI, 13 he had said:

In the whole of architecture the primary ornament is the column, for grouped together they adorn porticoes, walls, and any kind of opening, and placed singly they have a decorative function too; they lend distinction to crossroads, theatres, and piazzas, they serve as trophies and as monuments, they give visual pleasure, and they bring dignity with them. It is difficult to record how much the ancients spent on this most elegant of forms.

Alberti was evidently anxious to make the status of the Corinthian door doubly clear: not only did it have more elements from its order than either Doric or Ionic, but its pediment and half-columns were the most explicit attribute of authority.

In spite of the care shown in building up this scale of the orders, Alberti almost never gives a precise recommendation for when they should be used. Only once does he give a clear rule. This is for the use of the orders on the openings in private houses: "The windows you will decorate with Corinthian work, the main door with Ionic, and the doors of triclinia and minor rooms [*cellarum*] with Doric" (IX, 3). This passage is curious because, although it is fairly obvious that the doors of inner rooms are of lower status than the main door, it is not so easy to understand the association of Corinthian with windows. The explanation may lie in the extremely high valuation put by Alberti on light. The windows were perhaps thought of as providing access for God in the person of the Divine Radiance of Medieval and Neo-Platonic thought, just as the doors provided access for man. Otherwise Alberti may be thinking of the importance of windows in the exclusive upper floors of palaces. In either case his recommendations reflect, even if tentatively, a clear hierarchy of the orders with Corinthian at the top.

This tentativeness when he comes to particulars is strange considering Alberti's interest in formulating general theories of architectural decorum. However, a closer examination of the treatise suggests that his caution stems from a fundamental difficulty. We have already seen how Alberti, when discussing temples, noted that those to female deities should have *venustas* and those to male ones *gravitas*:

What they [the ancients] say is relevant: temples to Venus, Diana, the Muses, the Nymphs, and the more delicate divinities should imitate a virginal slenderness and the blooming softness of youth; temples to Hercules, Mars, and the greatest gods should be so designed that they show more importance in their dignity [*auctoritatem ex gravitate*] than grace in their prettiness [*gratiam ex venustate*]. (VII, 3)

The text he is paraphrasing, albeit in a simplified form, is obviously Vitruvius' rule for the use of orders in temples, and the opposition referred to between *venustas* and *gravitas* is based on that between Corinthian and Doric. But *gravitas* (Cicero's word for serious dignity) is much the higher quality, and Alberti suggests as much here by attributing it specifically to temples "to the greatest gods." Doric, then, in terms of Ciceronian morality would be the highest of the orders and Corinthian the lowest, in complete opposition to established opinion. Alberti must have recognized this, which explains why he omits any mention of the orders themselves at this point. Elsewhere, though, the contradiction surfaces again. In his account of the origin of Italic Alberti had ascribed the property of *festivitas* to Corinthian. He also uses *festivitas* consistently in opposition to *gravitas* as the character appropriate to minor contexts: gardens as opposed to houses, villas as opposed to town residences, private inner rooms as opposed to public outer rooms. Thus, when he specifies Corinthian columns for garden porticoes (IX, 4) he is, in these terms, quite correctly expressing the character of the environment. This is the only point at which he actually gets as far as contradicting the other scale. Otherwise he avoids the problem by merely insisting that this or that major building should have *gravitas* and this or that minor building *festivitas*, carefully omitting any mention of what these words imply in terms of the choice of order. As his application of the other scale is extremely hesitant, there is never a direct confrontation between the two opposed systems. We can only sense the tension within Alberti himself as he wrestled vainly with the problem of reconciling the conventional assumptions on the expression of status in architecture—assumptions with which he, like everyone else, worked every day in his approach to clothing and manners—with his enthusiasm for the creation of a new architectural theory based on the Stoic values of Cicero's *De officiis*. Many of his contemporaries faced similar problems.

Alberti is much less ambivalent when giving rules for when to use round columns and when square columns or piers, and for when to use horizontal entablatures and when arches. "It is very important whether you use columns or piers, arched or trabeated openings. Arches and piers should be used in theatres, and arches may also be used in basilicas; but in temples, which are the most important buildings, only trabeated porticoes are found" (VII, 6). What he describes corresponds roughly with Roman usage. For Alberti, though, there is an underlying principle. Columns would be appropriate in temples as the "primary ornament of architecture," while they should not be surmounted by arches for the reason given later: "Square columns should be used with arches. For with round columns the work would be false [*mendosum*]" (VII, 15). This is because the angles of the square form found where the arches came down on the round column would not be supported by anything underneath, and a general prohibition against putting a solid over a void had been formulated earlier at VII, 7. According to Alberti's strange logic this meant that only a horizontal entablature could be used with the true column. There are thus two extremes, the temple with trabeated columns and the theatre with piers and arches. "But the basilica, because by its nature it has something of the quality of the temple, will claim for itself many of the ornaments due to temples. It will, however, rival the temple in such a way that it will seem to want to imitate rather than to equal it" (VII, 14). In this spirit Alberti declares that the basilica should have arches but may have columns as well, provided an impost block is inserted between the top of the column and the bottom of the arch (VII, 15). Its intermediate position as a building type can thus be read from its mixture of forms. In the case of temples and theatres the basis of the theory is ancient practice. Alberti, however, also applies the same principle to private houses: "Besides, it is appropriate that the houses of leading citizens should have trabeated porticoes, while those of the middle rank should be arched" (IX, 4). As always, Alberti is attempting to build up a complete theory of architectural decorum. The same concern for decorum also governs his rules for the height of podia. The temple should be raised above the whole city, and the basilica should be raised in the same way, but the height of its podium should be an eighth less (VII, 5); while the platforms on which private houses stand should not rise above those of their neighbours (IX, 2). A town laid out on these principles would be the very image of a stable republic in which the citizens were all equal, the constitution was respected, and God was given his rightful place above everything. Architecture would thus become the expression of sound moral and social values. Such a situation was sadly denied by the appearance of most Italian towns, which mirrored the near anarchy of reality. As Pontanus (a later enthusiast for decorum) said of the towers which were such a typical feature of fourteenth- and fifteenth-century towns, "they seem to show that it was thought praiseworthy for the most prominent citizens to raise square towers by which they could compete with each other in loftiness."[21]

Alberti's treatise, then, is founded on Vitruvius but aspires to be more truly Italian/Roman in its language and its values. It is also significantly affected by the tradition of Medieval writings on architecture and takes account of the conventions of Early Christian and later architectural practice. The diversity of these sources often makes it difficult for Alberti to achieve the clarity and coherence which he sought, and results in inconsistencies and even contradictions. Yet one feature unites the whole work: the moral tone which emerges not only in the theories themselves but in the way they are communicated. Words which would be more appropriate to the moralist—words such as *improbare*, *modestia*, *sobrietas*, *vitium*, *mendosus*, and especially the recurrent use of *opportet*, *debet* (it is morally necessary), and *decet* (it is fitting)—give the *De re aedificatoria* a character new to architectural writing. In fact the critical tone had been consistently rising from Vitruvius' attack on false combinations of details in the orders, through the Elder Pliny's invectives against extravagant building, up to the spirited indictments of Saint Bernard and Petrus Cantor. But Alberti's integration of such an approach into a large and often technical treatise represents a new stage. Moreover, his book's role as the first full discussion of the art after the Medieval encyclopaedias, and indeed the fullest ever up to its own time, combined with the fact that it was printed by 1485 and translated into Italian in the following century, guaranteed that it should set the tone for subsequent treatments of the subject. More recent theoreticians, whether they are promoters of Neo-Classicism or of the International Movement, often seem to echo the great humanist.

XI

Filarete

◆

The first modern treatise

ALBERTI'S is the first Renaissance treatise on architecture; yet it is also in a sense the last Classical treatise. In spite of a few incidental references to Christianity and the contemporary world, it is essentially dateless; it gives the impression of having been written for a republican aristocracy who worship *superi* (the gods), and whose main buildings are the *basilica*, the *curia*, the *theatrum*, and the *templum*. Composed in ten books, in Classical Latin, it is presented as a revised Vitruvius. The treatise of Antonio Averlino, otherwise known as Filarete, on the other hand, emerges directly out of the reality of fifteenth-century Italy.[1] It proclaims explicitly that it was written in a Christian context, for a duke, about the year 1460. Its author was highly conscious that he wrote in a time of linguistic, religious, and political change. Composed in twenty-four books, in dialogue form, in Italian, and heavily illustrated, it has little to do with Vitruvius. It also has little to do with the Medieval encyclopaedias. In short it represents a new stage in the development of writings on architecture.

The novelty of Filarete, particularly in contrast to Alberti, can be seen to depend largely on the difference in their backgrounds. Alberti was highly educated, and being educated meant then as now, being well informed about the past. It meant also being conscious that the past provides us with models for all aspects of our thought and activity. Filarete was not well educated. As a craftsman, although he had picked up a smattering of Latin, he knew little of other cultures besides his own. Unlike Alberti, he was familiar with no patrons but those whom he met in Florence, where he was trained, in Rome, where he worked in the 1440s, in Venice, where he stayed briefly, and finally in Milan,

where he worked for Francesco Sforza from 1451 until about 1465. The only language in which he could formulate his thoughts was the Tuscan dialect of his daily life—not even the purified Tuscan of Dante and his successors, but the much more truly "vulgar" spoken language of his own day. He thus contrasts with Alberti, the grammar both of whose language and of whose thought is much more limpid. Yet what Filarete loses in clarity he makes up for in effectiveness. Alberti, although he constructed elaborate themes using high-sounding terms such as *gravitas*, *auctoritas*, and *festivitas*, was largely unable to show how they could be given architectural expression. Filarete's spelling and grammar are often execrable, but the language of his theories can readily be translated back into the architectural practice from which it was derived. Equally, while Alberti shows an admirable intellectual rigour in applying an archaic and traditional vocabulary to artistic theory, Filarete frequently surprises us by the creative imagination he reveals in coaxing the Italian language into dealing with a whole new area of activity and a new set of ideas. It is Filarete who writes the first modern theory of architecture.

Filarete's treatise, or *libro architettonico* as he calls it, may not be directly in the tradition of Latin architectural writings. Nonetheless, as a long and complicated work of literature, it is certainly more than the stream of consciousness of a Florentine sculptor-architect, and it must have a source, or sources, all its own. These emerge from a study of the contents and structure of the work. Filarete's awareness of earlier literature is revealed right at the outset when he refers to both Vitruvius and Alberti, and indeed he is indebted to them for many details. They have, however, little influence on the general composition. Already in the preface—which, like that of Vitruvius, is dedicated to a prince

(Francesco Sforza in the original version, and Piero de' Medici in the manuscript now in Florence)—he asserts that all the proportions (*proportioni*), measures (*misure*), qualities (*qualità*), and origins (*origini*) of buildings derive from the figure and form of man (1ᵛ). This has echoes of his predecessors but already strikes a new and personal note, both in the ideas and in the manner of their presentation. Book I begins with an account of how Filarete found himself at a dinner where a certain gentleman had denied that architecture was such a noble art as it had been made out to be. A knowledge of geometrical principles was not, as Vitruvius had claimed, essential to its practice. This point of view was attacked by another more serious person, who knew that such knowledge was essential but wished he could find someone to explain why. Filarete then rose to the challenge as the only member of his profession present. After first praising ancient architects and criticizing his contemporaries, he proceeds to deal with the origins of the art. These go back, in true Christian fashion, to the Creation: "As is known to everyone, man was created by God; his body, his soul, his intellect, his innate quality of mind [*ingegnio*], and everything were brought forth in their perfection by Him, and thus the body was organized and measured and all its members endowed with proportion according to their qualities [*qualità*] and measurements" (2ᵛ). Habitation was, after food, the first necessity for man. "Thus, man having been made in terms of measure, . . . he wished to take from himself these measures and members and proportions and qualities and adapt them for building. . . ." (2ᵛ). Filarete then goes on to explain how these "measures and members and proportions and qualities" became the basis of architecture.

The lord, a thinly disguised Francesco Sforza, is so struck by Filarete and his anthropomorphic theory that he decides to employ him to construct a city, Sforzinda. This is well advanced when at the end of Book XII a new site suitable for another city is found on the coast. At the beginning of Book XIII it is decided that building should begin there too. Preliminary site exploration is carried out, and this brings to light some ruins and a Golden Book, which is the record of a city that existed on the site many years before, and which contains elaborate descriptions of its monuments. The book is written in Greek and has to be deciphered by the court scholar. The decision is taken to rebuild this city, Plou-

siapolis, in all its former magnificence, and this the lord is enabled to do by the discovery together with the book of some dust which turns out to be exceedingly valuable. Work on the two cities then proceeds concurrently, but particular attention is paid to expounding the economic, social, and educational organization of Sforzinda. The last two books contain an account of the art of *disegno*, drawing, based largely on Alberti's *De pictura*. The treatise proper terminates with the twenty-fourth book. The twenty-fifth, an account of Medici building activity, was added only when Filarete decided to offer a copy of the treatise to Piero de' Medici. The dialogue, involving usually the architect and either the lord or his son, continues throughout, although it is broken by delightful narrative sections describing such experiences as journeys, hunts, and dinners.

Plato and the Golden Book

In the last feature the work has much of the character of a Medieval romance or novel, and that is hardly surprising since fiction was perhaps the literary genre which the vulgar tongue had made most particularly its own. The same tradition seems to lie behind some of Filarete's extravagant architectural descriptions, since fantastic palaces and temples often feature in these writings. Yet a much more fundamental influence seems to have been exercised by a more surprising group of sources. The use of the dialogue form establishes a possible connection with Plato, and a number of the new elements of the treatise can be paralleled in three dialogues in particular. The description of two cities recalls the *Critias*. The notion of God as the first architect is reminiscent of the theme of the *Timaeus*. The account of an imaginary city in terms of its laws, its educational structure, and its economy is anticipated in the *Laws*.[2]

At first sight these may seem impossibly sophisticated sources for a work which has often been ridiculed for its lack of intellectual fibre. After all, Filarete mentions Plato only once, and then in a very insignificant context. Moreover, there is no evidence that he knew Greek. In 1460, none of the dialogues concerned were available in Latin translation except part of the *Timaeus*. Even Greek manuscript copies of the dialogues were extremely rare. Fortunately Filarete does actually hint at his dependence on an unidentified Greek text in his references to the Golden Book which is dug up at the coastal site. Moreover, Filarete also tells how he learned of its contents. It was translated for him by the lord's poet, Iscofrance Notilento, whose name is a near anagram of Francesco da Tolentino, better known as Filelfo, the most famous Greek scholar at the Sforza court. From Filelfo's correspondence we know that he was proud to be a friend of Filarete and that in 1456, just before Filarete started to write his treatise, he was anxious to consult a manuscript of Plato in the library at nearby Pavia, which contained all three dialogues as well as several others. It is thus not hard to identify Filelfo as the intermediary who gave the architect access to the Platonic material.

Filarete's use of this material is extremely varied. From the *Critias*, with its account of two contrasting cities, Athens and Atlantis, he took the idea of describing two communities, the one, Sforzinda, relatively sober and the other, Plousiapolis ("rich-city"), much more opulent as its name implies. From the *Timaeus*, with its account of how a divine "architect" designed the universe after his own image, Filarete took the idea that human architects should imitate God by designing columns based on the perfect proportions of the first man, Adam. Also from the *Timaeus*, where the human head is said to be copied from the perfect shape of the divine sphere, he probably took his insistence, new to architectural theory, that all capitals should copy the head in their proportions. Finally, from the *Laws*, an account of an imaginary society in twelve books, Filarete probably took his idea of writing about two communities in twenty-four books, with the first twelve devoted to Sforzinda and most of the remainder to Plousiapolis. From the *Laws* too he took one of his most innovative ideas, that of describing not just buildings but the educational, penal, and other institutions which they housed. The influence of the Platonic dialogues is pervasive.

How the humble Filarete came to exploit such a lofty source is unclear. It is possible that he had already decided to compose a treatise on building, and that this is why Filelfo introduced him to the ancient writings. What is perhaps more likely is that only after a discussion of the Platonic material, and at Filelfo's instigation, did Filarete have the idea of writing at all. Nothing in his background explains why he should suddenly

sit down to write a book about his art. Further evidence for Filelfo's seminal role is provided by the parallel between Filarete's treatise and the *Sforziad*, a work on which Filelfo was engaged at this time. The *Sforziad* glorified the ducal family of Milan, was modelled on the *Iliad*, and consequently was to be in twenty-four books. Filarete's treatise was also in honour of the Sforzas, was also in twenty-four books, and was also modelled on the work of a Greek writer.

Greek versus Latin

It is this last feature which points most clearly to the decisive role played by Filelfo in the conception of the treatise. Only he can have been responsible for its many Greek elements. Indeed, we should speak not of Greek elements but rather of Greek character. Since the Golden Book is in Greek, the ancient architecture that is reconstructed is specifically Greek architecture. The port and the coastal city inherit Greek names, Limen Galenokairen and Plousiapolis, and are decorated with Greek inscriptions. Moreover the treatise's Greek character is implied right at the beginning, where Filarete mentions only Doric, Ionic, and Corinthian columns omitting all mention of either Vitruvius's Tuscan or Alberti's Italic.

Our recognition of the Greek character of the treatise and of its Platonic character in particular also enables us to understand the significance of the name Filarete. This is not a family or baptismal name but was adopted by Antonio Averlino himself, as a derivative of the Greek *philaretos* ("lover of virtue"). This word occurs rarely in ancient literature. Much the most accessible example of it was one in the *Nicomachean Ethics* of Aristotle. But the ancient writer who had attributed most significance to the word *aretē* was Plato, and the last pages of the *Laws* are entirely devoted to it: the development of *aretē* in the citizens is the one object of all the laws in the city. We have already observed that Filarete modelled several of his institutions on those described in the *Laws*. He even went so far in adopting a Platonic tone as to call his main educational centre the Casa Areti. If the values of his treatise are, at least in this case, the same as those of the *Laws* it is not surprising that Averlino should have claimed them as his own too. It is probably not insignificant that the first association of a form of the word *filarete* with Averlino is in the introduction to the treatise itself and that it is used there as an adjective applied by the writer to himself—"your *filareto* architect"—not as a name. It is likely that Averlino only acquired this attribute at the time that he was writing his modern architectural version of the *Laws*. Presumably he was "christened" by the high priest of Greek culture in Milan, Filfelfo.

In his concern for *aretē*, displayed both in the treatise and in his own choice of a pseudonym, Filarete came closer to being truly Platonic than in anything else except his belief in a God who created man with a body that was ordered and proportioned. He could most easily grasp and accept these two aspects of Plato's thought because both could be related to current beliefs. The importance of virtue was a commonplace of moral thought, and the theory of human proportions had been transmitted from Vitruvius and others into conventional workshop training.[3] But his penetration of Platonic ideas is amazing if we consider that Filarete must have relied throughout on Filelfo as his interpreter and could never have studied and assimilated the works for himself. Few even of the most learned humanists could have got as much as Filarete did from Plato at this period, since Ficino had yet to make his complete translation. This helps to explain the difference between the influence of Plato on Filarete and that of Cicero on Alberti. Alberti assimilates and applies much of the system of thought of the *De officiis*. Filarete takes from the *Critias*, *Timaeus*, and *Laws* the structure of composition of his treatise, his didactic method, and his major themes; but he could never assimilate Plato's ideas.

Yet the same significance attaches to each author's choice of model. Both, when trying to discuss Classical architecture in a way that would lend it authority in the mid-fifteenth century, turned to texts of ethical philosophy. In view of this common approach it becomes important to establish why their choices were so different. We have seen that Alberti's choice was not surprising. The explanation of Filarete's choice lies, probably, in the very reason why Filarete should have chosen in the first place to write a treatise on architecture only a few years after Alberti. If we consider that Filarete had a Greek name, reconstructed Greek buildings, and dealt only with Greek columns, we notice a striking contrast with Alberti, who deliberately removed all Greek words from his Latin vocabulary, claimed that archi-

tecture reached perfection only in ancient Italy, and even went to the length of inventing an "Italic" column to prove the point. Filarete's attitude is as assertively Greek as Alberti's is Roman. Because of the chronological sequence, the contrast must have a polemical intention.

To find out what that was we must turn again to Filelfo. The same reasons that led us to him as the person responsible for the Greek elements of the treatise lead us again to propose him as the man who had the initial idea of writing a specifically Greek treatise. He was well aware that it was his understanding of that language that gave him a position of authority in the humanistic world. As one of the few Italian scholars who had actually studied in Constantinople and married a Greek wife, his sense of identification with Greek culture must have been uniquely strong. Filelfo had public as well as personal reasons for urging his friend to write a Greek complement to Alberti's Roman treatise. Earlier in the century, the Milanese scholar Decembrio had used a knowledge of Greek to put the Florentine Bruni to shame,[4] and Filelfo himself was probably parading his much greater knowledge when he sent the first four books of the *Sforziad* to Piero de' Medici in 1454. Indeed, if he knew of the founding of the Florentine Academy in 1455, he may well have sought to win his way back to the lucrative intellectual environment of Florence by demonstrating the usefulness of his Greek expertise to the new group. Filarete, for his part, will have had even more personal reasons for negotiating an eventual return to his native city; though he never succeeded as did Filfelfo. What is certain is that when the Florentine Academy achieved its full development under Lorenzo de' Medici after 1469, the preparation of a translation of Plato was one of its main concerns, and one of its members was also given the name Filarete. Finally, what above all gave urgency and significance to the reanimation of a specifically Greek culture was the Fall of Constantinople to the Turks in 1453. The Greek tradition which Filfelfo and Filarete were anxious to develop was not something dead, but until that year very much alive. The break in continuity between Classical Greece and Byzantine Constantinople, of which we are acutely aware, could hardly have been understood by a generation that looked to that city not only for its teachers of Classical Greek but for the manuscripts that preserved ancient

Greek wisdom. Constantinople was a Greek-speaking *polis*, and "Greek" was commonly used as a synonym for "Byzantine." With the Fall of Constantinople it was necessary to transplant Greek civilization to Italian soil. What Filarete urges on Francesco Sforza is nothing less than the construction of a new Byzantium where all that was best in Greek art could be preserved.

Filarete's treatise is thus the first work to assume that the highest achievement of ancient art was embodied in Greek rather than in Roman civilization. In this Filarete looks forward to Winckelmann and attempts to inspire European art with a new breath which only truly arrived with Neo-Classicism. If the architecture that he describes does not have the qualities which we think of as Greek, that is not his fault. Its opulence and complexity derive from Plato's Atlantis with its gold and polychrome edifices. The truncated form in which Plato left the *Critias* effectively prevented Filelfo and Filarete from realizing that Atlantis had been presented as a warning rather than as a model. Instead, confirmation that the qualities it embodied were really Greek could be found in the buildings of Constantinople. It has been dimly perceived hitherto that Filarete's architecture is influenced by Byzantine churches. It is now apparent that the domes, mosaics, and gold backgrounds which are recurring features of his buildings are introduced as essential to an architecture that was distinctively Greek. Filarete had seen only St Mark's in Venice, but Filfelfo could provide glowing descriptions of Haghia Sophia, which would only whet the architect's appetite. By 1465, Filarete had plans to see the buildings for himself, as we know from a letter in which Filfelfo recommends him to a friend in Constantinople.[5] It is the last we hear of the first Greek Revival architect.

Scholars often judge by intellectual appearances; so it is not surprising that Filarete's treatise, unlike Alberti's, has been either neglected or misunderstood. Vasari even called it "probably the most stupid book ever written."[6] If Filarete's accent had been less coarse and his punctuation less erratic, the importance of the Greek Golden Book and the role of Notilento (Filelfo) might have been acknowledged long ago. It has to be admitted that the work is also a good demonstration of the disturbing consequences of such collaborations. There remains a fundamental split between Antonio Averlino, the Italian craftsman, and Filarete, the Neo-

Platonist who dreamed of a revived Greek culture. Our writer may well have aspired to the latter role, but in his language and in his mentality he remained essentially as he had been brought up. As a result, the Platonism and the Hellenism have little effect on the detail of his theories.

Anthropomorphism and the *qualità*

As was observed at the beginning, the key to Filarete's opinions is his belief that the proportions, members, and qualities (*qualità*) of buildings "derive from man himself" (1ᵛ). This was because man, being God's handiwork, constituted an authoritative model. Under the inspiration of the *Timaeus*, Filarete has found a way of integrating Vitruvius (*natura* had given man his proportions) and Alberti (the justification for the use of human proportions in columns lay in their use in Noah's Ark) into a new and convincing justification of the whole apparatus of Antique architecture. There could hardly have been a better response both to the dinner-table criticism with which the book begins and to the more general current of moral architectural criticism. The theory of architecture was now firmly integrated into the structure of Christian belief.

The completeness and persuasiveness of Filarete's argument emerge as the treatise continues and he fulfills his promise to demonstrate how all the elements of architecture derive from man. An example of *misure* is the *braccio* or arm, a regular unit of measurement. For *membri* one amongst many is the *capitello*, its name derived from the Latin for "head." Among many *proportioni* which should be transferred from man to buildings is the ratio of 1:1 coming from the Vitruvian scheme of man inscribed in the square. All these examples would have been understood by Alberti. The introduction of *qualità*, on the other hand, is without precedent in an architectural context and requires further explanation.

Fortunately Filarete explains at an early stage that they correspond in some way to the three Vitruvian orders. The Roman writer, he says (1,3ʳ), talks of three architectural *misure*, Doric, Corinthian, and Ionic. These, according to Filarete, can be shown to relate to the usual classification of things into large, medium, and small, and particularly to such a classification of human types or *qualità*. It is even possible to talk of

Doric men who are the tallest, being nine times as tall as their head is high, Ionic who are the shortest, being only of seven heads, and Corinthian who are intermediate, of eight heads. These are the main *qualità* of men which served as models for the main *qualità* in architecture. Dwarfs and giants are other *qualità*, but they are either too small or too large to be used. Filarete's debt to Vitruvius in all this only serves to emphasize his disagreement with the ancient authority in two important aspects. One is in the concentration on head heights: since Filarete also states that the heights of capitals correspond to the diameters of columns, he is evidently rejecting the Vitruvian forms of Doric and Ionic capitals whose heights were only a half or a third of a diameter. An even more striking divergence from Vitruvius is the assertion that Doric, being nine capital-heights or column-diameters, is the tallest of the orders and not the shortest.

The rejection of the low capital forms must be a direct consequence of his insistence on the anthropomorphic basis of architectural forms. He could accept only those capitals whose proportions could be seen to correspond quite closely to those of the human head. He thus adjusted the Vitruvian rules in order to make this possible. His reasons for making Doric into the tallest of the orders are more obscure but are probably to be looked for in the same area. Its proportion of 1:9 heads/diameters is, as Tigler has observed, almost certainly based on the popular workshop canon of human proportions.[7] Since the canon of perfect proportions would have been thought to be best represented in the male form, and since Doric was said by Vitruvius also to be related to the male body, Filarete may have found it easy to change the ancient rule for the order, especially since Vitruvius had given Doric as the first order created by men and Filarete was well aware that the first man, Adam, having been made by God in his image, was the most perfectly formed. Filarete's anthropomorphism led him to give Doric new proportions by re-interpreting Vitruvius in the light both of Christian tradition and of the canon of workshop practice.

One reason why Filarete could so easily tamper with the theory of the orders is that he was probably extremely vague both about the exact meaning of Vitruvius' descriptions and about how they related to the capitals and columns which had survived from Antiquity. In 1460 Alberti was perhaps the only person who knew what a Doric capital looked like. Filarete's ignorance is evident in his interpretation of the Vitruvian theory of *decor* (48r). Vitruvius, he says, describes three *ragioni* of temples:

One, which they used for temples dedicated to Hercules, Minerva, and Mars, they called Doric, and these were severe and rugged, of rough stone, that is not finished with too much care or attention to prettiness, but rather dark and frightening. They also used another *ragione* or *maniera* which they called Corinthian: such temples were very ornate and pretty and were carefully finished, and these they dedicated to Venus and Proserpina and the goddess Flora, that is Ceres. They also made temples in another *maniera* which they called Ionic, and these were lower, of a humbler *qualità* and less grandiose, and these they dedicated to Juno, Diana, and Bacchus and other similar gods. I think (although Vitruvius does not say so) that they had another *ragione* made of branches and other fantastic materials, which they used for the sylvan gods such as Pan and Faun and other similar wild deities whom they worshipped.

There is admittedly a distant dependence on Vitruvius in these characterizations of the different types of temples. However, Filarete has taken the Roman writer's few cautious metaphors applied to capitals and, using these as a basis, has evolved an accurate descriptive vocabulary for the "style" of a building as a whole, in terms of degree of decoration, roughness of stonework, and degree of finish. The notion that a building can have an overall *maniera* in this way is new and important. It illustrates Filarete's ability to make perceptive generalizations which significantly enrich the vocabulary of art theory, just as he did when he introduced for the first time the idea that it is possible to distinguish the *stile* or *maniera* of an individual architect or artist (5ᵛ). Characteristically the advance here does not depend, as often with Alberti, on the fruitful application of a metaphor from another field of human activity but rather on his direct experience of buildings. He apparently related Vitruvius' characterization of the different capitals to his own experience of Roman monuments, some of which seemed simple and rough and others refined and delicate—a contrast which is still striking today. If anything in his background prepared him to describe architectural style in this way it must have been Medieval fairy stories and romances, which often contrasted the dwellings of monsters and princesses in similar terms.

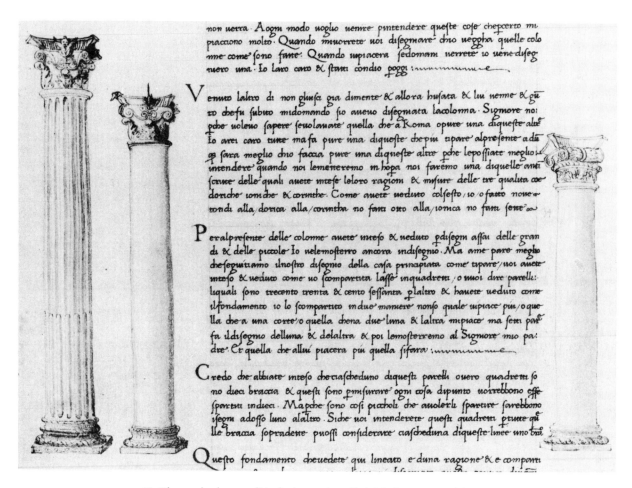

88. Filarete: the three *qualità* of columns, from Cod. Magl. II, IV, 140, fol. 57ᵛ.
From left to right: Doric, Corinthian, Ionic

Filarete's independence of Vitruvius is particularly clear in his placing of Ionic lower than the other two orders instead of treating it as an intermediate form. This transposition, which occurs both in his rephrasing of the Vitruvian rule for *decor* and in his own theory of the *qualità*, must depend on the convention, which had grown up through the Middle Ages and which was still very much alive, that Ionic was the lowest of three forms, being inferior to Corinthian and Composite, which were the only other forms known. In the treatment of Ionic there is thus a similarity between Filarete's account of the ancient *ragioni* and his own theory of the *qualità*, but in his treatment of Doric there is just as complete a contrast. For while the ancient form was "severe and rugged" his own version is refined and decorated, as can be seen in the illustration of the three column types at 57ᵛ (Fig. 88). There the series from left to right corresponds to Filarete's large, medium, and small *qualità*. The small form is identifiable as Ionic by its volutes, though additional elements are placed below to give it the full one-diameter height demanded for all capitals. Corinthian in the middle is as we should expect, but Doric is only a taller, richer form of the same type. The contradiction in character with his ancient Doric is striking. Yet this is also consistent with his view of a change in the aesthetics of religious architecture from the pagan to the Christian world. At 48ʳ, after describing the use of Doric, Corinthian, and Ionic for different gods in Antiquity, he goes on to tell how the ancients made their temples low because they felt that man should humble himself before the gods, "and then the Christians made their churches tall so that when a man entered he should raise his heart on high towards God and raise his mind and soul in contemplation of Him." Filarete's "dark and frightening" ancient Doric would have been highly appropriate to the ancient world, while the tall, ornate Doric which he himself uses fits well with the Christian one. Filarete's lack of understanding of Vitruvius thus left him free to theorize about Doric in particular and about architectural style in general in a new and important way.

More important than his interpretation of the *ragioni* or *maniere*, as they were used by the Romans, are the details of his own notions of the *qualità*, as illustrated by the three columns. The differentiation by absolute distinctions in the forms and proportions of capitals and bases has almost entirely gone. Instead we become more conscious of relative differences in height and in the degree of surface decoration. This last point is well worked out. His Ionic, on the right, has the simplest ornaments on both capital and base. His Corinthian has richer textures on both elements. His Doric, on the left, has more mouldings on the base, more detail on the capital, and also rich fluting on the shaft. It had, of course, been possible to see such relative differences as underlying the traditional series of the orders. However, neither Vitruvius nor Alberti had thought of them consistently in this way, largely because they accepted the mythological explanations of the origin of each order in an absolutely different human type. Alberti had, it is true, revised the proportions of the orders into a continuous progression, but Filarete goes much further. This is clear in his application of the scales of relative variation to other architectural elements. In Book IV (22ʳ) he takes up a remark in Vitruvius that there are three different sizes of bricks and adapts it to mean that there are three different proportions, large, medium, and small, called also Doric, Corinthian, and Ionic. Bricks are thus brought into his system of the *qualità*. So too are openings. In Book VIII (60ʳ) he gives three proportions for doorways: two squares (1:2), a square plus a half (1:1.5), and a square plus a diagonal (c.1:1.414). These he says are called Doric, Corinthian, and Ionic, with Doric presumably having the tallest proportion (1:2) and Ionic the lowest

(1:1.414). Again he goes beyond Alberti in the reorganization of Vitruvius, for Alberti had indeed introduced the idea of Doric, Ionic, and Corinthian doors but had given them all the same proportion of 1:2. Filarete also went beyond the humanist by applying his proportions to arched as well as rectangular apertures.

It is clear from all these applications that Filarete is concerned to define architectural forms as Doric, Corinthian, or Ionic in terms of their position on two sliding scales, one of increasing attenuation of proportion and the other of increasing decoration. We are now closer to understanding why the key to all this is the use of the term *qualità*. For Vitruvius, Doric, Ionic, etc. were different *genera*, separated by absolute and biologically immutable distinctions. Such a point of view was natural to someone who knew that the different architectural styles so described had grown up separately as the architectures of different Greek tribes. Alberti's use of the term *species* also implies a biological distinction, if a less rigid one. By his use of the term *qualità*, Filarete introduces a flexibility that the earlier terms did not have. The referents of *genus* and *species* were substantival: an element either was Doric or was not, depending on its origins. The Doric "quality," on the other hand, has an adjectival reference: it can be applied to anything which is either more attenuated or more decorated, whether it be as small as a brick or as large as a column, regardless of what was Doric in ancient usage.

Architectural *qualità* and social classes

These connotations of *qualità* are of only underlying importance for Filarete, but there is another function of the word which is of explicit value for him.[8]

There are several *qualità* of buildings just as there are several *qualità* of men. . . . As there are men some of whom have more status than others, so it is with buildings according to who lives in them or who uses them, and just as men should be dressed and adorned according to their status [*dignità*] so too should buildings. (40ᵛ)

These "qualities" are in fact parallel, and in the same passage he explains how: just as the officiating clergy in a church are dressed in vestments adorned with gold, silver, pearls, and other precious stones, so too the church itself should be decorated with beautiful stones, carvings, and paintings. The supreme magnificence of the clergy must be matched by the magnificent architecture of the church. Filarete's appeal to the norms of dress as guides for architectural decoration would have been readily understood at the time. The principle that rank in both secular and religious society should be reflected in dress was widely accepted, and in fifteenth-century Italy the degree of richness allowed to each class was frequently prescribed by law. Filarete gives only this one example of how clothing and decoration should be matched, but it is presumably the same notion that led him to make the Doric column, as being the most noble, also the most ornate. By making this analogy for the first time, Filarete found a simple key by which to decide on the ornaments of any building. Many later writers took up the metaphor of architectural decoration as clothing, and it proved extremely fruitful. Its simplicity and comprehensiveness exposes the clumsiness and inadequacy of the theories of Vitruvius and Alberti, who needed to make piecemeal recommendations on the suitable decoration of each structure.

It would have been difficult for Filarete to have this insight if he had not first chosen as his term for architectural style the world *qualità*, which had long been established as a regular word for "social class." This made it easy for him to see a connection between a building and its occupant in the first place. In Book VIII he explores this connection:

There are different *qualità* of men, such as *gentili* who are near the lords to serve for support and for ornament; the *mezzani* [middle] are also both useful and decorative, yet are not so decorative as the *gentili*. The other people who are *più infimi* are for use and necessity and for the service of the lord, and they are not as beautiful to look at as the higher groups. (56ᵛ)

It is exactly the same with the different types of columns, Filarete continues: Doric ones are of *maggiore grandezza*, Corinthian are *della mezzana*, and Ionic are *come quegli infimi*. Thus Ionic should be used where columns have to work hard supporting a heavy weight, Corinthian should also have a load-bearing function, and Doric "columns are placed where they have both to support and to adorn the building but do not have as fatiguing a function as the other two *ragioni*" (56ᵛ).

The parallelism between the orders and the classes could not be more precise. The lowest column and the lowest class are both chiefly designed for utility and hardly at all for ornament. The highest column and the highest class are both suited for positions requiring maximum elegance and minimum effort. The key to the parallelisms lies not only in the use of the word *qualità* for both, but also in the classification into *grande*, *mezzana*, and *piccola*. The three columns are explicitly so characterized at 56ᵛ, and these terms were traditional for differentiating the social classes: "the population of the city is divided anew into *grandi*, *mezzani*, and *piccolini*."[9] It is now clear why both Doric columns and Doric openings have to be tall and thin: they must be literally "higher" than the other types. In the same way, Ionic has to be low; it is a happy coincidence that the lowness of Ionic also produces a form structurally better able to bear weights. Contemporary practice had actually been moving towards establishing a hierarchy of the columns with the taller and more decorated ones used in the more honourable positions, and Alberti had at one stage characterized traditional Corinthian as *lepidus* ("elegant") in contradistinction to the traditional Doric which was *ad laborem aptius* ("more suited for work"), but he had given no hint of the neat theory developed here. The strength of Filarete's theory lies in its foundation on the simple premiss that the forms and relationships found in architecture correspond to and depend on similar forms and relationships in man and society. Its simple consistency springs from a brilliantly appropriate choice of terminology which lends constant support to this premiss. Its attractiveness is revealed in the way it shows how the forms of Classical architecture can be used perfectly to express the norms and conventions of Medieval society.

The significance of Filarete's achievement emerges most clearly if we compare it with Alberti's attempts to deal with the same problems. Alberti had produced only a few hesitant and inconsistent notions on how the use of the orders could be related to particular architectural contexts. His failure was particularly poignant in view of his statement that "in architecture the most praiseworthy quality is the ability to judge what is suitable." Filarete was certainly fortunate in having Alberti's unsuccessful example to learn from, but the main reason why he succeeded where the humanist had not must lie elsewhere. In view of the importance of his choice of terminology for all elements in his theory, it seems certain that the use of his native Italian to for-

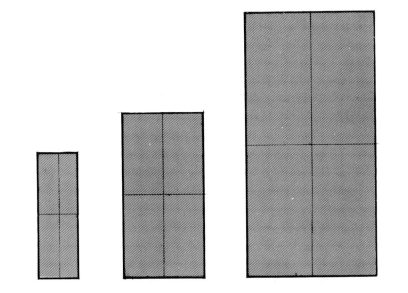
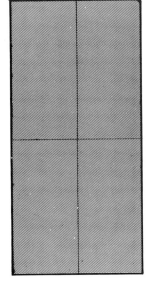

89. House plans, after Filarete. From left to right: poor man,
artisan, merchant, gentleman, bishop, duke

mulate his ideas is essential to their consistency and clarity. Alberti using his laboriously learned Latin could never attain the same level of instinctive rightness. It was impossible for him to match Classical architecture to contemporary society, since he thought about them in different languages, the former in Ciceronian Latin and the latter in church Latin or street Italian. The vocabulary of one world would not fit the other. For Filarete, on the other hand, no thought was possible that was not expressible in the vulgar tongue. If this meant that he lost some of the nuances of Vitruvius, it also meant that inconsistencies and vagueness were kept to a minimum. Seeing everything with the same eye he could see clear correspondences. Alberti, like other humanists, constantly suffered from double vision.

Filarete, unlike Alberti, knew that the society that he was writing about was his own. Hence the facility with which he brings in such references as those to the vestments of priests. Hence too the ease with which, having once formulated his theory, he goes on to apply it. At the beginning of Book XI he states his intention to design a house for "each class [*facultà*] of people" (84^{r}). He begins with a palace for a *gentilhuomo* (Figs. 89

and 90b). The plan is to be of 100 × 200 *braccia*, with a main façade on the short side. The door in the centre is to be 4 *braccia* broad and 8 tall,

and so all its members will be given the same proportions; that is, all the other doors will be double squares, in the Doric or "big" measure. I do this because the *qualità* of the owner is of the upper class.

The quality of Doric matches that of a gentleman; so his house should be Doric. Fundamental is the proportion of the groundplan: two squares or 1:2. This appeared earlier as the proportion of the Doric door, and it is also the proportion of all the openings here. Apparently, we must consider it as the proportion of other rectangles in Doric buildings too, even including the overall plan or elevation. Nor does the Doric quality reveal itself only in these rather rigid formulas. Of the four towers that he puts on top of the palace he says that they are a *cosa degnia* and that they too correspond "to the *qualità* of the Doric measure." Evidently the gentleman class being the highest and the Doric proportion being consequently the tallest, the tower as the form most clearly expressing height belongs with that *qualità*.

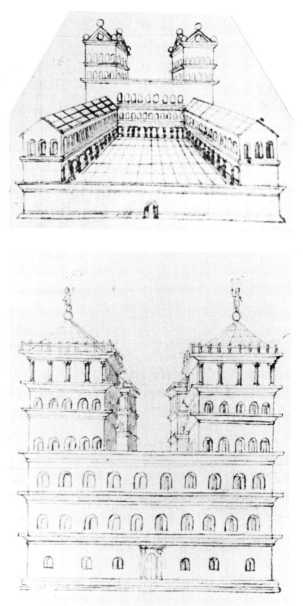

90. Filarete: top (a) Merchant's house, fol. 86ʳ;
bottom (b) Gentleman's house, fol. 84ᵛ

columns) recur almost exactly in the ducal and episcopal palaces. In the ducal palace described in Book VIII (57ᵛ) the groundplan is 160 × 330 *braccia*, which is only slightly more attenuated than 1:2 (Figs. 89 and 91b). The latter is again the proportion which is explicitly stated to underly the relation between the height of the arch on the façade (12 *br.*) and the height of the whole ground floor (24 *br.*). The palace also uses two sets of columns (or possibly Filarete gives two sets of proportions for the same colonnade). The proportion of one set is exactly 1:9 (2 × 18 *br.*), while that of the other is slightly more attenuated (2½ × 24 *br.*). The fact that in both groundplan and column height we find proportions slightly taller than 1:2 can almost certainly be seen as expressive of the fact that the duke is socially on a level even above the gentleman. The fact that the episcopal palace (66ʳ) returns to the normal Doric ratios for its plan (160 × 320 *br.*) while still preserving more slender proportions of 1¼ × 12 *br.* (Figs. 89 and 91c) for its columns is equally well calculated to mark it as inferior to the ducal residence but still superior to that of an ordinary gentleman. The similarity in absolute measurements, on the other hand, preserves the general equality of status between secular and religious leaders. The differences between the different Doric buildings on the index of measurements are precisely matched by differences in the scale of decoration. Just as the ducal and episcopal palaces are absolutely larger than the gentleman's house, so they are also both adorned with large pilasters on the *piano nobile*, a feature absent from the simplest Doric building. They are also the only two secular buildings in Sforzinda which are raised on three steps. Again, however, in decoration as in proportion the superiority of the duke is made quite clear. He has three towers on his façade, while the bishop, like the gentleman, has only two. The duke also has more sculpture. Filarete's theory of the "qualities" with its flexible indices of proportion and decoration is thus capable not only of producing an architecture appropriate to a class, but even of articulating differences of status within it.

The admirable consistency in the treatment of the Doric "quality" begins to break up in the exposition of Corinthian and Ionic houses which follows in Book XI. These turn out to be the houses of the merchant (85ᵛ) and artisan (86ʳ) classes. But the merchant's house has a ground plan of 50 × 150 *br.*, a proportion of 1:3

Filarete does not think of Doric as appropriate only to gentlemen on a one-to-one basis. It is suited to all buildings of a comparable degree of nobility. Although he does not actually use the word "Doric," its proportions (that is, 1:2 for apertures and plan and 1:9 for

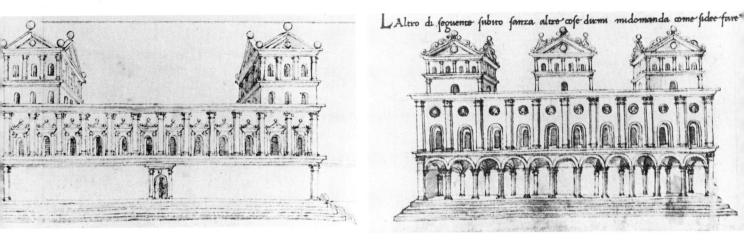

91. Filarete: left (a) Bishop's palace, fol. 66ʳ; right (b) Duke's palace, fol. 58ᵛ

which is far from the Corinthian "square plus a half" (1:1.5) (Figs. 89 and 90a). Instead it is apparently the façade of the building which approaches "Corinthian" proportions in its dimensions of 32 × 50 *br.* (only 2 *braccia* out), while 1:1.5 is specifically said to be the proportion of the main door. A puzzling element is that the windows and inner doors have the Doric ratio. Equally odd are the dimensions of the groundplan of the house of the artisan, which should produce the Ionic "square plus a diagonal" (1:1.414) but are in reality closer to 1:1.7 (30 × 50 *br.*). Still, when Filarete goes on to discuss the house of a poor man (86ᵛ) the progression toward more stumpy proportions is continued and a square plan (of 10 or 12 *braccia*) is recommended (Fig. 89). The poor man's house thus constitutes a sub-Ionic quality just as the duke's palace is super-Doric.

There are no other buildings for which Filarete gives the *qualità*. There is, indeed, only one other building for which he gives enough information for us to establish what *qualità* he intended for it. This is the castle inside Sforzinda described at 38ʳ. The plan is square, but the gateways have a proportion of 1:1.5 (6 × 9 *br.*), and the columns of an internal portico have a proportion of 1:8 (1 × 8 *br.*). This consistency between the two proportions suggest that they are specifically intended as the attributes of the Corinthian *qualità*. There is no compelling reason in the rules why this

should be appropriate here. The men-at-arms who occupy the buildings are not mentioned in the discussion of classes. We can only guess that Filarete thought they belonged with the *mezzani*, and a passage in Book XX confirms that this is so. In an explanation of the importance of different members of society to their lord he uses the simile of a wall:

The large outer stones which support the wall and which are the carved ones are the *gentilhuomini* and *persone da bene* and *virtuosi*, and the columns are the captains of the men-at-arms. The other stones are the soldiers and the bricks are the citizens. The filling of the wall is the country people, and the skin is the artisans. (168ᵛ)

From this it is clear that men-at-arms come below gentlemen and above artisans. Filarete's association of them with Corinthian is thus part of a consistent relation of architectural "qualities" to social classes.

This last passage, with its explicit analogy between the structure of a wall and the structure of society, well illustrates how fundamental for Filarete is the correlation between social organization and architecture. Indeed, it is an interest in this correlation which links the two most remarkable features of this treatise, his use of Plato, the first great social theorist, and his invention of a theory of architectural *qualità*. It is difficult to demonstrate a precise connection between these two features, but his contact with Plato may have alerted him to the possible interdependence between forms of society and forms of buildings, an interdependence which is especially clear in the *Critias*. Even a general knowledge of Plato could have encouraged Filarete to make explicit a system of relationships between architecture and class which was already implicit in so many contemporary and earlier buildings. He was thus inspired by the most exotic of sources to formulate the most realistic of theories. His acceptance of social realities is a refreshing change after the pretentiously rhetorical, mystical, and ethical theories of Vitruvius, Hrabanus, and Alberti. His comparison of the aristocracy to large, finely carved exterior blocks and of peasants to a rough rubble filling is more revealing of perennial attitudes both to buildings and classes than all the abstractions of his predecessors.

XII

Francesco di Giorgio Martini

◆

The manuscripts: from notebook to textbook

THE THIRD writer to deal extensively with architecture in the fifteenth century, Francesco di Giorgio, had a wider involvement with architectural activity than either of his predecessors.[1] Also, unlike Alberti and Filarete, he came not from Florence but from Siena, and he seems never to have become drawn into Florentine circles. Born in 1439, he was trained in his native city as a painter and sculptor. By the early 1470s, however, he was working also as a water engineer, and from 1477, when he arrived in Urbino, he seems to have been active chiefly as engineer and architect. Until 1489 he worked alternately at Urbino and Siena, with important excursions to Cortona in 1484–85, and to Rome, where he probably was in 1486. Although he then returned to settle in Siena, his fame as an expert in fortification and structural problems brought him many invitations to travel. He made journeys to Milan in 1490 (where he met Leonardo), to Naples in 1492 and 1496, and finally to Rome in 1501, the year in which he died.

The most striking aspect of Francesco's achievement is his contribution to architectural literature. Many manuscripts associated with his name survive, and after the recent work by Maltese, Scaglia, and Betts their dating and the connections between them have been fairly well established.[2] A small notebook in the Vatican Library was probably composed in the 1470s. Another small book of drawings in the British Museum Department of Prints and Drawings was probably made shortly afterwards and before 1477, when Francesco went to Urbino. The first version of a full treatise is represented (as Maltese has shown) by two other manuscripts both dating from the 1470s one in the Laurenziana in Florence, Ashburnham 361 (henceforth

L), and the other in Turin, Saluzziano 148 (henceforth T). The latter contains an additional collection of illustrations of Roman monuments largely made in 1485–86. Betts has introduced into the literature a small improved version of this text, now in the New York Public Library, but this too was superseded by a developed second version of the treatise found in two other manuscripts, Magliabecchiano II, I, 141 (henceforth M) in the Biblioteca Nazionale in Florence, and S.IV, 4 (henceforth S) in Siena, which is shorter and contains significant variations. Bound in with M is a translation of Vitruvius (the only text in Francesco's holograph apart from the Vatican notebook), and Maltese has convincingly suggested that this second version was prepared by Francesco after the appearance of the first printed texts of Alberti in 1485 and of Vitruvius in 1486 had made him aware of the serious deficiencies of the first version, in both form and content. In the first version not only is the Italian extremely rough but many passages consist of very ill-digested attempts at translating or paraphrasing a bad text of the Roman writer. The second version is improved all round and shows how much he benefited from the new translation which Francesco must have made with the help of a Latin scholar. This second version will have been written in the 1490s, which would fit with the references to sites which he could have seen on his visits to Naples in that period. Throughout the series of manuscripts there is a steady increase both in the coherence of the verbal presentation and in the proportion of space devoted to purely architectural material. The first version of the treatise consists of a large number of unconnected sections dealing with subjects as diverse as columns and hydraulic apparatus. Only about a third of the pages are concerned with architecture proper. In the second version there is a much more clear and balanced division into seven sections called *trattati*, each with a prologue, and with a preface at the beginning and a conclusion at the end of the whole. The majority of pages now also deal with strictly architectural material.

Francesco's approach is different from both Alberti's and Filarete's. The difference can partly be explained in terms of his background, which was even humbler than that of Filarete. The Florentine was the son of a metalworker, Francesco of a poulterer. His education and command of the written language must have been correspondingly inferior. The progressive improvement in his capacity to articulate his ideas reflects the efforts of a man self-taught in his mature years. Indeed, Francesco belongs to the first generation for whom the introduction of the printed book made such self-education relatively easy. The way his treatises reflect the successive influences of Valturius' *De re militari* published at Verona in 1472, of Alberti (1485), and of Vitruvius (1486) provides an excellent illustration of the way the introduction of printing after the mid-1460s opened up general education.[3] It made accessible to many readers works both ancient and modern which would otherwise have been in restricted circulation, and stimulated the preparation of reliable and clear versions of texts which were otherwise corrupted by generations of scribal error. Moreover, the rapid dissemination of each new volume must have stimulated a discussion of its contents far more intense than that occasioned by the slow passing from hand to hand of a laboriously copied manuscript. Argument about architecture must have reached an unprecedented pitch in 1485 and 1486, and it is no wonder that Francesco de Giorgio's approach to the subject was transformed as a result.

The importance of drawings

One of the most obvious differences between Francesco's treatises and those of his predecessors is the developed use of illustrations. Vitruvius had used a few diagrams, Alberti none; Filarete, although he did give them a new prominence, still reserved them for selected occasions. Francesco, on the other hand, fills whole pages and often borders too with drawings which range from the quick sketch to the elaborate portrayal of whole buildings. Francesco's use of drawings is also

highly purposeful. The clearest statements of his aims and ideas are found in his most articulate pronouncements in the final version of the treatise, especially in the fuller source M. There the prologue to the first *trattato* serves as a preface to the whole. It begins with the statement (derived from Eupompus) that no art attains perfection without using arithmetic and geometry and goes on to insist that *disegno* (drawing) is just as important for every useful science. This point is backed up by further references to the high status of drawing in Antiquity:

And, although in our own day it is held to be unworthy and inferior to many other mechanical arts, nonetheless anyone who reflects on how useful and necessary it is for every human activity, whether for the process of invention or for the exposition of ideas, whether for working purposes or for art—and whoever considers too how closely related it is to geometry, arithmetic, and optics [*prospettiva*]—will easily judge, and with good reason, that drawing is a necessary means in every theoretical and practical aspect [*cognizione e opera*] of the arts. (II, pp. 293–94)

The emphasis on *aritmetica, geometria,* and *disegno* is new. Mathematics had been important for Alberti, and Filarete had referred to *geometria* and *disegni* at the outset as important elements of architecture, but here they are given absolute preeminence.

A major influence on the thought Francesco expresses here is likely to have been his contact with Urbino between 1477 and 1489. His predecessor as architect of the ducal palace, Luciano Laurana, had received a patent from Federigo da Montefeltro in 1468 in which he is praised for his *virtù*, especially for his *virtù* in architecture, "which is founded in the art of arithmetic and geometry, which are among the seven liberal arts and among the most important of them being of the highest level of certainty [*in primo gradu certitudinis*]."[4] But the person who had above all established a connection between geometry, drawing, and architecture was the most important painter employed at Urbino, Piero della Francesca. In the introduction to his *De prospectiva pingendi*, dedicated to Federigo da Montefeltro at some time before the duke's death in 1482, he declares that the treatise deals with *commensuratione* and *disegno*—a pair of words similar to Francesco's *geometria* and *disegno*.[5] Since there is a close correspondence between some of Francesco's drawings, especially those of Composite capitals, and those of Piero, there may even be a direct dependence of the Sienese on the Umbrian master. There is certainly a community of spirit between the *De prospectiva* and Francesco's writings in the way each sets out to provide a clear and almost scientific account of one of the visual arts, using *disegni* which are closely assimilated to *geometria*.

The largest number of drawings is to be found in Francesco's earlier version as represented by T, but they actually have greater importance in the later version represented by M, where each drawing is usually larger and where, on some pages, they even replace words entirely. An increasing interest in the use of drawings between the two versions is also demonstrated by the more frequent references to them in the later text. Already in the preface Francesco had referred to the usefulness of drawing "in the explanation of ideas [*nell'esplicare i concetti*]." Elsewhere he indicates what he means in more detail. In the second *trattato*, talking of houses in the country he says in S, "and to provide better information [*migliore notizia*] I will draw some" (II, 343). This is expanded in M to become "I will draw some according to these rules so that the eye can represent them to the imagination, because examples move the imagination more than do words" (II, 517). In the fourth *trattato* he again compares words unfavourably to drawings, saying in S "as will better appear in the illustration," to which he adds in M "because it would take too long to explain every detail in words; so let it be found acceptable to make up for the deficiencies of words with painting" (II, 393). Later in the same *trattato*, again only in M, he gives a more ambitious justification for the use of drawings "in which," he says, "the sense of sight will judge better than the sense of hearing, as it is the more noble sense and is more sensible to differentiating characteristics, as Aristotle affirms in the prologue to the *Metaphysics*, a point which is especially true in this art which above all deals with the visible as well as the invisible" (II, 399). This argument is found elaborated in the fifth *trattato*, in both S and M, when Francesco wishes to introduce a novel feature, a series of *esempli* of fortresses consisting of large drawings accompanied by short written commentaries:

Because every intellectual observation has its origin in sensation, as Aristotle testifies in the first book of the *Posterior Analytics* and in the second and third books of *On the Soul*, and

because among the senses that of sight is the most spiritual, pure, and perfect and shows us more things and differences between things, it seems that our intellect is unable to understand anything or remember it for long if it has not perceived it with the sense of sight, or at least seen something like it through perceiving which the intellect can rise to know the first object as well. Thus, when philosophers and calculators [*calculatori*] wish to deal with variable qualities [*qualità intense*] they talk of them as if the quality was expressible as a visible and continuous line, a method that also improves the memory, since it arranges the matter being considered with brevity and order, accessible for frequent meditation. Hence, when all the general and special rules have been given, it is necessary to draw some examples, through which the intellect may more easily judge and with greater certainty remember; because examples affect the intellect more than general words, especially the intellect of those who are not very expert or learned. (II, 444–45)

Illustrations contain both more and more accurate information than words and are more memorable. They also have a good pedigree in the diagrams of scientific writers. Finally, in the conclusion to the whole work, which exists only in M, the last paragraph is again devoted to drawing. All who read this *operetta* must endeavour to understand *disegno*, "because without it it is impossible to comprehend the composition and detailing of buildings, since exterior surfaces cover interior ones and it would take a long time to give examples of all parts." Another reason is that "the complete architect needs to use invention for many undescribed cases which occur, and for this he requires drawings." Lastly, he says, "as I said at the beginning, he who has arranged in his imagination [*fantasia*] some rational building or machine which he wishes to put together and make is unable to communicate and describe his idea [*concetto*] without *disegno* . . . (II, 505–6). Drawings are not just a useful adjunct to architectural writings; they are also essential to the practice of architecture, and not just for the final working plans—a use which would be familiar to everyone—but also for the process of invention.

Francesco's treatise both begins and ends with *disegno*, and it is his use of drawings which he presents as his main claim to superiority over his predecessors in a passage found only in M:

There have often been worthy authors who have written at length about the art of architecture, but they have used characters and letters and not representational drawings [*figurato disegno*] and so, although to the writers themselves it seems that they have elucidated their designs according to their intentions, to us it seems that through lack of drawings there are few who can understand them. For, following the imaginative faculty each person makes different compositions, which are often more different from the truth of the first idea than day is from the darkness of night; as a result the readers are not a little confused, because, as it is said, "so many readers, so many diverse interpreters." But if such writers had matched their writings with drawings it would be possible to react to them much more directly, seeing at the same time both the signifier and the signified, and so every obscurity would be removed. (II, 489).

There have been many, he goes on, who have either invented things or rediscovered things from Antiquity and have described them, but because they do not use drawings it is difficult to understand them. Instead, they should have used the services of some expert painter. It is especially difficult to describe both the inside and outside of an object simultaneously without the use of perspective and straight lines or ordinary drawing (*natural disegno*) rather than some indirect method (*una certa via indiretta*). Thus many things are lost. "Consequently I consider drawing in this respect to be necessary to every other science as well as architecture" (II, 489–90). There can be little doubt that the main stimulus to Francesco's argument for the use of drawings was his awareness of the inadequacy of the two purely verbal texts of Alberti and Vitruvius which had just been printed. Not that he had neglected drawings in the first version, written before those editions appeared. As we saw, there were many already in the earlier manuscripts, and in the text he referred to the use of both words and images. But he never sets drawing above words until the second version. It is, moreover, only in M, which represents a later stage than S, that he makes his most assertive claims.

Aristotle and the scientific treatise

An awareness of the shortcomings of his predecessors may have provided Francesco di Giorgio with a stimulus to develop the use of drawings, but a more elaborate explanation is needed for the articulate justification of this interest. This is to be found in his study of Aristotle. Francesco frequently links the name of the Greek philosopher to his enthusiasm for drawing. More particularly, the emphasis on the primacy of the sense of sight, on the visual nature of memory, and on

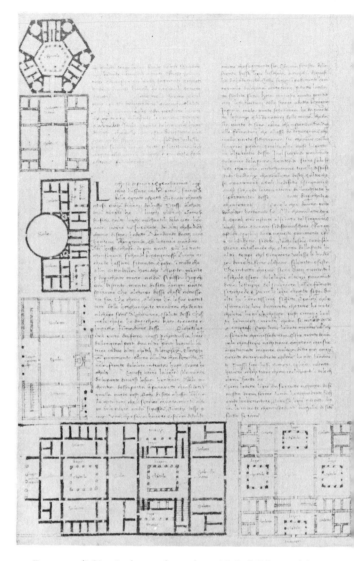

92. Francesco di Giorgio: house plans: above (a) Cod. Sal. 148, fol. 17ᵛ; right (b) Cod. Magl. II, I, 141, fol. 21ʳ

the role of the *fantasia*, as well as the notion of a signifier and signified, can all be directly traced to his works, even if his references are not always correct. Indeed, his developing interest in drawing precisely parallels the growth in his knowledge of Aristotle. For the latter is cited in the manuscripts of the early version only once, and there it is clear that he has been encountered through an intermediary, Saint Thomas Aquinas. In S, on the other hand, he is referred to more than ten

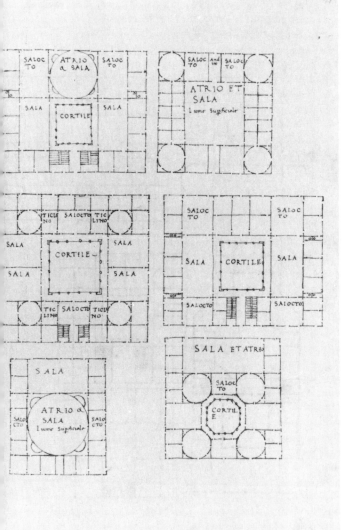

the two versions of the treatise (Fig. 92). Essentially, many more in the second version are reduced to geometrical diagrams. In the first version, all the house plans are drawn, like those in Filarete, showing the actual thicknesses of the walls; in M and S, they appear as networks of single lines. The same is true, though to a lesser extent, of the church plans. Francesco set out to turn his notes on architecture into the first scientific treatment of the subject. The use of drawings, especially those of a diagrammatic character, was a part of this. He was anxious to find a more reliable format for an architectural treatise than that provided by his predecessors; and he succeeded. Most later works on the subject, rejecting the approach of Vitruvius and Alberti, continue to emphasize the essential role of illustration.

Francesco's interest in drawings as an aid to clear and accurate communication led not only to his exploitation of linear diagrams but also to the development of a quite new type of drawing, the cutaway view, in which the external wall of a building was removed in order to make it possible to show the interior. Already in the first version he refers to the way in which in a drawing one part may conceal another, and in the second version he expands on this notion. We thus observe Francesco first isolating and then solving the problem. In the first version of his treatise he remarks incidentally that one difficulty with drawings is that one part of a building hides another, a point which is certainly true of the perspective drawings which he was using at that time. In the second version, he has come to terms with the difficulty and talks instead of the fact that whether you show the exterior or the interior something will always be missing. If it is possible to show the interior the problem is much less serious, and a number of drawings in M show that he had learned precisely how to do just that. Indeed, the best examples of this are to be found in his drawings of Roman structures made in the late 1480s. Once introduced, these drawings were to prove essential to the next generation of draughtsmen from Leonardo to Raphael, as Lotz has shown.[6]

In the precise way he uses drawings Francesco is influenced by Aristotle only in a general sense, but when it came to the organization of the written text the Greek writer could serve as a more useful guide. Once again this is more apparent in M, as the preface reveals. The prefaces of both S and M state that the Platonic

times, while in M there are as many references again, several in the context of the newly expanded justification of illustration. In general, M shows the results of a deepening study of the scientific literature of the Aristotelian tradition; for there are also further references to Averroes and Avicenna beyond those in S, where they appear for the first time.

This interest in scientific writings also puts into a clearer context a critical shift in drawing style between

and Peripatetic philosophers agree that one of the best ways of analysing an unfamiliar subject is to divide it into its parts, and that Francesco has accordingly divided his work into seven *trattati*, with the first devoted to "general properties" and the next six to "particular" ones, "following the opinion of Aristotle in the *Physics*, where he instructs us that in the sciences it is necessary to proceed from universals to particulars" (II, 299). The subsequent account of the division of *Trattati* Two to Seven in S, where he begins with cities and ends with houses and war machines, is not as well ordered as that in M, where Francesco begins: "After this, because the first building a man needs is his house or habitation the second treatise should detail the parts which are required in commodious and convenient dwellings, from houses to palaces, since man is a sociable animal and cannot comfortably live apart" (II, 299). Francesco is rethinking the whole problem of the architectural treatise under the inspiration of Aristotle. Alberti and Filarete had divided their works (into ten and twenty-four books respectively) according to literary models. Francesco works out his own scheme based on internal needs. General principles are grouped into the first *trattato* and more clearly separated from the rest of the work than in any of the earlier treatises.

If, moreover, we turn to the second *trattato* in M, the one on houses, the consequences of Francesco's new interest in method are striking. Once again the division between *proprietà communi* and *proprietà particolari* is used to organize the material, with the different types of houses being grouped under the latter heading. The greatest novelty is that houses are dealt with at this stage at all; but equally important is that houses of less important people are dealt with before houses of more important ones. Both innovations not only break with tradition but turn it on its head. Previously writers had always dealt with the higher-status types first and the lower last, which meant that temples and churches were the first buildings to be described, and when eventually it was the turn of houses, it was palaces which came first too. Francesco's rejection of this order depends on the new scientific method of his approach. The houses of private persons are dealt with first before those of people in public life "because naturally they come first" (II, 342). Among private houses those of farmers come before those of artisans, which come be-

fore those of merchants, etc. for the same reason: because the first houses were those of farmers, and so on. In the same way, houses in general come before public buildings, since houses must have been the earlier type of building. How far Francesco went in applying schemes of developmental morphology to architecture is well demonstrated by a page of church plans (Fig. 93).[7] The plans are arranged in two series, one of centralized type along the bottom of the page and the other of longitudinal type up the side. Not only do the two series meet in a composite form which can be seen as centralized on its short axis (thus linking with the centralized series) and longitudinal in the vertical axis (thus leading into the longitudinal group), but each series shows a steady growth in complexity away from the basic form-type; as in diagrams of the slow growth of a multi-cell organism in a modern biological textbook, one new space or columnar grouping after another is added until an ultimate "maturity" is reached. The insistence that a study of architecture has to follow the "natural history" of buildings can again only be derived from Aristotle, who regularly describes historical developments in terms of growth—as in the *Poetics*, where contemporary tragedy is dealt with only after earlier dramatic forms have first been gone through. As with Aristotle's earlier theory of literature, so with Francesco's theory of architecture: the introduction of a new and self-consciously scientific method has far-reaching implications.

Francesco was evidently well aware that the house was the most morally questionable architectural form, and he devotes the first section of the *trattato* to this problem. After rehearsing all the moral and religious objections he refutes them one by one, often in the same terms that are found in contemporary inscriptions on real palaces: a house is constructed not just for its builder but for his descendants; a house reflects glory not on the individual who puts it up but on God who gave man the power and knowledge to do such a thing in the first place. His main argument, however, is characteristically drawn not from morality but from natural science and invokes the special physical and psychological needs of man as an animal, a term which he has already used:

Because man is more delicately balanced [*temperato*] than any other animal, it follows that he is more vulnerable to the elements and their excesses than other creatures, and conse-

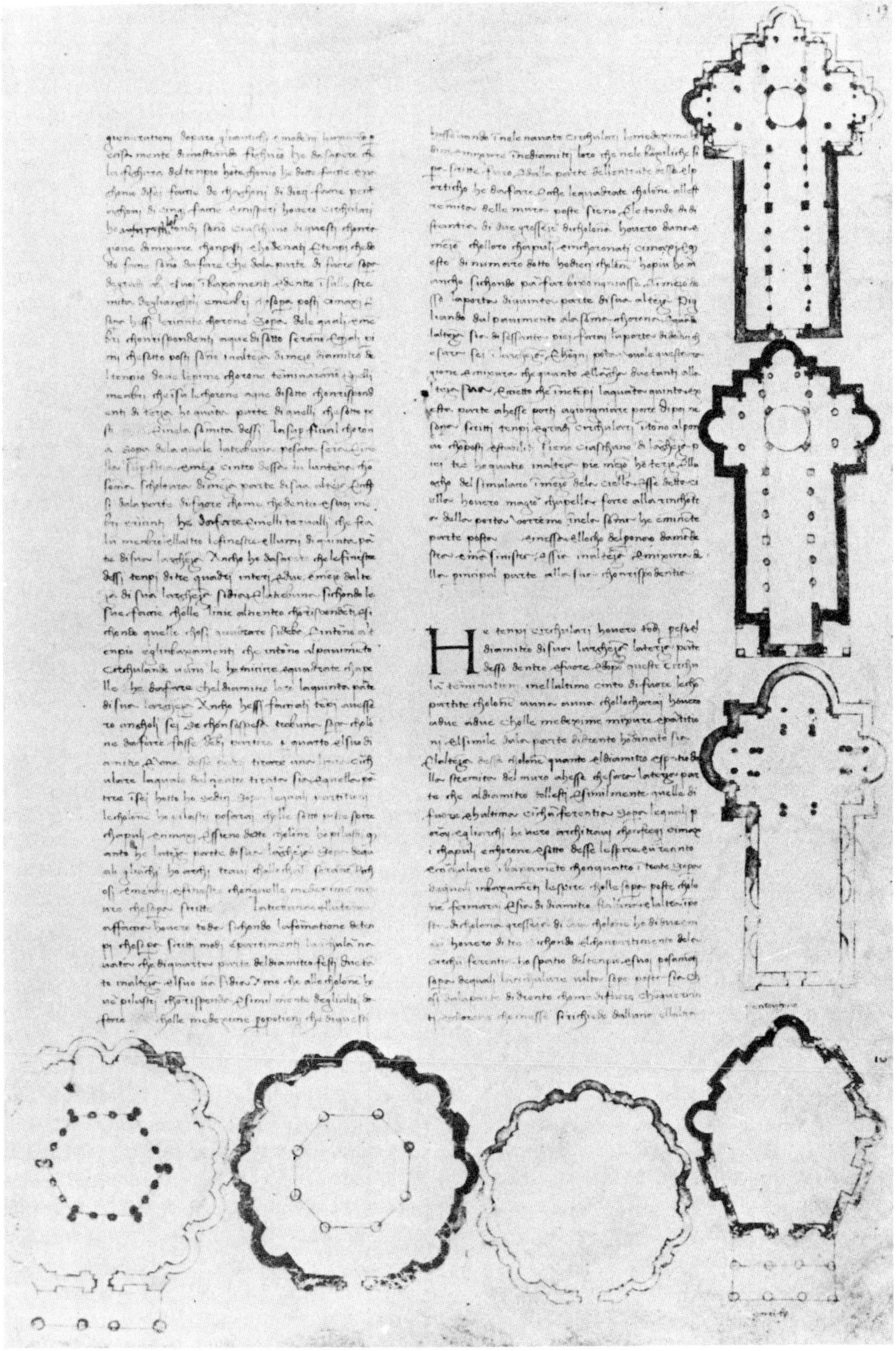

93. Francesco di Giorgio: church plans, Cod. Sal. 148, fol. 13r

quently he needs a home which is more artificial [*artifizioso*] than theirs, one which will be better proportioned and more appropriate to him the more art is employed in its design. (II, 326)

The lower a creature is, the less comfort it requires to find peace (*con meno commodità . . . si quieta*). Man is so demanding because of the perfection of his intellect and the loftiness of his goals. Francesco is not explicit about the type of artistic refinement he demands, but he appears to believe that a comfortable dwelling is necessary to stabilize the delicate balance in man's humours, and a well-proportioned one to satisfy man's needs for intellectual refinement.

For Francesco, the general difference between man and other animals is more important than the minor distinctions between classes. In so far as he does devise different houses for different social groups, he does little more than provide for their different functional needs, hardly referring to the ornaments which had absorbed his predecessors. This is particularly true of the second version and especially of M, where only linear schemes of groundplans are found and these give no information on decoration, showing only the abstract geometry which for him was the main essential in the well-designed house. The same is generally true of the account of churches. The influence of the Aristotelian tradition thus affects the nature of his theories as well as their presentation. Aristotle is as important for him as Cicero was for Alberti and Plato for Filarete —perhaps more so, since for the first time it is possible to talk of a decisive influence in the area of basic method.

Some further ways in which this affects the use of illustration and the organization of material can be added to those already mentioned. Right at the beginning of S and M, Francesco apologizes for his shortcomings and voices the hope that he will be not a *determinatore*, someone who lays down rules, but a *motore*, a stimulating influence on higher minds (II, 298). Clearly the *scienzia* he often talks about is more the pursuit of knowledge than its attainment. He often just presents different arguments without arriving at a solution, as in the discussion of the siting of the image in a temple, where he is clear that the points are *suasive* (persuasive) rather than *dimostrative* (compelling) (II, 408–9). He is fully prepared to change his own mind and to let others reach independent conclusions on the

basis of his evidence. It was this approach to the science of architecture which had enabled him to critically update his own ideas from his first manuscripts to the last.

The orders

Enough has been said so far to prepare us for the fact that Francesco's approach to the orders is quite different from that of his predecessors. His drawings of ancient monuments and his slowly deepening understanding of the text of Vitruvius meant that his knowledge of the orders went through several stages. His lack of interest in surface decoration and his concern instead for geometry, especially in the second version, meant that his treatment of them as decorative forms was insubstantial. His general neglect of the moral and social uses of architecture meant that his recommendations on using them appropriately were few.

The main discussion of the orders is contained in a separate book on columns in the first version (T and L) and forms a major part of the *trattato* on *templi* in the second (S and M). This change between the two versions is made more marked by the change in the word used to refer to the orders, from *generatione* to *specie*. The first term must be simply a translation of the Vitruvian *genus*, reflecting the basis of the text of T and L. The second, on the other hand, resembles Alberti's *species* and probably reflects the recent publication of his work. But since there was no particular reason why Francesco should have adopted the Albertian term, the influence of Aristotle may once again be detected, for *species* was a key word in the Aristotelian tradition of scientific writing which Francesco aspired to join.

The material in the first version consists largely of a confused and distorted paraphrase of Vitruvius. In spite of Francesco's fluency and air of conviction, we are left with the impression that he understood little of what the ancient author said on the origins and the forms of Ionic and Corinthian, and nothing of what he said on Doric. The illustrations all seem to show variations of Corinthian/Composite forms. The chief points of interest are the introduction of a number of features which had never been referred to before, some of which derive from Francesco's misapplication of ancient terms to forms which he had observed in ancient and modern structures, such as the consoles and brackets which he calls *metofe*, *mutoli*, and *tigrafi*. Others are his own invention based upon his observations, such as the *colonne pulvinate* which have a larger entasis than usual, and the *colonne a balausti* and *a candeliere* which derive from the forms of ancient lamps.[8] The account of the orders in the second version is much more rewarding, as we should expect, since by then he had had Vitruvius properly translated and had made a detailed study of ancient monuments. Yet although his translation of Vitruvius is fairly accurate and he does draw correct Doric capitals and entablatures, he still fails to connect text to monument. One reason for this is that he was much more interested in the proportional differences between the orders than in the differences in their forms. This is manifest in the illustrations in M, where a Doric capital is labelled Ionic and an Ionic example Doric, simply because he has established that Doric forms are ⅓ diameter high and Ionic ones ⅔ diameter and the examples illustrated have those proportions (Fig. 94). Indeed, his main concern throughout is to establish the proportions of each form in detail. When he refers to his systematic study of Roman remains it is in pursuit of these proportions: "which proportions I have personally [*per sperienza*] found, examined, and many times measured with great care and no little effort"; to which is added in M alone "so that from many examples, none of which is discrepant, it is possible to arrive at general conclusions, just as other universal conclusions are based on and confirmed by the observation of particulars" (II, 378). Francesco clearly realized that the methodical collection of evidence could advance the knowledge of ancient architecture, and although the peculiar nature of his interests led to rather idiosyncratic conclusions, the scientific value of his work is demonstrated by the fact that text and drawings contain all the information necessary for anyone coming after him to make correct identifications.

Apart from providing the first correct illustrations of several forms of capital, base, and entablature, the main contribution of Francesco's work in this area is to give new prominence to the *stilobata* or pedestal and to introduce the *gocciola* or corbel. In both cases he was led to record them after observing their frequent use in practice. The pedestal was, as he says, "frequently used by ancient sculptors" and so demands a special mention (II, 527). The *gocciola*, on the other

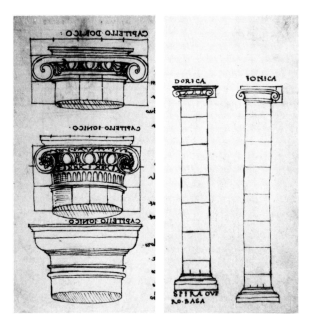

94. Francesco di Giorgio: column types, Cod. Magl. II, I, 141: left: fol. 33ʳ; right: fol. 32ʳ, details

hand, was a form which he had noticed often in modern buildings and which he had been hard pressed to find used in Antiquity: "and these I have not found in any author, nor in any ancient building except in a ruined church at Veii or Civita Castellana, where I saw two very beautiful specimens" (II, 390). Francesco, the first writer to place so much value on personal observations, in this case is led by them to give prominence to forms which add a new flexibility to the orders as described by previous writers.

Francesco's few remarks on the *use* of the orders are to be found almost exclusively in his second version. The only remark of any interest in the earlier T and L concerns the design of columns which have to bear heavy weights: "in some basements and low situations where the columns have to bear a heavy weight they used the *pulvinate* [with large entasis] and *nane* [dwarf] types, with capitals following the same principle having volutes, bound-up leaves [*lenguazzi legati*], flutings, basket shapes, or some other simple treatment; and above these columns they put very short bases in the role of cornices, because they would be more solid and continuous" (I, 65). Francesco seems to have observed that Doric or Tuscan columns, which have the largest entasis, were sometimes placed below other orders. He also reveals a more fully developed awareness of what makes forms look strong than any of his predecessors. In the second version, it is only when talking of churches that he makes any reference to the appropriate use of columns, capitals, or entablatures. He begins with a general guide to the principles to be followed in the decoration of churches. In S he says that the higher the status of the occupant of a house the more magnificent the house should be, and consequently a temple should have as much *proportione* and *ornamento* as any building. The basic principle is rephrased in M: "if the more important the person to whom a place is dedicated the more *ornato* and *perfetto* it should be, then it follows that we should use all our ingenuity and strength unstintingly to observe the rules [*operare regulatamente*] in building temples more than in any secular structure" (II, 523). The essential notion is the same as that found in Alberti and Filarete and in most contemporary buildings—that the more important a building is the richer it should be—but there is a significant stress on proportion, perfection, and regularity. There is no necessary connection between being *ornato* and being *perfetto*. Indeed, in his characterization of the orders in M, Francesco had suggested that they might even be opposed. Commenting on the fact that Doric is derived from man and Ionic from woman, he had noted that "although woman is an imperfect animal and is, as Aristotle asserts in several places, a defective man [*maschio occasionato*], nevertheless she is more beautiful [*vagha*] in appearance, especially when young, than the male, and so columns derived from woman will be more ornate [*ornate*]" (II, 375). This implies that Doric, being based on man, would in contrast be more perfect. In other words, to make a building *perfetto* would demand Doric and to make it *ornato* would demand Ionic and Corinthian. Not being interested in the whole problem of appropriateness, Francesco is not troubled by the inconsistency, which is similar to that which affected the theories of Alberti. But it is characteristic that his formulation has the clarity to force such an inconsistency out into the open at last; and it is noteworthy that, as we shall see, in the very years when he was writing the inconsistency came to the surface in practice, as archi-

tects made conscious choices whether to make a building either more ornate *or* more perfect.

Francesco did not mind in which direction the choice of order was made. He only insisted that the same order should be used throughout:

Although Doric and Ionic columns are less often used than Corinthian, nevertheless they can correctly be used, provided that Doric is not used inside and then Corinthian outside, or vice versa; but since a building is an artificial body resembling man in many respects, similar members should have similar measures and not different ones. And for the same reason I conclude that in a temple only one species of column should be used, although to many the reverse seems true, using the argument that the more grades and diverse forms of perfection are found in a work the more perfect it is, just as the theologians claim that the reason why many species of strange animals were created was to make the universe more perfect. But to this argument it is possible to reply easily that this is relevant in an accidental collection of different things, such as a city, which is more beautiful the more different forms of temples, houses, and other features it has; but in individual works where each part is either for decoration or functionally necessary, this argument has no place, since it could well be used to prove that man should have wings. (II, 397–98).

Francesco's statement on the relative frequency of the use of the orders is equally correct whether it rests on observation of ancient or modern practice, but in either case his reluctance to support the prevalence of Corinthian suggests that he is conscious of the winds of change and would prefer to see the simpler orders more extensively used. His insistence that only one order should be used in any one building is much more positive; although the idea of a whole building in a single order is found in both Vitruvius and Filarete, it is here stated as a principle for the first time and must be a reflection of Francesco's strong anthropomorphism. As a principle it also demonstrates his lack of interest in exploiting the rich range of Antique decorative forms.

He goes on to give two rules for the decoration of cornices; the first confirms his attitude to the building as an integrated unit, but the second offers a grudging qualification: "The first is that all the string courses and cornices of the temple, both inside and out, should be either more simple or the reverse. The second is that if one set should be more ornate it should be those on the inside rather than those on the outside" (II, 530). In the first he seems to dissociate himself once again from the whole question of how values can be expressed in ornament, while in the second it is clear that he is giving in to the habit of mind which had been established since Roman times.

Apart from these few observations Francesco di Giorgio never formulated the elaborate rules for architectural *decorum* which had absorbed Alberti and Filarete. He represents a different generation. Their task had been to show the superiority of Classical architecture over Gothic and at the same time to make expenditure on building, and on private building in particular, an attractive and moral activity. Their works had to be elaborately literary in order to be persuasive, and both modelled their works not only on Vitruvius but on Classical ethical writings. Francesco's position was different, as he sums up:

Although I am not unaware that some modern writers have written and commented on this art, yet in the end I find that they have touched but lightly on useful and difficult passages. Whence, although to some it appears that this art of architecture has been rediscovered in our days, and its principles, rules, and goals understood, it will be easy to recognize the multitude of errors and deficiencies which there are in all modern buildings. (II, 509)

Classical architecture has been rediscovered—or so people think. In fact the discipline as a whole, including writing on the subject, is still full of errors. Francesco saw himself as a corrector rather than as an innovator. The way to put the subject on a correct basis was to make it more scientific. To do this he turned to the greatest scientist of all, Aristotle, just as his predecessors had turned to the greatest ethical writers. He thus became the first scientific writer on architecture. The nature of his contribution can be seen in the way he used his guide. Unlike his predecessors, he took from his model neither form nor content. What he took was something less definable but more essential: method.

Yet among all his reductive methodical paragraphs there are two which suggest the possibility of a more creative approach than anything earlier. One is in the first version, when he is discussing the architect's need to understand music. This point had already been made by Vitruvius, but only for such tasks as tuning catapults. Francesco, on the other hand, says: "Music too appears necessary for the relationships and proportions of each building. And as music has its long and very long intervals, its breves and semibreves which correspond in their proportions, so too the same is necessary in a building. And when there is a dissonant note in music the whole tune is discordant, and the same happens in a building: it will be badly composed and discordant if all the elements do not correspond" (II, 37–38). Alberti had talked generally about musical harmony in buildings, but Francesco pushes the analogy between the two arts further. The second passage is in the second version, when he talks about how Callimachus invented the Corinthian capital, "just as sculptors and painters expand on natural reality, as has always been permitted both to them and to poets to make artificial things more elaborate" (II, 525). Although he does not actually say that architecture has the licence of poetry, he does imply that a respectable architectural form was created by something like poetic licence, and this brings architecture closer to poetry than it had ever been. Architecture as music and architecture as poetry are two exciting possibilities. Given Francesco's claims for the superiority of vision over hearing, there is every stimulus for the architect and writer on architecture to realize both possibilities, and both would indeed be taken up in the years around 1500.

XIII

Architects and theories in the later fifteenth century

◆

Alberti

THE *De re aedificatoria* was, as we saw, somewhat equivocal on the principles governing the application of the orders to individual buildings. The clash between the values of Ciceronian morality and those of contemporary society made it impossible to give whole-hearted backing to either. Still, the few precise recommendations which Alberti made reflect closely the contemporary practice according to which the richest orders were used for the most important parts of the most important buildings, and the same preferences are seen in the earliest works with which Alberti's name can be associated. Yet even in his acknowledgement of the superiority of the richer forms there are signs of uncertainty, with his earlier buildings giving precedence to Composite and his later ones to Corinthian. Composite, for example, are the capitals on the base of the horse monument in Ferrara on which he advised in 1443, and Composite too are the half-columns on the façade of S. Francesco at Rimini after 1450 (Fig. 95). Since in the latter structure the introduction of Composite represents a change from the Corinthian of the neighbouring Arch of Augustus, on which the design is based, the stress on the order must be emphatic. If so this stress can probably be related to Alberti's observation in the *De re aedificatoria* that Italic (his name for Composite) is the order to be preferred to all the others. The nationalism which affected the treatise, composed before 1452, also affected the buildings he was involved with at the same period. However, Alberti may already have started to have doubts about the merits of his preferred form. If he knew of Michelozzo's use of the orders in the Medici

palace he is likely to have worried about its possible secular associations, and this may be why he was at pains to introduce prominent cherub heads between the Composite volutes at S. Francesco.[1] This, though, was apparently not enough to sanctify them, and in all his subsequent religious buildings he passes over his preferred Italic in favour of Corinthian, as if acknowledging that Michelozzo's reading of Tuscan Romanesque was better than his. His façade for S. Maria Novella, the chapel and the Holy Sepulchre reconstruction in S. Pancrazio (Fig. 97)—all for Giovanni Rucellai— S. Sebastiano and S. Andrea at Mantua and the choir of Ss. Annunziata at Florence—all for Lodovico Gonzaga—are Corinthian throughout. The fact that Alberti alluded to the superiority of Italic only once in his treatise already suggests a lack of conviction in the matter, and his practice bears this out. The same lack of conviction is indicated by his use of the column carrying an entablature, described in the treatise as his preferred form for religious structures, only once in such a context, in the chapel in S. Pancrazio.

There is, indeed, only one major building attributed to Alberti in which we find a more self-conscious use of the orders. This is the Palazzo Rucellai, probably of the late 1450s (Fig. 96).[2] Alberti certainly designed other works for the family, and, although some doubt has been cast on his role here and the courtyard can hardly be his, the correspondence between the palace façade and his treatise makes it hard to reject the attribution, which has been traditional since Vasari. The most explicitly Albertian feature is (as Wittkower saw) the insertion of a horizontal entablature above the columns dividing the *bifora* windows.[3] This avoids the error of having a column directly supporting an arch, as had

95. Alberti: S. Francesco, Rimini, after 1450

happened on the windows of the Palazzo Medici. The main doors also correspond to Alberti's treatise, being (as Heydenreich noted) identical with his Ionic type.[4] They thus conform to the specific recommendation in the treatise of Ionic doors for principal entrances.[5] The most remarkable feature of the façade is the pilaster articulation which is applied to all three floors, and within this new scheme there is a further innovation, the simple capital type on the ground floor. With its square abacus, echinus, and low vertical element be-low, it invites identification with the Doric order, which is clearly understood in the *De re aedificatoria*. Since this is the first appearance of something like true Doric, its introduction requires an explanation. The two floors above both have a form of Corinthian, the capital usually associated with high status, and when it is remembered that Alberti recommended Doric for the least important doors, such as those of *cellae* or store-rooms,[6] and describes it as "more suitable for work,"[7] it is easy to see the simple form as having a low-status

183

96. Alberti: Palazzo Rucellai, Florence, 1450s

reference here. The ground floors of fifteenth-century palaces were usually reserved for service and storage facilities, while the family itself occupied the upper floors; so the two orders could be seen as aptly chosen to express this difference of function. Alberti is also at pains to differentiate even between the two upper floors. The Corinthian capitals of the first floor have finely carved leaves while those on the second are smooth and plain. The first floor contained the main reception rooms of the family and carried their emblem in its frieze and their crest between the windows. The top floor was occupied by less important family rooms and also those of the servants. To emphasize the difference in status between the two floors even further, Alberti has used Composite capitals on the first-floor windows but reverted to a simple Doric form for those above. The top floor is thus as assertively differentiated from the first by its window columns as they both are from the ground floor by the main pilaster order. By using the two sets of forms together Alberti has been able considerably to extend Michelozzo's principle of differentiation. He has also gone beyond anything expressed in his treatise.

Bernardo Rossellino at Pienza

The other name which has been connected with the Palazzo Rucellai is that of Bernardo Rossellino. Trained under Michelozzo in Florence, and then architect to Nicholas V in Rome at the time when Alberti presented his treatise to the pope, he had the right background to produce the mixture of Michelozzian and Albertian features which the palace embodies. Possibly he worked as executant architect, with Alberti as adviser on the façade. Such a relationship may already have existed at the papal *curia*. Certainly the Palazzo Piccolomini at Pienza 1461–64, indubitably by him, is so similar to the Florentine palace that the connection between the two buildings must be very close.

The Palazzo Piccolomini is only one of a whole group of structures round the town square of Pienza which were erected by Rossellino for Pius II when the latter rebuilt his birthplace, Corsignano, and renamed it during his papacy from 1458 to 1464 (Figs. 98–100). The palace, destined to house the pope's family and its heirs, represents an application of the Rucellai palace façade to a rectangular block around a courtyard, with

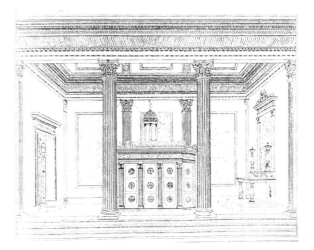

97. Alberti: Rucellai Chapel, S. Pancrazio, Florence, c.1467 (after Seroux d'Agincourt)

the addition of a three-storey loggia over the garden giving views to the distant hills (Fig. 100). There are thus three series of orders—one on the three street façades, one in the court, and one on the rear—and for the first time all are related in a complex articulation using Composite, Corinthian, Ionic, and Doric. The main façade corresponds, as has been said, to the Palazzo Rucellai, with three orders of pilasters, Doric below, a rich Corinthian above, and a simpler Corinthian above that. There are, however, significant changes. One is that the Doric pilasters are now covered with the same channelled masonry as the rest of the façade, a feature which is so unusual as to be difficult to interpret. The capitals of these pilasters are also lower and simpler, with no egg-and-dart moulding or fluting, as if to increase the difference of status with the upper orders. The court relates to Michelozzo's in the Palazzo Medici, though again with modifications. The ground floor has a rich Composite arcade as in the Palazzo Medici, but the colonnade at the top has a mixture of a sub-Corinthian and Ionic forms. The rear façade has a completely new arrangement. The lowest loggia is Corinthian, the middle sub-Corinthian with down-turned leaves, and the top simple Doric, in a regularly declining series which roughly inverts that of the main façade. The lowest loggia, being Corinthian, is evidently of slightly lower status than the main cortile, as is appropriate to the garden which might be used for

98. Pienza, Piazza, early 1460s

nade," the second has an "elaborately painted wooden ceiling" and is "a very pleasant place to sit in winter," and the third is similar to the second "but less elaborate in its coffering."[8]

The articulation of the building in terms of the orders is highly elaborate. The street façade, the court, and the garden loggias all have to be read separately. The street façade gives the passer-by or approaching visitor a general classification of the status of the three floors. The court and garden loggias, on the other hand, are to be read by the visitor after he has entered and as he moves from area to area. The specific function of individual spaces now overrides the general characterization of the floors. Thus, although the whole ground floor, with its storage and service rooms, is regarded as Doric at the bottom of the scale, the Composite court, as the principal reception area, is still the most magnificent public space, and the Corinthian garden loggia is only marginally less important. The orders are varied in a way which can be seen to relate to the varying status of the different environments as described by Pius in his *Commentaries*. Pius himself notes the "appropriate" use of capitals and bases on the exterior of the palace, and he may have particularly encouraged Rossellino to use capitals carefully and appropriately throughout.[9] The relative status of the different spaces could be read from their capitals, just as the status of a person could be read from his clothes and the importance of a religious ceremony judged from the opulence of the vestments worn for its performance. In earlier buildings we have seen horizontal and vertical articulations working separately, but never with the three-dimensional integration found here.

The use of the orders to articulate the building in three dimensions reflects the developing capacity of Renaissance architects to think of buildings not just in terms of two-dimensional elevations or groundplans. This is seen not only in the handling of solids such as palaces and churches but also in the control of open spaces such as piazzas. The best example of this is the Piazza of Pienza itself, which is virtually completely surrounded by buildings designed by Rossellino. Its coherent treatment as an ensemble is manifest first in the placing of the buildings. The square is dominated by the cathedral to the east. Opposite stands the Palazzo Communale. On the other two sides, which are not parallel, the palace of the Piccolomini and of the bishop

receptions but of a less formal kind than those in the courtyard. The middle loggia on the main living floor would be slightly lower in status again, as the private retreat of the most important members of the family, while the top—Doric—loggia would naturally be the resort of the least important members and even of servants. Pius' own description of the three loggias clearly brings out their relative importance. The lowest has "high and splendid vaulting, a most delightful prome-

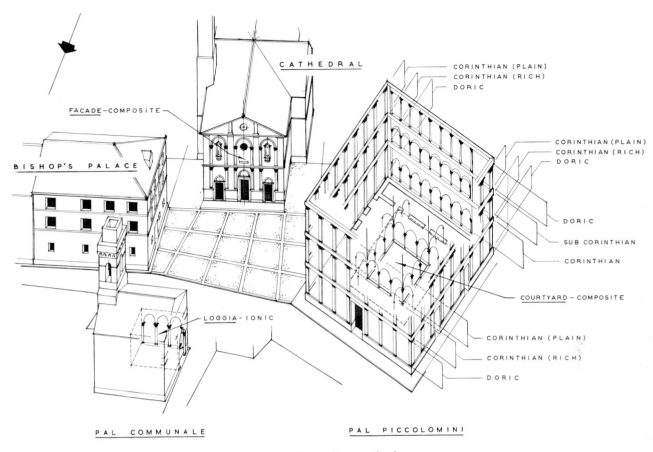

CATHEDRAL

FAÇADE-COMPOSITE

BISHOP'S PALACE

CORINTHIAN (PLAIN)
CORINTHIAN (RICH)
DORIC

CORINTHIAN (PLAIN)
CORINTHIAN (RICH)
DORIC

DORIC
SUB CORINTHIAN
CORINTHIAN

COURTYARD - COMPOSITE

LOGGIA - IONIC

CORINTHIAN (PLAIN)
CORINTHIAN (RICH)
DORIC

PAL COMMUNALE

PAL PICCOLOMINI

99. Pienza, Piazza: diagram of orders

face each other. The buildings of the chief religious and secular institutions of the town thus stand at either end of the main axis, with the church occupying the broad base of the trapezium. The residences of the chief secular and spiritual individuals then oppose each other on the minor axis formed by the trapezium's sloping sides. The relations between spiritual and secular, institution and individual, thus create in the square a microcosmic unity. Moreover, the articulation of these relationships depends not just on the siting of the buildings but on their architectural decoration. This is manifest first in the choice of materials. The church façade is entirely in light travertine, which is also found in decreasing quantities in the Palazzo Communale and the Palazzo Piccolomini. The amount of ordinary dark

tufa, on the other hand, increases steadily from the Palazzo Communale and Palazzo Piccolomini to the bishop's residence, where it is used almost exclusively. This differentiation of status is further articulated by the use of the orders. The two institutional buildings both have full columns on their façades, but while the church has many, with Composite capitals, the Palazzo Communale has but three, and Ionic ones at that. The two residential palaces are both on an absolutely lower plane, since neither has full columns; but while the Palazzo Piccolomini has Doric and Corinthian pilasters, the bishop's palace has no columnar forms at all. The use of the columnar forms thus cleverly shows that the Piccolomini palace is inferior to the Palazzo Communale in one sense and superior to it in another. Public comes

100. Bernardo Rossellino: Palazzo Piccolomini,
Pienza, early 1460s

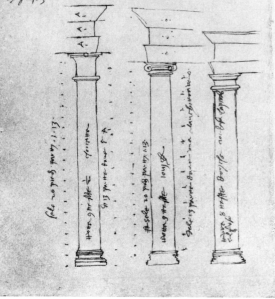

101. Giuliano da Sangallo: three orders,
Cod. Senese s.IV 8, fol. 31ᵛ

before private, but the aristocracy comes before the ordinary citizen. The columnar forms also show clearly,
as does the use of materials, that while religious comes
before secular in the world of institutions, still, as an
individual, the prince comes before the prelate. The relationship between the bishop's and the Piccolomini
palace here is similar to that between the episcopal and
ducal palaces in Filarete's Sforzinda. There is indeed a
close similarity of spirit not only between the ideas of
Pius' Pienza and of the Sforzas' contemporary Sforzinda, but between the approaches of Rossellino and of
Filarete to the problem of expressing the structure of
society through the layout and decoration of different

buildings. Both take the appropriate use of the orders
farther than it had been taken before. They surpass Alberti's contribution both in theory and in practice as
easily as Michelozzo did that of Brunelleschi.

Nor should we think of Rossellino simply as a fol-
lower of Alberti. The degree of his independence is evident in one of the most important aspects of the architecture of Pienza, the use of the arch as a positive
emblem of high status. This is apparent in the use of an
arch moulding only over the rectangular *main* door of
the Palazzo Piccolomini, which is thus distinguished
from the minor entrances on the piazza. It is most striking in the church façade, where the triple arch motif

102. Giuliano da Sangallo: Villa Medici, Poggio a Cajano, 1480s

and the use of arch mouldings over both major and minor doors give the façade much of the massive energy which distinguishes it from the palace with its grid of thin entablatures. It even influences the design of the palace's garden loggia. The Corinthian ground floor has full rounded arches, the Doric top floor has a horizontal entablature, and the sub-Corinthian middle floor has an unusual flat arch-form intermediate between the two. The variation relates in part to the diminishing height of the storeys, but that factor could have been handled in other ways. The contradiction of Alberti's rule could not be more abrupt. In his treatise he was insistent on the superiority of the horizontal en-

tablature over the arch, and he employed the horizontal entablature, though only in relief form, on all his church façades. The reason for Rossellino's preference for the arch will emerge in the next chapter, when we examine the Duomo's interior.

Giuliano da Sangallo

The use of the orders in the mid-fifteenth century generally follows principles which derive, through Michelozzo, from Tuscan Romanesque buildings. There were no ancient Roman buildings which could have taught them how to use Composite, Corinthian,

103. Giuliano da Sangallo: S. Maria delle
Carceri, Prato, after 1484: exterior

104. S. Maria delle Carceri, Prato: interior

and Ionic as they did, to differentiate status. Equally there were no Roman monuments known to them which could have taught them normally to put the richest order lowest in a vertical series as they did, following models such as the Florence Baptistery. There are thus at first no buildings which follow the familiar Classical usage of the Theatre of Marcellus (Ionic above Doric) and the Colosseum (Corinthian above Ionic above Doric)—none, that is, until those of Giuliano da Sangallo. The reason for the sudden change must be connected with the fact that he is also the first architect whom we know to have devoted much time and effort to making a collection of accurate drawings of the monuments of Rome. One of the fruits of this effort, begun during his stay in Rome from 1465 to 1472, was the first correct illustration of the three columnar forms (Fig. 101). It is even possible, as we suggested earlier, that both the visit to Rome and the subsequent modification of contemporary usage reflect a conscious programme to improve Tuscan style by making it more Classical, following the recommendation of Cristoforo Landino.[10] Landino was the teacher of Lorenzo de' Medici, who was responsible for Sangallo's appointment at one of the buildings where the new usage appears, S. Maria delle Carceri at Prato (Figs. 103 and 104),[11] and who was an associate of the patron of the other, Bartolomeo Scala. It is certainly easy to see the first building with the new usage, Scala's suburban villa at Florence (1470s), with its grand Roman-style reliefs illustrating a Latin poem written by its owner, as a consciously Latinizing monument.[12]

It is worth noting that although the relationship of superposition is new and contrasts with earlier practice, the introduction of Doric and Ionic in a villa context can be understood in terms of contemporary values, as can the subsequent similar combination of Ionic full columns above simple square piers at Lorenzo's own villa at Poggio a Cajano (1480s), also by Giuliano (Fig. 102).[13] Michelozzo had already used Ionic on the first floor of the Medici villa at Carreggi, and piers in the Medici villa at Fiesole, thus firmly associating simpler forms with the simple villa life, perhaps by analogy with the use of the simple Ionic in monasteries. Certainly the general conformity of the choice of Doric and Ionic in these buildings to contemporary taste is shown in the recurrence of Doric and Ionic in a series of major villas of the 1480s and 1490s. Doric forms were used both on the grand villa of Poggio Reale at Naples, begun by Giuliano da Majano in 1487, and on the Belvedere villa of Innocent VIII in Rome, after 1484. Ionic columns are found in the so-called Villa of Bessarion on the Via Appia. Just as this wave of villas reflects a new interest in simple country living as admired by the ancient Romans, so the choice of the simpler architectural forms for their decoration creates a suitable environment for the moderation and restraint associated with such a life in the writings of Horace and others. In fact, of course, these villas were often lavishly decorated and were the settings for extravagant entertainments; so the use of Doric and Ionic for their architecture represents the beginning of a significant shift from the use of the orders as a simple scale for expressing relative importance. Instead one can talk for the first time of the simpler orders being used to indicate not low social status but high moral values. The possibilities which Alberti had hinted at in theory are at last affecting architectural practice.

Francesco di Giorgio

As Millon has shown, the church of S. Maria del Calcinaio, which Francesco designed for Cortona in 1485, is a rare example of a building which follows the written theory of its architect, being a close approximation to the church which is laid out according to the proportions of the human body as illustrated by Francesco in his treatise (Fig. 105).[14] There is also a further important correspondence between the building and the text. Francesco strongly disagreed with those who argued that a building should use all the orders, by analogy with the universe which God had filled with many animals to increase its perfection. For him a building, like an animal, should have a uniformity in all its members.[15] One of the most remarkable features of S. Maria del Calcinaio is that it is the first building to use the same forms for all its parts, with an identical scheme of Corinthian-type pilaster and pedimented windows

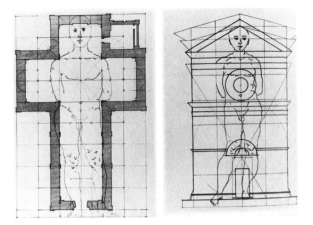

105. Francesco di Giorgio: plan and elevation of S. Maria del Calcinaio (1485) superimposed on his drawings of the church-man assimilation (after Millon)

both inside and out and from façade to sanctuary. The elevation thus assimilated the building to a single man just as does the plan.

Since Francesco's other buildings do not have this property of coherence, it is tempting to see it as having a deliberately polemical intention. Sangallo's church of S. Maria delle Carceri (Figs. 103 and 104), also commemorating a miracle of the Virgin, was being designed at the same moment with the principle of variety pushed to its utmost. For there not only was the wall articulation Doric and Ionic on the exterior and Corinthian on the interior, but also the inner pilasters were fluted and the outer ones not. Moreover, the main altar contrasted with the wall articulation in using full columns with Composite capitals. There was a general competition among cities throughout Italy in the construction of churches dedicated to the Virgin, and these two would naturally have invited comparison. Francesco may have intended his church to be a statement as explicit as his later written remarks would be. Indeed, both designers may have seen themselves as operating in a culture in which for the first time there were several conflicting theories to choose from. The appearance of the printed Alberti in 1485 and Vitruvius in 1486, just as the final decisions were being taken for both buildings, must have brought a new intensity to the discussion of architectural theory.

XIV

A new Christian architecture

◆

WITH GIULIANO de Sangallo and his combination for the first time of Classical forms with Classical usage, Renaissance architecture comes closer than ever to the apparent imitation of Antiquity, and, whatever positive association such an imitation may have had in the secular world, for a true Christian the associations could only be negative. In paintings by contemporaries, such as Botticelli's *Adoration* in the Uffizi, Classical architecture is emblematic of all that Christ came to sweep away. The background to this situation has already been reviewed in Chapter IX, where it was pointed out how the increasingly Antique forms of later fifteenth-century architecture brought forth a series of defensive inscriptions on palaces and a revival of Gothic ornament as an antidote in churches. But these were at best palliatives. What was necessary was a moral purification of the ancient forms themselves. Alberti had already hinted in the *De re aedificatoria* at how this might be done, implying that the strong and simple forms of Doric could be seen as expressing the ancient virtue of *gravitas*, sober dignity; but the pressure of contemporary social values prevented him, as we saw, from following this idea up. For the popes, however, the Christian moral pressures were stronger and the need to conform to worldly standards less predominant. Not surprisingly, then, it was they who faced up to and dealt with the problem.

Nicholas V (1447–55)

The first pope to try to develop a genuinely Christian architecture in a Renaissance context was Nicholas V. Firmly established as sole claimant to the title, he was also the first since the return from Avignon to celebrate a jubilee in Rome, in 1450.[1] As a first step to giving the Church a new material face he planned to rebuild not only the Vatican but the old church of St Peter's itself. (Fig. 106). The small beginning which he made in reconstructing the east end of St Peter's, with an architecture of massive walls and vaults, was later swept away in the grander reconstruction of the sixteenth century, but we can learn much of how the new church was viewed from Giannozzo Manetti's elaborate biography of the pope.[2] The most important point is that Manetti is at pains to assert that the new works should be related not to the Roman but to the Old Testament Jewish tradition, while making it equally explicit that they are a clear advance on the latter. The only two structures from the past which are fit to be compared with those of Nicholas are the Temple and palace of Solomon.[3] Indeed, he consistently shows that Solomon has been surpassed by Nicholas. If Hiram, who was only a bronzeworker, is highly praised in the Bible, "how much greater praise must we lavish and bestow on our Nicholas, who set Bernardo Rossellino to superintend each group of workers."[4] If Nicholas had completed his scheme "of a divine temple and a royal palace, he would have equalled Solomon with an ever greater magnificence or rather would have reached ever greater heights."[5] To prove his point he quotes the biblical descriptions of Solomon's buildings and compares them detail by detail with his own account of Nicholas' project.

He first compares church and Temple. The church enormously exceeds the Temple in its dimensions. Its windows are not splayed (*obliquus*) but pierce the wall at right angles (*transversus*), and they are also circular in shape.[6] There are three vestibules instead of one portico, and instead of three trabeated storeys there are a multitude of arches in the seven *cruces* (probably meaning the aisles and transepts) and a vault above.[7] Whether in terms of architectural elements (as in the preference for the arch over the beam), of geometrical perfection (as in the contrast between splayed and square-set windows), or in simple numerical terms (as in the dimensions), the church emerges as the more impressive building. The comparison of the two palaces is developed in the same vein.[8] Large stones are superior to small ones, and blocks formed to the geometrical right-angle are to be admired more than those only finished with an adze. A simple door is also surpassed by one which is flanked by two towers and covered with an arch. Three simple rooms, one above the other, are more than matched by three superimposed arcades of three arches each. A lead roof is superior to cedar coffering.

Why should Nicholas and his architect have taken such trouble to surpass the buildings of Solomon? The reason emerges in the final sentence. Nicholas' plan surpasses that of Solomon in the same way that the "new religion of Christ" surpasses the "old law."[9] His buildings represent the religion of the New Testament just as Solomon's do that of the Old. As Solomon's Temple/palace complex was approved by God to be His own residence, chosen by Him as a mark of His recognition of Solomon's authority, it was clearly an appropriate model for Nicholas as it had been for Charlemagne. Equally, the identification of the Vatican complex with the "new religion of Christ" as opposed to that of the Old Testament made it just as appropriate that the Jewish model should be surpassed there. Manetti does not explain the precise need for the new buildings to match the "new religion," but there can be little doubt that his thinking echoes Nicholas' ambitions to establish the position of the pope as head of the Church in a more permanent and fundamental sense than had been done previously. Christ had said "Thou art Peter [Petrus] and upon this rock [petram] I will build My Church" (Matthew 16, 18–19). This text had always given a special significance to Rome's possession of Peter's body. Taken literally, it meant that the new Church of Christ, as opposed to the Temple of the old Law, could only be erected over Peter's tomb. Nicholas' decision to move the chief papal residence from the Lateran, where it had always been, to the Vatican was a calculated step.[10] It reflected his conviction that it was less important now to appear as successor to the Roman emperors, who had previously occupied the Lateran, than as the head of the new Church

founded over Saint Peter's body. The grandiose reconstruction of the old basilica, whose flimsy walls and wooden roofs recalled the Old Testament structures, emphasized the power of the *nova religio*, and the introduction of features from Solomon's palace into the residence itself emphasized the inheritance of a Salomonic authority.

Manetti defines a new Christian architecture whose arches, vaults, large square stones, and square-cut windows are all intended to express the inauguration of a new era. Although to us these features may all be Roman in character, Manetti avoids this suggestion, implying only that they are an improvement on Salomonic forms and on Old St Peter's itself. In fact they had already been anticipated in building work under Eugenius IV (1431–47). The columns of S. Giovanni in Laterano had at that time been replaced by great square piers,[11] and the little church of S. Onofrio had been built with thick walls supporting groined vaulting.[12] Both Eugenius and Nicholas—members of a *curia* only lately returned from France, and themselves fresh from attending councils in the North—probably had Romanesque and Gothic models as much in mind as Roman when creating the new style. Old St Peter's with its flimsy colonnades, horizontal entablature, and wooden roof would have compared as unfavourably with the great churches north of the Alps as with the ruins of the Eternal City. Nothing would give the new architecture a greater authority than for it to be seen as embodying the best qualities of both Medieval and ancient styles. Thus the large stones and thick walls are essentially Roman, while the idea of a long choir with a polygonal apse and external buttresses is decisively Gothic. No one could have regarded Nicholas' building as emphatically Classical, and so as pagan. They were reconstructions of Solomon's divinely approved Temple and palace, in a style whose permanence and universality would match the permanence and universality of Christ's victory.

Pius II (1458–64)

Pius II's architect at Pienza was the same Bernardo Rossellino who had worked for Nicholas, and we can now see why, in contradiction to Alberti, he accorded such importance to the arch over the architrave. The cathedral recalls directly the new architecture of the re-

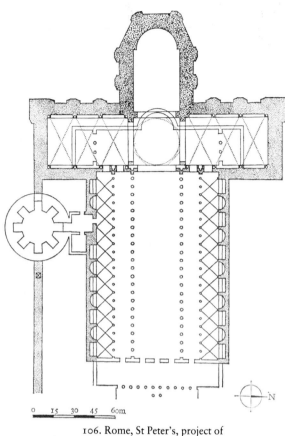

106. Rome, St Peter's, project of
Nicholas V (after Urban)

amount of tracery, are exactly intermediate between the plain and untraceried windows of the palace and the pointed and elaborately traceried windows at the church's east end. The use of such intermediate forms to indicate the nave's participation in both the spiritual and the secular world is not new.

The dichotomy involved in Pius' decision to use the Classical style—the most authoritative in worldly terms—on the worldly façade and the Gothic—the most authoritative in spiritual terms—in the holy interior also affects his use of the orders. While the columns of the façade are the richest of those around the piazza, marking the church out as the most important building in the terms of the world, those used on the interior revert to the bottom of the same scale. With their square abacus, egg-and-dart echinus, and fluted lower section, the capitals correspond exactly to those of the Doric pilasters at the bottom of the Palazzo Rucellai. They are thus of the same general order as those on the basement of the Palazzo Piccolomini itself. The shafts also have simple bases with a single torus moulding, as specified by Vitruvius for Tuscan and by Alberti for Doric. Since there is no possibility that the order here expresses lowness of status, the conclusion is unavoidable that it has the other available reference implied by Alberti, that of *gravitas*, sober moral excellence. In other words, the conflict between social and moral values which was embodied in Alberti's *De re aedificatoria* is equally apparent at Pienza; but here the conflict is resolved. In the piazza social values are predominant, in the church moral ones. The only explicit hint that the Doric inside the church is to be read differently from that outside the palace is the use of the more elaborate capital with flutes and egg-and-dart in the ecclesiastical context. The order is thus able to carry the absolute moral overtones of Doric, while distancing itself by its refinement from the socially inferior elements of the palace.

The logic behind Rossellino's use of the orders here should not make us take it for granted. It has to be remembered that the use of Doric on the interior of the church clashes not only with the buildings outside but with every other contemporary building and can only have been forced upon Rossellino by exceptional pressures. In view of all that has been said earlier, it is clear that these pressures must have been those of conventional contemporary Christianity, which viewed Clas-

built St Peter's (Figs. 98, 99, and 106). Besides being a vaulted, aisled structure with a polygonal apse, it combines Classical and Gothic features throughout in the most striking way. Pius himself tells how the façade recalls an "ancient temple" and the interior is modelled on a "German" church, and a closer study shows that the opposition implicit in these two terms is carefully exploited.[13] The façade does indeed conform to Classical values, having the Composite columns which mark its relative status in worldly terms in the context of the secular piazza. The interior, on the other hand, declares the primacy of Christian spiritual values, above all in the great Gothic tracery windows, which dominate the holiest area around the high altar. Indeed it is possible to demonstrate how self-conscious this contrast was by looking at the windows in the nave (Fig. 107). These, with their round heads and limited

107. Pienza, section of cathedral and piazza (after Cataldi et al.)

sical forms as being fundamentally tainted by paganism. Pius II showed his alertness to these pressures not
only by using Doric as an emblem of Christian morality
and by introducing prominent Gothic features, but also
by leaving the columns and walls a puritanical white
and laying a curse on anyone who changed them. As
pope, he apparently felt that he needed to observe
higher standards than his contemporaries, at least as
far as church design was concerned—even if this meant
using a form which was liable to a negative interpretation in terms of social status. Possibly Pius was conscious of the vainglorious arrogance of his extravagant
rebuilding and renaming of his home town and was
anxious to compensate for it. His explicit criticism of
the Tempio Malatestiano at Rimini as "so full of pagan
images that it seems less a Christian shrine than a temple of pagan devil-worshippers" shows that he was
well aware of the dangers associated with the use of the
Classical style.[14]

Sixtus IV (1471–84)

When Francesco della Rovere, head of the Franciscan order, was elected pope as Sixtus IV, there was still
little agreement on the precise character of an appropriately Christian architecture. Classical forms carried
the aura of world domination but lacked spiritual associations. Gothic had spiritual associations but carried little secular authority. Corinthian was magnificent but immoral. Doric was moral but lacked worldly
dignity. In the circumstances it is not surprising that
Sixtus seems only slowly to have arrived at a more de-
finitive formulation. An early church, S. Maria del Popolo, begun in 1472 in order to be ready to impress the
pilgrims arriving for the Jubilee in 1475, is a careful
compromise. To the thousands of pilgrims who found
it the first church they met as they streamed into the
city from the north, it could be all things to all men. Its
compound piers and its basilica plan both derived from

109. Ospedale di S. Spirito, Rome, 1474–82

the Gothic S. Maria sopra Minerva. Its vaults and mouldings and the loosely Corinthian capitals of both the façade and the interior, might evoke either an Antique or a Romanesque past. In S. Maria della Pace, dedicated by the pope in gratitude for the defeat of the Pazzi conspiracy in 1478, Corinthian is still the major order, being used for the octagon at the east end. Doric pilasters do, however, have an important role, being used both on the exterior and, for the first time, on the interior of the nave. The contrast in the orders is similar to that between Corinthian and Ionic in Michelozzo's Chapel of the Novitiate at S. Croce, but the use of Doric in such an important monument implies a new acknowledgement of its acceptability. In S. Agostino

nearby, built by Cardinal d'Estouteville in 1479–83, Doric seems even to tip the scale against the more elaborate forms (Fig. 108). With its narrow nave and aisles and its unusually high vault carried on a system of alternating piers, it is even more Medieval than S. Maria del Popolo, perhaps reflecting the Gothic tastes of its French patron. But there is little Gothic about its wall articulation. The nave arcade is carried on simple square piers, and the crossing arches also rise from rectangular pier forms with low moulded capitals. These low capitals with their unusual rosettes correspond closely to those on the Doric pilasters of the Basilica Aemilia, which were drawn by Giuliano de Sangallo about the same time. The main supports of the church

108 (at left). S. Agostino, Rome, interior, 1479–83

110. Perugino: *Charge to Peter*, 1480s, Sistine Chapel, Rome

are thus more or less Doric, as at Pienza, but an even more austere rectangular form. Corinthian is, however, still used on the façade, and, in an unusual arrangement, small Composite half-columns with short Corinthian pilasters above are attached to every other pier along the nave. Outside, as at Pienza, the even more temple-like façade competed on a worldly scale with the other buildings in the city. Inside, although there was just enough in the way of half-columns and Composite capitals to make the church's status apparent, its essential character, especially at the east end, was of an unparalleled Doric sobriety. The contrast between the worldly values of the exterior and the spiritual ones of the interior is subtly expressed also in the disparity between their relative proportions. The façade, with its steps, is broader than anything yet seen. The interior,

is exceptional in its Gothic loftiness. Perhaps the new Christian simplicity of the interior is an emblem of a late repentance by d'Estouteville, whom Pius II had called "fat" and a "devotee of luxury."[15] But almost certainly the design was also intended as one of the first monuments in the programme of Christian architectural reform introduced by Sixtus. D'Estouteville was a chief instrument of papal policy in the replanning of Rome, issuing an important edict on the subject in January 1480.[16] In his church he sought to work through example.

S. Agostino, however, being one of a hundred churches scattered through the eternal city, could not invite identification with the Church in the same way as the buildings in the Vatican and the Borgo which Sixtus himself erected in fulfillment of Nicholas' gen-

111. Botticelli: *Temptation of Christ*, 1480s, Sistine Chapel, Rome

eral plan. The grandest of these were the Sistine Chapel, already anticipated by Nicholas, and the Ospedale di S. Spirito, which evoked the spirit if not the letter of Nicholas' porticoed streets running down to the Tiber (Fig. 109). Both structures represent further steps in the Christianization of Classical architecture. In the Ospedale not only is the whole edifice, with its two long wards meeting in a domed chapel, built almost entirely of simple brick, but it also uses Gothic windows and Doric pilasters throughout, both on the façade and on the interior of the chapel's octagon. The combination of traceried Gothic windows and Doric pilasters in the chapel interior, a contrast with the octagon of S. Maria della Pace only a mile away, which still used Corinthian, directly takes up the two essential features of Pius' church at Pienza. Only here there is no concession at all to contemporary worldly values, with the austere brickwork and the use of Doric throughout on portal, portico, and upper elevation all contributing to a sober impression.

It might be thought that this sobriety was partly a reflection of the building's function, were it not for the even greater simplicity of the massive brick walls of the pope's great new chapel. Here too the windows had Gothic tracery, and, although Corinthian pilasters have a decorative role inside, the paintings they frame make it clear that Sixtus was anxious to associate himself with simplicity in general and Doric forms in particular.[17] The clearest statement of Sixtus' programme is found in the inscriptions on the two triumphal arches in the background of Perugino's *Charge to Peter*, where Peter, the first pope, receives the keys of authority from Christ (Fig. 110). The inscription reads IMMENSUM SALOMO TEMPLUM TU HOC QUARTE SACRASTI SIXTE OPIBUS DISPAR RELIGIONE PRIOR: "You, Sixtus IV, have dedicated this temple, unequal to Solomon in your wealth but superior to him in your religion." Like Nicholas, Sixtus compares himself with Solomon. The chapel is in some sense a new Temple, and indeed Battisti has shown that its proportions of $1 \times 1\frac{1}{2} \times 3$ are copied precisely from Solomon's building. One main difference, though, is that the new structure has massive brick walls and a heavy vault, and in this it takes up exactly the distinction first exploited by Nicholas. As with Nicholas, the new style explicitly represents the superior new religion. But the other main difference between Solomon and Sixtus, that of wealth, is new. Sixtus' pride in the poverty of his structure goes beyond the virtuous restraint of Pius. Perhaps it has its source in his Franciscan background, for Sixtus had been a reformist head of that order. Its implication for architectural taste is evident from the fresco. The inscriptions being written on two extravagant marble arches resembling the Arch of Constantine, are emblems of Roman ostentation. Yet the setting as a whole represents the Temple area at Jerusalem as it then was, with an octagonal structure in the centre clearly based on the Dome of the Rock, at the time commonly identified with Solomon's Temple.[18] The extravagant marble decoration of the Temple itself matches that of the two Roman arches, and it is significant that all three monuments have Corinthian free-standing columns as the most striking symbol of opulent display. There could not be a more striking contrast between them and the plain brick exterior of the Sistine Chapel.

The message of Sixtus' architecture is stated even more precisely in the *Temptation* fresco by Botticelli (Fig. 111), for the Temple on which Christ stands—the Temple which he promised to rebuild—is represented by the neighbouring Ospedale. Since this fresco with its symmetrical architecture is the central one of a group of three at the altar end of the chapel, just as the *Charge to Peter* is the central one of a group of three near the entrance, it is likely that the Ospedale is seen as the New Temple near the altar, replacing the Old outside the screen. It is a building virtuous not only in its function, the care of the sick, but above all in its architecture. It may seem strange that Sixtus used the Ospedale rather than St Peter's to represent the New Temple. But he had pointedly stopped work on the new church, as

if conscious that Christ wished money to be spent rather on the care of the poor and weak than on building. He had also required that the façade and orientation of the new hospital recall the church nearby, so that it might be thought of as in a sense its successor.

There are, finally, two paintings of a more personal kind in which Sixtus' architectural tastes are expressed. One is Melozzo da Forlì's great work showing Platina being appointed as librarian at the Vatican.[19] Sixtus IV is seen seated in a room flanked by massive square piers which, although elaborately decorated, are fundamentally simple and strong in contrast to the single Corinthian column in the background. It is the piers which are identified with Sixtus, the first pair being covered with a riotous ornament of oak-leaves (*rovere* = oak); if our explanation of S. Agostino was correct, the single Corinthian column is there just to remove any doubts the viewer might have about the pope's status and authority. Certainly when Sixtus IV, or perhaps his nephew Cardinal Giuliano della Rovere, commissioned an altarpiece for the family chapel in Savona Cathedral his fundamental contempt for the Corinthian column and all it represented is clearly shown. The two donors kneel either side of the central *Adoration* with behind them an extravagant marble colonnade whose rich capitals and broken arches lie in ruins on the ground (Fig. 112).[20] The artist Giovanni Mazone must surely, like Perugino and Botticelli, have received specific instructions on how architecture should be used to express the della Roveres' values. Sixtus still found it necessary to use Corinthian columns in some real buildings, but in a painting he could expose them to moral scorn.

Sixtus' nephews

As pope, Sixtus had to keep up institutional pretensions of magnificence. His family, however, were bolder in putting his principles into practice, conducting what was almost an architectural crusade. The first building which can be associated, if indirectly, with one of his nephews and which ambitiously asserts the family's tastes is a surprising one, the cathedral at Urbino. This church, begun by Francesco di Giorgio before the death of Duke Federigo in 1482, has been drastically reconstructed since, but the original character of its interior is recorded in an eighteenth-century drawing. For a great church associated with one of the richest princes of Italy and built next door to his magnificent palace, the building seems to have been of a staggering simplicity. With walls bare but for two entablature mouldings, and with a plain barrel vault, the only articulation was a row of tall square piers carrying the arches separating nave and aisles. The capitals of these piers consisted of thin mouldings echoing the entablature along the walls. Although not strictly Doric, the plain piers most closely recall the wall piers of S. Agostino of the same date, and there can be little doubt that the exceptional character of the whole reflects the same reformist intentions. It may seem odd that such a remote structure should be used for these demonstration purposes, but it should be remembered that Pius' cathedral at isolated Pienza was also the very first church to introduce a consciously austere Classical mode. There were, besides, particular reasons why Federigo should have felt the winds of change blowing from Rome. He was, like the pope, directly identified with the Church, being its Captain General. He was also directly linked to Sixtus, having received from him the title of duke in 1472 and having betrothed his daughter to the pope's nephew, Giovanni della Rovere, in the same year. His cathedral was thus an appropriate structure in which to illustrate the pope's new approach to church architecture. Francesco di Giorgio's response to the commission is decidedly different from that of the builder of S. Agostino, but reveals the same interest in the use of the plain rectangular pier and arch. There must indeed be a direct connection between the two churches, since the resemblance in plan is considerable, especially in the use of a five-bay nave supported on piers with corresponding apsed chapels in the aisles. Without a firmer date for Urbino Cathedral there is no certainty which was first, though perhaps Federigo's church is best seen as a refinement on the Roman building.

Federigo's church at Urbino reminds us that we are not dealing with a general moral revivalism of Christianity which comes out in particular buildings. There is nothing uniquely spiritual about the latter half of the fifteenth century. The rise of austerity in church building can only be related to a particular problem: how can Classical architecture be made acceptable in a Christian context? It is no accident that three of the churches which we have reviewed—the cathedral at Pienza, S. Agostino, and the cathedral at Urbino, each more austere than its predecessor—were put up adjoining palaces celebrated for their magnificence; and al-

112. Giovanni Mazone: *Adoration*, 1491, Petit Palais, Avignon: detail with Cardinal Giuliano della Rovere

113. Palazzo della Cancelleria, Rome, after 1486: courtyard

though d'Estouteville's is lost and so cannot be discussed in detail, the other two survive as arguably the two grandest Classical palaces of their time. In each case the church is a sort of antidote to the palace.

Until now the new moral architecture has not been applied to the palaces themselves because of its negative associations in terms of social status. This, however, was to change as the new forms gained their own authority from their use in an ecclesiastical context. The first building where this occurs is the next grand Classical palace, that of one of Sixtus' cardinal nephews, Raffaele Riario. The present Palazzo della Cancelleria was built by him, together with the church of S. Lorenzo in Damaso, on a vast site in Rome after 1485 (Figs. 113 and 114). The façade which contains the entrances to both the palace and the church is based on those of the Palazzo Rucellai and the Palazzo Piccolomini. It has channelled masonry throughout with Corinthian pilasters on the upper two floors, but the ground floor has lost its Doric order and on entering the palace it soon becomes clear why. Doric has now replaced Composite for the magnificent two-storeyed loggia of the cortile and thus clearly no longer carries any association of inferior status. Indeed, it is clearly thought of as superior to Corinthian, which is used for the meagre pilaster order at the top of the court elevation. Riario has thus resolved the manifest contradiction of the double-standard use of Doric at Pienza. He seems to accept that a form which has positive moral status in an ecclesiastical context can only have positive social status in a secular work. Over and above his knowledge of the way Doric had been brought to the foreground by Pius, d'Estouteville, and Sixtus, Riario must also have known both the text of Alberti, published in 1485, in which Doric is by implication credited with *gravitas*, and the text of Vitruvius, published in 1486, where it was said that Doric was appropriate to temples of manly gods *propter virtutem* ("because of their manly virtue"). Both books were printed in the same years when the palace was planned, and the Vitruvius was dedicated to Riario himself.

Even more remarkable than the use of Doric for the palace cortile is the order of the church (Fig. 114). This consists of massive square piers like those in the corners of the court and with similar plain capitals decorated only with rosettes. The rosettes on the plain rectangular capitals established a direct link with the

114. S. Lorenzo in Damaso, Rome, after 1486: detail

forms of S. Agostino, but now the form is used much more assertively. Instead of being pushed away high up under the vault it is now brought right down to the level of the piers, which also have their origin in d'Estouteville's church, and there are now no token Corinthian or Composite attached columnar forms. Riario has had the courage to let the virtue of his forms speak for itself, eschewing all conventional expressions of status. The contrast between the stumpy piers of the

115. Duomo, Turin, 1490s: façade

church and the more slender and rather more ornate columns and piers of the palace court makes it absolutely certain that strength and simplicity are the attributes of status here, just as elegance and richness had been in most earlier buildings. In the same spirit, the windows of the palace on the façade also have the same piers and Doric capitals on either side, replacing the Corinthian and Composite forms always found on the main floor of earlier palaces. The Corinthian pilasters of the façade represent the only concession to traditional usage. Presumably, like Pius with his church at Pienza or d'Estouteville at S. Agostino, Riario felt that on the outside, where the building was competing with others in a worldly environment, it was still necessary to register its status in traditional terms. Once inside, the visitor would be able to assess the meaning of the

building in its own terms. Just how far Riario has gone in inverting the traditional values of Antiquity and his own period is most apparent in the assertive use of piers and arches for the church. Throughout Antiquity, the Early Christian period, and the earlier fifteenth century the column had always been regarded as the noblest support appropriate to a religious building—preferably, as Alberti recognized, combined with a horizontal entablature. The very structural weakness of that combination was an important element in its authority. By choosing the pier and arch, the combination associated with the most basic ancient structures such as bridges, and the one recommended by Alberti for secular structures, Riario indicated in the clearest terms that, however much the language of his architecture may owe to the Antique, it owed nothing to pagan materialistic values. His building corresponded to the best of ancient morality and above all to the values of Christianity as presented by Sixtus in his chapel.

Riario was not the only nephew to use the new forms. The palace of another relative, Cardinal Domenico della Rovere, had been begun too early to reflect the new vocabulary, but its present well-head uses the same square piers as Riario's church. Elsewhere, in the grand new cathedral of Turin, which Domenico erected in the 1490s, the façade is decorated with Doric pilasters, and the interior has a simpler version of the Doric shafts of Pienza (Fig. 115). It is a measure of the status which Doric has now achieved that it can be used even for such a conventionally popular church as the cathedral of a major city, the type of religious structure which down the ages had made the greatest accommodation with worldly values. Even here, though, a small concession is made in the three western portals, which are Corinthian at the sides and Composite in the centre. The concession is similar to that made in the façades of the church at Pienza and Raffaele Riario's palace, though smaller, since the main orders of the façade are clearly Doric. People were so used to telling the status of a building from its façade, and above all from its portal, that it was still necessary to take account of that habit.

Exactly the same concession is made in the family palace built in the 1490s at Savona by Giuliano della Rovere, the most important cardinal nephew, who was later to achieve such prominence as Pope Julius II (Fig. 116). This building by Giuliano da Sangallo is the first major palace to have an entirely Doric façade, just as the cathedral at Turin was the first major church to employ such an order both inside and out. The lofty elevation, which makes extensive use of marble, has three rows of Doric pilasters, the lowest having the most elaborate capitals, of the same fluted variety as that used by Alberti and Bernardo Rossellino. The only modifications to the overwhelmingly Doric character of the façade are two columns with Corinthian variant capitals, which stand free of the structure flanking the doorway. They thus mark the status of the building without actually affecting its character. One advantage of the choice of Doric here is that with its moral pedigree it defends the Cardinal's extravagant use of a marble revetment from the possible charge of vainglorious

116. Giuliano da Sangallo: Palazzo della Rovere, Savona, 1490s: detail of façade

display. In the contemporary Corinthian portals at Genoa, just up the coast, and in the contemporary Corinthian marble façades of Venice, on the other side of the peninsula, prominent inscriptions were necessary to provide a more explicit protection. Doric now proved its worth as the means by which Classical architecture could finally be made acceptable in terms of Christian morality.

One final work in the same group, also commissioned by Giuliano della Rovere, is the great altarpiece of the *Adoration*, now in the Albani collection (Fig. 117). The painting, which the Cardinal commissioned from Perugino probably in 1491, is almost a programmatic complement to the same artist's earlier *Charge to Peter* (Fig. 110). In an almost oppressive way each panel is filled with yet another version of the massive square piers found in S. Lorenzo in Damaso. Both the forms and their repetition are without parallel in an altarpiece, and there can be no doubt that the intention is to represent the architecture of the true Christian Church. It takes its cue not only from S. Lorenzo in Damaso, but also from the simple wooden structures which rise newly built out of the ruins of Classical architecture in earlier Adoration scenes. Perugino was obviously so delighted with the power of his new forms that he used them in a whole series of later paintings.

117. Perugino: *Adoration*, 1491, Villa Albani, Rome

Their meaning is repeatedly made clear, as in the predella of the Fano altarpiece of 1497, where the simple square piers of the Christian *Annunciation* are opposed to the richer Ionic decoration of the Jewish temple shown in the *Presentation*. Strong pier replaces weak column, plain capital replaces ornamental form, and simple stone replaces coloured marble. The new architecture is designed to be more moral in structure, in decoration, and in material. The initial idea for a Christian Classical architecture which had been first introduced in the church at Pienza had, thanks to the efforts of the della Rovere pope and his nephews, achieved an initial acceptance. This acceptance meant that from now on Classical forms no longer needed the protection of either defensive inscriptions or dilution with Gothic.

XV

Francesco Colonna

Two loves: sex and architecture

THE *Hypnerotomachia Poliphili* was printed in Venice at the Aldine Press in 1499.[1] It thus belongs literally to the fifteenth century. Yet, since it does not emerge from the world of architectural practice, its relevance is not so much to preceding buildings as to the works of those who may later have come under the spell of its ideas. Much mystery veils its background. The identification of its author rests on little more than the hazardous traditional connection of the FRATER FRANCISCUS COLUMNA whose name is concealed in the first letters of successive chapter headings with a Dominican friar who spent much of his life as a member of the community of SS. Giovanni e Paolo in Venice. An alternative identification with the Colonna prince of Palestrina is unconvincing.[2] Whoever the author was, it is hard to explain the appearance of this large and lavishly printed work at this time except as one manifestation of the antiquarian humanism of the Veneto in the later fifteenth century. From its title, which may be loosely translated "Dream-love-fight of Poliphilus," to the colophon which claims that the work was completed in Treviso in 1467, the book has an hallucinatory character. Only the diligent work of scholars, culminating in that of Pozzi and Ciapponi, has revealed the detailed dependence of the *Hypnerotomachia* on a number of Classical and Renaissance texts including Alberti's *De re aedificatoria*.[3] Pozzi convincingly argues that it was the publication of the latter work in 1485 which in large measure inspired the enrichment of the basic love story with an important body of architectural material. The authors of the magnificent series of woodcut illustrations, however, still elude identification. The role of these highly inventive blocks in what is only the third architectural book to

be printed after Alberti and Vitruvius, and the first to be illustrated, gives them a place of importance in the history of architecture.

The story on which the *Hypnerotomachia* is based has nothing directly to do with architecture. It is the autobiographical account of Colonna's love for a member of a nunnery in Treviso in the 1460s, a love which ended tragically with the girl's death from the plague. The affair is scantily concealed under the trappings of Classical Antiquity, with the nunnery being represented by a temple of Diana, the chaste goddess. The work as a whole is divided into two books. The first, and much the longer, in the form of a dream, tells of Poliphilus' pursuit of the girl, Polia, and of his adventures once he found her. The second tells more simply the story of Polia herself. Only the first is of architectural interest. In the course of it Poliphilus comes across many strange and wonderful buildings. Some are clearly based on ancient structures described by Vitruvius, Pliny, and others. Others are much closer to fifteenth-century architecture. Some of the buildings are ruined and others not. The tradition of introducing fantastic structures into a love story relates the work directly to Medieval romances, as does the dream idea, but the buildings in those romances had never been so numerous or so ruinous, and were never so accurately described. Moreover, the ruins here are explicitly ancient, and all are described with the full language of Classical architecture. There is also a further confusion of time scale, since Poliphilus seems sometimes to be present in a living Classical world and sometimes to be objectively contemplating the ruins of a vanished civilization. There is a similar confusion in the cultural setting, as Egyptian, Greek, Latin, Hebrew, and Arabic inscriptions are mixed together. All this contributes to the mysteriousness and universality of the whole. The vagueness of the cultural environment depicted is increased by Colonna's interspersing through the Italian of many Latin forms. Yet, however inconsistent is the evidence, the basic function of the architectural part of the work as an exercise in the recovery of Classical architecture and its theoretical background is clear and unambiguous.

Liniamento and prattica

This emerges most clearly in the pages describing the first great monument with which Poliphilus is confronted. His dream begins when he wakes to find himself in a strange place. Frightened, he runs through the wild countryside until he comes to a large architectural complex. The description and illustration of this occupy many pages, but the most important part is an account of a doorway which occupies the base of the monument and which is approached across a large piazza (Figs. 118 and 119). Poliphilus is so struck by it that he declares how,

being inclined to study, and inflamed with desire to understand the fertile intellect and the sharp awareness of him who had been the perceptive architect of its proportions, being interested in both its *liniamento* and its *prattica*, analysing it carefully, I did as follows: I precisely measured the square form under the coupled columns either side of the door. From this measurement I readily grasped the system of proportions [*symmetria*] of the aforesaid gateway, which I will briefly explain. Divide a rectangular figure A B C D by three equally spaced lines both vertically and horizontally and there will be sixteen squares . . . (c1ᵛ)

It is clear from this what is meant by *liniamento*. The meaning of *prattica* emerges after he has gone through all the details of measurements and proportions.

In the following part it seems opportune to go through the pleasing and extremely pretty ornaments of the gate. For, to the hard-working architect, being, or essence [*essere*], is of more concern than well-being [*bene essere*]. This means that he best concerns himself first with arranging the mass of the complete structure and defining it in his mind (as was said above), rather than with laying out the ornaments which are accessories to his principal concern. For the first the fertile expertise of one person alone is required; in the second many manual labourers or individual workers, called by the Greeks *ergati*, will collaborate and these, as has been said, are the instruments of the architect. (c3ᵛ)

The second section, on *prattica*, thus deals with all the decorative details of the gateway, while the *liniamento* discussed earlier is its underlying geometrical scheme.

The idea of making this fundamental division into *liniamento* and *prattica* must derive from Alberti's distinction between *utilitas* and *pulchritudo*, but Colonna has seriously modified Alberti's polarity. There had always been something inconsistent in Albert's pairing of *liniamentum* and *opus* in the first half of his treatise and of *pulchritudo* and *ornamentum* in the second. Although Alberti's division could be explained in terms of a desire to apply to architecture Cicero's distinction between *utilitas* and *honestas*, it was evident that in a sense *liniamentum*, the geometrical layout of a building, and *pulchritudo*, the high form of beauty which derives from harmonious proportions, also form a pair, while *opus* and *ornamentum* could be paired in opposition. This is very much what Colonna has done. He was concerned not with Cicero's moral dualism but with the intellectual status of the discipline. For him the most important division is that between architectural planning, in so far as it is a mental operation of the architect, and the physical execution of the construction and its ornaments, which is in the hands of manual labourers. This distinction between the mental and physical sides of architecture virtually reverses Alberti's between *opus* and *pulchritudo*. The prime reason for the change must be the recent acknowledgement of the essentially intellectual character of the Renaissance architect, which was apparent both from Laurana's patent and from Francesco de Giorgio's whole approach. In music a similar distinction was being made at the same time by Gaffurio, whose *Theoricum opus musicae disciplinae* appeared in 1480 and his *Practica musicae* in 1496. Although not precise, there is a general correspondence between his division of music into *theoria* and *practica* and Colonna's division of architecture into *liniamento* and *prattica*.

Architecture and music

The notion that Colonna's approach to architecture may have been influenced by recent writings on music receives direct support from a crucial linking passage at the beginning of his account of *prattica*. Here he excuses himself for the length and dryness of the first part and explains his reasons for writing as he did. The prime goal of the architect is to invent a scheme

118. Francesco Colonna: *Hypnerotomachia Poliphili*, 1499: gateway, fol. c8ʳ

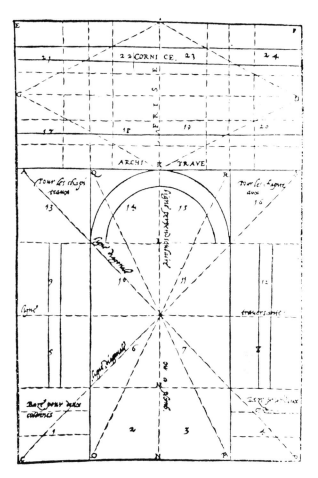

119. *Quadratura* of gateway in Fig. 118 (after French ed., 1546)

to achieve a modulated treatment of the solid body of the building. The architect then reduces this by a process of minute division, in exactly the same way as the musician, after he has decided on the key [*intonatione*] and the measured time [*mensurato tempo*] then divides up this basis [*solido*] proportionately into small chromatic divisions [*chromatice minute*]. Following this simile the principal rule for the architect after he has invented the design is the organization by squares [*quadratura*], dividing these up into the smallest units; this provides the harmony [*harmonia*] of the building and its modulation [*commodulatione*] . . . (c4ʳ)

Colonna argues for a precise similarity between the working processes of the architect and those of the musician. Each first "invents" a basic structure, and each

then needs to find some system for organizing the details. The musician uses the chromatic scale (*chromatice minute*) and the architect *quadratura*. His elaborate account of the geometrical layout of the gate was a demonstration of how this *quadratura* works.

The notion that the geometrical proportions found in a building could be thought of as creating a harmony such as is found in music had already been developed by Alberti and by Francesco di Giorgio. This, however, remained virtually the only connection between the two arts. Colonna, on the other hand, implies the possibility of a much wider parallel between music and architecture. Are there, then, architectural equivalents for *intonatione* and *mensurato tempo* as well as for *chromatice minute*? Colonna does not identify them at this point, but we are justified in looking for them in his other architectural passages, especially where other musical terms such as *harmonia, modulata,* and *emusicatamente* appear.

Intonatione and the orders

In Renaissance music theory the *intonatione* was the tone or mode which, like the modern key, determined a series of notes on which a composition was based. Colonna himself refers frequently to such musical *toni*. Right at the beginning Poliphilus is wandering tired and frightened through a wood when he hears a *dorio* (sc. *tono*) being sung (a5ʳ). Later he hears Dorian music again. This time he is being guided by two ladies, Logistica and Thelemia, through a rocky and stormy mountain landscape when he meets five more formidable females:

The place and situation seemed very difficult [*laborioso*]. Logistica accordingly, noticing this, immediately began to sing in a Dorian mode [*dorio modo et tono*] and, taking the lyre from the hands of Thelemia, sweetly sang: "O Poliphilus, do not let yourself become worried by this place since once the strain [*fatica*] has passed only good will remain." Her song was so intense that I would have agreed to stay with these maidens. (i1ʳ).

The Dorian mode is designed to enable our hero to cope with the *laborioso* environment and the associated *fatica*. It is evidently effective. The situation is so similar to that in the earlier passage that there too the Dorian mode presumably had the same function. The Phrygian mode also occurs twice. The first time it is found as an accompaniment to a dance of the nymphs (e7ᵛ). Later it is a chorus of girls who dance to the "stimulating Phrygian" (*excitante phrygio*) mode, and they are inspired by it to represent a battle, "a tournament which was delightful in its sudden and spontaneous vehemence" (h1ʳ). Phrygian is thus associated with dancing, and especially with vigorous and violent movements. When Poliphilus, by now in the company of his beloved Polia, comes to the temple of Venus there is more dancing while sacrifice is made, but now the dance is led by two maidens playing Lydian pipes in a sweet Lydian vein, singing "O holy scented fire, melt the ice of every soul; placate Venus with love and let it be charged with her heat" (o5ᵛ). The Lydian mode is

linked with the same erotic theme when Polia sings alone on the voyage to the island of Cythera. In a highly wrought poem with an exquisite vocabulary she sings of "the supremely sweet pleasures of the holy and gentle Venus" (s5ʳ). Lydian is thus usually entwined with love.

These characterizations of the modes according to their expressive qualities and their effects are in a general sense traditional. Plato had classified Lydian as "soft" and both Phrygian and Dorian as "warlike." Aristotle had described Dorian as having a "manly" character. Aristides Quintilianus said that Dorian covered the lower vocal range, Lydian the upper, and Phrygian the middle, which would tally with the first being manly and the second virginal.[4] There is little evidence that Colonna was concerned with the elaborate technicalities of the four authentic and four plagal modes; instead, he restricts himself to the three which were best known and which had the clearest characters.

There can be little doubt as to what Colonna would have seen as the architectural equivalent of *intonatione*. The Classical orders with their similar tribal names formed a comparable scale of alternatives. Like the modes they occur frequently throughout the book. It is, moreover, clear that Colonna was extremely interested in discovering principles governing their application, since an extensive passage in his account of the gateway is devoted to their use in that context. The door was flanked, as in the illustration, by two pairs of free-standing columns, the inner two of porphyry and the outer of ophite. The detailed description of them (c5ʳ⁻ᵛ) seems at first confused. The four free-standing columns are called Doric of seven diameters, but their capitals are such as Callimachus designed with acanthus leaves in the Corinthian or Roman manner, like those on the Pantheon, one diameter high. This strange mixture is, however, explained by the comments on the fluting of the shafts. There are twenty-four flutes—the number Vitruvius gives for Ionic and Corinthian—and these are filled for the lower third with "rope" forms. The reason for this, Poliphilus observes, is that

this superb structure or temple must have been dedicated to individuals of both sexes, either a god and goddess, or a mother and son, or a father and mother, or a father and daughter, or a similar combination. For the wise ancients associated a high degree of hollowing-out with the female sex, in contrast to the rope form which they associated with the male, because the slippery feminine nature exceeds the male in lasciviousness. The flutes, which indicated the folds of the female costume, were required for the temple of a goddess . . . (c5^{r-v})

There is no clear source for this curious commentary on the fluting of the columns, in which our over-sexed friar saw in the rounded moulding nestling in the flute an expression of sexual union. At all events, if the nature of the fluting was so specifically intended to indicate the bisexual dedication of the building the same explanation may be invoked to deal with the mixture of columns of Doric proportions with Corinthian capitals. The Vitruvian association of the two orders with the two sexes had never been applied to real or imaginery buildings before, and the idea of mixing the orders had certainly never been recommended. Colonna takes up for the first time Vitruvius' theory of architectural *decor* and at once develops it to a new level of expressiveness. In this way his appropriate use of the orders exactly parallels his use of the modes. By his study of the architectural details of the gate Colonna prepares us for the inscription (given at c6v) which records the dedication of the structure to Aphrodite and her son Eros. His careful presentation of the principle involved beforehand shows that he had a real interest in contributing to architectural theory in this area.

The use of the orders on this gateway encourages us to look for them also elsewhere in the book. The first reference to a particular type of column is in the description of the ruined portico which flanks the gate. The columns there are described (b4^r) as having an araeostyle spacing (that is, the widest possible), with capitals which are "Doric or pulvinate with bark [*cortici*] or spiral volutes." The passage is confusing, since Colonna seems to imply that Doric capitals have volutes, but such confusion was also found in Francesco de Giorgio, and Doric is obviously the order which is intended. Exactly why it is used here is made clear in a later passage, apparently referring to the same portico, which immediately follows the analysis of the gate:

. . . in the lower part were some dwarf columns [*nane columne*] intended to be resistant to an enormous weight, and there were other Corinthian ones . . . as good proportions [*symmetria*] demanded and as the need for strength and for ornament required, as if the artistic principle [*artificiosa ragione*] was derived and cleverly adapted from a correspondence with man. Just as a man who bears a heavy load should

have large feet and strong legs, so too in a properly measured building dwarf columns should be used to bear weight, and Corinthian and slender Ionic ones should be introduced for decoration! And according to the demands both of harmony and of structure all the parts of the building were endowed with a correct elegance. (c8^v)

From the opposition between *nane columne* and Ionic and Corinthian it seems that this is another expression for Doric. Colonna thus presents a general principle that short, thick columns, such as Doric, are to be used where strength is required and slender ones, such as Ionic and Corinthian, where the need is only for ornament. In doing this he is taking up the observations both of Alberti, who had said that Doric was *ad laborem aptius*, and of Filarete, who had made the analogy between the orders and the classes, but here for the first time the implications of this view are followed up in terms of rules for practice; more particularly, Colonna is here the first writer to approach the problem of superposition of the orders, and in his recommendation that Doric should be used in the lower parts of buildings he directly contradicts the usual fifteenth-century habit of putting the richest order at the bottom.

In later passages when the orders are mentioned no reasons are given, but in most cases the particular choice can be explained in terms of one of the two principles already discussed. Thus, as Poliphilus continues on his travels he comes to a "wonderful octagonal bath building" (e5^r), with pilasters on the outside and a free-standing Corinthian colonnette in each corner of the interior. Since the main piece of sculpture inside is a statue of a nymph by a fountain, the use of Corinthian can be explained in the same Vitruvian terms as in the gateway. For Vitruvius recommends Corinthian not only for temples to Aphrodite but also for temples to "Fountains and Nymphs." Nor is Colonna's interest in architectural *decor* limited to the choice of order. Every detail of the building is calculated to emphasize its aqueous associations. The frieze above the colonnettes is decorated with "naked boys playing in the water with little sea monsters." Mosaics on the seats round the sides show swimming fish and shells. Sculptures of Poseidon and of dolphins with more little boys surround the Nymph herself. Even the materials are consistently water-like. The columns are of green jasper figured with wavy veins, the roof is covered with "leaves of pure crystal," the inner walls are of *verdis-*

n iii

120. *Hypnerotomachia Poliphili*: Temple
of Venus, fol. n3ʳ

in the gate dedicated to Aphrodite earlier. Moreover, the constant recurrence of the same materials, porphyry, ophite and bronze, suggests that they too are thought of as explicitly appropriate. Both porphryry and bronze are traditionally reddish in colour, and bronze is wrought with the aid of fire. Here indeed the bronze is explicitly fire-gilt, *causticamente inaurato*. The materials may thus all be connected with the scarlet and fiery nature of love. This suggestion is supported by the candelabra round the exterior, "the orifice of which [i.e. each candelabrum] was expanded into a shell form, in which some inconsumable material burned with a perpetual and inextinguishable fire, a fire which neither wind nor rain could put out" (n2ᵛ). Here the shell that once gave birth to the goddess puts forth the flames of unquenchable desire.

In these buildings Colonna seems to develop the Vitruvian principles enunciated in connection with the gateway. In the remaining structures, on the other hand, it is the principles that were articulated in connection with the flanking porticoes which seem more relevant. Indeed the Vitruvian principles were appropriate only when a building had a particular dedicatee, and none of the later buildings do. One called Polyandrion, which serves as a cemetery, is also situated on the seashore. All that we are told of its order is that its underground vault is supported by *columne nane* (p8ʳ). Whether necessarily Doric or not, they follow precisely the rule for dwarf columns given earlier. After this Poliphilus sails with his beloved Polia for the *deliciosa insula cytherea*, "the delightful isle of Venus." This is described and illustrated as circular and is laid out as a vast garden with separate enclosures divided by paths running both orbitally and radially (Fig. 121b). These paths are covered with pergolas, and where they meet four Ionic columns are set up with shafts of nine diameters (t1ʳ). There is no clear reason for the choice of order, but Doric would have been inappropriate since their function was only for ornament and not support, and Corinthian may have been thought too emphatic and dignified. The same could be said of the similar use of Ionic for the colonnade which runs along the circular canal halfway to the centre of the island (Fig. 122). On the other hand, the use of Doric for the octagonal fountain structures in the centre of each section between the paths could again be explained by the order's function of support, since these columns carry vases

simo iaspro and of "coral-coloured jasper decorated with veins like double whirlpools," and the doors are again "brightest crystal." Never before had architecture been made so expressively appropriate.

A similar spirit governs the design of the temple of Venus Physizoa which Poliphilus later finds on the seashore (Fig. 120). This extravagant structure, which is beautifully illustrated, has an opulent decoration of pilasters and columns which are repeatedly described as Corinthian. The order would be as appropriate here as

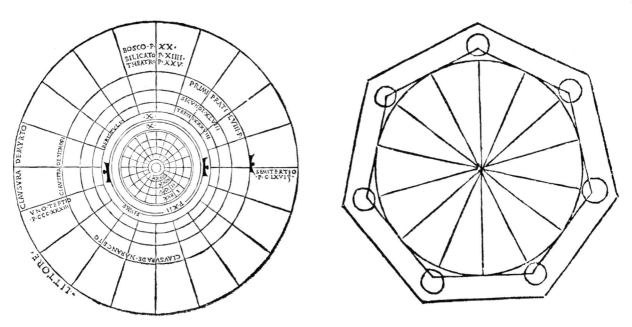

121. *Hypnerotomachia Poliphili*: left (a) map of *Insula cytherea*, fol. t8ʳ;
right (b) plan of shrine of Venus at its centre, fol. y8ʳ

out of which rise an upper storey of piers. Colonna thus found a fairly consistent way of applying the orders even when there was no question of sexual appropriateness.

There is a precise parallel between Colonna's use of the musical modes and that of the architectural orders: in both arts he is concerned with the choice of an expressively appropriate style. As we should expect from his initial remarks that the architect follows the same procedures as the musician, it is the development of an expressive theory of architecture to match the established one in music that is his special concern. Hence it is the theory of the appropriate use of the orders which he carefully elaborates, while he assumes a general familiarity with the traditional theory of the choice of mode in music. But this does not mean that there is no reverse influence from the theory of the orders on that of the modes. In fact it seems likely that his introduction of a Dorian mode when Poliphilus is faced with a *laborioso* situation is intended as exactly parallel to the use of Doric where a strong support is necessary. For, although the general character of the Dorian mode had long been recognized, it had probably never been treated quite like this. Also, the association of Lydian with the song to Venus reminds one so precisely of the matching of Corinthian to that goddess that perhaps it too is inspired more by the recommendation of Vitruvius than by any text of music theory. The soft property of Lydian was well known, but it had arguably never been connected so precisely with the goddess of love. This however, should not distract from Colonna's main achievement, which is the extension of the expressive range of architecture, not just by developing available if unexploited theories of the orders, but by inventing a new theory of flutes, and above all by taking to new lengths the idea of the appropriate use of colours, materials, and figural decoration.

A final freakish touch to his theory of expressive architecture is provided by the heptagonal shrine which stands in the middle of an amphitheatre in the centre of the island (Fig. 121b). It is yet another shrine of Venus and contains a statue of the goddess, which is suddenly revealed to the two lovers at the climax of the story when a curtain is removed. The erotic overtones of this moment are beautifully illustrated by the sculptures attached to the seven columns. On the three to the right are figures of boys, and on the three to the left are girls (or quite possibly female genitals: *il foemello sexo*,

122. *Hypnerotomachia Poliphili*: colonnade
on island, fol. t6ᵛ

y8ʳ). The seventh at the rear, which is hexagonal and not round as are the others, is adorned with a hermaphrodite child, as if as an emblem of final sexual union. The choice of seven columns recalls *Proverbs* 9, 1: "Wisdom hath builded her house, she hath hewn out her seven pillars"; only here our wayward friar has changed the house of wisdom into a temple of carnal knowledge.

Mensurato tempo and intercolumniation

Mensurato tempo, "measured time" or tempo, was the other element which, according to Colonna, had to be decided by the musician before he could set about the detailed composition of his piece. As with *intonatione*, an architectural equivalent is ready to hand. If an order constitutes the mode of a colonnade, then the spacing of the columns must constitute its time. The tempo of a colonnade could be said to be varied as the columns are spaced at more or less close intervals. Vitruvius had long before catalogued the main types of spacings which were usable in temples.[5] These were pycnostyle (1½ diameters), systyle (2 dias.) eustyle (2¼ dias.), diastyle (3 dias.) and araeostyle (3 + dias.). We have already seen that Colonna called the first Doric colonnade outside the gateway araeostyle (b4ʳ). Later he talks again of another araeostyle colonnade (h4ᵛ). Much later the Ionic pergolas on the island have

columns placed "every four diameters" (t1ᵛ), that is with three diameters between them in the diastyle spacing. The next series of Ionic columns, on the other hand, those along the canal, are said to be eustyle (t7ᵛ), while the last colonnade between the canal and the amphitheatre is referred to as pycnostyle (u2ʳ). Colonna thus shows a considerable interest in column spacing, a subject which had hardly concerned his predecessors. He also appears to arrange them in a mathematical order from araeostyle, the widest, to pycnostyle, the narrowest, so that not only does the series running through the book give it a greater unity and coherence, but the changing intercolumniations actually seem to form a rhythmical accompaniment to the narrative. The tempo of the colonnades quickens with the tempo of the love story. As Poliphilus and his lover come ever closer to the final revelation, and particularly as they come ever closer to the centre of the island with its converging paths, the columns too become closer. There is even an equally expressive conclusion to the narrative in the heptagonal shrine, where the separately carved sexes on the front six columns find union in the hermaphrodite column at the back, echoing the consummation of the lovers' relationship. The accelerating tempo of the colonnades acts, like the accelerating tempo of a fertility dance, as an expressive accompaniment to the book's theme.

Colonna was thus able to show how each individual

building could be said to have a *mensurato tempo* just as it had an *intonatione*. He also showed how their succeeding *tempi* could be used to give an overall structure to his literary composition. Indeed, his choice of *intonationi* was probably planned to function in the same way. Certainly the series of the modes, Dorian, Phrygian, Phrygian, Dorian, Lydian, Lydian, seems intended as a similarly expressive sequence leading irresistibly to the erotic climax.

Colonna showed how the architect, by closely imitating the musician, could considerably increase the potentiality of his art. One major influence on his approach must have been the tradition of the Medieval romance into which his work so clearly fits. For in compositions such as the *Roman de la Rose*, and many others, buildings were often introduced and frequently were endowed with some expressive character in order to make them frighten or entice or fascinate. Probably, however, the main inspiration for his innovative approach came from the current dispute on the relative status of the different arts, especially the relative status of painting compared to poetry, and of architecture compared to music. This dispute encouraged people to compare the methods of the rival techniques, and in the next chapter we shall consider its influence in more detail. For the present we may only note how eloquently Colonna testifies to the essential community which unites all the arts. The *Hypnerotomachia* is more than

a bizarre union of love story and antiquarian fantasy, and its importance does not reside chiefly in its contribution to architectural theory. It is above all a new creation in which four arts play an almost equal part. It is written in words and pictures, and it has an accompaniment of music and architecture.

Indeed, the music and architecture can be seen to have an even more fundamental role. In a way they, being the only two arts which are truly geometrical, can be seen to provide the whole work with a literary equivalent of the *liniamento* or geometrical framework which Colonna said was so important for the architect. It is as if the commentary on the gateway is also a commentary on the whole book to which it serves as an introduction. Having once entered the book through the gate, the reader recognizes that the rhythmic series of the modes, Dorian, Phrygian, Phrygian, Dorian, Lydian, Lydian, and the accelerating tempo of the colonnades from araeostyle to pycnostyle provide the book with a remarkable structure. Colonna plans the book as he might plan a building. Vitruvius had long ago noted in passing how the Pythagoreans had laid out their writings on mathematical principles deriving from the cube. Colonna's principles are not just mathematical but musical and architectural as well. Music and architecture are for him the highest of the arts, and it is on them that the compositional procedures of the writer should be based.

XVI

Luca Pacioli

◆

The *De divina proportione* and the superiority of the eye

EXACTLY ten years after the publication of the *Hypnerotomachia* another friar produced a book containing architectural material, also in Venice. Entitled *De divina proportione*, it was written by Luca Pacioli and published by Paganino da Brescia in 1509.[1] Pacioli was born in 1445 in Borgo San Sepolcro, the native town of Piero della Francesca. He studied chiefly in Venice and later, like a true friar, he travelled from city to city as a teacher, visiting, among others, Zara, Florence, and Perugia. Not surprisingly, he came into contact with his countryman Piero. Baldi describes the friendship between the two, and Pacioli's admiring references to the artist, as well as his plagiarism of his writings, show how much he learned from him. After going on to teach mathematics in Rome and Naples he returned to Venice in 1494 to publish an elaborate mathematical treatise called the *Summa de arithmetica geometria et proportionalità*. Then, from 1496 to 1499, he held the chair of mathematics at Milan and became a friend of that other learned painter Leonardo. It was during this time that he prepared a manuscript of what was to be the first section of the *De divina proportione*, completed in December 1498 and subsequently presented to Duke Lodovico Sforza.[2] This work was accompanied by drawings after models of the solids made for Pacioli by Leonardo himself. It was with Leonardo that he left Milan at the fall of the Sforzas in 1499 and with Leonardo that he lived for a time in Florence. After this he returned to Venice; he was teaching there in 1508, and in 1509 he published, as well as a Latin edition of Euclid's *Elements*, the full *De divina proportione*. To the text of the original 1498 manuscript was added a whole treatise on architecture,

and at the end appeared as a separate work an Italian translation of Piero della Francesca's *De corporibus regularibus*, printed without any acknowledgement. Thereafter, little is known of the energetic friar who had also written the first book (never printed) on double-entry bookkeeping and who was so brilliantly portrayed in a painting attributed to Jacopo de' Barbari (Fig. 123).

The interest of the *De divina proportione* ia apparent from the title itself, which was already prefixed to the Milan manuscript dedicated to Duke Lodovico Sforza. The work is described thus:

Concerning Divine Proportion, a work which is necessary for all perceptive and curious minds, wherein every student of Philosophy, Perspective, Painting, Sculpture, Architecture, Music, and other mathematical disciplines will find most sweet, subtle, and admirable learning, and wherein he will delight in the varied researches into the most secret science.[3]

In this title the roll-call of mathematical disciplines is quite remarkable. Of philosophy, perspective, painting, sculpture, architecture, and music, the middle four are unusual at all in such a list, and in any case we should expect music to come first after philosophy. Evidently Pacioli is already eager to make a specific point, and this he later explains in some detail. What the odd four subjects have in common is their dependence on the sense of sight, and it is his new attitude to sight which causes him to break with convention.

This word "mathematical," most noble duke, is Greek by its derivation and in our language means something like "susceptible of systematic learning" and for our purposes the sciences and disciplines we understand as mathematical are arithmetic, geometry, astrology, music, perspective [*prospectiva*], architecture, and cosmography, and any which depend from these. However, the general opinion of sages is that the

123. Attr. to Jacopo de' Barbari: *Luca Pacioli*, 1495,
Museo Nazionale di Capodimonte, Naples

first four are arithmetic, geometry, astronomy, and music, and the others are considered as subsidiary, that is dependent on these. This is the opinion of Plato and Aristotle, and of Isidore in his *Etymologies*, and of Severinus Boethius in his *Arithmetic*. But in my judgement, weak and humble as it is, they are limited to a set of either three or five: the set of three is arithmetic, geometry, and astronomy, omitting music for the same reason that they omit perspective, while I add perspective to their four for the same reasons that they include music. If they say that music satisfies the hearing, which is a natural sense, I say that perspective satisfies the sight, which is more noble inasmuch as it is the "first gate of the intellect." If they assert that music consists of number expressed in sound and of measure applied to the time of its duration, I assert that perspective by any definition relies on natural number and on measure applied to the line of sight [*linea visuale*]. If they claim that music recreates the soul by its harmony, I say that perspective delights by the use of due distances and by the use of varied colours. If music reflects harmonic proportions, perspective reflects arithmetical and geometrical ones . . . So from this argument, if from no other, I insist that either there are three principal arts and that the

217

others are subsidiary, or that, if they want to include music, then there are five, since perspective is in no sense lower than music nor less worthy of praise. (pp. 40–41)

Pacioli is bent on a complete reappraisal of the traditional view of the arts. He would abolish the *quadrivium* of arithmetic, geometry, astronomy, and music, the keystones of the higher educational system from Late Antiquity onwards. The superiority of the first three he acknowledges, but he would deny any superiority of music over what he calls *prospectiva*. Although he does not explain precisely what he means by this word, he evidently refers to the scientific view of vision which had been developed over the preceding two hundred years and which had enabled practitioners of the visual arts, especially in the latter years of the fifteenth century, to consider their skills as having a mathematical basis. Pacioli could justly believe that works such as Piero's *De prospectiva pingendi* of around 1480 had done for painting what Pythagoras long ago had done for music and that this required a restructuring of the system of the arts. In this restructuring not only is perspective grouped with music but it and the arts dependent on it are actually considered as in some sense superior to it, since they rely on sight rather than hearing. This is why perspective and the three visual arts are placed before music in the title.

The introduction of perspective as an art equivalent to music is dependent on the superiority of the sense of sight over that of hearing, which had already been insisted on by Francesco di Giorgio. The connection with Francesco's point of view is indicated by the recurrence of the Aristotelian quotation about the eye being the first gate of the intellect and, indeed, the general dependence on an Aristotelian position. At *De divina proportione* I, 2, Pacioli turns again to Aristotle. "The master of those who know," he tells us, says that "knowledge begins with seeing" and that "nothing is in the intellect which is not first experienced by sensation"—an opinion which he glosses with the observation that wise men recognize that the noblest sense is sight. The Aristotelian material would have been familiar to Pacioli, since, from the time of Aquinas, Aristotle had had a prominent place in education. There is no direct evidence that Pacioli knew Francesco di Giorgio or his writings; but their paths must often have crossed in central and northern Italy, and they had common contacts in Piero and Leonardo.

An even more striking parallel to Pacioli's approach is in the work of Leonardo. The latter's defence of the visual arts is familiar, but the similarity of approach is such that it is worth quoting it here once again.[3] Leonardo often insists on the superiority of the sense of sight: "The eye, which is called the window of the soul . . ."[4] "The eye is the highest sense and prince of the others . . ."[5] Sight is specifically favourably compared to hearing, and poetry is consequently adversely compared to painting: "Painting represents the works of nature to the senses with greater truth and certainty than do words or letters . . ."[6] "The eye with its due distances and its due means is less deceptive in its function than any other sense, because [we do not] see except by straight lines which compose the pyramid; but the ear is deceived in judging the situation and distances of its objects, because these are represented to it not by straight lines such as those of the eye but by ones which are twisting and bent . . ."[7] Leonardo quotes extensively the comments on the relative merits of painting and poetry which were addressed to a poet by Matthias Corvinus, King of Hungary:

Don't you know that our mind is composed of a harmony and that harmony is not generated except when the proportions of things are seen or heard in an instant? Don't you see that in your science there is no proportionality created in an instant; instead one part comes out of the other in succession, the later element is not born unless the earlier dies? For this reason I judge your invention [the poem] to be inferior to that of the painter, simply because it is not composed of harmonic proportions.[8]

Matthias Corvinus is here evidently referring to the theory of musical harmony which was essential to fifteenth-century polyphony, that is the notion of several voices singing different notes together to create a unity which is richer than anything possible with one voice alone. Elsewhere Leonardo even argues that painting is more harmonious than music, since all parts of a painting can be enjoyed at once, while a piece of music has the same disadvantage as the poem of only existing as an experience in time; and, besides, one musician cannot sing in four voices at the same time.[9] He also argues that the way a painter records the distance of objects on receding perspective lines is closely comparable to the musician's use of a series of intervals to compose a series of notes.[10] Clearly his ambition is exactly the same as Pacioli's; "So since you place music among the liberal arts, you must either include painting as well or else withdraw music."[11] Most of these passages are dated by Pedretti to the early 1490s; so Pacioli is only providing a more systematic and theoretical support to a point of view which had already been firmly articulated at the Sforza court, and doing for all the visual arts what Leonardo had done for painting.

One of Pacioli's most powerful reasons for supporting the visual arts was his recognition that geometry could only be understood through the eye, while arithmetic could as well be appreciated through the ear. This emerges in his explanation of what he means by his title, in chapters III–VI of the *De divina proportione*. The "divine proportion" is the golden section (*ab* is to *bc* as *bc* is to *ac*). The proportion is irrational. It cannot be written down arithmetically. It only exists as a geometrical figure, the divided line. The divine proportion is thus as mysterious and ineffable as God. It is also embodied in the geometrical solid the dodecahedron, which can contain the other figures, the tetrahedron, the cube, the octahedron, and the icosahedron; and just as these four can be related to the four ancient elements, so it can be seen as constituting a higher *quinta essentia* (fifth essence). The divine proportion is thus, like God, a ruling principle visible everywhere. It is its irrationality and its geometrical character which give it its potency, and these are precisely the qualities of all the visual arts. Unlike music, which employs intervals which are rational proportions expressible in numbers such as 1:2 (the octave), 2:3 (the fifth), etc., the lines of perspective embody continuous and irrational proportions. Pacioli is fascinated by the mysterious music of geometry: "figures and forms with a certain irrational harmony [*certa irrationale simphonia*]" The irrationality of geometry becomes a touchstone of excellence, and at several points in the book on architecture Pacioli commends the use of irrational proportions.

Architecture

In the first and main part of the *De divina proportione*, dealing with the regular solids, there is no anticipation of a separate section on architecture, and when it appears it represents an abrupt change of tone. It is, for example, dedicated not to the Duke of Milan but to some stonecarvers [*lapicidi*] in provincial Borgo San

Sepolcro who are described as "experienced in the pursuit of sculpture and architecture" (p. 123). He is writing in 1509 in response to their request not just for information on arithmetic and geometry but for "some rule and way of arriving at the desired architectural effect." Yet, although there is a strong contrast in the character of his audience and the tone is more practical, there is probably an intimate connection between this and the earlier section. For such simple artisans as those he here addresses must have been shocked to learn that they were really practising not a mechanical but a liberal art, and they must have wanted to know more of how they could be worthy of their new status. Pacioli's response is to deal with an aspect of architecture which will be particularly useful for his stonemason friends, that is architectural ornament.

For no part of the said art of architecture can be correctly decorated if it does not employ gay mouldings, or marble, porphyry, and serpentine and other different sorts of stone, as on columns, cornices, and frontispieces, and the other ornamental details which are required for defensive works and public buildings as well as sacred ones; and because these details afford greater adornment the more they are executed with due diligence in their proportions and proportional relationships, these elements are very necessary both for you and for anyone who is involved in such buildings. (p. 129)

He is going to deal with columns, entablatures, and pediments that is all the architectural details which are most relevant to his audience of stonecarvers. He goes on to explain more precisely how his work is going to be divided up: "and we will make of our account three succinct parts corresponding to the number of the illustrated examples set at the beginning of this work entitled 'On divine proportion'" (p. 130). The first part will deal with human proportions, since not only do all measures and their names derive from the human body, but also God has endowed it with all sorts of proportions and relationships [*proportionalità*]. These he will describe first, as they are essential to the design of the details which stonecarvers have to use on the façades of churches and palaces. Vitruvius, he admits, had already dealt with them, but he will try to give an account in a language that is easier to understand. The second part will deal with round columns, which are required both for strength and ornament. The third will cover the entablature. Finally these details will be employed in a representation "of a gate which is based

124. Luca Pacioli, *De divina proportione*, 1509:
Beautiful Gate of the Temple at Jerusalem

ception of the change from double to single columns, both gates employ the same compositional elements and both appear to be designed on a similar *quadratura* scheme of a square and a half. Neither illustration embodies the geometry precisely, but since we know those proportions were intended by Colonna but never followed by the draughtsman the same may be true with Pacioli. If Pacioli's gate had been bound in at the beginning of the book as he wanted, the reader would have entered the treatise through it even more directly than would the reader of Colonna. In any case, a contemporary would surely have sensed the correspondence between the two designs and recognized it as placing the later work in the tradition of its predecessor.

Orders and characters

Pacioli may begin his series of illustrations with one showing human proportions, and end with one showing a complete work of architecture, but those in between show details of column and entablature, and it is, correspondingly, an account of the ancient orders which forms the bulk of his text. After the first three chapters on the human body, Pacioli turns in chapter IV to the subject of columns. These, he says, are called by Vitruvius Doric, Ionic, and Corinthian after the areas where they were first found. Then, adopting a more condescending tone, he explains that Vitruvius makes it all rather difficult and advises his readers to remember

how in our Christian religion we have different male and female saints, and how we give to each of these attributes referring to their strife on behalf of the faith; thus to Saint George we give arms, lance, breastplate, helmet, sword, and horse with all its trappings, and similarly to Saint Maurice, Saint Eustace, the Macabees, and others; Saint Catherine has her wheel because through that she received the crown of martyrdom for her faith, and Saint Barbara the tower in which she was imprisoned; and so with all the saints, male and female, the Church permits that in their memory we should be inflamed with the holy faith through our eyes so that we do the same, careless of potentates. For "the saints of the Lord did not fear the lashes of their executioners." In exactly the same way [the ancients] according to their mistaken rituals made ornaments for their idols and gods, now in one way, now in another, according to their characters, and applied them to trophies, temples, and columns, calling them after the countries where these forms originated . . . and they made such

on that of the Temple of Solomon at Jerusalem as it is described by the prophet Ezekiel . . ." (p. 130). The four accompanying woodcuts, which were apparently intended to be bound in at the beginning of the whole work, do indeed roughly correspond to this scheme. There is one illustration of the proportions of the human head; then a pair, one showing the pedestal and shaft of a column and the other a section of entablature; and, finally, one showing a gate entitled PORTA TEMPLI DOMINI DICTA SPECIOSA (Gate of the Temple of the Lord called Beautiful) (Fig. 124).

One tantalizing feature of the gate is its correspondence both in form and function to the gate which provides the key to Colonna's theory (Figs. 118 and 119). The shared idea of having an illustration of a gateway as the key to a text on architecture is remarkable enough. Even more remarkable is it that, with the ex-works the one more decorated than the other according to the moral excellence which he or she may have revealed in his or her mighty deeds, as for Hercules, Mars, Jupiter, and the rest, and for Diana, Minerva, Ceres, and suchlike, as is explained fully by Vitruvius. (p. 139)

Pacioli's comparison of the Vitruvian principle of *decor* with Christian practice represents a significant new approach. He explains the use of different attributes for different saints in terms of the emotive effect of these attributes on the Christian spectator, who should be moved to imitation. In other words, the attributes are not simply appropriate appurtenances: they are dynamic and expressive in their function. What makes this approach important is that Pacioli apparently intends us to consider the orders as functioning in the same way. They are no longer for him, as they were not only for Vitruvius but for Alberti and Filarete too, simply sets of appropriate architectural forms. He thinks of them as having a more active role.

Another important aspect of his approach is that he seems to recognize that the Vitruvian rule of *decor* can be brought up to date so that the orders could be matched to male and female saints just as they had been before to male and female pagan divinities. The close parallel between the lists of gods and of saints certainly suggests this, and the desire to conceive of the orders as functioning in the same way as saintly attributes points in the same direction. This may seem an obvious step, but, with the possible single exception of Pizzolpasso in his letter, no earlier writer had taken it. If, however, we remember that Colonna in his work published only ten years earlier had for the first time shown a real interest in the Vitruvian principle of matching orders to deities, it is quite understandable that this second step should follow soon afterwards. A subsidiary, but important, implication of Pacioli's comparison between the orders and the attributes of saints is that an order is no longer just linked to a "type," such as a masculine divinity, but is connected in some way with a specific "individual," so that a Doric building for Saint George would be different from one for Saint Eustace just as their attributes would differ. He does not tell us how this could be done, but once again there is a precise parallel to what Colonna had done in differentiating, for instance, a Corinthian shrine for a nymph from one for Venus by the use of appropriate sculpture and materials. Pacioli

thus shows the same interest in the expressive potential of architectural forms that we found in the *Hypnerotomachia*. As with Colonna, the interest is likely to derive from the concern to develop the analogy between architecture and music.

Orders and emotions

In chapter VII Pacioli returns to the orders in an elaborate study of the differences between them.

You must note too that the said types of column, that is Ionic, Doric, and Corinthian, are made in the same way as far as their bases and pedestals are concerned, but their capitals are different. The Ionic or so-called pulvinate capital is melancholic, since it does not raise itself upwards, but makes a melancholic and mournful impression like a window; it is only half a head high, that is half the diameter of the column, without another abacus or other moulding; it only has volutes turned downwards in the length of the column like a distraught hatless woman. But Corinthian has a tall capital decorated with leaves and volutes with its own abacus and cornice, as it is said, like the elegant and gay girls adorned with their headbands for whom they were put up . . . and such columns they did not use for very solemn [*gravi*] buildings, but they kept them for gay [*ligiadri*] situations as in *logge*, gardens, galleries, and other places for walking. Doric columns have capitals of the height and proportion already given, but without so much ornament, a pure and simple drum of a masculine appearance, like Mars, Hercules, etc., in whose honour such buildings were erected. And this type (although it is little used today) because it is smooth and simple [*schietto e semplice*] is stronger than Corinthian and better at bearing weights, and the ancients used to divide its height into six equal parts . . . and sometimes seven depending on where they were put. . . . And so too Ionic columns, which are divided the same way as Doric, are very suitable for bearing weights. Although, as was said of Doric, because they are not beautiful to the eye they are [not] used today, you may use them in buildings which are utilitarian [*utili*] rather than grand [*pompose*], if you have freedom of choice; otherwise do what the patron wants and that is all. (pp. 144–45)

This passage contains a strange blend of new and old ideas. There are still references to the masculine and girlish characters of Doric and Corinthian, following Vitruvius, and various fifteenth-century notions are alluded to. Alberti had first suggested that stumpier columns were more suitable for utility and strength, and the idea has been taken up by Filarete and Colonna. Never before, however, had the general principle been stated that the shorter types of columns were more suitable for utilitarian buildings and the taller types for grand ones. Also Albertian in origin is the opposition between solemn (*gravi*) and gay (*ligiadri*) buildings which occurs in the discussion of Corinthian. This must derive from the opposition between *festivitas* and *gravitas*. But once again a general rule is presented with greater forcefulness. One result of this presentation of the two Albertian oppositions in the same passage is that their inconsistency emerges even more clearly. Saying that shorter columns such as Doric are recommended for utilitarian buildings, and taller ones such as Corinthian are suitable for grand ones, hardly fits with the advice that Corinthian should be used only for gay structures such as garden *logge* or with the associated suggestion that the opposite type of column, Doric, should be used for solemn ones. We should expect the same order to be suited to both "solemn" and "grand" buildings, rather than two different orders which embody a strong contrast. Pacioli, like Alberti, is still unable to resolve the fundamental problem of whether it is the richest or the simplest order which is most suited to the most important buildings. He can only restate in clearer terms the essential point that Doric is appropriate to morally superior buildings (*difficii gravi*) and Corinthian to socially superior ones (*cose pompose*).

The only completely new element in this passage is the characterization of Ionic as "melancholic" with which it begins. Not only has this order never been described in this way; none of the orders had before been directly associated with an emotion. Although Pacioli may have been influenced by the Vitruvian story of the origin of Caryatids in the figures of humiliated widows, the specific interpretation of the volutes as the attributes of mourning women is all his own. No clue is given as to why he should have introduced such a characterization in terms of emotion, but the most obvious parallel is with the musical modes. Indeed, it is now possible to see that the characterization of the other orders are influenced by the same approach. Although the terms *ligiadro* and *grave* may be derived from Alberti's opposition of *festivitas* and *gravitas*, as adjectives they are much more expressive than Alberti's abstract nouns, which are technical terms derived from the language of rhetoric and ethics. Pacioli is thus developing a fairly consistent emotional characterization of the three orders, Doric, Ionic, and Corinthian, as respectively solemn, sad, and gay. In so doing he can only be extending the assimilation of the orders and the modes found in Colonna.

Just how far Pacioli has gone in assimilating the theory of the orders to that of the modes is apparent from a comparison of his remarks on the orders with the modal theories of the greatest contemporary musical theorist, Franchino Gaffurio. There is every reason to expect a connection between the two men, since Gaffurio also worked at the Sforza court, being professor of music in Milan in the same years when Pacioli was professor of mathematics. Also, Pacioli's publications closely parallel those of Gaffurio: thus while Pacioli's *Summa arithmetica*, reviewing arithmetical knowledge, appeared in 1494, Gaffurio's equally comprehensive treatment of music appeared in two parts, the *Theoricum opus*, already printed in Naples in 1480, and the *Practica musicae*, printed in Milan in 1496. More precisely, the *De divina proportione*, printed in 1509 and with its architectural section written for a popular audience, seems to provide a deliberate match for Gaffurio's *Angelicum ac divinum opus musicae* (1508), also written as an Italian popularization of parts of the Latin *Practica*. Gaffurio's other great work, the *De harmonia musicorum instrumentorum*, written by 1500 (and referred to as complete in the 1508 frontispiece of the *Angelicum ac divinum opus*: Fig. 126) but not printed till 1518, is the one with the fullest account of the modes. In it he explains modal theory in a vocabulary very similar to that of Pacioli. Thus his statement that Dorian was thought appropriate for *graviores res*, "more serious matters,"[12] can be related to Pacioli's that Corinthian should not be used for *difficii gravi*, "serious buildings." While his remarks on the mournful nature of Lydian, which was invented *lamentationis et fletus causa*, "for lamentation and weeping,"[13] reminds us of Pacioli's characterization of Ionic as *malenconico* ("melancholic") and *flebile* ("mournful"). Since the *De harmonia* was not published till 1518, Pacioli may either have seen it in manuscript or, more likely, have arrived at his own theories as a result of oral discussion. Gaffurio certainly has an interest both in Pacioli's mathematical work and in the visual arts. Not only did he possess a copy of the *Summa arithmetica*,[14] but he was involved in an advisory role in the design of the *tiburio* of Milan Cathedral already in 1490.[15] Moreover, the *De harmonia* has a number of cross-references to painters and their practices and seems, in one specific detail, to show a reverse influence from the world of architectural theory. This is when it is said that the Dorian mode was used for songs about Mars and Minerva, an idea for which there seems to be no musicological source but which takes up Vitruvius' idea that temples to those gods should be in the Doric order. Contact between architectural and musical theory seems to have been not entirely one-sided.

Whatever the mechanics of that contact, it seems to have led to one of Pacioli's most remarkable contributions not just to the theory of the orders but to the whole theory of architecture, the introduction of the notion of emotional expressiveness. What had been hinted at in Colonna's association of Lydian with love songs now becomes explicit. The power of music to control our emotions had, along with its mathematical basis, always been one of the strongest reasons for its generally high status in the ancient world. Since Pacioli went to such lengths to assert the mathematical basis of the visual arts it is hardly surprising that he should also ascribe to them emotive force. At the same time Leonardo made similar claims for painting in its rivalry with poetry. "Painting moves the senses more quickly than poetry. And if you say that with words you will bring people to tears or laughter, I tell you that it is not you who move them, but it is the orator, and a science which is not poetry."[16] His fascination with the emotions as a limited series is revealed too in his notes on anatomy, where he proposes four illustrations to show the four universal conditions of men: happiness (*letitia*), weeping (*pianto*), contention (*contentione*), and labour (*fatica*).[17] This rather strange series of conditions involving the distortion of the normal human physiognomy has a curious correspondence with Pacioli's characterization of the orders in terms of gaiety, sadness, and the suitability for bearing weights. An interest in the emotions and their expression through the visual arts is thus yet another link between Pacioli and Leonardo. Once again we can sense the importance of the competition with the more established arts of music and poetry.

Architectural criticism and the eye

The following chapter (VIII) introduces yet another new element into the theory of architecture. It is headed "Where are now found the most correctly made columns in Italy both ancient and modern" and consists chiefly of a list of columns in the most famous cities of the peninsula together with remarks pointing out their good and bad qualities. Earlier writers had contented themselves with the formulation of general rules and had hardly referred to individual buildings of any period. Pacioli, on the other hand, sets out to establish aesthetic criteria, if not for whole buildings, at least for columns which are his main concern.

He begins with a strange passage criticizing Alberti, with whom he had stayed in Rome in the days of Paul II, for his lack of patriotism in substituting the term "Italic" for Vitruvius' "Tuscan," an observation which reveals his own failure to understand that the two terms refer to quite different forms. He goes on to praise the architecture of Florence, especially under Lorenzo de' Medici who, he implies, even became involved in making designs himself. Florence is thus the city to visit to find the best columns, which are those in the chapter house of S. Croce (the Pazzi Chapel), in S. Spirito, and especially in S. Lorenzo, where the best contemporary examples are to be found. He also admires those in the Duomo of Pisa, although their variety shows that they have been brought together from different sites. As for those of the Pantheon, he says that "although they are of the greatest size, nevertheless they do not have the correct proportions between height, base, and capital, that is, correct in the judgement of one who is expert in the art" (p. 149). Of the spiral vine columns in front of the altar of St Peter's he says that although they can serve as models in their height, their capitals, and their bases, the same cannot be said of the spiral shaft, "since it can be seen as either narrower or broader, as the eye pleases." In the twin columns in the Piazzetta at Venice he notices a similar weakness in the shaft design, "since if you look closely they seem to come to a point" (p. 149). Then, as if not to abuse Venice's hospitality he concludes that nowhere in Italy is there a column which surpasses that in the chapter house of the Frari in that city. For although it stands on a capital rather than a base, it "answers the eye with every beauty" (p. 149). Criticism is thus throughout in terms not of an objective correspondence to Vitruvian or other rules but of a subjective response to the column by the eye.

The significance of this passage of architectural criticism becomes clear if it is compared with the passage in Alberti which deals with the faults in bad architecture. There the emphasis is always on rational errors: structurally weak design, lack of mathematical regularity, incompatability between form and function. No examples are given since everything can be formulated in general rules. Pacioli, by contrast, needs to introduce examples since his point is precisely that only in front of the building itself can the faults which interest him be recognized. The faculty where the judgement takes place is the *giudizio*, whose dependence on the evidence of the senses is discussed by Leonardo: "The soul seems to reside in the judicial faculty [*parte giudiziale*], and the judicial faculty seems to be in the place where all the senses come together, that is the place called the common sense [*senso commune*]."[18] The chain of experience runs from *senso* (eye) to *giudizio* to *anima* (soul), and *giudizio* is the area where all sense experience is processed. Its response to the visual experience of something like a building is thus of decisive importance. It is not surprising to find this faculty, which is central to Aristotelian psychology, receiving a new attention at the same time as the sense of sight, which had also been so important to the Greek philosopher. The central importance of *giudizio* in the circle of Pacioli and Leonardo is illustrated by its use by Leonardo in a passage where he draws attention to one of his most important contributions to artistic development. Talking of the need to employ a series of free drawings to experiment with a figure or composition until a satisfactory solution is found, Leonardo explains how we often make figures like ourselves because "our *giudizio* is that which moves our hands in the creation of the outlines of such figures through a series of different ap-

pearances until they satisfy us."[19] The judgement which guides the painter in his sequence of creation and correction is the same as that which guides the architect in his selection of a satisfying column.

PACIOLI's importance is not that he formulates a new theory of architecture nor that his writings have a great influence. It lies rather in the fact that his contact with a whole range of artists and writers from Alberti and Piero to Leonardo means that through his writings we can get precious glimpses into the artistic culture of the late fifteenth century, and especially into the Milanese background of Bramante, who was to be the most important architect of the early sixteenth century. We will have to bear Pacioli's ideas in mind when considering the architecture of the latter after his arrival in Rome. We have all the more reason for taking them seriously since their main theme, the predominance of the eye over the other senses and the consequent elevation of the status of the visual arts, is one which is found not only in Leonardo but elsewhere. We have already seen how Colonna, like Pacioli, attempted to endow architecture with the expressive potential of music, just as Leonardo sought to match painting to poetry. Other common elements between Pacioli and Colonna are no less significant, such as the importance that both attach to the use of coloured marbles, as stressed by Pacioli in his introduction to the architectural section of his work, as well as their common interest in illustrations. Both features must stem from the new concern for visual effect. In the same way Pacioli's desire to have full-page illustrations bound in at the front of his treatise parallels Dürer's similar placing of the large blocks of his 1498 *Apocalypse* before the text, presumably for the same reasons. The emphasis on visual communication which, for Francesco di Giorgio, had only been for the sake of instructional clarity now begins to influence the higher realm of artistic expression.

XVII

Bramante

◆

THE WRITINGS of Colonna (1499) and of Pacioli (1509) roughly bracket the first decade of the sixteenth century, a decade which marks that peak of achievement in the visual arts known as the High Renaissance, as represented by the painting of Leonardo and Giorgione, the sculpture of Michelangelo, and the architecture of Bramante. It would be strange if they did not provide us with some clues to the understanding of this remarkable phenomenon, especially since Leonardo and Bramante were both with Pacioli in Milan and Giorgione was working in Colonna's Venice. Since Colonna and Pacioli both wrote on architecture, the hope that they can shed some light on Bramante's intentions must be particularly high.

Architectural polyphony

Nothing certain is known of Bramante's activity in his native environment of Urbino. His earliest documented work is in the Milan area, where he was employed from about 1477 to 1499. His first major building, S. Maria presso S. Satiro (1482 onwards), is entirely consistent with normal practice, being Corinthian inside and out. The same is true of his ambitious extension of S. Maria delle Grazie and the Canonica of S. Ambrogio, where the most striking novel feature are the columns carved to look like tree-trunks, perhaps following Alberti's recommendation that such columns are appropriate to gardens.[1] Both these works are of the early 1490s, but when in 1497 Bramante made a completely new design for the monastic buildings behind S. Ambrogio he seems to have departed from established principles. His project included two large cloisters to be erected on the opposite side of the church to the existing Canonica. The odd element in their elevation is that, while both have Doric pilasters on the upper floor, on the lower storey one is Doric and the other Ionic. It is difficult to explain the difference in order between the two cloisters as indicative of a difference of either status or function. Ionic was, of course, the traditional order for cloisters, and Doric here may also have been introduced because of its appropriate simplicity. Yet there is no apparent reason for the change from one to the other. The only readily available explanation is that for some reason Bramante desired variety. This effect of variety is further enhanced if the monastic cloisters are taken together with the Corinthian Canonica to create a series of three similar elevations using three different orders (Fig. 125). The layout of Bramante's first work in Rome, the cloister of S. Maria della Pace begun in 1500, confirms an unusual interest in the use of a series of the orders (Fig. 127). For this cloister, although only a single square, combines Doric, Ionic, Corinthian, and Composite in a highly self-conscious way. On the ground floor the pilasters of the main arcade are Ionic, while the upper floor consists of an alternation of Corinthian columns and cross-shaped piers with Composite capitals. It is likely also, as Bruschi has argued, that the square piers of the lower floor should be recognized as Doric.[2] The four orders would thus be compressed into one two-storey building depriving them individually of any distinctive expressive function. What makes this use of the orders particularly strange is the use of the two orders of similar height under the same architrave on the top floor, which denies one of the main rules of Classical architecture.

Bramante must have had a very positive reason for this innovation. To say that he simply wanted to combine all the orders is not enough; but no other explanation for the innovation emerges out of either the ancient world or recent practice. We must instead look at

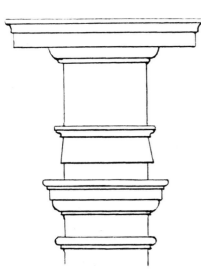

125. Bramante: three orders from S. Maria delle Grazie,
Milan, 1490s (after Förster)

contemporary theoretical interests. The major feature shared by Colonna and Pacioli was their insistence on the analogy between architecture and music, and although neither of them uses this analogy as an argument for multiple combinations of orders it is easy to see how the analogy could have led in exactly that direction. Leonardo, in an important passage (cited in the last chapter) which compares poetry unfavourably with painting, stresses how in a painting, unlike in a poem, all the elements can be enjoyed together, thus producing just such a quality of harmony as is essential to the beauty of music: "just as from many different voices joined together at one time a harmonious proportional relationship develops."[3] The pleasure offered by a poem, on the other hand, is no greater than music would provide "if one caused each voice to be heard separately at different times, so that there was no concord."[4] The same point is repeated more explicitly when Leonardo describes how a poet is like a musician "who sings by himself a song composed of four voices and sings first the soprano, then the tenor, after that the alto [*contralto*], and then the bass: he is unable to produce a harmonic proportionality. . . ."[5] Leonardo's use of polyphonic harmony as a metaphor for the painter's capacity to show several parts of a body at the same time is of rather questionable validity. If, however, the same metaphor is applied to architecture, the correspondence between the different voices and the voices of the traditional human models of the orders—virile, matronly, and virginal—makes a direct application of the musical principle to building both obvious and easy. The assimilation of Doric to the bass voice, Ionic to the alto, and so on, would seem especially natural in view of the fact that the modes had conventionally constituted a scale of sound with Dorian at the bottom. Bramante may thus have seen his task as an architect in the same way that Leonardo saw his as a painter, that is as an artist whose concern it was to make the closest possible parallels between architecture and polyphonic music.

It may seem strange to us that both Leonardo and Bramante should have attached so much importance to polyphonic harmony. In fact, they were only taking up the principle which Gaffurio, whom we have already met as an influence on Pacioli, had placed at the very centre of his theory of music. As he says in the *Practica musicae* (1496): "harmony is the sweet and congruous sonority of distant and contrary voices embracing consonances by a common mean: it is made up out of high and low and intermediate notes."[6] Here he is only restating an accepted view. But his interest in harmony as a combination of disparate elements leads him to go on

126. Franchino Gaffurio, *Angelicum ac divinum opus musicae*, 1508:
frontispiece (re-used in *De harmonia*, 1518)

to give a new character to the ancient Mixolydian mode as a mixture of the elements of all the others, and to invent a new *genus* (alongside the diatonic, the chromatic, and the harmonic) called the *permixtum*, or "mixed."[7] He was also busy in the late 1490s composing a new musical treatise, the *De harmonia musicorum instrumentorum*, whose title accorded to harmony an unprecedented prominence. The importance he attached to this idea of harmony was illustrated in the frontispiece affixed to the 1508 *Angelicum ac divinum opus* (and re-used for the 1518 publication of the *De harmonia*), where Gaffurio is shown teaching with the words *Harmonia est discordia concors* ("Harmony is a concordant discord") coming out of his mouth, and where three organ pipes of different lengths are emblematic of the harmonic relationship of three different notes (Fig. 126). It is easy to see how the three organ pipes could be assimilated to columns of three different

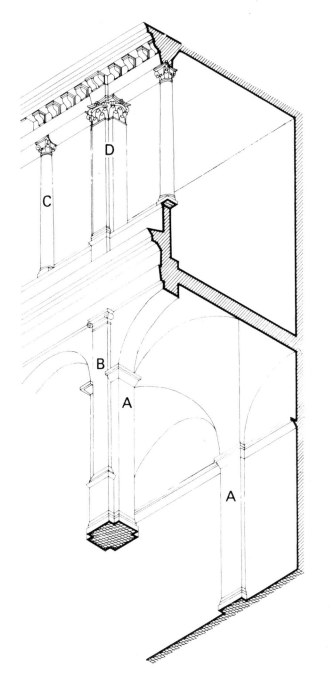

127. Bramante: S. Maria della Pace, Rome, 1499:
left (a) cloister; above (b) diagram of four
orders—Doric (A), Ionic (B), Corinthian (C),
Composite (D) (after Bruschi)

orders. Bramante, like Leonardo, will have had no difficulty in having access to Gaffurio's ideas. The musician was involved with Bramante in the design of the Milan Cathedral *tiburio*, and Vasari tells us that music was one of the architect's main interests.[8] There is thus likely to have been the same kind of contact between the two men that there was between Gaffurio and Pacioli.

Further evidence of Bramante's interest in combining the orders in a series is found in three later buildings in Rome, all part of the Vatican complex which he extended on a vast scale for Julius II (1503–13). The first of these is the interior elevation of the Belvedere Court.[9] When Bramante enclosed the sloping ground between the wing of Nicholas V and the villa of Innocent VIII after 1504, he planned an elevation of three rows of galleries either side, Doric at the bottom, Ionic in the middle, and Corinthian at the top. The fact that this was the first Renaissance building to employ the same series of orders as on the bottom three arcades of the Colosseum should not be taken as a sign of Bramante's interest in that monument. Not only does the articulation not correspond with that of the ancient structure, but the other two series of orders in adjoining buildings are different again. In the grand spiral stair ramp, which gave direct access from outside the palace to the upper Belvedere, and which was under construction in 1511, four different column types succeed each other supporting the continuous turning architrave (Fig. 129b). The lowest group of capitals are very simple and were probably thought of as Tuscan, those above are slightly more elaborate and were probably thought of as Doric, the next group are Ionic, and the final set Composite. Different again is the series decorating the exterior of the Logge in the Cortile di S. Damaso (Fig 128). These Logge, which replaced a more modest loggia on the site, were under construction in 1509 but were only finished by Raphael in 1518. The ground floor originally seems to have had plain open arches. Above that came two rows of arcades, the lower decorated with Doric pilasters and the upper with Ionic. Finally at the top came a trabeated colonnade with Composite capitals. Each of the three Vatican structures thus had a different series of the orders, and none of them had the same series as the S. Maria della Pace cloister. Yet all four buildings show an entirely new interest in the combination of three or

128. Cortile di S. Damaso, Vatican, c.1509–18

four orders in a consistent series with no concern for the expression of relative status. It is as if Bramante wanted to try out as many variations on the theme as possible: Doric, Ionic, Corinthian, Composite (S. Maria della Pace); Doric, Ionic, Corinthian (Belvedere); Tuscan, Doric, Ionic, Composite (spiral stair); Doric, Ionic, Composite (Cortile di S. Damaso). In the same way different combinations of voices might be used by a composer in order to produce a rich variety of effects. Since Bramante never takes from the Colosseum either its formal language or the entire series found there (Doric, Ionic, Corinthian, Corinthian) it is unlikely that its imitation was his prime concern. It may, however, have given him an idea for the most apposite architectural equivalent of a series of voices. For scores of polyphonic music which displayed three or four parts one above the other with the bass at the bottom were just coming in at this time, and Bramante could easily have been struck by the fact that the successive orders of the Colosseum provided a similar scheme (Fig. 129a). Hence his fondness for such score-like combinations after the less obviously musical effects of the cloister of S. Maria della Pace.

There is no direct evidence that Bramante identified a vertically rising series of the orders with polyphonic

harmony. It is striking, however, that when Serlio, who was a great admirer of Bramante, sought to justify a variation in the treatment of different floors of an elevation he did this by saying that the result had the advantage of being a *discordia concordante* (concordant discord), referring directly to Gaffurio's celebrated phrase.[10] It is also true that there is no direct parallel between Bramante's "polyphony" and anything in either Colonna or Pacioli. Nevertheless there is a remarkable correspondence between Colonna's gateway and the cloister of S. Maria della Pace (Fig. 131a). The latter structure is arguably the most elaborate example of a layout in terms of *quadratura* such as Colonna recommended as an equivalent to the *chromatice minute* of the musician. Bramante's interest in using a grid of squares to organize both plan and elevation has produced the solecism of a court with an even number of bays on all sides; also each elevation seems to consist of two units, each containing a square and a half, which happens to be precisely the proportional layout of the door in the *Hypnerotomachia*. Another possible connection between Bramante and Colonna is provided by the project (recorded by Serlio)[11] to place the Tempietto within a circular colonnaded court—a scheme which recalls the temple at the centre of the island of Cythera surrounded by its circular peristyle, and one which produces the same progressive narrowing of intercolumniation effectively intensifying the experience of the approaching worshipper. Gombrich showed how features of the Belvedere project too depended on the *Hypnerotomachia*.[12] Coming from the Milan of Pacioli, Leonardo, and Gaffurio, Bramante might naturally have been interested in a musical theory of architecture such as that presented by Colonna. Moreover, Colonna's book came out just as Bramante arrived in Rome and began designing the cloister of S. Maria della Pace.

If there is no direct proof that Bramante was familiar with Gaffurio's ideas on polyphony and was interested in relating them to architecture, the same is not true of Cesare Cesariano, who was Bramante's intellectual heir in Milan. In his great commentary on Vitruvius, published in Como in 1521, Cesariano gives musical theory a prominent place alongside that of architecture and repeatedly refers his reader to the writings of Gaffurio.[13] Indeed he constantly calls Gaffurio his *preceptore* (teacher) for music just as he calls Bramante his

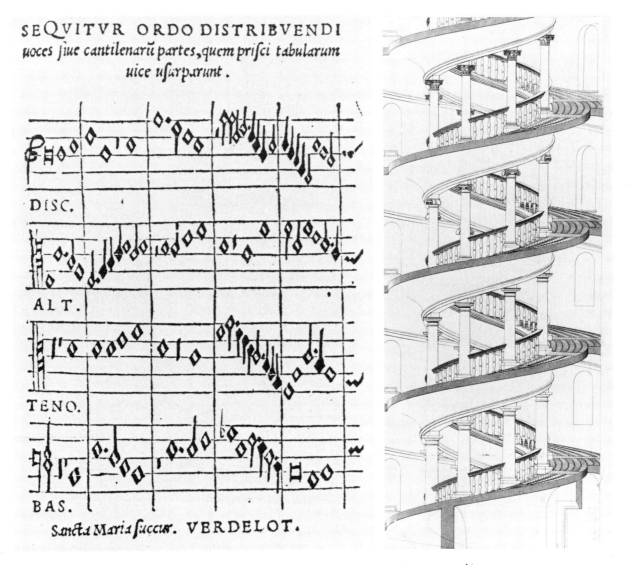

129. Left (a) four voices of Verdelot's motet *Sancta Maria, succurre nobis,*
c.1510–15, as published by Lampadius (1537); right (b) spiral stair,
Vatican, c.1511 (after Letarouilly)

preceptore for architecture. Cesariano at least felt that the two were compatible figures. He was also sure about the need to apply Gaffurio's theories to architecture, as when he insists that the architect "should not only know how to commodulate the proportions of buildings, but their *intonantie* [resonances] as well,"[14] referring the reader directly to the theorist. Although in the context of Vitruvius it was not appropriate to dis-

cuss combinations of orders, Cesariano shows a particular interest in polyphonic harmony. When Vitruvius remarks that the architect should understand music, Cesariano notes among other things that a *symphonia* is made "when voices sing proportionately and being in a commodulation are most sweet to hear; in which by using high and low voices they make the appropriate concords."[15] Later he seems to assimilate the modes

130. Leonardo da Vinci: *Last Supper*, 1495–98,
S. Maria delle Grazie, Milan

to the seven notes of the octave: "They call this harmony, that is the concent of the universe, and in it Saturn is moved by the Dorian, Jupiter by the Phrygian, etc."[16] Much later again he talks of the tetrachords: "Which tetrachords are each made up of four voices, that is one is low, the second medium, the third high, and the fourth very high, as with the *contrabasso, tenore, contralto* and *soprano*."[17] His readiness to see harmonies in different types of combinations—of the notes of the octave, of different modes, and of four voices—directly recalls Bramante's apparent readiness to assimilate the Classical orders now to a series of modes and now to a series of voices. His enthusiasm for relating architecture to music does sometimes carry him wildly away, as when he interprets Vitruvius' *barycephalae* temples as tall churches of cathedral size which have a great resonance for low notes![18] Still, as Bramante's most articulate pupil he provides hard evidence for his master's likely musical interests. Since his contact with Bramante must have ceased with the lat-

ter's departure from Milan, it is not surprising that he shows no explicit knowledge of his particular musical exploitation of the orders.

Cesariano provides useful support for our connection of Bramante with Gaffurio. But he does not indicate what might have led the architect to take an interest in musical theory in the first place. Responsibility for this probably lies with Leonardo, who so explicitly favoured visual polyphony. Leonardo may even have directly anticipated Bramante in showing how polyphonic harmony could be achieved visually. He may also have anticipated him in showing how harmony could be combined with musical *quadratura* in a single work. The *Last Supper* was painted on the end wall of the refectory of S. Maria delle Grazie at Milan in 1496–97 (Fig. 130). Luca Pacioli observed already in the *De divina proportione* that in the *Last Supper* Leonardo had made a triumphant demonstration of the ability of the visual arts to rival the aural arts by representing the emotional responses of the disciples to

232

Christ's words: "One of you shall betray me."[19] This response is articulated by a division of the disciples into four groups of three, and in three of these groups all three men react almost with one voice. The men on the left all stretch out their hands as if to say "Did you hear what He said?" and those on the right hold up theirs in a gesture of aversion as if to say "What a shocking idea!" while the third group to the left of Christ all seem to protest their innocence. The fourth group, on the other hand, introduces the sinister figure of Judas expressively jarring the harmony of the whole. Each group contributes an element to the response, but we must look at all together to get the rich total effect. The four male groups thus recall the organization of a contemporary choir with its four sections, treble, alto, tenor, and bass, and the whole can be said to rival the harmony of a contemporary musical setting of a religious drama. If Leonardo wanted to make a polyphonic painting he could hardly have found a better way of doing it. Others have recently and quite independently argued the influence of Gaffurio's theory on Leonardo, especially in this painting. They have also pointed out what may well be intended as another musical feature.[20] This is the grid of squares underlying the composition. The end of the room is square, and this square is divided into four with Christ's head at the centre (Fig. 131b). This scheme then provides the geometric key to the whole painting which can be described as consisting of three units of a square and a half repeated horizontally. We have already noted that the square and a half was the key to the musical *quadratura* of Colonna's gate and that it recurred in Bramante's S. Maria della Pace cloister (Fig. 131a). Both writer and architect may have known of the principle underlying Leonardo's painting. It may not be irrelevant that the same 2:1 proportion (that of the octave) also underlies the chief musical diagram of Cesariano's Vitruvius commentary.[21] The polyphonic effect of the *Last Supper* is another encouragement to see Bramante's contemporary project for the cloisters of S. Ambrogio a few hundred yards away as embodying the same musical properties. If Bramante's interest in rivalling the aural arts was principally inspired by Leonardo at this date, this may also explain why the one surviving piece of evidence for his attempt to master the art of poetry is a manuscript collection of sonnets also dated 1497.[22]

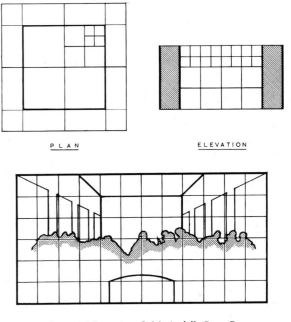

PLAN   ELEVATION

131. At top (a) Bramante: S. Maria della Pace, Rome, 1499, cloister, diagrams of plan and elevation; below (b) *Quadratura* of Fig. 130

The orders and the modes

If one group of buildings by Bramante is characterized by a new interest in combining the orders together in a series, another group is characterized by a new and more assertive use of one order alone. This group requires a different explanation, and one readily emerges from the writings of Colonna and Pacioli, both of whom had developed theories on the emphatic use of individual orders by analogy with the musical modes.

Bramante's most famous building in a single order is the Tempietto (Fig. 132). This remarkable round structure in the cloister of S. Pietro in Montorio marks the spot where, according to one tradition, Saint Peter had been crucified. An inscription records that it was founded by the King and Queen of Spain in 1502, and this date still seems most likely. The Tempietto is Doric both inside and out, and the exterior order is adorned with a prominent series of triglyphs and metopes, the latter filled with sculpture. It has often been suggested that the choice of order represents a christianization of the Vitruvian rule of *decor*, with Doric being used for

132. Bramante: Tempietto, S. Pietro in Montorio, Rome, after 1502

Saint Peter on the same grounds that it would be for Mars. This can now be supported by reference to contemporary theory. Not only did Colonna in 1499 make the first explicit revival of the theory of *decor* since Antiquity, and Pacioli compare the matching of order to temple with the Christian habit of matching attributes to saints, but Gaffurio even applied the same idea to the musical context, matching the Dorian mode to Mars and Minerva. Bramante should thus be seen not simply as updating Vitruvius but as going beyond him, once again following up the musical theory of Gaffurio. Hence the architecture and its decoration take on a role of active significance. Just as Colonna had extended the Vitruvian rule by using materials, colour, and sculpture to increase the Venereal aspects of his Corinthian temple of Venus, so Bramante uses the symbols of the metopes with their allusions to Saint Peter, the papacy, and the Christian Church to intensify the Petrine and Christian meaning of his Tempietto. Vitruvius only wished that the orders should not be used inappropriately: Bramante wishes them to be actively expressive. Vitruvius only wanted architecture to conform to the laws of nature: Bramante wanted architecture to rival music.

A close parallel to the use of Doric in the Tempietto was provided by the structure of peperino which Bramante built to protect the tomb of Saint Peter while the crossing of the new church was being erected (Figs. 35 [p. 60] and 139). It too was executed in a full Classical Doric, with its metopes adorned with reliefs referring to its Petrine and papal associations. Like the Tempietto, it both matched and expressed the character of the Prince of Apostles in its strong simple forms. In this work we can also confirm that we are not just dealing with a use of Doric as a morally superior form, in the general sense that had been understood in the late fifteenth century, by comparing it with a structure of similar function, the marble casing of the Santa Casa, the supposed house of the Virgin, around which had been built the great church at Loreto (Fig. 133). This has a similar role within the church, being the facing of the holy shrine which stands at its centre. Designed by Bramante for Julius after 1508, the marble casing was not actually erected until the years after 1513 under the supervision of Andrea Sansovino. The wall surfaces are framed by half-columns as at St Peter's, but the order is now Corinthian of a most elaborate variety with fluted columns and a heavily carved entablature. In Vitruvian terms, the architecture is as appropriate to the glorious Virgin as was the simple Doric to Saint Peter. Statues of the prophets and sibyls who foretold Christ's coming and large reliefs of the life of the Virgin all draw attention to the importance of the Santa Casa for the Christian community. Never at the period had there been such an eloquent piece of sculpted architecture. The contrast between the two buildings at Rome and Loreto may in part be due to their different life expectancies, since it is possible that the altar house in St Peter's was only temporary, but the striking differences in their ornamentation call for more specific explanation in terms of the expression of character. The way that the differentiation of the two buildings in terms of materials, sculpture, and order parallels the differentiation of buildings in the *Hypnerotomachia*, where the desire to imitate modal theory is more or less explicit, and the way that the association of the order with *segni* and *instrumenti* associated with Christian saints parallels the text of the *De divina proportione*, where the analogy with music is implicit, make it likely that Bramante's intention was the same.

On the pre-eminence of Doric

Two of the three buildings just discussed were Doric, and one of the most striking features of Bramante's architecture is his fondness for that order. A major group of Doric works are those put up for Julius II, and in one sense this is not remarkable given the pope's preference for the simple order when he was a cardinal. Now, however, the use is both more personal and more assertive. The order is linked with the pope's name in a whole group of works by both Bramante and Giuliano da Sangallo. Julius' name is inscribed in large letters on Giuliano's design for a Doric loggia for the papal trumpeters of 1505 and on the grand loggia on the Castel S. Angelo, overlooking the Tiber, of the same year. Also Doric were the cupola added to the Torre Borgia about 1510 by either Giuliano or Bramante, and Bramante's "Serlian" windows both in the Sala Regia (Fig. 134) and in the choir of S. Maria del Popolo, all of which are prominently marked with the pope's name. It is clear that the specifically Doric character of this simple order is more important than it had been before. This is even more true of the palace Bramante designed for the ap-

133. Bramante: exterior of Santa Casa, Basilica della Santa Casa, Loreto, begun 1509

ostolic protonotary Caprini around 1510. Its triglyphs, metopes, and half-columns rival the rich articulation of the Tempietto (Fig. 135).

It is just possible that all these buildings only represent an extension of the della Rovere style of the late fifteenth century, but they are different in character from the earlier structures, and reference instead to the musical theory of Gaffurio provides a general reason for a new preference for a Greek order equivalent to the Dorian mode. In his *De harmonia*, the great theorist provides a remarkable eulogy of Dorian. An important chapter is headed "De proprietatibus quattuor modorum et de praestantia Dorii" (On the properties of the four modes and on the pre-eminence of Dorian).[23] Another whole chapter is devoted to Dorian usage,[24] while the three remaining modes are all cramped into one. Never, even in Antiquity, had the mode received such attention. By bringing together many of the Classical references to it and elaborating on them, Gaffurio places Dorian in an unrivalled position. The Dorians who developed the mode had, he says, a taste for the permanent, the constant, and the severe, and they thought it appropriate to the loftiness and greatness of a noble mind. Plato admired it for its "manliness and good behaviour." It was used for songs about Mars and Minerva "because these, by their tem-

236

peraments, should endow a man's mind with a great strength [*ingenti robure*]." The ancients thus with remarkable perception claimed that the Dorian mode was a "leader and guide in the direction of a good and correct life."[25] We have already seen that Pacioli seems to be influenced by Gaffurio's theory of the modes in saying that Corinthian should not be used for *difficii gravi* and taking up Gaffurio's recommendation of Dorian for *graviores res*. We have also seen that Gaffurio's own ideas seem to reflect a knowledge of Vitruvian theory in the matching of modes to divinities. Given these and the other examples of contact between musical and architectural theory in Milan, it is likely that Bramante (who was, Vasari tells us, active as a musician) would also have known of the new evaluation of the Dorian mode. He may well have recognized how easily it could be used to give a further expression to Julius II's tastes. As a cardinal Julius had favoured an architecture of Christian simplicity; Gaffurio's theory suggested how, by being made more specifically Doric, this architecture could be made not only a more positive expression of moral greatness, but even an effective instrument for encouraging such moral excellence in others. His identification of the Dorian mode with *ingens robur* could have made it especially appropriate to a member of the della Rovere family.

All this is speculation. But it would explain why Bramante's buildings for Julius are more assertively Doric than any previous structures. It would also explain why not only Julius but many other members of the Roman establishment, from the Caprini family onwards, confidently adopted the same forms. The lofty credentials with which anything Doric was endowed by extension from Gaffurio's theory made it unnecessary any longer to add Corinthian and Composite attributes, as had still been done on the Palazzo della Cancelleria façade and on the portals of the Savona palace or Turin Cathedral. If Doric was the emblem of "the loftiness and greatness of a noble mind," it needed no trappings of authority. After the example set by the apostolic protonotary Caprini, many others felt that it was the only appropriate attribute of their elevated status. By using it they could even feel that, like Plato's guardians playing Dorian music, they were helping to raise the moral level of the whole community.

In this sense there may also be a parallel with the effect of polyphonic harmony in the buildings of the

134. Bramante: window of Sala Regia, Vatican, after 1504

Vatican. Gaffurio had noted that the skills which the musician employs to create a harmony out of different voices were similar to the skills which a doctor should use in creating a harmonic balance of elements in the human body and those which a statesman should use in creating harmony out of the different classes in society. Since Early Christian times it had been argued that a principal role of the ecclesiastical hierarchy was to bring harmony to the disparate elements of the Church.[26] The repeated emphasis on a harmony of different orders in the Vatican, seat of the Church's government, may have been seen as an expression of a new harmony brought by Julius. It may even have been thought of as expressing that harmony so powerfully as to communicate it to those who saw it and so to actually help in spreading it.

Some may find the proposed influence from musical theory unlikely on internal grounds, since it may seem implausible that Bramante would have used the orders as an equivalent of several polyphonic voices in one set of buildings and as an equivalent of modes in another. But it must be remembered that Bramante would never have argued that architecture was an art which exactly

135. Bramante: Palazzo Caprini, Rome, c.1510: engraving by Lafreri

corresponded in its elements of music, only that it was possible to produce in it analogous effects, such as those of polyphonic harmony and modal expressiveness. It is also important to remember that when Bramante uses the orders to mean two completely different things he is only doing what Pacioli and Colonna did in their theories. Colonna had one theory that the orders were equivalent to people of different sexes and another that their appropriateness depended on whether their function was to support or to adorn. Pacioli had one theory that the orders should be matched with associated emotions, another that they should be matched with types of divinity, and yet another that they should be matched with buildings according to a scale from utility to pomp. Such ambiguities and contradictions were always inherent in attempts to enrich the significance of forms by attaching to them metaphorical meanings. Almost every treatise provides ex-

amples of such apparent inconsistencies, and we should not be surprised to find them in practice.

A possible influence of musical theory on Bramante's architecture thus would provide an explanation for three of the most striking characteristics of his style after 1497: his combination of a series of three or four different orders in one building, his emphatic use of a single order together with associated sculpture, and his preference for Doric. There is no direct evidence for this musical influence: all that can be said is that Bramante the musician is unlikely to have been ignorant of the ideas of Gaffurio, or of Leonardo's and Pacioli's efforts to apply those ideas to painting and architecture. The only direct links between Gaffurio and Bramante are established by their collaboration on the design of Milan Cathedral and by Cesariano's reference to them both as his teachers. There is, though, one odd piece of evidence which comes close to demonstrating

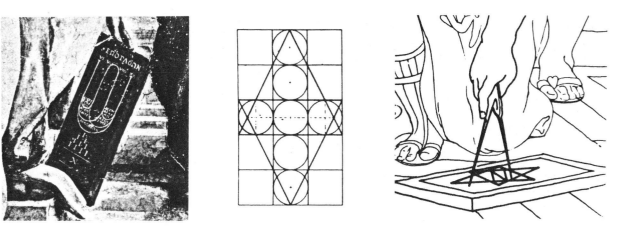

136. Raphael, *School of Athens*, Stanza della Segnatura, Vatican: left to right
(a) musical diagram of Pythagoras; (b) diagram of background architecture;
(c) diagram of Archimedes (Bramante) (b and c after Bruschi)

that there is an exact parallel between Bramante's architecture and music. This is Raphael's fresco of the *School of Athens* in the Stanza della Segnatura. In the foreground on the right-hand side Bramante is shown in the guise of Archimedes leaning forward to draw a diagram of intersecting triangles on a tablet in front of him, a diagram which has been shown to represent the underlying geometry of the architectural background to the whole scene (Figs. 136 and 142).[27] Since Vasari tells us that Bramante did indeed help Raphael with this architecture, Raphael is here evidently recording that special debt. But Raphael also appears to be telling us something else. The tablet containing Bramante's diagram is exactly paralleled by a similar tablet on the left-hand side of the fresco in front of Pythagoras, which contains another diagram, this time a representation of the geometry underlying the harmonies of the Greek tetrachord, the basic device of musical instruction. Raphael seems to use the explicit pairing of these images to show that Bramante's architecture is an exact equivalent of Greek music, both being governed by the same simple geometry. It is significant that he does not make Bramante's diagram copy the proportions of the tetrachord, since the point is not that architecture follows music but that both have, as Pacioli pointed out, a common mathematical basis. Bramante, as Raphael presents him to us, is not copying the musician; he is only achieving similar effects.

Modes of rustication

Bramante's expressive use of orders, materials, and carved ornaments seems to have a close parallel in his expressive use of rough masonry. When applied earlier to Florentine palaces from the Palazzo Vecchio onwards, bossed masonry was probably intended to convey a general impression of strength and authority, taking as its models the castles of Frederick II in southern Italy.[28] It was presumably still with the same association that it had been used on the Palazzo Medici and a whole series of later fifteenth-century structures. There had, however, been a tendency on important buildings for the roughness of the individual blocks to be progressively reduced, so that by the end of the century bossed masonry was either faceted as on the Palazzo dei Diamanti at Ferrara, or channelled as on the Palazzo della Cancelleria, or rounded as on the Palazzo Strozzi. It is as if people felt that whatever its past associations its roughness made it somehow incompatible with the refinement associated with the upper classes.

Bramante, on the other hand, had perhaps found a more convincingly appropriate way of using it. One of the best examples of this is the basement of the Palazzo di Giustizia, the "ministry of justice" building begun for Julius II about 1508 but never finished (Fig. 137). The gigantic basement on the Via Giulia still testifies to

137. Bramante: Palazzo di Giustizia, Rome, incomplete basement, c.1508

the power and rigour of Julius' urban government. The intended towered façade, shown on the foundation medal, conveys the weight of traditional military authority. The massive and rough rustication dwarfs and oppresses the passer-by. Size, roughness, and regularity of coursing are intended as vivid expressions of the power, remorselessness, and discipline of the law. Another new form of rustic masonry is used around the great gate through the north wall of the Belvedere Court. Underneath the inscription, which is framed between two great rounded string courses which had already been used on the tower of Nicholas V and which were to become emblematic of fortification, the arch is framed by a massive series of voussoirs. Being more rounded and smoother than those of the Palazzo di Giustizia, they embody the more passive strength of defence in contrast to the aggressively punitive quality of justice. The bossed masonry of the basement of the Palazzo Caprini was different again (Fig. 135). Being

made only of a stucco covering applied to bricks, it is unlikely to have had connotations of strength. In an unusual way it combined rough and pitted surfaces with sharply bevelled edges. The difference of form suggests that the reference is different again, and, since the bossing is restricted to the basement which is occupied by shops, it is possible that it serves (as Doric had served earlier) as an expression of the simplicity and coarseness of the lower classes who would occupy it. Evidence to support this suggestion is provided by subsequent residential palaces such as the Palazzo Vidoni and the Palazzo Cicciaporci, which also exclude rustication from floors above the basement but which often use it there in connection with commercial premises. One factor which may have influenced the use of rustication in this context is that Doric, which had earlier been used for a similar purpose as on the Palazzo Rucellai, had now acquired complete respectability. By the replacement of Doric with rustication the distinction of status between ground and upper floors, as on the Palazzo Rucellai, could still be made. Similar considerations led to the introduction of rough masonry in rural buildings. Now that Doric was an emblem of urban civilization, it was necessary to find a new badge of rustic simplicity. Rough masonry was an obvious possibility, and it is probably with this purpose that Bramante used it in his unusual rural nymphaeum at Genazzano. There it is not only applied to window frames for the first time, but rough masonry is also left on sections of entablature; and although it has been suggested that the building may be genuinely unfinished, the rough simplicity of many of the mouldings seems to suggest that the coarse overall effect is intended. When Bramante introduced rough masonry as an expression of rural simplicity, he hit upon an idea which was to strike a ready response in the European mind. Already in the nearby church of Capranica Praenestina a similar set of coarse unfinished forms with blocks of raw stone still attached is applied to the *tribuna* of 1520. Such a use of rustication on a church can only be understood as an early and overenthusiastic demonstration of the building's rural character, and the gesture was to prove exceptional. But such rough masonry did rapidly become associated with secular rural buildings, and it would soon be classified by Serlio as *opera rustica*. Once again it is important to notice the precise character of the rustication of the nymphaeum. Instead of the large surfaces covered with self-conscious and artificial projections that are found in varying forms in all the urban examples, here the surface roughness—found, for instance, in the entablature where it looks as if an outer layer still has to be removed—gives more the impression of the unfinished and untamed. Further finishing, like further education for the countryman, would produce considerably greater refinement, though all the forms are deliberately more simply moulded than the urban examples—the bumpkin will remain a countryman. Each of these four types of rustication communicates something about the building or part of a building to which it is attached. Bramante realized that the qualities of simplicity, strength, and even roughness are applicable equally to judges, soldiers, the lower classes, and country dwellers, but knowing that they are applicable in each case for different reasons he has varied the types of rustication accordingly. His use of rustication cannot be directly related to a particular musical device as can the use of the orders, but it does show how he was looking for any possible way to express the character of different buildings.

The new St Peter's: the history of religion and the history of architecture

Nothing that has been said so far sheds any light on the use of the orders in Bramante's greatest building, the new St Peter's (Fig. 139), or for that matter in the church of S. Biagio planned for the centre of the Palazzo di Giustizia. Both buildings are dedicated to male saints, but both were intended to have magnificent Corinthian interiors. Both too were put up by Julius, who in so many other buildings favoured sober Doric. The simplest explanation in the case of St Peter's would be that Julius just could not risk using Doric for the church which he was rebuilding as such a clear statement of the new power and authority of the Church and the papacy.[29] If so, he was of course adopting an approach opposed to that which he inherited from his uncle, and it is indeed certain that he saw his activity at St Peter's in a very different light. Sixtus, who actually stopped work on St Peter's, boasted in his chapel that he was inferior to Solomon in his wealth, but superior in his religion. Julius, on the other hand, in the last bull of his reign affirmed his intention to imitate the Old Testament ruler precisely in sparing no expense to build a church worthy of God.[30] If it was important for him to spare no expense and to be seen to be doing so, he could hardly use Doric and was almost required to use Corinthian. He had already shown a new confidence in the value of architectural magnificence in commissioning such a project. Perhaps Julius was even particularly inspired by a text at the end of the Old Testament urging the people to rebuild the Temple: "The glory of this latter house shall be greater than of the former, saith the Lord of hosts: and in this place will I give peace, saith the Lord of hosts" (*Haggai* 2, 9). This was always read as a reference to the Christian Church and could easily be seen as looking forward to a day when it would receive an architectural expression which would surpass that of Solomon's Temple. It might then also explain Bramante's remarkable introduction of olive leaves into the Corinthian capitals of the new church, as described by Vasari.[31] Just as the

Corinthian form was an appropriate expression of a greater glory, so the olive leaf would be a neat allusion to the peace that was to be given there. Jerusalem was, of course, the "city of peace" and the Christian Church, as the New Jerusalem founded by Christ the *rex pacificus*, was its more perfect realization. Allusions to the New Jerusalem, to the new Temple, and to the pope as a new *rex pacificus* abound in texts written to celebrate the pontificates of both Julius II and his successor, Leo X, as Shearman has demonstrated.[32] Typical is the speech of Thomas de Vio at the Lateran Council inaugurated by Julius II in 1511: "This is that Jerusalem . . . in which . . . the *rex pacificus* leaves peace unto us and gives his peace unto us.[33]

The suggestion that the Corinthian order of the new St Peter's may have been seen as an expression of the "greater glory" of the new Church compared to the old Jewish Temple receives express confirmation in another great work commissioned by Julius II. The organ shutters for the church of the Santa Casa at Loreto were ordered by the pope when he was in Loreto with Bramante in 1510 (Fig. 138). The most remarkable features of the two panels by Antonio Liberi are their architectural backgrounds. Liberi's interest in architecture is shown by the fact that at his death he possessed not only Vitruvius and Alberti but even Pacioli's *De divina proportione*;[34] and he is said to have studied architecture with Antonio da Gamberino around 1516.[35] However, since Bramante was with the pope at the time the work was commissioned it is likely that he was involved, and it is hard to see who else could have instructed Liberi in the mysteries of Doric triglyphs and metopes. The scene itself is the Annunciation, but it is the architecture which is more dramatic than the figures. On the left, two Old Testament prophets stand in a flat-ceilinged building whose long wooden entablature is carried on columns; on the right, the Virgin awaits the dove in a lofty vaulted space adorned with much richer shafts. The architectural contrast between the largely wooden Temple and the stone church, first expounded by Manetti in his writing on St Peter's, here attains even fuller expression. The structural differentiation is matched by the change in ornament. The wooden architecture is Doric and the stone Corinthian, the Doric columns plain and the Corinthian fluted. The matching of order to material must be based on an understanding of the Vitruvian comments on the wooden

138. Above and far right, Antonio Liberi: *Annunciation*, after 1510, organ shutters, Basilica della Santa Casa, Loreto

origin of Doric as the earliest of the orders. Doric could easily be linked to the biblical description of the wooden order of Solomon's Temple, while the ox-skulls of the Basilica Aemilia could be aptly re-used to refer to the blood sacrifices of the Old Testament. Such sacrifices had been rendered unnecessary by Christ's victory, and this victory is alluded to with equal clarity in the frieze of weapons and armour above the Virgin's head. The vaults and free-standing columns with projecting entablatures which readily recall a triumphal arch take up the same theme. Since Vitruvius makes it clear that Corinthian was invented by a stone sculptor, it was as appropriate for it to be a masonic order as for Doric to be wooden.

The contrast between the buildings of the Old and New Testaments could not be more striking, and there can be little doubt that, just as the wooden architecture of the one is inspired by descriptions of Solomon's Temple, so the vaults and domes of the other are intended to refer to the new St Peter's. The idea of using two chronologically successive styles of architecture in paintings of the Annunciation to express the revolutionary importance of the Incarnation was, as Panofsky showed, a regular device of fifteenth-century Flemish art.[36] The transformation of Romanesque forms into Gothic, as in the Friedsam *Annunciation* (Fig. 86), reminds us forcibly that the age of the Law passes and the age of Grace begins. Now a Doric-Corinthian transformation appears as an equivalent to the Romanesque-Gothic one. Whether or not this idea had already been anticipated in the Ionic-Corinthian and Composite-Corinthian mixtures of Fra Angelico and Michelozzo,[37] in Liberi's painting the message conveyed through the change of order is reinforced by the contrast between primitive wooden and sophisticated masonic forms. Never had assumptions about architectural history been exploited to such expressive purpose.

There is another important contrast in the two architectures of the Loreto *Annunciation*. Although the Doric Old Testament building is wooden, it is shown as elaborately painted as if to look like stone, and the columns are either painted or real marble. The architecture of the "church," on the other hand, hardly uses colour or paint, thus implying the use of natural materials. Savonarola, a decade or so earlier, had contrasted the early church, which was made of genuine precious

materials, with its corrupt successor, which was only made of wood but was painted to look as if made of valuable stones, and which soon collapsed.[38] The friar's criticism of the corruption of the Medieval church may here be transferred to the Jewish faith. The falseness of their respective interpretations of God's message is manifest in their pretentious skin-deep appearance of excellence. The true Christian architecture is both strong in its forms and true in its materials.

The use of Corinthian in the organ shutters shows that by 1510 Julius II had good reason to see that order, in religious architecture at least, as the best emblem of the fulfilment of the Church's promise. Doric on the other hand could be seen as emblematic of primitive ignorance. This represents an inversion of his previous preference, while still a cardinal, for Doric as an order of Christian virtue opposed to the pagan worldliness of Corinthian, and it is worth briefly speculating on the reasons for the change of approach. A major factor may have been the passing of the half-millennium. The years before 1500 were accompanied by great forebodings of doom which were encouraged by the preaching of Savonarola and others, and there was every reason to avoid the architecture of Antichrist which was one of the "last things." After the critical year had passed, people might reasonably heave a sigh of relief and feel that the moral pressure was off. Whatever the reason, the re-emergence of Corinthian, whether in Bramante's St Peter's or in Liberi's organ shutters, demonstrates that the need for restraint was no longer predominant. The pressure to avoid using Corinthian in the late fifteenth century had always posed a problem, and now, by exploiting a new historical awareness of the development of the ancient orders, it was possible to use Corinthian in a way which expressed not worldly magnificence but the ultimate fulfilment of a divine message. Corinthian could thus be Christianized as Doric already had been. Julius could now use not just Corinthian but the whole structural vocabulary of mature Roman Imperial architecture to communicate the fact that the Christian Church had achieved its full and permanent perfection. The development of Classical architecture could be employed as a paradigm of the unfolding of God's plan for humanity.

All of which helps us to understand how the pope could erect such a grand Corinthian structure as the new St Peter's at the centre of the Christian world. In its forms it may seem perilously close to the architecture of Jewish and pagan error in Perugino's *Charge to Peter* (Fig. 110), and to that of the Antichrist in Signorelli's fresco at Orvieto, but its message relates to the internal development of religion and not to the opposition between Christians and unbelievers. Moreover, although it is big and Corinthian it conspicuously avoids the use of extravagant marbles and free-standing columns bearing architraves which were the most tell-tale attributes in the earlier paintings.

Liberi's *Annunciation* also helps us to understand why it was just as appropriate for the Tempietto and the altar house of St Peter's to be Doric and to make prominent use of the horizontal entablature as it was for the church to have a Corinthian order associated with arches and vaults. The Tempietto built on the site of Saint Peter's martyrdom and the altar house around his tomb were above all monuments of *early* Christianity, a primitive period long before the Roman Church had achieved world authority under the Renaissance popes. Once Doric and Corinthian, beam and vault, were seen as the two ends of a chronological polarity they could as easily be used to express the growth of Christianity alone as the development of Christianity out of Judaism. The austerity of the materials and decoration of both Tempietto and altar house made it clear that they were only primitive, and not both primitive and corrupt as was the painted marble Doric of the Loreto painting.

As so often, the meaning of a piece of architecture is neither inherent in its form nor attributed to it by a text, but derives entirely from its context and from the changing feelings and expectations of the typical spectator. If it strained credulity that Doric at Pienza could be an emblem of low status in the palace and of high morality in the church, the reader may be even more reluctant to accept the variability of the meaning of Doric in Bramante's works for Julius II. In Loreto it is an expression of the incomplete vision of the Jews, in the altar house an expression of primitive faith; in the Vatican it is not only a mode tuned to virtue's key but a voice singing in harmony with others. Yet we know that in the modern world the colour red can within a limited environment change its meaning from "health" to "death" to "danger" to "stop" to "come on." We must not expect the past to be simpler than the present

139. St Peter's, Rome, interior with remains of old basilica, 320s (foreground) and
Bramante's crossing and altar house: drawing, c.1570, Kunsthalle, Hamburg

and art simpler than life. Bramante knew that the typical visitor to St Peter's might first gape at the massive nave as an expression of contemporary papal authority and then within a few steps bow his head in contemplation at the tomb of the fisherman whose simple faith fifteen hundred years earlier had launched Christianity in the West. The change of order, like the change of scale and change of materials, could both reflect and stimulate the change of mood.

One way of describing the difference between Bramante's architecture and that of his predecessors—and indeed his own before 1496—is that its richness and variety both assume and invite a more alert response on the part of the viewer. Whether or not the reader accepts all the individual explanations here proposed for Bramante's modulation of architectural form, it is hard to deny that he seems constantly to be trying to tell us something. Otherwise the changes of order, material, and structural form would be completely wasted. In this sense Bramante seems to expect an active response from the viewer's eye just as the musician expects an active response from the listener's ear. Leonardo's paintings may be said to operate in the same way, and we know that both he and Pacioli were intent on claiming for the eye a new receptivity. In the end, the most compelling argument for the influence of musical theory on Bramante is that it makes available to us a coherent network of interpretations of the type of response he might have expected: it suggests meanings for forms which are manifestly significant. The sense that Bramante's practice needed a theory is of long standing. As early as the mid-sixteenth century Doni was so conscious that Bramante's architecture looked as if it must have underlying principles that he invented spurious treatises by the master on rustication and the different orders and listed them in the second edition of his *Libreria*.[39] Doni was guessing in the right area, and in epitomizing Vasari's headings on the orders which were themselves derived from Serlio, who was close to High Renaissance Rome, his invention is along the right lines. The invention offered here attempts to get closer to Bramante's historical context. Leonardo's own writings provide him with his intellectual credentials. We have to provide Bramante with his.

XVIII

Raphael

◇

WHEN BRAMANTE died in 1514 it was Raphael who succeeded him as architect in charge of the work at St Peter's, and from that time the young painter became one of the most important architects in Rome. He must have already developed a close contact with the older master, who, as a distant relative from the same city, Urbino, had probably brought him to Rome in the first place. Indeed, Raphael may from the start have been groomed as his successor.[1] Raphael probably portrayed himself listening to an exposition of Bramante on the left-hand side of the *Disputa* and he certainly showed himself standing in a direct line behind Bramante/Archimedes on the right of the *School of Athens*. His relation to Bramante there is exactly the same as that of Cardinal Giulio de' Medici to his uncle Leo X in Raphael's portrait of them. That painting depicts the Cardinal, the future Clement VII, as Leo's successor as pope, and by analogy the fresco would show Raphael as his relative's successor as a "musical" architect.

The letter to Leo X

Potentially the most revealing document for Raphael's ideas on architecture is the letter he wrote to Leo X in connection with a survey of the ruins of Rome.[2] Although not principally concerned with contemporary practice, it at least alludes to a number of ideas, some of which can be related to those of Bramante. One feature of it, for example, is the extraordinary sophistication of Raphael's understanding of architectural history both in the ancient world, where he clearly recognized Doric as the earliest of the orders, and in the Medieval period. Less clearly Bramantesque is the letter's most startling innovation, the use of the word *ordine* for the first time to describe the different types of ancient columnar architecture. The term appears without emphasis in the phrase "the five orders used by the ancients; that is Doric, Ionic, Corinthian, Tuscan, and Attic."[3] There is no hint that the term is new, and there is no hint of the causes which may have encouraged its introduction. *Ordine* had many meanings—"arrangement," "class," "law"—any of which could be applicable as a replacement for Vitruvius' *genus*, Alberti's *species*, or Filarete's *qualità*. It is thus difficult to know which sense may have been uppermost in the mind of whoever introduced the term. There is, however, a temptation to look for a meaning which had already been used with musical analogies by Gaffurio, and it is remarkable that the musical writer does indeed use the Latin *ordo* for "class" in the passage where he compares the varied elements in a harmonious society with the varied notes in harmonic music. "In the same way, the middle position between the 'deliberative' and 'popular' classes [*ordines*] is occupied by the 'warrior' class. . . . There are some things which are common to other arts which are especially properties of music. Indeed, what is above all such a property is its being made up of opposites, thus conveying an image of the universe and of natural harmony."[4] Although neither Bramante nor his contemporaries seem to have used the orders primarily with a class analogy in mind, the analogy had already been used by Filarete in Milan. Besides which, Gaffurio's musical interpretation of the structure of society provides an appropriate context for the belief in the harmonizing effect of columnar polyphony which we earlier attributed to Bramante. Given that Vitruvius had long ago talked of an *ordo* or "row" of columns, and that the term also could be understood to mean "arrangement," the word may have seemed felicitous for a number of reasons. Certainly once introduced it seemed much more pre-

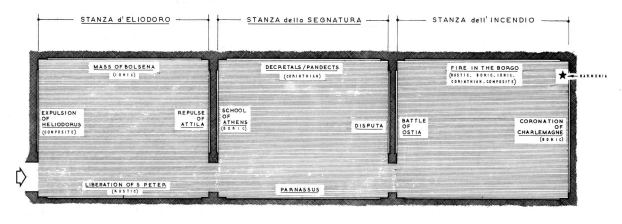

140. Diagram of Vatican Stanze

cisely appropriate than the looser terms used earlier, and it rapidly established itself in most European languages. One of the explanations for this must be revealed by Machiavelli, who in his *Florentine Histories* written in the early 1520s repeatedly stresses the need to strengthen and maintain the *ordini*, the laws and institutions which alone guarantee the survival and prosperity of the state.[5] The magical multivalence of this word, which must have seemed almost like a talisman of social stability in a time of turmoil throughout Europe, ensured that it would soon replace all previous terms for the columnar forms both in Italian and in other languages.

Raphael's brief account of the three main orders, Doric, Ionic, and Corinthian consists basically of a compressed description of their origins. His reference to the other two, Attic and Tuscan, is even more cursory. But the letter ends with a final sentence on the orders which is highly suggestive: "And many buildings are found which use several styles [*maniere*], such as Ionic and Corinthian, Doric and Corinthian, Tuscan and Doric, as it seemed best to the architect to make buildings appropriate to their functions [*appropriati alla loro intentione*], especially in temples."[6] Raphael does not hesitate to explain the choice of orders in a

particular building, and even their mixture, as a conscious expression of the structure's function. Such a statement would have been out of place at any time before the theories of Colonna and Pacioli and the buildings of Bramante, whose achievements it eloquently sums up. It is also noteworthy that Raphael here uses the term *maniera* rather than *ordine*: the latter term is well suited to describe an order as a standard collection of forms and proportions, the former is better adapted to the definition of an expressive style. It is even possible to see the use of the two terms *ordine* and *maniera* as matching the two main approaches to the orders found in Bramante. *Ordine* is the more appropriate term in the context of a harmonious combination of different columns, as an equivalent to Gaffurio's harmony in music and society. *Maniera* is more appropriate to the use of an individual order as a vehicle of expression, as an equivalent to a musical mode.

The Stanza della Segnatura and the Stanza d'Eliodoro

Raphael is likely, then, to have been familiar with both of the ways in which Bramante used the orders, and it is not inappropriate to look for a continuation

141. Raphael: *Liberation of Saint Peter*, Stanza d'Eliodoro, Vatican

of his teacher's interest in his own work. Nowhere should we expect to find this more fully worked out than in the frescoes in the three rooms or *stanze* in the Vatican, where he conspicuously presents himself as Bramante's pupil and heir apparent—most especially in the frescoes for the first two rooms, which were executed in his lifetime. Of the eight walls in these first two rooms three have little architecture depicted within the fresco decoration, but the remaining five all have striking architectural settings, each unique and differentiated from the others (Figs. 140–145). Most remarkably the five can be seen to create a complete series of the five architectural "modes" used by Bramante; rusticated in the *Liberation of Saint Peter* (Fig. 141), Doric in the *School of Athens* (Fig. 142), Ionic in the *Mass of Bolsena* (Fig. 143), Corinthian in the double scene of the *Giving of the Pandects and Decretals* (Fig. 144), and Composite in the *Expulsion of Heliodorus* (Fig. 145). There can be no question of Raphael having intended to create such a series when he initially received the commission to decorate the Stanza della Segnatura. At that stage he could only have planned the Doric setting of the *School of Athens* and the Corinthian of the *Pandects and Decretals*. But there can be

142. Raphael: *School of Athens*, Stanza della Segnatura, Vatican

equally little doubt that when he was given the second *stanza* too he realized, perhaps prompted by Bramante, that he could produce precisely the same effect of harmony that the great architect was achieving elsewhere in the Vatican complex. Evidence that the idea was developed only in the process of detailed planning is provided by the fact that the original drawing for the *Mass of Bolsena* has no order at all; and the masonry of the prison in the *Liberation of Saint Peter* is also much less emphatic in the first compositional sketch. By 1514, however, the two rooms contained a richer "concordant discord" than any in Bramante's buildings, and like Gaffurio's society with its different *ordines*, and

music with its different voices, they created a true image "of the universe and of natural harmony." The use of the orders thus completed the microcosmic universality of the separate iconographic programmes of the two rooms by uniting them in a grander scheme. Underlying the whole are the religious and political ambitions of Julius II, who figures in most of the scenes, and it may not be irrelevant that the painted piers in the corners of the room take up the plain architectural style which he had first encouraged as a cardinal. His bass voice provides the theme around which the harmony is built.

Since the architectural backgrounds of the *School of*

143. Raphael: *Mass of Bolsena*, Stanza d'Eliodoro, Vatican

Athens (Fig. 142) and the *Giving of the Pandects and Decretals* (Fig. 144) were designed before the idea of an overall harmony can have been introduced, it is in those scenes that we would most expect the choice of order to have followed from the subject. In the *School of Athens*, where the most famous sages of Antiquity are grouped together, the link is most obvious. The plain Doric pilasters aptly express the moral qualities of simplicity and restraint which were cultivated by the best of ancient philosophers and which Plato and Aristotle, who stand together at the centre, had both recognized as proper to the Dorian mode. The fluted Corinthian pilasters framing the *Giving of the Pandects*

and Decretals (the two texts which formed the basis of secular and canon law respectively) should, on the other hand, be understood, along with the apses in which the two scenes take place, as the emblems of status and authority which they had always been—besides evoking the new St Peter's in particular. In the Stanza d'Eliodoro, however, we have to reckon with the possibility that Raphael may have rather forced his choice of order to achieve a complete series. There can be no doubt that the magnificent rustication of Saint Peter's prison in the *Liberation* scene, with its concave facets and deep projection, is a brilliantly appropriate expression of the oppressive containment of prison. There is

251

144. Raphael: *The Giving of the Pandects and Decretals*, Stanza della Segnatura, Vatican

equally little doubt that the choice of a magnificent Composite order associated with marble columns and a gold vault in the Temple of the *Expulsion of Heliodorus* (Fig. 145) is intended to be emblematic of the material extravagance so often associated with the Jewish religion, though the choice of order may have gained some further justification from the capitals of the spiral columns around the altar of St Peter's, which were supposed to have come from the Jewish Temple and which combined Ionic corner volutes with a ring of acanthus leaves (Fig. 35 left, p. 60). The choice of Ionic for the church dedicated to Saint Christina at Bolsena, the setting of the miraculous *Mass*, is more diffi-

cult to explain, but the order was not out of place in the relatively unimportant church of a modest saint. Doric might have been too manly, and Corinthian or Composite too pompous. Thus in each scene Raphael has more or less carefully employed a single order to individualize the setting. In no case is the architecture in any sense an historical or archaeological reconstruction; in each it is an imaginary creation designed to enhance or elaborate on the message of the fresco. Further examples of how this is done are offered by the vaulted architectures of the structure housing the ancient philosophers and of the Temple. Each is designed to anticipate the new St Peter's and charge that build-

145. Raphael: *Expulsion of Heliodorus*, Stanza d'Eliodoro, Vatican

ing with additional authority from the pagan and Jewish worlds, while their avoidance of Corinthian shows that the new church is more developed than the former and less extravagant than the latter. Never before had painted architecture been used to such calculated effect. Raphael's efforts are unthinkable without the precedent of the musically harmonious and expressive buildings of Bramante, but they have the freedom to go beyond them, incorporating the more dynamic expressive interests of Leonardo.

Although the main influence on Bramante's use of the orders seems to have been Gaffurio's musical theories of the uses of the voices and of the modes, Bra-

mante had also acknowledged the Vitruvian theory of *decor* as in the Tempietto and the altar house of St Peter's. Raphael too seems to follow the same theory, as in the cartoon for the tapestry of *Paul Preaching at Athens* of 1515–16, which shows a round Doric temple with a statue of Ares (Mars) close by. There can be little doubt that this structure and statue are intended (as has been suggested) to help identify the scene as the assembly on the Areopagus or Hill of Ares.[7] More uncertainty must surround the reasons for the choice of Corinthian for the chapel of Agostino Chigi in S. Maria del Popolo in about 1515, but Fabio Chigi's claim in 1626 that it was intended to be appropriate to the Vir-

253

146. Raphael: *Coronation of Charlemagne*, Stanza dell'Incendio, Vatican

gin is so unusual that it is likely to rest on a substantial tradition.[8] Indeed, since the chapel is dedicated to the Virgin of Loreto and copies Bramante's magnificent Santa Casa, Raphael is here only following his master.

The Stanza dell'Incendio

Only two walls of the third *stanza* decorated for Julius' successor, Leo X, make a prominent use of architecture. One, the *Coronation of Charlemagne*, shows a single structure, Old St Peter's (Fig. 146). It may at first seem surprising that it is shown as a low barrel-vaulted building with an order of Doric half-columns equally unlike either the old church or the new. But when it is recognized that the architecture is adapted from that of

Bramante's altar house it can be understood in the same way as that structure, as an expression both of Petrine strength and of the primitive simplicity of early Christianity. The other fresco, on the other hand (the one after which the room is named), is architecturally the most complex of the whole series.

The *Fire in the Borgo* was conceived and executed between 1514 and 1517 (Fig. 147). It records the miracle when Leo X's namesake Leo IV (847–855) succeeded in bringing to an end a terrible fire which threatened to destroy the Borgo, the fortified settlement which he had just established in front of St Peter's. In the background is the Medieval basilica as it still stood in the early sixteenth century. In front of this, to the right, is a structure inscribed with Leo IV's name. This

147. Raphael: *Fire in the Borgo*, Stanza dell'Incendio, Vatican

may be intended to recall the tower which he built and certainly invites identification with the Benediction Loggia recently completed in a similar position (Fig. 148). It is in this building, with its rusticated basement, that the pope appears framed by a Doric "Serlian" opening between Doric pilasters. Almost invisible on the left-hand end of this structure is a Corinthian column which is apparently one of two framing an aedicule. In front are two evidently older buildings, one Ionic with a cracked entablature, on the right, and an emphatically ruined Composite colonnade, on the left. The fresco evidently contains a range of architectural forms (Rusticated, Doric, Ionic, Corinthian, and Composite) similar to that which was represented in the separate architectures of the first two *stanze* planned un-

der Julius II. Leo X has trumped his predecessor by compressing a harmonic series into a single scene.

It is possible that Raphael was led to construct the "concordant discord" of the *Fire* by purely aesthetic considerations, but recent observations by Shearman on the *Coronation of Charlemagne* suggest that a higher political meaning was intended.[9] Pointing out that in the adjoining fresco a member of the choir holds a book whose inscription, beginning with the word *harmonia*, might possibly be reconstructable as the tag *Harmonia est discordia concors*, Shearman goes on to suggest that the concord referred to may be political as well as musical. Contemporaries, as he says, believed that it was the pope's musical talents which enabled him to establish *concordia* with the French king, and it

148. View of Piazza S. Pietro, Rome: drawing, F. Zuccaro,
J. Paul Getty Museum, Malibu

is certainly Leo's meeting with Francis which is alluded to by this fresco, in which Charlemagne is given the face of the modern monarch. If we remember Gaffurio's comparison of the harmony between the various classes (*ordines*) with the harmony of music and compare Raphael's use of a polyphonic series of the orders with that of Bramante, we may extend Shearman's propagandist interpetation so that the musical pope brings *concordia* to the world as a whole. One of the traditional interpretations of the *Fire in the Borgo* is that it alludes to Leo X's role in extinguishing the burning conflicts which then threatened to destroy the Church. The *concordant discord* of the orders in the setting of the fresco would be an appropriate expression of the new harmony which was referred to in the inscription on the adjoining left-hand side of the neighboring scene.

Whether this effect was desired or not, other aspects of the painting's meaning are certainly articulated through its architecture. This first becomes apparent when it is realized that besides St Peter's, which is accurately represented, the other structures are all adaptations of familiar groups of monuments in the ancient Forum. Raphael has not only referred explicitly to their separate forms and materials but has also preserved their relationship to each other. The most obvious correspondence is between the Composite structure and the remains of the temple of Castor and Pollux, which has since the Middle Ages dominated the centre of the Forum Romanum. The only major difference in the triple columniation is the introduction of veining to the marble and the change of order from Corinthian to Composite. Following this identification it next becomes apparent that the Ionic and Doric structures be-

149. View of Forum, Rome: drawing, Maarten van Heemskerck

hind correspond, in order, articulation, and position, to the temple of Saturn and the Tabularium as seen in a view past the temple of Castor and Pollux towards the Capitol. The temple of Saturn is rare as a surviving Ionic trabeated structure. The Tabularium has a Doric upper floor above a blank wall of rough masonry, thus anticipating the main features of Leo IV's building (Fig. 46, p. 72). In no case is the equivalence exact, but the correspondences are too remarkable not to be intentional. The viewpoint assumed was as familiar in the Renaissance as it is today, as can be seen in the drawing by Heemskerck which shows how even the relative heights of the buildings coincide (Fig. 149). Raphael made significant adjustments for compositional reasons, as by changing the direction of the three columns of the Temple of Castor so that they lead back to the heart of the picture, and of the columns of the Temple

of Saturn so that they moderate the recession. Other major buildings, such as the Temple of Vespasian, have been omitted because they would have disturbed the desired sequence of the orders. Yet the essential correspondence is obvious, and the buildings of the Forum would have been particularly familiar to Raphael in his role as superintendent of antiquities.

The reasons for the reference to the Forum are not far to seek. The Borgo is portrayed as the Christian successor to the city's pagan centre. It was Leo IV, whose name is inscribed like a founder's inscription on the Loggia itself, who first established the Borgo and surrounded it with walls. By this act he finally surrendered the hope of maintaining the old city across the Tiber and effectively inaugurated a new city round St Peter's. The plan of Nicholas V to rebuild the Borgo had only reinforced the decision. By the time of Julius II not only

257

had the Borgo become typologically the successor to old Rome, with the Piazza S. Pietro as a new Forum, but the whole institution of the papacy was seen as a successor to the imperial authority. Julius was a new Caesar, ruling temporally as well as spiritually. Paolo Cortese in his book *De cardinalatu* reinforced an ancient convention by consistently referring to the cardinals as senators.[10] Fulvius, whose *Antiquitates* (published in 1527) was written with the assistance of Raphael himself, concluded his great work with a glorification of Rome reborn:

Rome still has some shadow of her former majesty, for peoples from all over the world return to her, as limbs do to the head. She has the most gentle *imperium* of Christ and his vicar, the pope, the highest authority in the whole world . . . which authority, having surpassed the kings in word and example, and having buried the images of the pagans, has taken over the government of the world.

Rome has the apostolic senate, the clergy and the holy cardinals. It contains

the citadel [*arx*] and home of the Christian religion and the head of the state . . . the apostolic church [*aedes*] and the *curia*, pre-eminent among those that have existed.[11]

The vocabulary throughout is intended to remind us of the glories of ancient Rome and to convince us that they are returned in a more worthy if slightly less magnificent form. The references to the Vatican as a new *arx* and to St Peter's as an *aedes apostolica* is intended to imply that the ancient citadel and the temple of Jupiter, above the ancient Forum, have been directly supplanted by the new buildings across the Tiber. This would give added point to Raphael's transposition of the view towards the Capitol to the new context of a view towards the two main buildings of the Mons Vaticanus, where, as on the Capitol, the *aedes* and *arx* are situated right and left of the main axis. St Peter's is the successor to the main temple of ancient Rome, and the Vatican fortress is the successor of its ultimate defence.

So far we have established the importance of the orders as a series and pointed out the significance of correspondences to real buildings. There is, however, a further level at which the two elements are combined. To appreciate this it is necessary to recognize that the rusticated basement and the barely visible aedicule of the Leo IV building are peripheral to its main characterization as a Doric building. Once identified as an es-

sentially Doric structure, it can be seen to form part of a coherent series of three with the other two, Ionic and Composite, in front of it. Together they embody a consistent increase in richness of order and richness of materials from background to foreground. The Doric pilasters are travertine and unfluted, the Ionic columns are still unfluted but of coloured marble, and the Composite shafts are both of coloured marble and fluted. The arrangement is both visually and intellectually neat. It also cleverly establishes a polarization between the Doric structure and the Composite one, a polarization of evident meaning. The Doric structure with its inscriptions is clearly a new building put up by the Christian pope, while the other two are half ruined and so are clearly intended as vestiges of imperial magnificence. The sobriety of order, material, and ornament of the Christian building is in emblematic contrast to the extravagance of order, material, and ornament of the pagan ruins. The Doric of the ninth-century papal loggia also appropriately matches the Doric interior of Old St Peter's as shown in the *Coronation of Charlemagne* in the same room. The architecture of early Medieval Christianity is repeatedly and consistently contrasted with that of the Roman Empire.

It is important that the contrast is with *early* Christianity. For the contemporary viewer will have known that the new St Peter's and the new Benediction Loggia were both in fact Corinthian/Composite, though of simple travertine, and thus contrasted almost equally strongly with the Christian architectures of the frescoes. Raphael evidently intends us to perceive that, although the architecture of Leo IV is a moral improvement on that of pagan Rome, it is in turn only a primitive anticipation of the new Christian architecture of Leo X. The change from the Doric of the early Leo to the Corinthian of his Renaissance successor is an expression of the historical development of the Christian Church from simple origins to a perfect fulfilment. In his letter to Leo, Raphael showed an unparalleled awareness of architectural history as a sequential development.[12] He was clear that Doric was "the most ancient" order, originating in simple wooden forms, to be followed by Ionic and then Corinthian. He also describes the decline of architecture during the Empire and the Middle Ages and its subsequent revival until, under Bramante, it almost rivals ancient Rome—almost, but not quite. This last account could be taken as an eloquent commentary on the sequence of buildings in the fresco, which begins with the Augustan temple of Castor, whose order is enriched to make it even more magnificent, and declines through the temple of Saturn, whose crude details betray it as a late imperial monument, until the ultimate simplicity of Leo's loggia is reached; while the barely visible Corinthian aedicule looks forward to the modest but mature revival of ancient forms in Bramante's new St Peter's.

The *Fire in the Borgo* is a powerfully compressed image of the historical development which leads from ancient to Medieval to modern Rome. The viewer standing in the room would have been carried by the perspective system past the ruins of the ancient city in the foreground and the simple structures of the Medieval city in the middle ground to the modern façade of St Peter's in the background, behind which was rising the new church. Held in the grip of the receding orthogonals the viewer was carried through fifteen hundred years of architectural history, from the Composite splendours of paganism past the modest Doric structures of early Christianity to the early sixteenth century, when a new and splendid Corinthian building was to complete the cycle of decline and revival. The remarkable receding axis of the painting took the viewer on a journey through time, with its conclusion, like the vanishing point, invisible but certain.

It may at first seem surprising that Raphael should have revealed such a strong sense of history in his fresco. After all, where could he have got the idea of using an account of what had happened centuries earlier to present both a view of an even earlier past and a vision of the contemporary world? Fortunately Raphael has himself answered this question. Vasari noted long ago that the group on the left with a young man carrying an older one recalls the image of Aeneas carrying Anchises, and it has since been recognized that the whole group of four people is an exact illustration of *Aeneid* II, lines 721-25, when Aeneas flees the burning city of Troy with his family.[13] Now, the historical structure of the *Aeneid* anticipates that of the *Fire in the Borgo* precisely. It is an account of a past event—the journey of Aeneas from Carthage to Italy—elaborated in such a way as to present both a record of an even earlier past—the destruction of Troy—and a vision of the future—Virgil's own world of Augustan Rome. Its central theme, which is the story of how

Rome came to be the vehicle of Italian destiny, is prefaced by a record of how Troy was destroyed by fire and includes an outline of Augustus' plans for world empire. The correspondence is exact. Although the fire from which the family is escaping is supposed to have happened in the ninth century near St Peter's, what is shown is a departure from the burning Forum, perhaps at the Fall of Rome in the fifth century. The significance of Leo IV's fortification of the Borgo is that it marks the foundation of a new centre which, under the rule of Julius and Leo, like Rome under Julius and Augustus, will achieve full development as the great seat of a great power. Just as it was divine intervention which brought first the destruction of Troy, then Aeneas' transfer to Latium, and finally the exaltation of Rome under Augustus, so it was God's will that the power which once resided in the Forum should be transferred to the vicinity of St Peter's and, after testing dangers, should in the end achieve permanent and visible establishment under Leo. Just as it was Aeneas' son Iulus (Ascanius) who founded Alba Longa, mother city of Rome, and his descendant Julius Caesar who was to be the instrument in the final establishment of empire, so it was one Leo who founded the new city around St Peter's and another who gave it its ultimate form. By showing a new Aeneas and his family leaving ancient Rome, Raphael can only have intended to present his painting as a new *Aeneid*, an exposition of the destiny of the pagan city. Since the *Aeneid* had always been liable to interpretation as a work prophetic of Christ's coming, it was all the more appropriate as the model for a Christian epic.

After Leonardo's vaunting of painting versus poetry and Bramante's attempt to show that architecture was the equal of music, Raphael had every reason to match the great Roman poet in his fresco. The rivalry of the visual with the aural arts was a recurrent theme of contemporary art theory from Leonardo to Pacioli, and Raphael, as the son of the court painter-poet of Urbino, may well have felt better qualified than anyone to lead painting to victory. He enters the contest with the aural arts on a number of fronts. By the use of open mouths and gestures he makes us hear the screams and prayers of the frightened women, thus taking up ideas found in Leonardo's *Last Supper* and in his own earlier works such as the *Disputa* and *School of Athens*, both of which are built around a painted "argument." But the

150. Marcantonio Raimondi: *Nativity* (upper half), engraving, British Museum

Fire is a much more thorough supplanting of aural communication. It goes beyond Leonardo in achieving a painted equivalent of poetry, and it goes beyond Bramante in generating an architectural equivalent of musical harmony. By combining the two effects together it takes the visual arts further into the territory of the aural arts than any earlier work. Like theatre (or, better, like opera) it comes close to being the ultimate *Gesamtkunstwerk*, in which effects of sight and sound work together to generate a new and more powerful form of expression.

The history of architecture and the history of religion, again

In both the letter to Leo and the *Fire in the Borgo*, Raphael reveals an even greater sense of the importance and meaning of architectural history than did Bramante, and in a work from his school we find the Bramantesque ideas of the relation between the history of architecture and the history of religion being developed in a new and more scientific way. The composition concerned, a *Nativity*, is preserved in two versions: one a drawing by Raphael's pupil and heir Penni, the other an engraving (with the scene in reverse) by Marcantonio Raimondi, who made many prints after Raphael's designs (Fig. 150). Since the print preserves the relationship between the architectural elements shown in the Liberi *Annunciation* at Loreto it probably represents the correct arrangement (Fig. 138).

Behind the group of the Holy Family rise two impressive and startlingly differentiated structures. That on the left (in the engraving) is a pedimented building which is recognizable as a remarkably scientific reconstruction of the wooden predecessor of the Doric temple as described by Vitruvius and as referred to by Raphael in his letter to Leo X. That on the right is a triple-arched structure adorned with four free-standing

151. Peruzzi: *Presentation of the Virgin in the Temple*, S. Maria della Pace, Rome, 1523–26

Corinthian columns, three of which bear sections of entablature. The missing section makes it look more like an unfinished building than a ruined one. Although the forms are not identical to those of the two buildings in Liberi's *Annunciation*, the similarity of the contrast between a wooden Doric structure and a masonic Corinthian one is so close as to suggest a similar interpretation. There is no difficulty in recognizing the incomplete vaulted structure on the right as the Christian Church which is to be. It is harder to be certain about

the structure on the left; but if its simple wooden forms, which are such a scrupulous reconstruction of the origins of the Doric temple, are seen to represent the primitiveness of Jewish architecture and the incompleteness of Jewish religion, then its closed windowless character would also illustrate the proverbial "blindness" of the Synagogue in its rejection of the Christian message, in evident contrast to the open arches of the Church.

This interpretation is supported by a slightly later

work less directly connected with the Raphael school but firmly in the same tradition. In the background of Peruzzi's large *Presentation of the Virgin at the Temple*, painted for S. Maria della Pace in Rome between 1523 and 1526, a similar relationship exists between a small pedimented Ionic temple towards the left and a much larger structure on the right with a foreshortened row of giant columns (Fig. 151). This juxtaposition is at first confusing, since both buildings clearly represent temples. The small Ionic building is clearly identified as the Jewish Temple by the figures of Moses, Samson, and Judith on the pediment and by the lights inside its dark interior, while it is at the larger temple-like structure on the right that the Virgin is in fact being received. Further analysis, however, clarifies the significance of the duality. The obelisk with a ball on top is identifiable as the one which was intended by Bramante and others to stand in the centre of the piazza in front of St Peter's, and the tower to the left of the hexastyle façade closely resembles the towers planned by Bramante to stand on either side of the new church. The right-hand temple where the Virgin is received thus stands for the Christian Church as represented by the new St Peter's. The dark little temple at the left stands for the Jewish religion which rejected Christ.

The Peruzzi painting exploits the same pairing of Jewish and Christian buildings which we found in Liberi's organ shutters and in the Raimondi print, but here for the first time the identification of St Peter's with the Christian Church is made explicit. What Peruzzi does is take up Raphael's idea, found in the *Fire in the Borgo*, of using the Piazza S. Pietro to illustrate a historical development; however, where Raphael illustrated the Church's relationship to paganism Peruzzi illustrates its relationship to Judaism. In both paintings movement through the piazza represents movement through time; in both the earlier religion is represented by simple trabeated structures, and in both the new vaulted Corinthian architecture of the Christian Church has to be imagined by the viewer for the contrast to be effective. Some paintings can be understood purely from an internal analysis, as they stand; these require completion by the viewer. Raphael and Peruzzi start our interpretation in the right direction, but it is we who must think it through. Such works, like those of other High Renaissance artists, demand a level of participation and response which was usual in the context of arts such as music and poetry but new in the context of painting, sculpture, or architecture.

XIX

Serlio

◆

A painter's treatise

SEBASTIANO Serlio is, in terms of background, productivity, and influence, much the most important writer on architecture of the sixteenth century. Born in Bologna in 1475, he was already an established painter when he went to Rome after 1514 to work with the painter-architect Peruzzi until the Sack in 1527. He then left for Venice, taking with him an intimate knowledge of High Renaissance artistic ideas, and there he developed those ideas in a series of publications planned already in 1528, working at the same time as both painter and architect and acting as adviser on architectural matters. By 1539 he was celebrated enough to be invited to France by Francis I, where his productivity as both writer and designer of buildings only increased, although from 1546, the year of his patron's death, until his own demise in 1554 he concentrated more on writing.

To trace Serlio's written *oeuvre* through all its stages of growth and transformation is a substantial task in itself.[1] Not only did his writings emerge in a piecemeal way during his lifetime, with new editions and translations into Latin and the languages of northern Europe appearing at the same time or following rapidly, but the volumes he left unpublished at his death have continued to emerge, both in the sixteenth century and the twentieth. Though even now the work is incomplete, its main stages are clear. His first venture, mentioned in a 1528 copyright application, was a series of nine engravings, consisting of three sets of three each, devoted to the columnar elements of the three main orders, Doric, Ionic, and Corinthian.[2] These copper plates appeared in several versions during the following years.[3] Then in 1537 he launched his main project, which is fully described both in a new copyright application and in an introduction to the first volume to appear. At this stage Serlio envisaged a set of seven *libri* each devoted to a separate subject: I, geometry; II, perspective; III, ancient buildings; IV, the five orders (*maniere*); V, temples; VI, habitations, from cottages to palaces; VII, architectural problems (*accidenti*). The book which bore this prospectus was in fact Book IV, which established the pattern of an extensive text accompanying a rich and well-organized set of woodcut illustrations. The next book to appear, in 1540, was III, with its illustrations of Roman monuments within and outside Italy, and a few buildings by Bramante, each with its own commentary. After that in 1545 came Books I and II together, followed in 1547 by Book V. At this point the series was broken by the appearance in 1551 of a "Libro Estraordinario" which had not been included in the original scheme. This book, entirely devoted to a series of gateways, was the last to be published in Serlio's lifetime. Book VII, on the different problems an architect may be faced with in (for example) handling an odd site or modernizing an existing building, was published by Jacopo Strada in 1575. Book VI survives in two manuscript versions, one in New York and one in Munich, both of which have been recently edited and published.[4] Both versions follow the original plan of dealing with the houses of the different classes, but both also show the extensive influence of Serlio's experiences in France, especially in the use of half-timbered architecture. Yet another book, which was apparently planned after the original prospectus but which (unlike the Libro Estraordinario) was to be added to the first seven as a Book VIII, was devoted to the design of Roman camps; it was based both on the text of Polybius and on surviving remains. It too exists in Munich in manuscript form but has never been published.[5] The closest Serlio's vision of a single coherent treatise ever came to fulfilment was when the first five books published in his lifetime were reprinted in 1619, together with the Book VII published by Strada, and with the Libro Estraordinario replacing the missing book on houses as Book VI.

Surprisingly, in view of the richness of its contents and its widespread diffusion in the sixteenth century, Serlio's work has never been treated seriously. One of the main reasons for this is one that should have only enhanced its importance, namely its partial dependence on Peruzzi. Both Vasari and Cellini implied that Serlio was little more than an incompetent plagiarist, and Serlio's own repeated modest acknowledgement of his debt to his great master only encouraged an underestimation of his independent achievement. It is certain that Serlio took with him to Venice a number of drawings which derive from Peruzzi's studio. However, the vitality of his activity long after he had left Peruzzi and his constantly flexible response to new environments, such as those of Venice or France, suggest that Peruzzi's influence only provided him with a starting point.

Otherwise the character of the work is Serlio's own. This special character is apparent right at the beginning of the first book which, although not the first published, was planned from the outset. The very first illustration is of a single point. This is followed by a line, that by parallel lines, and they in turn by a square. The limpidly rational organization of this first page continues throughout the book, as the reader is taken gently through the problems of Euclidean plane geometry which are relevant to the drawing of architecture. Book II moves into three dimensions with an equally carefully developed discussion of perspective. Serlio thus abandons the approach of his predecessors, who in their different ways had all begun with the fundamentals of architecture, its parts, its techniques, its materials, and so on. Serlio begins with the principles not of architecture but of architectural drawing. Nor does he make any excuses for this. He simply believes that the task of the architect is essentially to conceive and then put down on paper the design for a building. The execution of such a design, with all the problems of laying foundations, choosing materials, and erecting vaults, will be the responsibility of others. He has, moreover, a simple justification for approaching architecture first through drawing and perspective. As he says in the introduction to Book II (18ᵛ), virtually all the great ar-

chitects of his own century, the century which had seen the first flowering of good architecture, started out from precisely that background. Not only Bramante but Raphael, Peruzzi, Genga, Giulio Romano, and his humble self all began as painters. In other words, the architecture of his own period—the architecture of which he writes—is no longer the same art of Alberti, of Filarete, of Francesco di Giorgio, or of Vitruvius. Serlio's interests have something in common with those of Francesco Colonna and Luca Pacioli, neither of whom had bothered much with the technical side of architecture; but Serlio is the first to disregard technical issues in what claimed to be a comprehensive treatment of the art. He saw himself as the spokesman of the modern approach to architecture as illustrated by Bramante and his followers, and the first feature of this modern approach was its starting point in the sphere of painting and drawing.

Architectural judgement

Another new feature emerges in Book III. The purpose of this book is stated most precisely in the preface to Books I and II, where Serlio says that the third book should not be seen just as a collection of delightful and beautiful buildings, but that its text provides a guide to "the selection of the beautiful [*elettione del bello*]." The text is to be used as a critical commentary on the illustrations of ancient and modern buildings, which are already selected for their excellence.

Naturally, a prime criterion of quality is conformity to the rules of Vitruvius. Serlio frequently notes that a feature is or is not correct in Vitruvian terms. It is not enough for a modern architect to be able to point to Antique precedent as justification for a particular detail. The ancients often erred, and we should "hold to the doctrine of Vitruvius as guide and infallible rule." Who would deny that "in architecture he is at the highest level and that his writings (except where some other reason exists) should be sacrosanct and inviolable?" The Romans learned true architecture from the Greeks, and perhaps as conquerors they became "licentious" (*licentiosi*) in their use of Greek forms. Anyone who could see the buildings of the Greeks which have unfortunately been destroyed would judge them greatly superior to those of the Romans. So those architects who condemn Vitruvius, especially where he is most intelligible, as in the treatment of Doric, are "architectural heretics" (69ᵛ). Vitruvius' dependence on Greek sources gives him an authority which overrides the evidence of the monuments.

But Vitruvius alone is of limited use. There are many cases where some more complex criterion is needed, and in the discussion of the Arch of Titus (99ᵛ) we can see how Serlio moves out beyond a limited criticism in terms of the ancient writer. After noting that most Roman arches have incorrect elements, perhaps because they were made of spoils from other structures and were erected in a hurry, he goes on to analyse the entablature of the arch in detail (Fig. 152). The cornice is "licentious," not only because its combining of consoles and dentils had been forbidden by Vitruvius, but also because it has too many and too richly carved mouldings. "If I had to make a similar cornice I would observe the following arrangements: I would make the crowning *cima* smaller and the drip mouldings bigger; I would leave the consoles as they are and omit the carving of the dentils, but leave it on the *cima*." Going on to the impost of the arch he remarks that "it is so rich that one moulding confuses the other, but if they were so arranged that one moulding was carved [*scolpito d'intagli*] and the other left plain [*netto*] I would praise it more." Finally he defends his independent approach:

Perhaps it will seem to those who are intoxicated with Roman buildings that I am too bold in wanting to judge them . . . but it is one thing to imitate them exactly as they stand and another to know how to make a selection of the beautiful [*elettione del bello*] with the authority of Vitruvius and to reject the ugly [*bruto*] and badly understood [*mal inteso*]. And it is certain that the most beautiful quality in an architect is that he should not be deceived in his judgement [*giudicio*]. (99ᵛ)

Both the prominence given to *giudicio* and the specific application of it in the reduction of carved details on mouldings are new elements in the approach to architecture, and Serlio represents them as his own contribution.

Subsequently the same vocabulary keeps cropping up. When discussing the Arch of Trajan at Benevento he again criticizes the richness of the cornice mouldings: "I would praise it more if there were not so much sculpted detail and if it were so arranged that the mouldings were alternately smooth [*schietto*] and carved [*intagliato*]" (104ᵛ). This principle is taken up

152. Sebastiano Serlio, Book III (1540): Arch of Titus, details (from 1551 ed., fol. CVIIʳ)

again in the criticism of the highly ornate cornice of the Arch of the Argentarii, where he points out that the dentils and the *ovolo* underneath should be separated by a flat element, "something which is truly necessary to separate one element from another, especially when they are richly carved" (101ʳ). To prevent confusion, carved mouldings should always be framed by plain ones.

Other critical remarks concentrate on a moulding's projection or height. Serlio praises the crowning cornice of the Arch of Septimius Severus as reflecting great *giudicio* because the projection makes the whole element look bigger when seen from underneath, while he disapproves of the similar projection of the lower cornice at the base of the arch because it cuts off our view of the arch above (102ᵛ). In the same way he praises the base mouldings under the attic of the Arch at Benevento because they do not recede too much and so are more comprehensible from a low viewpoint. A concern with how things look from a low viewpoint, when that is the typical one, is a recurrent feature of his observations. On several buildings he points out, as he does on the Arch at Pola (110ᵛ), that mouldings high up above a cornice should be raised on a plain block, so that the cornice obstructs the view from underneath as little as possible. Equally he praises ancient architects for cutting down on the linear details of elements which are distant from the eye because this helps to prevent a confused effect. This can be a justification for breaking rules, as when he praises the architect of the Arco dei Leoni in Verona for cutting down the fascias of the uppermost frieze from three to two (115ᵛ), or the designer of the Pantheon for reducing the mouldings of the bases of the upper order to one because two would have "made the work too minute and confused" (53ʳ). Similarly, the Corinthian order high on the Colosseum is, he says, "of solid work [*opera soda*] without carved detail [*intaglio*] except for the capitals, and they too because of their height are not delicately detailed" (80ᵛ).

The consistency of the terms applied is impressive. Three considerations should guide an architect in the design of architectural details. The first is that mouldings with *intagli* should always be separated from each other by plain ones. The second is that mouldings and other elements seen from a distance should be simplified. The third is that the angle at which a feature is normally seen should influence its height or projection, and may even require the addition of elements to raise it above a cornice immediately below which might otherwise conceal it. Any of these considerations may allow an architect to depart from the rules of Vitruvius, because all of them can be documented in ancient buildings if they are carefully studied. The underlying point is that the way an element is seen by the eye is as important as—and may override—any considerations of geometry and regularity. There had been hints of this approach earlier. Luca Pacioli, especially, against the background of a new interest in the eye, wrote a

whole chapter collecting the best architectural forms using the visual response as a main criterion of excellence. But Pacioli's observations were very limited and were still based on his response to individual monuments. Only with Serlio is it possible to talk of principles with a demonstrably universal application. One key to this demonstrability is Serlio's use of illustrations, as in this third book where, besides the basic plans, sections, and elevations, a wealth of detailed analytical illustrations are used to make individual points. Using his draughtsman's eye rather like a zoom lens, Serlio picks out and focuses on any feature which particularly interests him, thus permitting himself to communicate clearly the basis for the types of critical remarks with which he was so concerned.

The other key is the attempt to formulate general rules, as in Book VII, where Serlio takes another step back from the material in order to indulge in what he calls a "Discussion and definition of some architectural terms." Here he sets out to discuss more theoretically both the faculty of *giudicio*, which took such a recurrently central place in his criticism of ancient buildings, and also the whole range of vocabulary used to describe a particular feature—*sodo*, *schietto*, *delicato*, and so on. This in itself breaks new ground, and the way Serlio proceeds is particularly novel. The whole seventh book is given a strikingly theoretical cast by being arranged, like a scientific work, as a series of "propositions." Most of these deal with solutions to particular problems with which an architect is likely to be confronted. Propositions Ten to Thirteen, however, are introduced as an *intermedio* or interlude, which will treat of

judicious architecture [*architettura judiciosa*] and especially of ornaments and decoration, and explain . . . the difference between an architecture which is solid [*soda*], simple [*semplice*], plain [*schietta*], sweet [*dolce*], and soft [*morbida*] and one which is weak [*debole*], flimsy [*gracile*], delicate [*delicata*], affected [*affettata*], harsh [*cruda*], in other words obscure [*oscura*] and confused [*confusa*], as I will make understood in the four following illustrations. (120)

Serlio sets out to describe and illustrate qualities of architectural style which had never been dealt with before, using as a tool a vocabulary consisting of a series of five pairs of words each referring to opposed characteristics. As becomes apparent, each pair tends to deal with a different aspect of style: for example, the first terms *soda* and *debole* refer to the presence or absence of structural strength, the middle terms *schietta* and *delicata* refer to the degree of incised detail, and the last pair *morbida* and *cruda* cover the degree of unity and softness of transitions involved in the overall effect. Just how precisely he believes these metaphorical polarities can be applied to architecture is revealed in his commentary on each of the four cuts. (The precision and consistency of language throughout is remarkable, and to enable this to emerge as clearly as possible the following paragraphs rely heavily on retaining the original Italian terms.)

Each illustration shows a wall articulated in a different way by a columnar order. The first is Ionic and, as Serlio says,

because it is Ionic it can be called *soda* [solid] since it is not weakened by *intagli*. It can also be called *morbida* [soft] and *dolce* [sweet] because it has not very much *crudezza* [harshness]. And even if the columns were fluted, the capitals given incised detail, and the dentils carved out, you still could not call it *cruda* [harsh]. And you can see that such a work is made with good *giudicio*. (120)

Serlio here begins with a fairly simple demonstration of how the terms can be applied to Ionic, and introduces an interesting technique of instruction. Not only does he refer to two possible treatments of the order, but he actually illustrates them both, since the central section of the illustration has added to it exactly those three modifications of shaft, capital, and entablature mentioned at the end. We are thus able immediately to test for ourselves the validity of his remarks. The next example is Doric and receives a slightly fuller analysis (Fig. 153):

It could be called *soda* and *semplice* and even *morbida*. It is *soda* because of the order, which is Doric. It is *semplice* because there is no incised detail, and if there were any, as with fluted columns and carved capitals, the *sodezza* would not be removed, but only the *semplicità*. For that part which has no *intagli* is always *soda* and *morbida* because of its unity [*unione*], as can be seen in the *schietta* part. (122)

With the transition to the next illustration, which is Composite, the complexity of the observations increases further:

It can be called *gracile* and *delicata* and also *cruda* and *secca* [dry]; it is *gracile* because of the thinness [*sottilità*] and slenderness [*sveltezza*] of the columns, which nevertheless are fitting in that order. It is also *delicata* because of the refinement

of the workmanship and because of the *intagli*. It can be called *cruda* because of the darkness of the columns and because of the coloured marbles set into the pedestals. It is dry [*secca*] because that is the opposite of *morbidezza*. And this can be seen in the part with the coloured marble columns. But the part which is *schietta* without *intagli*, and also without coloured marbles, is *gracile* like the rest but is not *cruda* or *secca*, but is rather *morbida*, *dolce*, and *semplice*. (124)

The text allows us to describe the overall character of the facing figure and also to differentiate the visual effects of the three different variations shown—plain Composite, plain Composite with coloured marbles, and carved Composite with coloured marbles. Finally the most ambitious text accompanies the last figure, which is also the one which shows the most variations (Fig. 154). It is Corinthian, and Serlio says that

it can be called rather *cruda* and *confusa* in that part where the columns are of coloured marble and dark; for elements which are dark and yet project forward when put in front of something light give the opposite effect. And that is the reason why the best painters when painting a history [*istoria*] or a story [*favola*] with many figures one behind the other always paint those nearest to our eyes in the lightest colour to give strength to their work. And if they did otherwise, making the nearer figures dark and the farther ones light, their painting would be *cruda* and *confusa*. And that is what happens in the work opposite for these same reasons. But I do not want the architect to reject columns of dark coloured marble, nor porphyry ones, nor serpentine ones, nor do I want him to reject the use of similar rich encrustations. They should be used extensively but with good *giudicio*. So, for example, if he should have to make a loggia or portico with free-standing columns, I would admire such a work if the walls were encrusted with fine stones well arranged, but it would not fit if he set coloured marbles into the pedestals because their darkness makes them look *deboli*. Such a work would also be *confusa* and *affettata* if it had many *intagli*, as can be seen in that part where all the mouldings of the entablature are carved, a treatment which *giudiciosi* find very *confusa*. But if the *intagli* are separated, as they are above the door, such a work could never be blamed for being *confusa*. (126)

In those four texts and illustrations Serlio makes an impressive attempt to develop a vocabulary which covers most of the possible variations of wall articulation available in the mid-sixteenth century. He covers not only all the orders, but all the alternatives within them as well. In the last illustration, for example, he shows not just Corinthian, but Corinthian with three degrees of surface carving and also with three degrees of mar-

153. Serlio, Book VII (1575): "Discussion and definition of some architectural terms" applied to Doric (from 1575 ed., p. 123)

ble encrustation, providing for an even wider range of combinations than he deals with in the text.

Serlio's introduction to these "propositions" made it clear that his goal was not just to develop what is in effect the first analytical vocabulary of architectural style, but specifically to develop the *giudicio* of his readers, so that they would be able not only to differentiate styles but to choose the best one. This had also been the purpose of the illustrations of ancient buildings in Book III. It is accordingly not surprising to find him returning to these works at the end of the last proposition. Addressing those who are not capable of understanding all his reasoning, he refers them back to the Pantheon and the Arch of Ancona, which are

among the most beautiful of ancient buildings. The Pantheon is Corinthian and has very few *intagli*, but is very well organized [*compartito*]. The arch at Ancona is also Corinthian, very well designed, and has *intagli* only on the capitals. From

which I conclude that these things which are *semplici* [simple] and well understood [*bene intese*] will be praised more than those which are *confusa* and *affettata*. (126)

Similar conclusions have been drawn in rather greater detail in Book III itself. Discussing Trajan's other arch, at Benevento, immediately after the passage describing the mouldings quoted earlier, Serlio goes on to make a general statement:

But there are architects, and especially today, who, to please the masses [*vulgo*] and to decorate their poorly understood buildings, add to them many *intagli* in such a way that often they confuse the architecture with these *intagli* and destroy the beauty of its form, and if there ever was a time when things which are *soda* and *semplice* are valued by *i giudiciosi* it is the present period (*secolo*). (104ᵛ)

Serlio's enthusiastic study of the visual response to architecture and the operation of the faculty of *giudicio* here emerge in a new light. For the statement is hard to

154. Serlio, Book VII: "Discussion and definition of some architectural
terms" applied to Corinthian (from 1575 ed., p. 127)

understand except in the context of rhetorical theory, where the idea of there being two opposed styles, one clear and well organized and the other confused and overwrought, the former admired for its association with the intellectual Athenians and the latter despised as the style designed for the mobs of Asia, was well established. In other words, Serlio's basic values can be seen to be derived from the already highly sophisticated world of literary criticism. The qualities of being *schietto*, *semplice*, and above all *bene inteso* are transferred from Attic rhetoric to architecture. Serlio's exercise with the "propositions" was intended to show for the latter art (as had already been shown for the former) that there were rational reasons for preferring those qualities. In rhetorical theory the elevation of Attic rhetoric was based on the functional argument that it was clearer and so better for putting across an argument. In architectural theory Serlio, by turning to the

analysis of the operation of the sense of sight, could show that simplicity and clarity might also be required for reasons internal to the art and the way it was experienced. Not only the propositions on *giudicio*, but the whole study of ancient architecture, can also be understood in this context. Just as Cicero and his contemporaries developed their own rhetorical style by studying that of the period and people whose speeches they most admired, so Serlio felt that the same could be done for architecture. This explains Serlio's quite unusual interest in the idea of a "correct period." Like a Roman discussing Greek oratory he is at pains to distinguish the good architecture of the earlier Roman Empire from the inferior later work, and the same approach leads him at the beginning of Book IV to say explicitly that "architecture in this our period [*secolo*] flourishes as did the Latin language in the time of Julius Caesar and of Cicero" (126^r). Yet he did not allow the

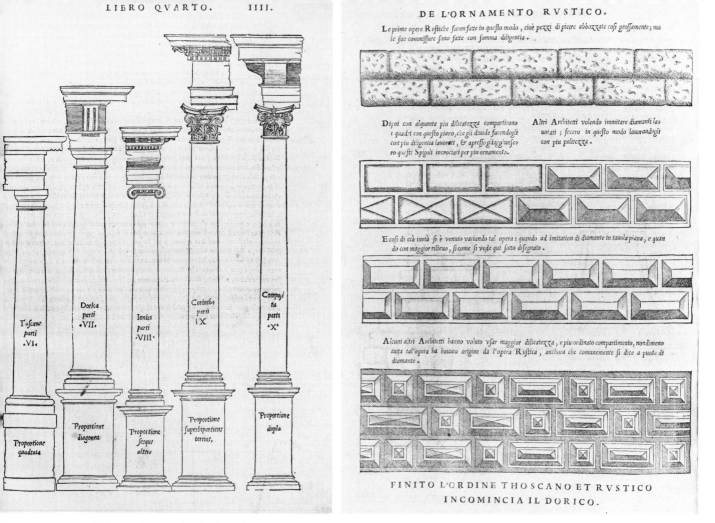

Toscano
parti
.VI.

Proportione
quadrata

Dorica
parti
.VII.

Proportione
diagonea

Ionica
parti
.VIII.

Proportione
sesqui
altera

Corintia
parti
IX

Proportione
superbipartiens
tertias,

Composi
ta
parti
.X.

Proportione
dupla

DE L'ORNAMENTO RVSTICO.

Le prime opere Rustiche furon fatte in questo modo, cioè pezzi di pietre abbozzate così grossamente; ma le sue commissure sono fatte con somma diligenza.

Dipoi con alquanta piu dilicatezza compartirono i quadri con questo piano, che gli diuide facendogli con piu diligentia lauorati, & appresso gi aggiunsero questi Spigoli incrociati per piu ornamenti.

Altri Architetti volendo immitare diamanti la uorati; fecero in questo modo lauorandogli con piu politezza.

E così di età in età si è venuto variando tal opera: quando ad imitation di diamante in tauola piana, e quando con maggior rilieuo, sì come si vede qui sotto disegnato.

Alcuni altri Architetti hanno voluto usar maggior dilicatezza, e piu ordinato compartimento, nondimeno tutta tal'opera ha hauuto origine da l'opera Rustica, anchora che comunemente si dice a punte di diamante.

FINITO L'ORDINE THOSCANO ET RVSTICO
INCOMINCIA IL DORICO.

155. Serlio, Book IV (1537): the five orders
(from 1551 ed., fol. IIII ͬ)

156. Serlio, Book IV: types of rustication
(from 1551 ed., fol. XVI ͮ)

influence of literary theories to do more than establish general guidelines. He left himself free to choose on the basis of his own analysis the best period of ancient architecture. This he placed not in the late Republic but in the early Empire, for Serlio almost certainly thought that the Pantheon, which he placed first and to which he devoted most pages and most praise, was Augustan (because of the appearance of Agrippa's name in its inscription), and he was well aware that the arches at Ancona and Benevento, which were the other monuments he most admired, were Trajanic.

Serlio's new critical approach to architecture both past and present is highly important. Inspired by the maturity of literary and especially rhetorical studies, he

applied for the first time to architecture such concepts as the best period and the best style. Indeed, he went beyond this in establishing a technical language for the description of the whole range of Classical architectural styles. He also went out of his way to define for the first time the contemporary style *par excellence* and was thus the first to isolate the character of the High Renaissance. Yet, throughout, he strengthened rather than weakened the autonomy of his own discipline by constantly returning to the specific criteria of excellence of architecture as above all a visual art. This ensured that his metaphors of stylistic description were rooted in direct sensory response rather than being transferred at second hand from the world of literature. In this he continues the tradition, begun by Colonna and Pacioli, according to which the visual arts should not see themselves in any sense as inferior to their more established sisters. Indeed, in his use of the illustrated book as a didactic tool, both in his analysis of ancient monuments and in his theoretical propositions on the definition of terms, he deploys educational techniques of a clarity and objectivity which were then rivalled in none of the arts and few of the sciences. Alberti had said that the most praiseworthy quality in an architect was the ability to judge what is appropriate, using a moral term ("praiseworthy") to qualify the essentially moral quality of decorum. Serlio says that the most beautiful quality in an architect is the ability to use visual judgement, employing an aesthetic term ("beautiful") to qualify an aesthetic gift. During the century which separated the two pronouncements, architecture had been largely removed from the traditional territory of ethics into the new one of aesthetics.

The credit for establishing the art in its new territory must go to Serlio himself. However, it is likely that the initial stimulus for such an approach came from Peruzzi. Cellini, one of Serlio's early detractors, says firmly that Peruzzi "turned to the investigation of beautiful architecture, and in order to determine the basis for the best style copied ancient monuments everywhere."[6] The motive for this statement might only have been a desire to damage Serlio's reputation as an original theorist, but the evidence suggests that it contains some truth. As Burns has shown, Peruzzi's annotated drawings clearly indicate that he was interested in architectural criticism.[7] Still, his vocabulary seems to have been much more idiosyncratic and hardly relates to that of his pupil; besides which it has also recently been shown that many of Serlio's drawings of Roman monuments derive not from Peruzzi, as was once thought, but from other sketchbooks.[8] Serlio almost certainly acquired his first interest in architectural criticism and the analytical study of Roman monuments from Peruzzi, but he went on to develop a language and system all his own. The character of his personal approach probably owes most to his contacts in the literary world of Bologna and Venice in the late 1520s and the 1530s.[9] Though often mistakenly caricatured as naive, Serlio moved in the most sophisticated intellectual circles.

The orders

His friends in these circles would have been delighted by the elegant way in which he introduced the magnificent block showing the five orders with which Book IV greeted its readers in 1537 (Fig. 155). It is, as he says, an imitation of the practice of ancient writers of comedy who often provided a prologue summarizing the contents of their plays. The information it carries is deliberately selected "so that a general rule is demonstrated at a single glance" (126ᵛ). The only written information on the illustration is the identification of each of the five orders shown and the arithmetical proportions of their respective columns and pedestals. The general rule is that there are five orders arranged in a regular mathematical progression, with each column being one diameter higher than its predecessor and with each pedestal being loftier in proportion than its neighbour in a similar way. The series rises from Tuscan, with its 1:6 column and its square pedestal, to Composite, with a column of 1:10 and a pedestal of two squares. However, already in his account of Tuscan Serlio makes it clear that the five orders form a series not only of rising proportions but also of increasing ornament and decoration. Tuscan is the "most solid [*sodo*] and the least ornate [*ornato*] order ... the most rustic [*rustico*] and the most strong and of the least thinness [*sottigliezza*] and slenderness [*gracilità*]" (126ᵛ). From what has been noted earlier it is easy to understand what Serlio means by all these terms, except *rustico*. This is soon explained; "since Tuscan work [*opera*] is the most rough [*rozza*] and least ornate, as it seems to me, rustic work suits it and matches it better than it does any other" (126ᵛ). "Rustication," as is apparent from the illustrations, is the word Serlio applies to rough stonework, and this can be recognized as appropriate to the coarse simplicity of the order. At the end of the section on Tuscan the whole problem of rustication is separately treated for the first time. On one page, four bands of masonry are shown, arranged in chronological order of development. The first, the original type, has blocks "coarsely roughed out" (*abbozzate grossamente*), and there is then a progressive increase in "polish" (*politezza*), "refinement" (*dilicatezza*), and "ornament" (*ornamento*) down the page (Fig. 156). Evidently Serlio was anxious to show not only that the columnar orders could be seen to com-

157. Serlio, Book IV: rustic
Tuscan portal (from 1551
ed., fol. XII^r)

statement that the order is appropriate to a whole set of buildings of defined functions: "Tuscan work, in my opinion, is appropriate for fortifications, that is for city gates, citadels, castles, treasuries and places for storing munitions and artillery, prisons, ports, and other such structures built for war" (126^v). Against the background of the expressive theory which was explicit in the writings of Colonna, Pacioli, and Raphael and implicit in the practice of High Renaissance Rome, such a recommendation is completely comprehensible. Nevertheless it reduces such principles to a new degree of definition, particularly in the context of the Tuscan order, which had previously been almost completely neglected. It also represents a new development in applying a theory of appropriate architectural expression to classes of buildings which had never before been thought worthy of such attention. Serlio's "in my opinion" further implies that the rule is his own, and, whatever influence there may be from his master Peruzzi, there is no reason to doubt that this is essentially true. He first seeks out some essential abstract property in a set of architectural forms, in this case "strength" (*fortezza*), and then, taking this as his key, matches these forms to a whole category of buildings in which that property is important. A similar logic led him to see rough rustication as fitting in the same context.[10] It explicitly reinforces the order's impression of *fortezza*. Commenting on a doorway which combines Tuscan half-columns with heavy rustication, he insists that it "represents great strength," and goes on to say that "the more coarsely the masonry is roughed out, as long as it is still done with art [*artificio*] it will match the character [*serverà il decoro*] of the order, especially, that is, when it is applied to the blocks which bind the columns and the keystones" (133^v) (Fig. 157). Not only are the order itself and the rough rustication expressive, but the particular way they are combined, as when here the great blocks "bind" the columns to the walls, is in a way emblematic of the strong containment of a fortress or prison. Moreover, the reference to *artificio* alerts us to yet another way in which the balance between rustication and order can be significant. Describing the same woodcut, Serlio tells us that the mixture of rustication with an order "represents . . . partly *opera di natura* and partly *opera di artificio*." The roughness of rusticated masonry presumably brings it close to natural raw stone, while the more the work is fin-

pose a scale from simplicity to refinement, but that masonry types could be varied in the same way. There may indeed be an intentional parallelism between the scale of the orders and the scale of masonry, since the richest and latest form of masonry is essentially a conflation of the preceding two forms, just as the Composite order is created by a final conflation of the preceding Ionic and Corinthian. This is all the more likely since Serlio seems to have been the first person to introduce the term "Composite" for Alberti's Italic order, thus drawing attention to its basically conflated character. If we analyse the page of masonry further, more of Serlio's principles can be discerned. Thus, reading from top to bottom and from left to right, there is a regular progression not only from rough to smooth but also from low relief to high relief and from no inscribed lines to many. This page, like that of the orders, can be seen to illustrate a *regola generale*.

So far Serlio's scales are only abstract schemata with a high level of coherence and consistency, seeming to aspire to the same level of theoretical purity as the analogous diagrams of the tetrachord which had long been customary in treatises on music. But Serlio intends them also to serve as the basis for establishing a language of architectural expression of a new precision. Accordingly, he begins his account of Tuscan with a

ished the more firmly it belongs in the world of art. This enables us to understand his comments on the next illustration, which employs coupled columns: "and because functional requirements are turned into ornaments, and ornament sometimes goes beyond the bounds of what is strictly necessary in order to show both art and the affluence of the patron, this *inventione* has been made" (134ᵛ). An increase in rustication gives an impression of natural strength, while an increase in carved ornament, even when applied to Tuscan, enhances an impression of artificial refinement and wealth.

In what he said about Tuscan and Rustic Serlio had to think out the problem largely on his own, indebted only to the practice of Bramante and his school. With Doric there was already a literary tradition going back to Vitruvius, and in his first general rule he adapts the Roman writer's individual observations on the orders to his own notion of architectural scales: "the ancients dedicated buildings to the gods, matching them to them according as their nature was either robust [*robusta*] or delicate [*delicata*]" (126ʳ). At the beginning of the discussion of Doric he goes on to show how the Vitruvian rule of *decor* can be brought up to date:

So, having to build a temple dedicated to Christ the Redeemer, or to Saint Paul or to Saint George, or to other such saints, Doric is the appropriate order; not because they were soldiers, but because they partook of the manly and the strong in sacrificing their lives for their Christian belief. And it is appropriate in this way not only for sacred buildings, but if you have to erect any building for any military or strong person whether they are of the upper, middle, or lower class, or whether the building is public or private, Doric is also suitable; and the more robust [*robusto*] is the person, the more the detailed handling should be solid [*soda*], and if the man, although military, still has something of the delicate [*delicato*] about him, then the handling too can show some refinement [*delicatezza*]. (139ʳ)

Serlio not only transfers the Vitruvian rule to the Christian context, as Pacioli had already hinted might be done, but goes on to show that a similar principle can be applied to the choice of order for secular buildings too. Moreover, using his concept of a scale from *sodo* to *delicato* he shows that the architecture can be matched to the man in a very precise way. Accordingly, for Doric, as for all the other orders from Tuscan on, he is careful to show at least two forms of the order,

the one more "solid" and the other more "refined," that is with more carved details.

Going on to Ionic he reveals a similar approach:

We Christians, if we should be involved in building temples in this order, should dedicate them to those saints whose life was intermediate between the robust [*robusta*] and the soft [*tenero*] and also to those female saints who led a matronly life. And if any building, whether public or private, has to be made for men of letters or those who lead a life of repose, being neither robust nor soft, for them too the Ionic will be suitable; and this manner will also be appropriate if you have to make any building for matronly women. (158ᵛ)

Since Vitruvius had recommended the order for the artistic Apollo and the almost effeminate Bacchus, and since it is more refined in character, it becomes appropriate for those men whose relation to life is primarily intellectual rather than physical. Francesco di Giorgio had already discussed the design of a separate type of house-plan suited for a similar class of people, called by him *studenti* (studious people), but this is the first time such people have been matched with a specific architectural form as well.

When he comes to Corinthian, Serlio deliberately misquotes the recommendation of the Roman writer, disregarding the association with Venus and other less serious divinities and saying only that because it was copied from the form of a virgin the ancients required that it should be "dedicated to the goddess Vesta, president of virgins" (126ʳ). This is done to facilitate the transposition of the rule to a modern Christian context. Thus, he prescribes:

If you are involved in building a temple in this order it should be dedicated to the Virgin Mary, Mother of Jesus Christ our Redeemer; and so too it should be used for all those saints, male and female, who led a virginal life; besides, this order is appropriate to monasteries; and convents housing virgins dedicated to divine worship should also be made in this style [*maniera*]. And if you make public buildings or private houses or tombs for people of a good and pure life you can use this type of ornament in order to match the character of the Corinthian capital. (169ʳ)

By restricting the ancient rule to Vesta he is able to turn Corinthian into an emphatically virginal order appropriate both specifically to monasteries and generally to all buildings associated with people of a pure and moral life. However, by taking his cue from the ancient text he loses the direct connection between the attributes of architectural forms and human types which was apparent with (for example) Doric, since the very prettiness of Corinthian makes it hardly directly expressive of goodness and purity.

The final order is Composite. As a form it had earlier been introduced by Alberti, who had called it Italic; but, apart from Pacioli's passing reference to the Alberti passage, it had not thereafter been properly discussed. The name "Composite" first appears in the 1528 copyright application, though the order was not then illustrated in the series of engravings. It was only the appearance of Book IV which brought final recognition both of the form and of its new name.

As far as I can see, Vitruvius never discusses Composite work [*opera*], which some call Latin and others Italic. Perhaps because the Romans were unable to surpass the invention of he Greeks who discovered the Doric column based on man, the Ionic imitated from matrons, and Corinthian derived from virgins, they made from Ionic and Corinthian a composition putting the Ionic volutes and egg-and-dart on to the Corinthian capital, and this they used more for triumphal arches than for any other structure. And this they did for a very good reason. For, having conquered all the countries where these forms originated, they could, being their masters, combine them at their pleasure, as they did in the great building, the Colosseum at Rome. There, having put three orders one above the other, Doric, Ionic, and Corinthian, they put on top of all these Composite work; as is said by everybody, although as far as one can see the capitals are Corinthian. (183ʳ)

Serlio's explanation of the origin of Composite is probably correct, as has already been observed. But the most remarkable feature of his commentary is that he evidently realized that the one monument which was supposed to prove its nationalistic meaning had in fact often been wrongly read, since the top capitals of the Colosseum were not Composite but Corinthian. His only way out of this difficulty was to identify the modillions under the cornice of the upper order as also a Composite feature. As he says in his account of the building in Book III: "The fourth order is Composite, and others call it Latin as having been invented by the Romans, and others Italic; nevertheless it can be called Composite, if for no other reason than because of the consoles in its frieze, since no other order has consoles in its frieze" (80ᵛ). It is as if Serlio thought that the theory about the placing of the orders on the Colosseum

was too attractive to lose, and so he rescued it by clinging to the consoles as a differentiating feature.

Perhaps, however, it was anxiety about the evidence for the theoretical justification for the name "Italic" which encouraged him to reject it in favour of his own, "Composite." This term preserved the essential element of Alberti's observation that that order was a combination of the others without adding a tendentious explanation. It also recalled a fourth "mixed" category which was known in the systems of classification of both music and literature. Mixolydian had already in Antiquity been accepted as the fourth "authentic" mode, above Dorian, Phrygian, and Lydian, and more recently Gaffurio had added a new set of modes called *permixtum* to the traditional "authentic" and "plagal" forms, and a *compositus* scale above the Diatonic, Harmonic, and Chromatic. And for literature Paolo Crinito (1504), for example, refers to a familiar convention of identifying four types of Latin: *prisca, Latina, Romana,* and *mista,* the last being the latest, developing only with the extension of citizenship to different races.

Whatever its origin, the name "Composite" reveals something of Serlio's general attitude to the order and its uses. He is at pains to point out, for example, that the triumphal arches on which it was so frequently found were often composite structures, being made "of elements taken from other buildings" (185ᵛ). He also tells us that the term can be applied to mixtures other than just Ionic and Corinthian, "since the ancient Romans made different mixtures" (184ʳ), and he even illustrates a whole range of strange forms involving leaf and animal elements (Fig. 158). This approach in turn leads him to make a series of bizarre inventions of his own, as in a fireplace on which he comments: "other Composite ornaments can be added to chimneys, and they can use varied forms because this way of building [*maniera di edificare*] is more licentious than the others" (186ᵛ). Evidently Serlio feels that it is in the nature of the Composite order that it is not tightly bound by rules as are the others, but is a sort of "free" style. He thus implicitly contrasts it with Doric at the other end of the scale, which is the most precisely "regular" of the orders. This contrast affects not only the internal design of the order; it also affects the way it is used. The rules governing the use of Doric were precise and detailed, those governing Composite almost non-

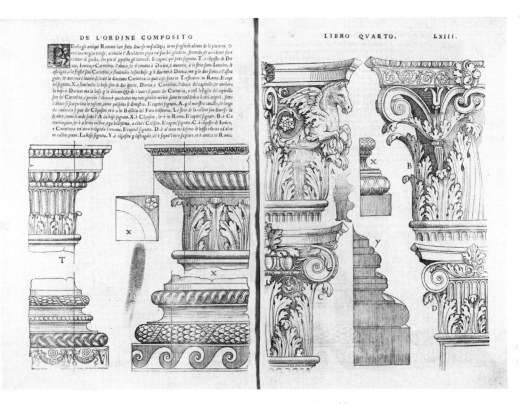

158. Serlio, Book IV: Composite capitals and bases
(from 1551 ed., fol. LXII^v and LXIII^r)

existent. Doric is the order of "decorum" and Composite the order of "licence." For Serlio the term "Composite" could cover a whole range of mixed and irregular creations which would otherwise have been beyond the pale.

The rules for the use of the different orders are based on varying principles. Those for Tuscan and Rustic are based on Serlio's own perception of the inherent nature of the forms, while those for Doric, Ionic, and Corinthian are based on the transposition and development of the observations of Vitruvius, and that for Composite on Serlio's interpretation of ancient usage following up the hints of Alberti. The resulting theory is disparate in character; but cumulatively the various recommendations on using the orders in fortifications, public buildings, palaces, and churches show a greater awareness than ever before that the choice of a particular order in a particular context might be taken to reveal something about the occupant, owner, or dedicatee of a particular structure.

In spite of this new awareness Serlio does not in his many detailed designs usually recommend them for particular uses, leaving the choice to the patron and architect. Guidance is only occasionally given. In Book IV itself, in the Tuscan chapter, two designs are shown which are suitable for "city gates or fortresses." The first has rusticated pilasters, while the second has smooth engaged columns; but the text on the latter also contains the advice that "the more coarsely bossed such a doorway is, the more it will match the quality of a fortress" (130^r). A simpler rusticated design is then recommended for a city or castle gate, and a less heavily rusticated one for supporting terraces in gardens (130^v, 131^r). Still later another single-arched opening, close in character to the first city gate (139^v), is recommended for the entry to a villa. Serlio appears to hesitate in distinguishing between the rural and defensive associations of rustication, and in his comments on a Tuscan door with flanking half-columns attached by rustic bands he observes: "I should judge that this

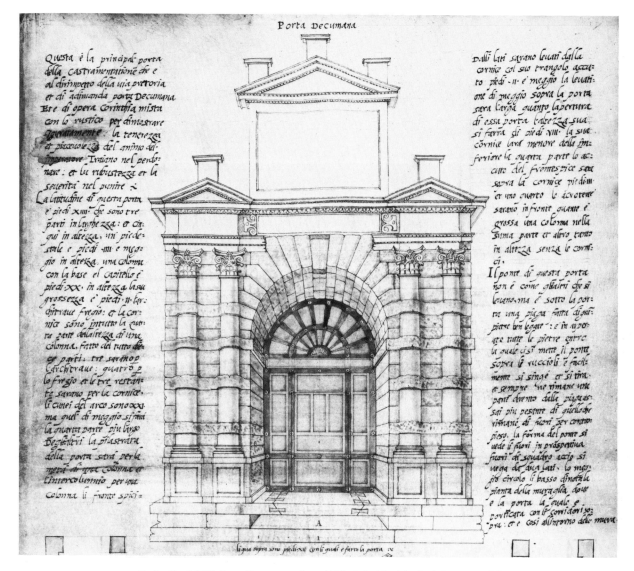

159. Serlio, Book VIII: Porta Decumana, Staatsbibliothek, Munich, Cod. Icon. 190, fol. 17ʳ

would be most suitable to a fortress; yet it would succeed well in any rustic building, as is seen by the use of similar work in Giulio Romano's buildings at Rome and at Mantua in the Palazzo del Te (133ᵛ, 134ʳ). As Gombrich noted long ago, the suitability of such a rusticated treatment to a villa may be due to its combination of *opera di natura* (the rustication) and *opera di artificio* (the finished columns).[11] A villa such as the Pa-

lazzo del Te was built for the enjoyment of "nature" by those who could not deny themselves the attributes of "art." Serlio is less communicative when discussing Doric. He does illustrate a Doric door with rusticated bands applied to the flanking engaged columns, adding a note that the refinement of the order makes it suitable for use only *inside* a fortress and that otherwise it might be used for the house of a soldier whether in the town or in the country (147^v). Otherwise his various façade designs are not matched to particular occupants, and the most interesting comments come when he recommends rustication on the ground floor of a Venetian palace because "it is appropriate over the water" (155^v)—presumably because the water is a "natural" element. With Ionic the observations are further reduced. The only detailed one is the recommendation that an Ionic portal with rusticated bands may be used for the residence of an intellectual (*letterato*) or merchant with a robust life-style (*di vita robusta*), in the country or even in the town (163^r). Ionic is the order appropriate to intellectuals and merchants, but it can be modified by rustication if their life-style requires it. The other pertinent comment on Ionic is that, since it derives from the form of matrons, mature women may be incorporated into the sculptural decorations of Ionic fireplaces (167^r). Corinthian is not recommended specifically for any buildings, but it is significant that only for this order does Serlio design churches, as if in acknowledgement of its frequent use in that context. He certainly admits to the general popularity of "Corinthian, which is universally loved by us all" (174^r) and goes on to note that it is particularly favoured by the Venetians (177^r). On Corinthian fireplaces he comments that they may incorporate girls for the same reason that Ionic may incorporate women. Apparently he felt that just as the orders should be matched to the character of the occupants, etc. of the buildings where they are used, so their sculptural adornments should be matched to their own internal properties. Figure sculpture and order can together reflect the nature of the owner.

In only one later book does Serlio go into greater detail in his theories on the use of the orders. This is Book VIII, on camps, which was never published. It consists chiefly of a reconstruction of a Roman camp, which basically follows the account in Polybius but which is also made to include features of camps erected by Trajan in Pannonia, as described to Serlio by Cardinal Grimani. The important passages for us are those which describe a series of gateways. Two of these are the main gate of the camp, the Porta Praetoria near the general's quarters, and the Porta Decumana opposite to it (Fig. 159). The first of these is described in the text:

The Praetorian Gate requires to be made in a serious style [*opera grave*] which will have a dignity appropriate to the

rank of the consul, and for this purpose Doric work is the most serious and is truly appropriate to a soldier. This gate will be entirely of delicate Doric, to suit the great emperor [Trajan] who so much loved the beauty of architecture. (18^r)

The Porta Decumana, on the other hand, "is of Corinthian work mixed with rustication to show figuratively the gentleness and mildness of the Emperor Trajan's mind in giving pardon" (17^r). Of these two gates the Praetoria is thus a direct personal expression of the emperor's Doric character and refined taste. The Decumana makes a more general statement about Trajan's clemency, using Corinthian as an emblem of gentleness, though combining it with rustication to make the military context quite clear. The third gate described is the side gate leading to the treasury looked after by the quaestor. This is both Doric and heavily rusticated below: "This gate which is so rusticated is appropriate at the side of the quaestorium, since very strong gates are necessary to preserve such valuable metals" (17^v). The rustication, which is in any case appropriate to a fortification, is emphasized as a symbolic protection of the emperor's bullion. But perhaps the most remarkable gates of all are those on a bridge nearby, which were explained to Grimani by the local inhabitants (Fig. 160). At one end was a rusticated Tuscan arch and at the other a Corinthian one without rustication, and Serlio insists that this is because the one looks towards the barbarians and the other towards Italy. Corinthian here thus has the same function as the same order on the Porta Decumana, which would also normally face away from the enemy and which expresses Trajan's gentleness towards his subjects. The rusticated Tuscan gate, on the other hand, presents a hostile barrier to the threatening hordes beyond the frontier. The two faces of the bridge represent the traditional two faces of the Roman government: "to spare the conquered and defeat [*debellare*] the proud" (Virgil, *Aeneid* VI). Serlio was a great admirer of Trajan, who of all emperors best embodied those virtues, and whose Arch at Ancona was for him the pinnacle of good taste. In his account of that arch he even took up the Virgilian language, noting how the emperor on top was shown "making a menacing gesture towards those peoples whom he had defeated [*che egli havea debellati*]" (107^v). For Serlio architecture had the power to express character and mood, a power long attributed to sculpture. The gateway was the primary vehicle for that expression.

Il render conto della casa dimostrata in apparente disegno
con la uiua scrittura e' molto gioueuole a coloroli
quali sono disposti al uolere imparare per il che io
trattaro breuemente le misure del arco qui dauanti,
la apertura del quale e' larga piedi xx. et in altezza
piedi . XL .   li piedestali sono alti piedi viii. le
colonne con le basi e capitelli sono in altezza piedi xxx.
la sua grossezza e' piedi . III . e tal grachtia non e' uic-
ciosa poi che uitruuio le mette tali nel tempio rhasoano:
l'altezza del architraue: fregio: et la cornice e' la quinta parte del altezza di una colonna. lo pilastro di
qua: e' di la dalle colonne sono due terzi di una
colonna fra le dua colonne sono piedi . v. li cunei
del arco sono xxi ma quello nel meggio e' la quarta parte piu largo de gli altri, li frontespici si faranno
con quella regola che nel mio quarta libro ho di-
mostrato, la leuatione di meggio senza le frontespici e' piedi xx. la sua larghezza e piedi xx. li
lati del arco sono quanto e' la sua apertura.

Li dua archi li g...
rano ne capi de...
per ostine alb...
era da gue...
ferroci...
corin...
la...

Ponte fu abbari...
triaua huomo c...
col suo truciman...
te a' ogni pietra c...
di modo che uen...
parole de piu u...
quano hauui mem...
huomo uenne in...
poi amie . et ic...
meria del Dignis...

Piedi se . c...

160. Serlio, Book VIII: Roman bridge at frontier of empire, with gates towards barbarians (left) and towards Italy (right),
Staatsbibliothek, Munich, Cod. Icon. 190, fols. 19ᵛ and 20ʳ

deferentia di opera e
con ponti fortissime
di opera rustica
ari erano pia
di opera
a uerso
re al
mia

chel buoni pa
in quei paesi
do minatamen
a quei paesani
et cose per
l suoi haue
l il gentil
quali uostro
ra a me
dimostrai

archi triomphali

L'arco qui alato di opera corinthia era al entrare del po-
te uerso Italia l'apertura del quale e piedi XX in lar
ghezza et in altezza piedi XL manco tri li piedestali
son alti piedi VIII l'altezza delle colonne con le basi
e capitelli e piedi XXXII la sua grossezza e la decima
parte del altezza l'architraue il fregio et la cornice so
in altezza la quinta parte della colonna partito il tut-
to in parti X tre sarano per l'architraue quatro per lo
fregio le tre restanti sarano per la cornice l'accepto del
frontespice sara leuato dalla cornice piedi VIII le pi-
lastrate della porta cosi le ale delle colonne sono
per meggia grossezza di colonna ghinterColonni doue
sono li nicchi son larghi piedi VII li lati del arco so
no quanto l'apertura

Ho uoluto dimostrare in maggior forma questi
archi accio chi si uegga quello é quanto
delle pietre et come sono li cunei acchiar-
chi et ho uoluto dimostrare quei pilastri con-
nellati sopra pilastroni et quei nicchi et
quei erni ouali ancora doue erano delli
pistoni Scolpiti quella apertura doa si vedi
sopra il pilastro et ne pilastri ancora
sono fatti accio che uenendo qualon emp
di acqui elle potessero shorare sifacilmenti
dubitando finfare il gran peso del aequa d'esso ponte

Apertura che e ne pilastroni per esalare l'acque

La figura qui sopra dimostra il fianco di qui pilastro sopra lo quale si ueggono
li parapetti dall uni et dall'altri con le ale dall lati per tenere lontani li nemici

Questo e lo diritto del ponte leuato dalla pianta ne capi del quale erano dua archi triomphali
di estrema grandezza et sopra ciascuno pilastro ui era un piedestale sopra li quali si mettiuano le spoglie
di nemici et gli pregioni ancora et in essi piedestali si sculpiuano a perpetua memoria

Licence and the rule

There can be little doubt that Serlio loved formulating and applying rules. But we have already seen in the discussion of Composite that he was also prepared to accord a place to "licence," both in the design process and in usage. Elsewhere he explores the idea of freedom of architectural composition and usage in a carefully constructed context. This is the Libro Estraordinario, published by him in the relatively civilized city of Lyons, but composed during the 1540s in the wilder environment of Fontainebleau. This environment, he says in his introduction, had a decisive influence both on the book's unplanned emergence and on its character:

in the solitude of Fontainebleau, in the company of wild beasts rather than of men . . . a desire came into my mind to represent in visual form some rustic portals. In a transport of architectural madness [*furore architettonico*] I produced thirty . . . with new fantasies surging in my mind. . . . I [also] made twenty of more delicate workmanship.

Later, at the end of the thirty rustic designs, as if exhausted by the fulfilment of some biological or psychological urge, he declares himself "already tired" (17ᵛ). Serlio stresses that the designs are not the result of a rational application but came almost willy-nilly to his mind, which had become unhinged by the wildness of his company. This explains not only why the book had never been planned, but also why the portals were all rather strange, especially the first thirty. Alberti would have despaired at the idea of designs produced in such a *furore architettonico*, and clearly Serlio himself was conscious of the boldness of his idea. Nevertheless his readiness to publish them proves his acceptance of such an uninhibited approach to composition. The reference to *furore* places him in the great tradition of inspired creators which was founded by the Greek poets whose *mania* resulted from divine possession. At the same time he presents his state as stemming from his savage surroundings in France. We can hardly fail to recognize the same conscious abandonment of self-control which Cellini's autobiography acknowledges at the same time in the more sordid sphere of his private passions.

It is certainly the savagery of his environment which causes him first to produce thirty "rustic" portals, which are the most direct expression of his state of mind. Admittedly they are given some respectability by being introduced by the design for the gate of the Cardinal Hippolito d'Este's house at Fontainebleau, but it might also be felt that the coarse rustication of the Cardinal's residence proved how even the loftiest spirits were affected by the bestial company. This would help to explain the Cardinal's attempt to prevent the portal's inclusion in the publication. Certainly it is as if the twenty delicate portals were added as an expression of Serlio's return to sanity after a crisis. As he says in his introduction to the first of these, "Now that I have given vent to the bizarre [*la bizzaria*] in mixed productions it is reasonable that I should give some treatment of the regular [*regolari*]" (18ʳ). In other words, the rustic examples represent extravagant irrational designs, and the delicate ones are relatively rational and correct. By publishing both sets Serlio acknowledges the value of both. This view, which is implicit in the layout of the whole book, is explicitly voiced in the commentary on rustic portal XXVIII (Fig. 161): "If it were not for the extravagance [*bizzaria*] of some men we would not recognize the restraint [*modestia*] of others . . . But because there always were, are, and will be, as I believe, bizarre people who seek after novelty, I have chosen to break and destroy the beautiful form of this Doric portal" (16ᵛ). The doorway is indeed of the purest and most refined Doric, but it has great rusticated bands breaking the shafts of the fluted columns, the lintel, and the entablature, while, to make the affront to manners even clearer, weeds are shown growing haphazardly from between the rough blocks. Just as the purity of the Doric forms represents the ultimate in correctness and restraint, so the rustication and weeds show the ultimate in the rejection of these standards. The next portal, XXIX, represents an even more striking polarization, the rough parts even rougher and the refined parts more refined (Fig. 162). Serlio himself points out that the rustication has become bestial (*opera bestiale*), with the addition of stones in the spandrels which are made by nature in the shape of monstrous animal heads, and that the Doric has become Corinthian, with all the detailed carving (*intagli*) of that order. If portal XXVIII was essentially an opposition of the correct and the incorrect, portal XXIX is essentially an opposition of the refined and the unrefined. Not only does each portal individually embody the same opposition as that between the two sections of the book, the rustic and the

161. Serlio, Libro Estraordinario (later Book VI) (1551): rustic portal XXVIII (from 1566 ed., fol. 30ʳ)

162. Serlio, Libro Estraordinario: rustic portal XXIX (from 1566 ed., fol. 31ʳ)

163. Serlio, Libro Estraordinario: rustic portal VI (from 1566 ed., fol. 8ʳ)

delicate, but the opposition between Doric and Corinthian represents a similar polarity. Rustication is particularly appropriate to Tuscan and Doric, and delicacy is especially the property of Corinthian. Hence the last rustic portal and the first delicate portal, which follow, are respectively Tuscan and Corinthian. Like the previous pair, they embody an opposition which is an epitome of the two sections, for almost all the rustic portals are Tuscan or Doric, and almost all the delicate ones are Ionic, Corinthian, or Composite.

It becomes apparent that, while in his treatment of the orders a decade earlier Serlio had regarded Composite as the most "licentious," being by implication opposed to a "regular" Doric, he has now adopted an opposite scale with the simpler orders being associated with the greatest licence and the richest ones with the least. It is the rustic gates with their predominantly simpler orders which are called bizarre and which collectively constitute a body of "licentious things" (*cose licenciose*) (15ʳ), while the delicate portals with their richer orders form a body of "regular things" (*cose regolari*) (18ʳ). This does not imply a contradiction in his

point of view. When the columnar orders are treated by themselves, Doric is clearly more regular and Composite more free; but when the accompanying variations of masonry types are brought in as well, rustication is clearly more free in its character than delicate work and consequently transforms the relative status of the orders. Emphatically rusticated Tuscan and Doric buildings are manifestly less restrained than emphatically delicate Ionic, Corinthian, and Composite ones. This is especially true in the Libro Estraordinario, where the rustication verging on bestiality is directly an expression of the animal savagery of rural France.

There is one final sophistication in Serlio's approach to his own mad creations. In the texts accompanying many of his rustic portals he is at pains to point out that if the rustication is removed the architecture underneath will be found to be quite correct. It is almost as if he is admitting that the *furore architettonico* is only a pose, a transitory state of mind. Thus, when describing the coating of rustication on the columns of portal VI he says they are "Doric, but dressed up differently [*stravestita*] and given a mask [*fatta maschera*]

... if these things were removed the portal would be pure and would have all its correct measurements" (5^v) (Fig. 163). Just as contemporary nobles would mask themselves for parties or for evening appearances on the streets in order to have the freedom of anonymity to indulge themselves, so Serlio has used the cloak of rustication to give himself a greater creative freedom, knowing that he can remove it at will if anyone should charge that such coarse and irregular features expressed his real self. It was natural that Serlio should draw an analogy between rustication and a pose of freedom adopted for a brief period. Country life was always thought to offer greater opportunity for freedom, and the Italian nobles of his day would often regard their brief stays in their villas as opportunities to relax after the formality demanded of them in town. Since town life constituted the norm, their rural relaxation could never be more than a conscious pose. Unlike modern man, who likes to think of himself as natural underneath and only dressing up formally to please others, being truly himself on the beach and in the country and stiff and unnatural in town, the sixteenth-century gentleman could never risk such a close identification with the natural life of animals and peasants and needed to show that his rustication was only a surface attribute. When Giulio Romano first cloaked the carefully carved columns of the entrance to the Palazzo del Te with rustication, perhaps he wished, in the same spirit as Serlio, to suggest that a rustic freedom could be enjoyed there by Federico Gonzaga and his guests, but that underneath they remained the embodiments of the best standards of correctness and restraint, standards which they would again proclaim as soon as they returned to the official life of the city.

Rustic, Gothic and the Classical orders

In the Libro Estraordinario (1551) Serlio explores the range of "licentious" and rustic architecture as inspired in him by the wild surroundings of Fontainebleau; but already in Book II (1545) he had made his views on rural life in general quite clear. The last illustrations of that book are three blocks depicting Tragic, Comic, and Satiric stage scenes (Figs. 165, 166, and 167). These and the accompanying commentaries are remarkable elaborations of the few sentences on the same subject in Vitruvius. The commentary on the Sa-

164. Serlio, Book VII: Remodelling a house, Proposition Eight (from 1575 ed., p. 157)

tiric scene is, indeed, developed into a general critique of country life. This critique grows out of a serious confusion of Greek satyric drama with Roman satire—a confusion already found in Cesariano's Vitruvius commentary of 1521, where the satiric scene is said to be a setting of *gente vitiosa e rustica* (immoral country people):[12]

The satiric scene is a setting for satires in which are presented (or rather mocked) all those who live licentiously and without inhibition [*rispetto*]. In ancient satires immoral and evil-living people were shown. Nevertheless, one can understand that such licence was permitted to those who talked without inhibition, that is, to rustic people [*gente rustica*]; hence Vitruvius, discussing stage design, says that this scene should be

165. Serlio, Book II (1545): Satiric scene (from 1551 ed., fol. 30ᵛ)

decorated with trees, rocks, hills, mountains, grass, flowers, and he also wishes there to be some cabins in rustic style [*alla rustica*]. (47ʳ)

Serlio's emphatic association of licence with rural life goes far beyond his Latin source, and his illustration leaves us in no doubt about what forms are appropriate to those who live without moral constraints. Scattered irregularly in a forest are huts roughly made of timber and stone, while loose unfinished rusticated blocks lie about in the foreground.

166. Serlio, Book II: Tragic scene (from 1551 ed., fol. 29ᵛ)

At the opposite end of the scale from the Satiric scene was the Tragic (Fig. 166): "its houses should be those of high-class personages, because chance love affairs, unexpected happenings, and violent and cruel deaths . . . always occur in the residences of lords, dukes, great princes, or even kings; and so, as I have said, in such stage sets no building will be shown which does not have something of the noble" (46ʳ). Accordingly, such lofty characters are given an appropriate background with all the apparatus of arcades and colonnades, pediments and niches, sculpture and inscriptions. Tragic architecture is as urban and correctly Classical as Satiric architecture is rural and rustic. The lofty actions of great personages have a setting which is as disciplined and refined as that of the low actions of the peasantry is rough and disordered.

Given this opposition, great interest attaches to the handling of the Comic scene (Fig. 167): "Its houses

167. Serlio, Book II: Comic scene (from 1551 ed., fol. 28ᵛ)

should be of private people, that is of citizens, lawyers, merchants, parasites, and other such persons; but above all it must not lack a brothel and an inn, and a temple is very necessary" (45ᵛ). The level of life in comedy is well indicated by its characters, members of the commercial classes, while the prostitute and innkeeper have essential roles. It is thus intermediate between tragedy and "satire" in terms of both social and moral values. This might appear to present Serlio with a prob-

lem when choosing an appropriate style, but with great wit he opts for a mixture of half-timber and Gothic. The pointed arch and the wooden beam, suitably irregular in form, serve as the leitmotifs of the scene.[13] Only the temple, isolated outpost of higher values, has a Classical dress of pediments and pilasters, though it too is in a state of evident neglect, with weeds growing from its tower. In general the whole set is clearly characterized as a more sophisticated version of low rustic architecture. Gothic is connected through woodwork with the primitive architectural forms of the Satiric scene and, though never discussed directly in the treatise, is definitely characterized as the architecture of the urban middle and lower classes, marked as they are by their appetites and weaknesses. Its disorder is as eloquent as is the regularity of Classical forms.

These three blocks not only serve to clarify Serlio's opinions on rustic architecture and the uninhibited nature of country life; they also provide the best possible propaganda for Classical architecture and against Gothic. From their first appearance in 1545 they would be spread in printing after printing throughout Europe, bringing shame and ridicule on all owners of Gothic buildings. In a sense they provided Serlio's whole treatise with its greatest *raison d'être*. Together, his whole collection of books could be seen as showing how the architecture of the immoral middle classes could be replaced by that of the noble aristocracy. Often such replacement would involve complete destruction and rebuilding, but Serlio also addressed himself to the more economical proposition of refacing. In the seventh book, his eighth and thirteenth "propositions" deal with the refashioning of asymmetrical Gothic dwellings into symmetrical Classical palaces (Fig. 164). Having revelled in designing imaginary Gothic monstrosities, he shows how with little inconvenience or expense they can be transformed into elevations as respectable as any in the book. In other words, he demonstrates how what once looked like a brothel or an inn can quickly look like a princely residence. These few wood-cuts in which Gothic is compared to Classical architecture do more than any text to explain the victory of the latter throughout Europe after 1550.

Serlio was an architectural theorist of exceptional talents and exceptional importance. He was the first to attempt to codify principles of genuinely visual aesthetic appreciation and to formulate a vocabulary to describe varying visual responses. He brought the characterization of the orders to a new level of refinement, establishing the canon of five which has survived to this day. He also established a parallel gradation of surface treatments for masonry which allowed a secondary modification of the basic scale. He acknowledged that not all types of architectural composition were governed by rules, that some orders were freer than others, and that some surface treatments were freer than others too. His observations on the relations between architecture and personal psychology are unique. In his wilder moments in France he even seemed to conceive of architectural equivalents of "inspired poetry" or "automatic writing." But, true to the Classical tradition in which he worked, he could only consider such procedures as an aberration brought on by an uncivilized environment. Finally, although in the unpublished Book VI he did design half-timbered buildings to suit the French market, he showed that only Classical architecture, with its permanent stone forms, its regular proportions, and its system of articulate characterization, could provide a frame for life which corresponded to the aspirations of disciplined individuals within an organized society.

XX

Serlio's Venice: Sansovino, Aretino, Titian, and Vasari

◆

Sansovino and the Piazzetta

IN 1537, the same year in which Serlio launched his treatise with the publication of Book IV, and in the same city, Venice, Jacopo Sansovino, the sculptor-architect from Florence, was designing three major buildings (Figs. 168 and 169).[1] Serlio, eleven years his senior, had already been involved in judging Sansovino's earlier design of S. Francesco della Vigna, and it is not inappropriate to look for the influence of Serlio's new and ambitious theory on the no less ambitious group of structures planned by Sansovino for the Piazzetta.[2] Understanding the architect's intentions is made easier by the fact that the three buildings—the Mint, the block containing the Library of St Mark's, and the Loggetta—were all described by figures closely associated with the architect. Francesco Sansovino, Jacopo's son, gave full accounts of them in the two versions of his Venetian guidebook,[3] and shorter descriptions are provided by Jacopo's friends Pietro Aretino[4] and Vasari.[5] All three writers bring us close to the ideas of the architect himself and make possible an unusually direct comparison of his vocabulary with that of the contemporary theorist.

Although the three buildings had different functions, and although the background to the construction of each was different, it is virtually certain that their façades were all designed together as a coherent scheme. For all three, the first evidence we have that their designs had been fixed in their present form is a letter of 20 November 1537 addressed to Jacopo Sansovino by Pietro Aretino,[6] which describes them with some precision. The Zecca or Mint was the first building

planned, in 1535, but there is no evidence that its façade design was fixed until the date of Aretino's letter. The moving forward of this façade in 1539 to accommodate a row of food stalls had probably always been intended by Sansovino, but the top floor added twenty years later was not. The building known as the Libreria was originally planned to house higher-class shops and offices for the Procurators, who owned the site and indeed controlled much of the building in the area. The decision to house the magnificent library of St Mark's in an appropriately splendid setting on the upper floor was taken only on 6 March 1537;[7] the forms of the façade were certainly fixed by the time of Aretino's letter later that year. Completion of the corner bays adjoining the Campanile in 1538 suggests that the decision had then already been taken to extend the elevation up the side of the Piazza di S. Marco itself on a new line, while the subsequent placing of the main door of the library opposite the Justice roundel on the Doge's Palace makes it clear that this was to be the central bay of a building which would extend, as now, down to the Molo. (Sansovino himself only managed to complete the section containing the Library.) The freeing of the Campanile made it highly desirable to simultaneously rebuild the decrepit loggia at its foot, where the nobles could display themselves to the populace from a strategic site just opposite the entrance to the Doge's Palace where they ruled in private. Aretino's letter again shows that the design had been agreed by November 1537. The Loggetta was complete structurally by 1540 and decoratively by 1545. Although modified in the seventeenth and eighteenth centuries by the widening of the attic and the addition of a terrace, and

168. Jacopo Sansovino: Mint and Library building,
Piazzetta, Venice, from 1537

although completely rebuilt after its destruction when the Campanile collapsed in 1902, it stands now substantially as Sansovino left it.

The most remarkable fact about the three buildings is that, although they were apparently planned more or less together in 1537, they are all strikingly different. Moreover, these differences were noted as important by those who first described them, Aretino, Francesco Sansovino, and Vasari. The first of the three buildings mentioned in Aretino's list is the Zecca. The arcade was constructed of deeply channelled rusticated masonry and made of white Istrian stone, as was the whole building. The upper floor of the façade con-

tained a row of enormous windows spanned by massive lintels and framed by a row of engaged columns decorated with heavy bands (Fig. 170). Their capitals and bases are Tuscan, but the entablature above has the triglyphs and metopes of the Doric order, though only roughly blocked out. This entablature was originally the crowning element of the entire structure until the present top floor was added. The main public entrance to the building was from the Piazzetta through the Libreria block. It consisted of an arch of masonry, again with deeply channelled rustication, flanked by two enormous figures with muscular torsos, the lower parts of their bodies encased in solid blocks of stone like ancient herms (Fig. 172). These figures bear a relatively finely detailed Doric entablature.

The main character of the Zecca is summed up by Aretino's phrase in the letter of 20 November 1537: *fabrica rustica e dorica*.[8] Since this was addressed to the architect himself it presumably reflects his terminology. Equally, the references to the building in Francesco Sansovino's first guidebook must also reflect the response his father wished the spectator to have. Francesco's *Delle cose notabili che sono in Venezia* (1556) takes the form of a conversation between a Venetian and a foreigner, and the latter's first reaction to the building is "This looks like a fortress in its outer entrance."[9] He then goes on to describe it as a "Worthy prison for most precious gold; and indeed the rustic treatment matches the character [*accompagna la qualità*] of the building." The visitor's first reaction is presumably to the side portal, which tells him that the building is some sort of fortress. Further examination enables him to elaborate this by seeing it as a "prison for gold," and to decide that in general the rustication precisely suits the building's function. A later and much bigger guide, *Venezia nobilissima*, drops the conversational format and reads like a simple description, but again the same point is made about the entry: "it shows at first encounter the solidity [*sodezza*] of the building, being made of the Rustic order mixed with the Doric and having two sculpted herms instead of columns or pilasters."[10] The main façade is described in a similar way, "partly rustic and partly refined [*gentile*]." Francesco feels that his father cleverly expressed an ambiguity in the building's function. As a factory and a strongroom, it requires the roughness of rustication to express *sodezza* and *fortezza*. As a container for

169. Jacopo Sansovino: Library building and Loggetta, Piazzetta, Venice, from 1537

"most precious gold" and a structure emblematic of the wealth and status of Venice, it also requires the more *gentile* forms of Doric. Numerous features of the building can thus be seen to embody this dualism: the combination of Tuscan and Doric elements in the façade columniation, the use of smooth column shafts with applied rustic bands, and the use throughout of heavy rustication modified by a smooth channelled treatment. Perhaps, too, Jacopo thought of the herms at the portal, with their torsos perfectly carved but with their lower limbs embedded in massive blocks, as expressing the same mixture.

The entire vocabulary of Francesco Sansovino's ob-

servations is so closely parallel to that of Serlio as to make a connection with that author virtually certain. We have already seen how the latter developed an elaborate theory of parallel scales from Tuscan to Composite and from *rustico* and *sodo* to *delicato* and *gentile*, scales which could be combined to allow the development of precise architectural characterizations. Serlio had, moreover, specified that rustication fitted Tuscan best and that that order was appropriate to "places for keeping treasure" among others.[11] He had also said that the rusticated portal "represents great strength"[12] (*rappresenta gran fortezza*) which directly anticipates Francesco's reaction to his father's Zecca door: "It

170. Mint, Venice: detail

Vigna in 1534. Since Serlio was developing his theories during the nine years he had been in Venice, and was just about to publish them there, and since Sansovino wished to make a name for himself by these first major commissions in 1536 and 1537, it would have been not unnatural for him to have adapted his designs to fit the senior architect's ideas.

The suggestion that Sansovino's buildings are deliberately intended to correspond with Serlio's theory is confirmed by the comments on the Libreria building by the same two writers (Fig. 171). The elevation, once again of Istrian stone, has a correct Doric order below and Ionic above, both richly articulated and with added relief sculpture. Aretino accordingly refers to the "Doric work with carved details [*intagliato*], having above the Ionic arrangement with the correct ornaments [*ornamenti dovuti*]."[14] The notion of "correct ornaments" implies correspondence to a rule, and the reference to a form of Doric which is *intagliato* takes up precisely Serlio's division of the orders into *intagliato* and non-*intagliato*. In particular, Serlio had claimed that *intagli* modify the inherent *sodezza* (solidity) of Doric forms by removing their *semplicità* (simplicity). Francesco Sansovino in the first version of his guidebook does not describe the architectural forms in detail, but he does point out that the lower Doric order has river gods in the spandrels while the Ionic has victories. (He might also have observed that the sexual differentiation of the two floors is found in alternating heads on the keystones of the two floors as well.) Though the careful matching of the orders with figures of the appropriate sex is unusual in the Renaissance, it corresponds precisely to Serlio's recommendations on the choice of figures for Ionic and Corinthian fireplaces. The use of victories in the Ionic order would thus be exactly what Aretino meant when he referred to *ornamenti dovuti*. In the 1581 guide Sansovino even says as much: "in the angles of the windows are victories, that is winged women, placed seated on the windows in the spandrels, to match [*accompagnare*] the Ionic order, which is much more slender [*scarmo*] and soft [*morbido*] than the Doric."[15] Not only is the general theory of an ornament "matching" an order Serlian, but the precise vocabulary in which Ionic is characterized as *scarmo* and *morbido* takes up that of Serlio in his "Discussion" of architectural terms. Francesco prefaces these detailed remarks on the orders by gen-

looks like a fortress" (*mi pare una fortezza*). It is true that Serlio's Book IV on the orders, in which his theories are first developed, itself appeared only in 1537, but we know that it was years in preparation. It was also being circulated in manuscript before printing, as we can gather from Aretino's letter about it to the publisher dated 18 September 1537.[13] Aretino even constitutes a possible link between the two architects, being a friend of both. It would not be surprising to find Serlio influencing Sansovino in this way. Not only was he considerably older, but he must also have derived substantial authority from his connection with Peruzzi. He had also been involved in a formal capacity in advising Sansovino over the design of S. Francesco della

171. Library building, Venice, with entries to Mint (left) and to Library (right)

eral ones on the appropriateness of the architectural forms of the building as a whole: "the architect, realizing that the site of the piazza was the noblest of any city anywhere, put all his efforts into making it rich in ornaments and details of every sort following the rules of the ancients; and he decided that the building should be of Doric and Ionic composition and full of dignified columns, friezes, and cornices."[16]

One problem is solved by neither Aretino nor Francesco Sansovino. Why were the orders chosen for the building Doric and Ionic? In fact, since the façade was to cover a multiplicity of functions, housing shops below and magistrates' offices and a library above on the Piazzetta—not to mention accommodating other facilities, such as apartments for procurators and others, if it continued up the side of the Piazza S. Marco—there could hardly be a specific appositeness in the choice of

the order as there was in the case of the Zecca. At least Doric and Ionic would not be in any sense inappropriate to such a range of functions. Besides, the Doric of the ground floor was clearly more refined than the Tuscan/Doric of the Zecca, just as commerce was a higher activity than metalworking, and the Ionic of the upper floor was yet one step more refined, as would be the activities conducted there. If there was some unifying feature for the whole building it was the ownership by the Procurators of St Mark—which explains why the saint's lion is found in the Doric metopes below and on alternating keystones of both lower and upper arcades. If it is remembered that Serlio said that both Doric and Ionic could be appropriate for the residences of males, Doric for soldiers and Ionic for scholars, then the two orders could easily reflect those two sides of the Procurators' personalities. The strongest evidence

172. Library building, Venice,
doorway to Mint

173. Library building, Venice,
doorway to Library, detail

that Ionic here is indeed emblematic of intellectual activity is its emphatic association with the Libreria. Not only is it the order of the upper floor of the structure and consequently the order of the outside of the library room itself, but in a quite unparalleled way the Ionic order is brought down the stairs inside the building to the main entrance to the library, in the central bay of the whole elevation. This entrance itself is flanked by two enormous female statues in place of columns, statues which are a striking accent in the Doric arcade and form a strong contrast to the two great herms at the entrance to the Zecca further along (Figs. 172 and 173). Just as those herms were supposed to announce the character of the Mint behind, so these women were intended to announce the character of the library—

something which would be difficult for us to understand without Serlio's association of Ionic with effeminate study.

With the Loggetta too, forms are presented as relating to its function (Fig. 174). As Aretino writes in his letter of 20 November, the "marble . . . , coloured stones . . . [and] large columns" all add up to a structure "composed of all the beauties of architecture, serving as a loggia for the use of persons of such great nobility."[17] The extreme visual beauty of the Loggetta matches the extreme nobility of birth and breeding of its occupants. More precisely, all the features of the building which set it apart from the other two carry the same message. The use of coloured marbles instead of Istrian stone and of free-standing columns for the ma-

174. Loggetta, Venice

jor order instead of engaged ones are both specifically mentioned by Aretino, while the bronze statues and marble reliefs can be seen to reflect the same spirit. The order itself is not explicitly named, but his reference to the building being *composta di tutte le bellezze di architectura* may well have been inspired by his knowledge that Sansovino planned to use the order that Serlio had called "Composite." Francesco Sansovino in his first guide does not comment on the architecture of the Loggetta, but he devotes an extended analysis to its sculpture. The visitor first says, "I was looking at these figures of bronze and stone only this morning, and I am sure that they mean something [*son significative di qualche cosa*]," reminding us that all of Sansovino's work in the Piazzetta is intended to be expressive.[18]

The Venetian then provides him with an explanation of the symbolism, first, of the four bronzes of Pallas, Mercury, Apollo, and Pax (which chiefly commemorate the virtues of the state) and then of the upper reliefs. These latter show Venice in the centre flanked by the rivers of the *terraferma*, with Venus on her left and Jupiter on her right: the two gods representing respectively Cyprus and Crete, the two main Venetian dominions in the East. Thus, "on this little façade is shown the empire of these lords [the nobles] on land and at sea." This passage reveals the intended articulateness of the whole programme, and also indirectly enables us to get a further glimpse of Sansovino's interest in the expressive use of architecture. For the building in the background of the Jupiter panel, identified by Francesco as the god's tomb, is Doric, while that shown with Venus, presumably her temple, is Corinthian. The orders are precisely matched to the divinities following the rules originally formulated by Vitruvius and most recently restated by Serlio. Since such matching is unusual in any context, it shows once again how interested Sansovino was in the appropriate use of the orders. Finally, the Loggetta is closely modelled on ancient triumphal arches, and this form provides an apt setting for the state's triumphal and imperial propaganda. This association probably also provides the decisive reason for the choice of Composite, rather than (for instance) Corinthian, since Serlio was at pains to stress that Composite was above all the order of ancient arches of triumph.

Each building separately shows a careful choice of both order and decoration following the rules of Serlio. If the three are also viewed together, these same differences unite them in a coherent series creating a crescendo of elaboration from Zecca to Loggetta. This is most manifest in the orders, which run from Tuscan/ Doric, through Doric and Ionic, to Composite. But it can also be seen, for example, in the gradation of the surface carving, or *intagli*, from virtually none on the Zecca, through a considerable amount on the Libreria building, to a great quantity on the Loggetta. There is also a parallel gradation in the degree of relief of the architectural and sculptural forms. The Zecca has an orderless ground floor and bound-in attached columns above; the Libreria has attached columns below and a combination of an attached major order and freestanding minor order above; the Loggetta has only free-standing columns. Again, the Mint has no figure sculpture, the Libreria a large amount of sculpture in relief, and only the Loggetta free-standing statues in bronze. All these variations represent consistent modulations on Serlio's scales from *sodo/semplice* to *delicato/gentile*, matching the consistent increase in the refinement of the buildings' occupants and the activities with which they are associated, from lower-class people involved in physical labour, through middle- and upper-class people doing commercial, intellectual, and administrative work, to the nobility doing nothing but displaying themselves. The same consistency is found in the application of another scale referred to by Serlio, that revealed in the number of steps leading up to a building. He says of a church the "the more its floor is raised above the ground the more dignity [*maestà*] it will have."[19] Again, in Book V, "I will always be of the opinion that every building, or rather its pavement, should be raised above the ground by several steps and that the more it is raised the better it will be."[20] If Sansovino's buildings are viewed in the light of this rule, it can be noted that the Zecca had originally only one step up to its front arcade, the Libreria building three, and the Loggetta five.

All of this suggests that Sansovino himself planned the three buildings as a single group forming a crescendo of importance, a suggestion which is confirmed by Aretino's description of the three buildings in the letter we have cited so frequently. In this letter of 20 November 1537, which is addressed to Sansovino himself and which was certainly intended to mark his recognition as the foremost architect in Venice following his obtaining these great state commissions, Aretino reviews all of Jacopo's major interventions in the city, whether executed or only planned. The list is, however, irregular in character except for the treatment of the three Piazzetta structures. These three are grouped together and are described in a rising series of rhetorical phrases, one and a half lines for the Zecca, two and a half for the Library, and four and a half for the Loggetta, with the language increasing in colour at the same time. Whether by drawings or descriptions, Sansovino had obviously succeeded in communicating to his publicist exactly the effect he wished to attain when the buildings were complete.

The Piazzetta as gateway

The only viewpoint from which the three buildings are visible together, and so function as a group, is the area of the Molo in front of the Piazzetta and the adjoining stretch of water (Fig. 175). It must, then, have been with this viewpoint in mind that Sansovino made his design, and indeed we know that this view into the Piazzetta had an extraordinary importance not only for Sansovino but for the whole Venetian community. Sansovino had revealed his interest in it from his first arrival in 1529 when, as Vasari tells us, he removed the ignominious booths from between the columns at the entrance to the Piazzetta because they were "ugly and shameful" for the dignity both of the palazzo and of the public piazza, and also for foreigners who, coming to Venice from the direction of S. Giorgio, saw such squalor at their first entrance to the city.[21] Most visitors to Venice would arrive by boat and approach the centre of the city directly from the water in front of S. Giorgio, landing near the two columns.

The importance of the view into the Piazzetta had long been recognized, from the thirteenth century, when those two great columns had been erected at its mouth, to the early sixteenth, when the entrance to the Merceria at its far end had been worthily marked by the Torre dell'Orologio flanked by its two wings. Indeed, in a whole series of woodcuts and paintings from the 1480s onwards the view into the Piazzetta had come to stand for the city as a whole. In a sense it had come to "represent" the city in much the same way as a portal might "represent" a palace or a church. Against this background it is hardly surprising that Sansovino should have found himself involved in the reconstruction of the one part of this composition which had not yet received a monumental treatment; but it is still unclear what might have prompted him first to the idea of total reorganization and then to the particular scheme of variety within unity which he eventually adopted.

Reference to Serlio solves both these problems. The chief hallmark of Sansovino's plan is the rich series of the orders running from Tuscan/Doric to Composite, and precisely such a series is found in Serlio's reconstruction of the Tragic scene (Fig. 165). At the front on the right there is a building with a rusticated arcade; behind it is one with a Doric colonnade. The temple behind this has an unfluted Corinthian porch, and the arch in the distance has fluted Composite columns. Ionic is missing, as Corinthian is in the Piazzetta, but the idea of a series is the same. The block was not published until 1545 as part of Book II, but it is likely to have been made much earlier, as were many others. There is even evidence that the whole idea of applying such a scene design to the Piazzetta also derived from Serlio. In the Uffizi there is a drawing attributed to Serlio which shows the Piazzetta itself adapted as a stage design (Fig. 176).[22] The Torre dell'Orologio, St Mark's, and the Campanile are all recognizable in the background, while in front are structures partly corresponding to those found in Serlio's Book II stage sets. There is no reminiscence of any of Sansovino's buildings, so the drawing was almost certainly made before

they were conceived, that is, in the early or middle 1530s. This being so, it is quite probable that it was an actual stage design by Serlio which directly inspired Sansovino to fundamentally reshape the Piazzetta by applying to it principles of arrangement already current in the theatre.

Serlio may well also have provided the theoretical motive for such a massive reconstruction. For, as we saw, his Tragic scene, with all its Classical architecture, is an explicit contrast to the Comic scene with its aberrant Gothic. Since the main difference between comedy and tragedy, as defined first by Vitruvius and restated by Serlio, was that comedy shows the low life of shopkeepers and tragedy the high life of kings and nobles, it is apparent that Serlio is arguing that Gothic forms are appropriate to such low life, with the irregularity matching the disorder produced by immorality and impulsiveness, while Classical forms with their order and regularity match the self-control and obedience to higher laws found in the deportment of the upper classes. Viewed in the light of Serlio's ideas, the butchers' and bakers' stalls with inns above, all housed in Medieval buildings, which occupied the Piazzetta when Sansovino arrived in Venice were hardly an advertisement for the city, sited as they were on its most public façade. The replacement of the architecture of the comic and immoral lower classes by one which evoked the higher values of the nobly born and bred must have seemed a matter of urgency in view of the imminent publication of Serlio's book. Serlio himself was to illustrate in Book VII how the misfortune of inheriting an irregular Gothic house could be overcome by giving it a Classical face-lift (Fig. 164), and that in a sense was precisely the problem of the Procurators. The imminent appearance of Serlio's treatise made it necessary to Classicize the city's "portal" just as Giotto's paintings in the Arena chapel may once have made it necessary to Gothicize St Mark's and the Doge's Palace. The Gothic details had made the city appear more Christian;[23] the Classical features now made the city appear more dignified and moral. The introduction of the new style was required to undo the damage done to the city's image by the old.

Ultimately the success of Sansovino's design depended on its ability to meet the needs of the city's rulers. Francesco Sansovino tells us how his father celebrated the nobles' qualities in the sculptures of the

176. Serlio: scene based on the Piazzetta, Uffizi, Florence

Loggetta. The armed Pallas recalled the government's wisdom, especially in things military. Mercury commemorated the practice of letters and of eloquence. Apollo represented the city's sun-like uniqueness and power, as well as its love of music. Pax was there to affirm the city's special right to peace, already promised to Venice in Christ's words to her patron: "Pax tibi, Marce." Such a group of statues might have been appropriate at any time, but they had a particular relevance in the 1530s. Read (as Francesco Sansovino reads them and as any visitor would) beginning on the left, the side towards the water, they would suggest a

cycle that moved from war to peace. To the Venetians, who had just emerged from the traumatic conflict with the League of Cambrai into the glorious recovery of the reign of Andrea Gritti, the sequence was reassuring indeed. Although not the same, the architectural sequence up the Piazzetta had a similar underlying range and brought a similar reassurance, presenting an image of strength in the Zecca near the water followed by a greater refinement further in. But the architectural sequence, with its range of orders, may also relate more directly to the theme of the sculptures. Francesco Sansovino emphasizes that Apollo refers above all to the

175 (at left). View of Piazzetta, Venice

297

177. Lorenzo Lotto: *Andrea Udone*, 1527, Hampton Court

musical talents of the Venetian magistrates who "are so well united by such an ineffable tuning that they produce a rare harmony, one which the government perpetuates," and he goes on to point out that Peace emerges from Venetian "religion, justice, and observance of the laws in the same way as a musical concent [emerges] from a concordant harmony." We suggested earlier that the exceptional exploitation by Bramante and Raphael of series of orders in the Vatican was intended to represent and increase the harmony of the universal Church at a time when its unity and coherence were seriously threatened. When Sansovino arrived in Venice from Rome he found the Venetian state in equal disarray, troubled by divisions among its sub-

ject cities on the *terraferma* and by doubts and dissent among its citizens at home. He may well have conceived of a similar use of a "concordant discord" as an effective means of improving both the city's atmosphere and its image. The series of buildings, with their different orders articulating the difference of their functions and of their occupants, evoked and encouraged a sense of social harmony. It did not matter that the image of a harmonious society might be an erroneous one, and in fact the reverse of the truth. It was the appearance that counted. Serlio in his discussion of the house restoration describes a situation very like that in the Piazzetta. The man who restored the house was in fact a miser who spent money on the façade only when forced to by the local prince, who felt that the old elevation brought shame on his city. Accordingly, when the owner put the facelift into effect he entered into the spirit of the enterprise, and instead of putting a statue of Avarice on the façade as he should have done he decided

to place in the four niches the four moral virtues, giving perhaps to understand that he had those moral qualities, and dressing himself up in Pharisaic garb . . . wishing the world to believe that he was good.

Serlio's commentary might almost be a satire on the Piazzetta, which had also received a new façade complete with four statues celebrating the virtues of the patrons (Fig. 164).

Aretino

Someone who could easily have developed this cynical vein, but who chose instead to advance his career more by flattery, was Pietro Aretino, who may have had a key role in the relationship between Serlio and Sansovino. A close friend of both men, he read Book IV before publication and wrote a laudatory epistle to accompany the first printing. What is more surprising is that he seems to have studied Serlio's ideas for his own purposes. Many of his letters reveal an approach to architecture which directly recalls the thought of the Bolognese theorist, especially his notion of the architectural expression of character.

The first and one of the most vigorous of these letters was written on 27 October 1537, to Domenico Bolani, in whose house on the Grand Canal he was living at that time. Describing his residence, he notes that

The entrance from the land, being dark, awkward, and bestial in scale [di scala bestiale], is like the frightening character [terribilità] of the reputation I have acquired in exposing the truth; but then anyone who gets to know me finds in my pure [pura], plain [schietta], and natural friendship that quiet contentment which one feels on entering the portico and in gazing at the balconies [over the Canal].[24]

Anyone familiar with Venice will recognize the contrast between land and water façades which Aretino is alluding to, but the development of the architectural simile is highly unusual in a literary context. A few months later in another letter, this time to the collector

Andrea Udone, written on 30 August 1538,[25] Aretino elaborates further on the idea of reading a person's character from his dwelling:

But for anyone who wants to see how clean [netto] and bright [candido] is his spirit, let him look at his face [fronte] and his house; let him look at them, I say, and he will see what calm and what beauty one can contemplate in a house and in a face.

He then goes on to describe his treasures, especially his sculptures:

Whence one may judge, with the testimony of such a noble and royal spectacle, the greatness of your generous and magnificent personality. For a delight in such refined carvings [intagli] and such casts does not spring from a rustic breast [petto rustico], nor from an unworthy heart.

To judge by Lotto's revealing portrait, Udone needed all the emblems of refinement he could acquire (Fig. 177). A similar point is made in a letter to Tommaso Cambi of January 1546:[26]

I like to think that your regal mansion in Naples is modelled on the great spirit which fills your breast; and the statues which adorn that beautiful palace represent the generosity which gives sustenance to your heart. Whence you are, truly, more a splendid aristocrat than a wealthy merchant.

Aretino repeatedly asserts the general principle that it is possible to know a man's animo from his habitazione.

The correspondence between the two façades of Bolani's house and the two sides of Aretino's own personality can only be fortuitous; but in the cases of Cambi and Udone both their houses may be said genuinely to express their personal tastes. This is particularly true of their collections, and Aretino is careful to differentiate them. Cambi's patronage of sculpture shows him to be more than a prosperous merchant, and Udone's sensitivity to the same art proves that he is no uncultivated rustic. The implication is that Cambi had a taste for large "statues," which were an appropriate expression of the princely scale of his liberality, while Udone seems to have built up a collection of relatively smaller pieces, such as those shown in Lotto's 1527 portrait, which illustrate instead refinement of appreciation. The same distinction is found in Aretino's comments on the actual architecture of their houses. Cambi's house shares with his animo the quality of grandezza (greatness). Udone's, on the other hand, shows how his *animo* is *netto* (clean) and *candido* (bright); equally, the *delicatura* of its floors conjures up the same images of refinement as do the *intagli* or carved details of his sculptures. Aretino characterizes the different living environments of the two men in such a way as to insert Cambi into a social and Udone into an aesthetic aristocracy. Doubtless Aretino's praises are carefully designed to respond to their different aspirations.

It is particularly interesting to find a taste for sculptures both large and small as an index of nobility whether of mind or rank, and to discover that a taste for *intagli* cannot be associated with a *petto rustico*. In the context of these ideas Serlio's opposition between "rustic" and "delicate" masonry takes on a new significance. The scale from rustication to refined carving reflects a scale of social status partly because only the upper classes have the ability to really appreciate refinement. Seen in this light, the contrast between the Zecca and the Loggetta becomes particularly evocative.

Any doubt that Serlio is the inspiration for Aretino's interest in architecture is removed by two other letters which include even more precise architectural descriptions. In one, a letter to Gianiacopo Lionardi of 16 December 1537,[27] he imagines himself with his friends and protectors on Mount Parnassus: "Then here I am with them in the church of Eternity made, as it seemed to me, in the Doric manner expressing [*significando*] in its solidity [*sodezza*] its permanence. No sooner had I entered than I met my two brothers, Sansovino and Titian . . ." In another letter, written to Filippo d'Asti on 27 June 1542,[28] he congratulates his friend: "and I for myself compare the firmness, integrity and capacity of your spirit to that solid [*sodo*], plain [*schietto*], and strong [*sufficiente*] order called Doric by architectural experts." Both texts show a direct knowledge of Serlio's characterization of Doric and reveal a careful attempt to understand his terms. This is most clear in the second letter, where the terms are deliberately chosen to match the three attributes of his friend's spirit: *fermo* becomes *sodo*, *intero* becomes *schietto*, and *capace* becomes *sufficiente*. Aretino was clearly fascinated by the language of architecture and had come to see it as a potent addition to traditional literary language.

He even uses Serlian architectural language and values to characterize a work of literature as well as the human personality. In June 1537 he writes to his friend the literary critic Sperone Speroni, complimenting him on one of his dialogues.[29] He compares it to the Pantheon in Rome,

which is the only paragon and perfect model of what can be realized or imagined in architecture . . . There is a measured simplicity in its most complicated elements. No fussiness disturbs the arrangement of the whole structure. Every decorative detail is in its proper place. Every part is pure and brilliant. One light alone descending from the top illuminates the whole temple, which has nothing too little and nothing too much. Your work has the same qualities.

The correspondence with Serlio's opinion of the Pantheon is exact. He placed that building at the beginning of his third book and gave it very extensive treatment. He described it as the most beautiful building in Rome and the best-understood structure he had seen. He particularly praised it for its single light source from above and noted that "the architect did not wish to confuse the work with many carved details; he distributed them with great *giudicio*." Admittedly Serlio's Book III appeared only in 1540, three years after the letter was written, but it must have been prepared earlier; and Aretino himself must have had access to it before publication, to judge from the fact that in 1539 he wrote to Lazzaro de Baïf asking him to persuade Francis I to accept the dedication of his friend's book. Evidently Serlio's architectural criticism, like his theory of architectural characterization, caught Aretino's imagination.

Of course the possibility remains that the influence may have been mutual, that Aretino may have himself been one of the sources of Serlio's knowledge of literary theory, especially of such concepts as *giudicio*. Certainly Aretino was already greatly interested in that idea in December 1537, when he wrote about it to Fausto di Longiano: "Nothing is more important in a man in my estimation than *giudicio*; a writer who lacks it is like a cupboard full of books."[30] The artist of the *Laocoön* had true *giudicio*, as he reveals in his treatment of the emotions of the three figures: "the artist deserves more praise for knowing how to express their emotions and their outward signs . . . fear in the first, suffering in the second, and death in the third, than for cleverly putting breath in their bodies." Aretino is here evidently campaigning for a greater understanding of characterization and expressiveness in both literature and the visual arts. His emphasis on *giudicio* in this context loosely parallels Serlio's in his "Discussion" of architectural terms, and, since he would have had a greater familiarity with the concept than the architectural theorist, he may have influenced the latter's approach.[31] Usually, however, the reverse influence from the architectural theorist on the littérateur is clearer and much more decisive, and further evidence of it may be found in the ideas put into Aretino's mouth by the writer Dolce in his dialogue on art named after him. There Dolce makes Aretino distinguish between two main types of figure style, one *robusto* and *muscoloso* and the other *delicato* and *gentile*.[32] The terms are similar to those used by Serlio in Book IV to distinguish between Doric and Corinthian and between rough masonry and smooth, and since the architect's elaboration of the opposition is the more developed and to the point, it is he who is likely to have taken the lead in formulating it.

The evidence is overwhelming that Serlio exerted a considerable influence on Aretino's thought on a wide range of ideas, from human characterization, to literary criticism, to the discrimination of figure style in painting. Apart from all the reminiscences of language, much the strongest proof of this influence is the relation of the pattern of architectural references to a lifetime of letter-writing from about 1526 to 1555. These references appear suddenly for the first time in three letters of 1537, not long before the one to Marcolini in which he records reading Serlio's Book IV, and then slowly fade out over the next ten years as Serlio himself fades into oblivion in France. The professional letter-writer seems to have been just as excited about the book's implications as was Sansovino. There must be few cases where a work of architectural theory has had such a directly stimulating effect on a writer in another field. Serlio's work must have seemed to Aretino to open up a genuinely new vein of metaphor and meaning, just as it seemed to Sansovino to inject new life into the obligatory forms of Classical architecture.

Titian

The two people Aretino met at the entrance to "the church of Eternity" were Sansovino and Titian, and it would not be surprising to find an impact of Serlio's publication on the great Venetian painter too. The painting which most invites a Serlian interpretation is the great canvas of the *Presentation of the Virgin* of 1534–38 in the Accademia (Fig. 178). Although it relates compositionally to earlier Venetian Presentations such as that of Cima, it has a grandeur of scale, especially in its architecture, which recalls more directly Peruzzi's great painting in Rome (Fig. 151, p. 261). Since that painting also provides a model for Sansovino's Zecca elevation, painter and architect can be seen as turning to the same source. Serlio, as Peruzzi's pupil, may well have been in possession of a drawing of the composition which he was able to show to his friends. Titian may have had a particular interest in learning how to employ such grand architecture, since Serlio's provision of architectural backgrounds for the painter Cariani in the early 1530s may have seemed to threaten his dominant position.[33] The *Presentation* was thus, perhaps, a direct response to the challenge of Serlio's presence, just as was Sansovino's redesigning of the Piazetta at the same time. Titian, like Sansovino, had good reason to take Serlio's theories very seriously. Although the *Presentation* was begun as early as 1534 it was in fact only finished in 1538, a year after the publication of Book IV, and Titian would have had ample opportunity to listen to Serlio's ideas from the time that they were both involved as judges of Sansovino's S. Francesco della Vigna in 1534, the year the painting was started.

The feature of the painting most suggestive of a Serlian inspiration is the way the figure of the Virgin relates to the receding colonnade behind her. Titian has gone to great lengths to precisely assimilate the luminosity and colour of her silken gown to the marble of the adjoining columns. The spectator cannot help perceiving the Virgin as yet another column in the row, an assimilation which is not inappropriate in Serlian terms since the columns are Corinthian, the correct order for Mary. It is possible that Titian is making no more than a visual pun, but a closer look at the extremely odd architecture behind suggests that more may be intended. Titian, like earlier artists, uses the movement of the Virgin up the Temple steps to symbolize the passing of her childhood. In the *Golden Legend*, the most popular source for her early life, it was claimed that after her Presentation at the age of three she stayed in the Temple until she was thirteen.[34] Accordingly Titian has placed the Virgin on a landing, having mounted a

178. Titian: *Presentation of the Virgin in the Temple*, 1534–38, Accademia, Venice

flight of eight steps, and with one foot on the lowest step of another flight rising from nine to thirteen. The Virgin on the ninth step has thus passed eight and still has four to go. Each step represents a year. Now, exactly the same is true of the columns. Mary has already passed eight complete columns and herself represents the ninth. In front of her there are still four years to complete, and these are effectively suggested by the four "incomplete" capitals attached to the blank wall

that fills the gap between her and the high priest. Although the interpretation may seem at first far-fetched, it provides an explanation for the strange and unparalleled arrangement of full columns and console half-capitals which have such a prominent role in the painting. It also explains the remarkable relation between the Virgin and the columns immediately behind her. To call the relationship between figure and architecture "Serlian" is not to imply that the building behind is as-

302

sociated with her as her residence, as it might be in rigidly Serlian terms. Titian's intention is much more loosely expressive. Aware of Serlio's notion of the potentially close parallel between a person and a building, he uses the architecture to develop and comment on the Virgin's situation at the time of the Presentation rather as a musical setting might develop and comment on the words of a poem. The connection between the Virgin and the building behind is, in a sense, the same as that between Aretino and Bolani's house. In both cases the buildings with which the two figures were fortuitously connected for a time seemed to communicate important ideas about them. But they could seem to do so only to someone alerted by Serlio to the particular expressive possibilities of architectural forms.

If the Virgin relates to the Corinthian columns behind her, then it is also tempting to look for a similar human connection for the four square Doric piers at the left-hand side of the painting. The most important figures in the crowd at the bottom of the steps are the four dignified gentlemen arranged in a formal group just in front of the arcade, readily identifiable as prominent officials of the Scuola della Carità which commissioned the work. Their four-square disposition and their sober clothing match the forms of the arcade as precisely as the Virgin matches the columns. Doric is as appropriately their order as Corinthian was the Virgin's. By these correspondences Titian uses the background architecture to subtly draw attention to the main characters in what is potentially a confused scene. As the background buildings are not directly integrated into the figure composition, they could easily have been added after the general layout had been decided, perhaps as late as 1537, the very year of Book IV.

There is one further juxtaposition which may be interpreted in a similar way, and that is the placing of the shattered torso of a Roman general or emperor against the heavily rusticated stair. The weeds growing between the blocks match the ruin of magnificence just as do the mutilations of the once haughty statue. Both are appropriately placed in obscurity under the feet of the brilliantly lit figures of Virgin and priests, whose meeting presages Christ's coming triumph. Serlio used similar masonry in the magnificent frontispiece for his Book III dealing with Roman antiquities, published in 1540, where the message of the architecture is explained in the attached inscription ROMA QUANTA FUIT

IPSA RUINA DOCET ("Rome's very ruins teach how great she was") (Fig. 179). The bossed masonry is emblematic of power, and its ruinous state is emblematic of its passing. Had the drawing for the block already been prepared? Or was it Serlio who this time was inspired by Titian?

In the Louvre *Crowning with Thorns* of the early 1540s Titian takes up the same imagery to even greater effect (Fig. 180). Above the scene of Christ's torture a bust of the Emperor Tiberius looks out unmoved from its frame of brutally roughened blocks. The connection between bust and building is emphasized by the massive lintel inscription TIBERIUS CAESAR. The character of the masonry matches the character of the emperor, while bust, inscription, and building together illustrate both the power and insensitivity of Roman rule. This creates a precise parallel with the passage in Serlio's eighth book where he describes a Roman gate which was Corinthian and rusticated in order "to show figuratively the gentleness and mildness of the Emperor Trajan's mind in giving pardon" (17ʳ) as well as his toughness. That eighth book was never published, but it is likely to have been largely composed in Venice, since it incorporates much material given Serlio by Cardinal Grimani and would probably have been discussed there along with Serlio's other writings.

Aretino too is likely to have known the same material from the eighth book, since it is so close to his own ideas on the expression of personality in architecture, and it is curious that in another painting by Titian which uses architecture expressively Aretino appears vicariously in the very guise in which he describes himself in his letter to Bolani. It was Ridolfi who first claimed that the figure of Pilate in the Vienna *Ecce Homo* (1543) was a portrait of Aretino (Fig. 181).[35] If the identification is correct, as seems likely, Titian is cleverly pointing out the similarity between his friend's relentless pursuit of the truth and that of the Roman judge who recognized Christ's innocence and presented the truth to the world. Aretino in his letter to Bolani had compared the land façade of the latter's house to the *terribilità* of his own personality in exposing the truth, and the rustication of Pilate's palace seems to convey the same severity, though it is probably important that the handling of the rustication is much more restrained than in the *Crowning with Thorns*, so as to match the greater humaneness of Pilate as the instrument of Roman power. At the other side of the scene, on the right, is a quite different piece of architecture, a pier with an attached column of dark polished marble, which can also be related to a character in the scene. In front of it, in the same relation to the column as the Virgin to hers, is a soldier on horseback whose burnished steel armour precisely echoes the shaft behind. This juxtaposition seems intended to mark out the soldier as someone of importance in Christian terms, someone such as the centurion Saint Longinus who, even in the act of carrying out the death sentence, was to acknowledge Christ's divinity. The polished marble column carries positive associations just as did the polished marble columns of the building in the *Presentation*—or, for that matter, of Sansovino's Loggetta, which was then nearing completion. Indeed, columns are found behind Christ himself in two other paintings of the early to mid-1540s, the *Supper at Emmaus* in the Louvre and the *Last Supper* at Urbino. In all these works the smooth column is used to mark out a person of strength and authority. The association is very similar to that between columns and nobles on the contemporary Loggetta. The column had long been an attribute of authority, and in the Middle Ages it had become the symbol of *fortitudo* (strength); but Titian by assimilating particular columns to particular people gives it a more clearly defined emblematic role. It is as if he realized that by introducing a column with its properties of "strength," "polish," and "height" he could communicate the essential qualities of a noble person in a most effective way. This explains his use of the column in portraiture. In the great Munich painting of the Emperor Charles V a column on a pedestal is placed exactly behind the emperor seated on his chair (Fig. 182). Charles and the column, the chair and the pedestal, are so assimilated as to communicate clearly to the unconscious viewer the stability (chair, pedestal) of authority (Charles, column). Two years later Titian was again to use the column on a pedestal as a symbol of authority in his *Philip II* in the Prado, though here the correspondence of the architecture to that in the previous painting and its shadowy character at a distance from the standing figure seem intended to suggest that the young prince has not yet acquired the authority of his father. Columns had often figured in paintings before, but it is their expressive use by Titian in these

works which guarantees their recurrence in many later images of European aristocracy.

Titian had inherited from the Venetian tradition a general taste for painted architecture, but neither in his earlier nor in his later works does it have the same prominence as it does in these paintings executed between 1534 and 1550. Titian's use of architecture as an important vehicle of communication is thus concentrated in about the same short period as was the related use of architecture by his friend Aretino, and it seems to be equally dependent on the active influence of Serlio. In a sense the same is true of Sansovino. His three buildings on the Piazzetta have always stood out as richer in language than those planned either before or afterwards. The impact of the Bolognese theorist on Venetian culture was brief but potent.

Vasari

Giorgio Vasari, the author of the great collection of *Lives* of Renaissance artists, may seem an odd addition to the group of three individuals who were directly connected with Serlio. Yet he was completely familiar with the particular details of Sansovino's buildings on the Piazzetta, and we know that he was a friend not only of the architect but of Titian and Aretino as well. Indeed, his friendship with all three was chiefly the result of his residence in Venice, probably at his countryman Aretino's suggestion, in 1541–42. He would thus have known them as a group at the very peak of their interest in Serlio's ideas, even though the great architectural writer had himself left a year or two earlier. This explains why, besides describing the different orders of the Piazzetta buildings, he also understood the importance of the principle underlying this differentiation. Talking of the Libreria block he pointed out that Sansovino had revolutionized Venetian architectural practice, since previously buildings in the city had not been varied "according to the site on which they were erected and according to their function."[36] It is hardly surprising that he credited this revolution to Sansovino rather than to Serlio. Not only did he not personally know the Bolognese architect, but, more important, by concentrating on the Florentine Sansovino he could strengthen his basic message that Florence was the chief fountain of the arts. His concentration on Sanso-

179. Serlio, Book III (1540): frontispiece

180. Titian: *Crowning with Thorns*,
early 1540s, Louvre, Paris

It might be thought that Vasari was genuinely ignorant of Serlio's importance, but for one substantial
fact. This is that his own accounts of the art of architecture, which, together with accounts of painting and
sculpture, form the introductions to the two editions of
the *Lives* (1st ed. 1550, 2nd ed. 1568), are closely dependent on Serlio's treatise. After a first chapter on materials he goes on to discuss architectural forms themselves in terms which are distinctly Serlian. Chapter 2
immediately points out that all squared masonry can
be classed as either *quadro semplice* (plain) or *quadro
intagliato* (carved) according to whether elements such
as cornices, friezes, leaves, dentils, etc. have received
detailed carving or not. This takes the traditional
stonemason's distinction between plain and carved masonry and uses it, as had Serlio, as a basic instrument
of classification. Already in chapter 2 Vasari describes
how this distinction can be applied to Rustic, Doric,
Ionic, Corinthian, and Composite, and even to *lavoro
tedesco* (German work, i.e. Gothic), and in chapter 3
he goes on to discuss the five orders and Gothic in
greater detail.

This chapter is, with some significant modifications,
essentially a compressed version of Serlio's Book IV.
Not only the proportions of all five orders but also the
rules governing their use—with, for example, Tuscan/
Rustic being used for prisons, fortresses, etc.—are all
taken from the earlier treatise. Vasari even elaborates
on Serlio's theories using his unpublished ideas. Thus,
talking of the ancients' use of Doric for the buildings of
military men and the temples of manly deities, he goes
on to point out that they always took care to differentiate the characters of their buildings as smooth or
carved, plainer or richer, "so that the rank and character of the emperor or other patron could be distinguished from that of others." This seems to reflect the
ideas used by Serlio in his eighth book on the Roman
camp, a work which though not printed seems to have
influenced Titian and Aretino at the very period of Vasari's residence in Venice.

Vasari's modifications and elaborations of Serlio's
ideas are few but revealing.[37] The first is his renaming
of the Tuscan order as "Rustic." Presumably he found
it embarrassing that the crudest of the orders should be
named after his beloved and admired Tuscany. A similar nationalistic urge led him to claim that it was the
Toscani who invented Composite. If the Tuscans were

vino is well illustrated by the way he alone, besides the
great hero Michelangelo, was awarded the honour of a
separately published *Life*. Vasari was probably right
that Sansovino's buildings did more to change the nature of Venetian architecture than did Serlio's books.
But the precise way he describes their innovatory character shows that he understood well those architectural
principles which Serlio took the lead in developing. His
reduction of those principles to one of "varying design
according to site and function" is remarkably perceptive.

181. Titian: *Ecce Homo*, 1543, Kunsthistorisches Museum, Vienna

the most refined people, they must have invented the most refined order. These modifications are already present in the 1550 edition, but in the 1568 text a more important one appears. There, discussing the *ordine composto*, he extends it to include the style of free invention which he attributes to Michelangelo. This requires doing real violence to the evidence, since almost all Michelangelo's buildings, including those mentioned by Vasari, such as the New Sacristy, the top floor of the Palazzo Farnese court, St Peter's, etc. use rather correct and conventional Corinthian capitals for their main order. The chief area of invention is in the tombs, niches, and window frames, which had traditionally been fields for the display of the sculptor's fantasy and technique. By neglecting the unpalatable truth that most of Michelangelo's works are repetitively Corinthian, Vasari is able to claim for his hero a freedom from Vitruvian laws. For the Composite order is, as he says, not mentioned by Vitruvius and is implicitly excluded from his canon by his criticism of mixed forms. Michelangelo is thus able to acquire an undeserved credit as a liberated "post-Vitruvian" and even "post-Classicist." In associating Composite with a style of free invention Vasari is only taking up an idea already articulated by Serlio, but he has made one small change in Serlio's nomenclature which makes it easier for him to develop it. Serlio's *composito* has become *composto*, and this shift from Latinization to Italian

182. Titian: *Charles V*, 1548, Alte
Pinakothek, Munich

alism. It is thus not surprising that Vasari at the end of the chapter on the five orders opposes to them a *lavoro tedesco* which we call Gothic. Already Filarete had found it natural to call the pointed arch "German"; but Vasari goes beyond this to accord "German work" almost the status of a style with its own principles, however perverse. Admittedly he condemns its use, but he was (as Panofsky showed) prepared to design in it when it was appropriate to the context.[38] He certainly goes beyond Serlio, who never gave Gothic any systematic treatment.

Serlio's ideas remain an important influence on Vasari's introduction on architecture even in his last chapter, though they are embedded in a discussion of proportion and anthropomorphism which derives largely from Alberti. The whole chapter is devoted to instructing the reader in how to tell a well-designed building from one that is not. One general rule recommended is that the "orders should be used according to the character and class of the patron."[39] Coming down to details, Vasari refers to an illustration of a palace which he planned (but failed) to insert as a guide, thus taking up directly Serlio's practice of using illustrations as an aid to architectural criticism. At the end, he insists on the importance of a "good eye" (*occhio buono*) which, if it has judgement (*giudicio*), can be considered "the true compass and measure because by it things are either praised or blamed." The faculty whose importance for architectural appreciation was first documented by Serlio here receives new emphasis, almost certainly in tribute to Michelangelo, who also claimed that the compass should be in the eyes.[40]

There is no better measure of Serlio's greatness as an individual thinker than his remarkable influence on four very different and very independent minds. That he inspired the design of one of the greatest architectural compositions of the Renaissance, the Piazzetta, and that he provided the basis for the architectural ideas in Vasari's *Vite* was, in a sense, no more than his due. But that he induced Aretino to exploit a new vein of architectural analogy in literature, and caused Titian to devote as much attention to the characterization of buildings as he had always devoted to that of people, places him in a more exceptional sphere. No earlier architectural theorist had such a striking effect on contemporary activity in such different fields.

If there was one reason above all others why he had

effectively shifts the focus of the word from the notion of the "composite" order formed by a mixture of the others to that of the "composed" order, that is one which is an exercise in free composition. Driven by his desire to glorify Tuscany and the greatest Tuscan artist, Michelangelo, Vasari thus modifies Serlio's account of the orders to make Michelangelo a free creator in a "Tuscan" style.

Nationalism played a prominent role in the history of the orders. Their revival by Brunelleschi was probably already motivated by Tuscan anti-German nation-

this effect, it was his uniquely felicitous perception of the relationship between the character of man and that of architecture. He showed, as no one had done previously, how critical terms for the analysis of human character and behaviour, ideas such as rule and licence, roughness and refinement, humanity and bestiality, could all be applied to buildings; so that a palace fa-

çade might tell you as much about its owner as would a face-to-face encounter with the man himself. If his ideas struck an immediate chord in his contemporaries it is because people had always felt the connection between a building and its occupant or function to be an important one, but had never understood so well how it could be expressed.

Sixteenth-century choices

◆

Status, morality, and character

BY THE mid-sixteenth century, in Italy at least, status, morality, and character were the three principal factors which were recognized as influencing the selection of architectural forms. The most important was the status either of the building's patron or occupant, or of the institution which it housed. This had always been the factor which most influenced a building's decoration, but only in the writings of Alberti and Filarete had it been extensively analysed. Filarete in particular had formulated precise rules for the expression of status by varying the degree of decoration and by adjusting proportions. The idea that a building might be read and criticized as an expression of the patron's morality had been introduced both in the Old Testament and in Greek philosophy and had been widely publicized in the Christian Middle Ages. Only in the late fifteenth and early sixteenth centuries had it been fully acknowledged and dealt with as a problem, a problem which was finally resolved when ancient theories of the musical modes were used as a guide in the choice of the tainted Classical orders. The concept of a building expressing the character or even the attitude of a patron or occupant was the most subtle and the most recent to receive an elaborate treatment. Already implied in the Vitruvian matching of different orders to different physical types and of different methods of architectural composition to different attitudes to life, it had gained prominence as a result of the influence of musical thought and had finally been used by Sebastiano Serlio as the key to a complete architectural theory.

Given the general acknowledgement of these and other factors, patrons and architects were faced with complicated and often embarrassing choices. An order which might be desirable in terms of one factor might be excluded in terms of another. There were, admittedly, yet other factors which served to mitigate the problem. One could decide that in the end most people would either never notice which order was used or would be too confused themselves to make sure critical judgements; or one might justifiably feel that the mere use of a Classical order at all would be so likely to improve people's assessment of one's status as a powerful person, of one's morality as someone who knew the rules, and of one's character as someone civilized that the choice between one order and another was of only marginal significance. In the long run, however, what greatly simplified the choice between forms was that in each context one of the three factors was likely to emerge as of overriding importance. In the majority of churches, for example, the expression of character was of little importance, morality could be taken for granted, and only status absolutely required expression. The strains were always there, but they affected some patrons and some buildings more than others.

Ecclesiastical buildings: the Church militant or triumphant?

By the 1520s the choice of which order to use in an ecclesiastical context had been largely resolved. Corinthian, always the emblem of the highest status, could now also be recognized as the emblem of the fulfilment of the Christian message. The great Corinthian order of St Peter's represented the final materialization of the Church. The doubts which had troubled the later fifteenth century were swept aside as Catholics proudly asserted the triumph of Christianity. The vast majority of sixteenth-century churches were thus Corinthian, as great churches had usually been. The only area where there were lingering hesitations about the morality of

183. Jacopo Sansovino: S. Francesco della Vigna, Venice, 1534

such extravagant forms was in the churches of religious orders, where, as Saint Bernard had long ago pointed out, extravagance could be less easily justified than in the more worldly churches of bishops. Sansovino's S. Francesco della Vigna in Venice (1534) still uses the plain Doric pilasters of the earlier Franciscan church of S. Salvatore al Monte in Florence (before 1490) in conscious expression of the Franciscan ideal of simplicity (Fig. 183). Even the enormous Basilica of S. Maria degli Angeli outside Assisi, designed in 1569 by Alessi, keeps within a sober Doric mode, quite exceptionally for a church of such importance and in contradiction of its architect's recommendation in another context of Corinthian for the Virgin (Fig. 184).[1] The restraint must certainly be a concession to the associations of the site as the place where Saint Francis first founded his order with a group of friars living in wattle-and-daub huts. The unusual design of the building, with a Doric entablature running uninterrupted across the façade and down the side, taking no account of the transept and creating a structure like an early Doric temple,

must be an attempt to recapture in masonry the essence of primitive Franciscanism. The same taste was shown by the austere and militant Jesuits in their early years. They acknowledged one of their members, Giovanni Tristano, as "skilled in the art of architecture which is appropriate to our colleges" (1564) and encouraged him to design and advise on their buildings throughout Italy.[2] His churches show a consistent taste for simple forms, from the Annunziatina (1561), the original church of the Collegio Romano in Rome, with its superimposed Doric pilasters, and the Gesù in Perugia of the same year, with its sober square piers reminiscent of S. Lorenzo in Damaso, to the Gesù of his home town of Ferrara (1570), with a single order of large Doric pilasters.[3] Only when Cardinal Farnese accepted Vignola's design for the Gesù (1568) in Rome over Tristano's head did its Composite and Corinthian forms set a new pattern for rich churches for the order. It was perhaps in modest response to this trend that Tristano made an essay in Ionic for the Gesù at Forlì (1570).[4] Certainly Ionic variants had been used earlier to ex-

184. Galeazzo Alessi: S. Maria degli Angeli, Assisi, 1569

ferent reasons.[5] Perhaps Zorzi got his particular reasons from Serlio, who was also an advisor on the project. One of the few architects who put themselves on record as claiming to apply the Serlian rules was Alessi. In a letter of January 1570 accompanying a design for the façade of the Gesù in Rome, he points out that the lower Doric order is "appropriate to a church dedicated to our Redeemer," while the upper Corinthian one "is appropriate to the Virgin Mother."[6] Though this reasoning may or may not be taken as embroidery applied after the fact, the letter does allow us to consider a similar explanation for his choice of Doric for the rebuilding of S. Rufino, the cathedral of Assisi, in 1571.[7] The order would there be an allusion to Saint Rufinus' character as a manly martyr. Certainly planned by Martino Bassi with "manly" associations in mind is S. Lorenzo, Milan, rebuilt in 1575 (after a fire) with a monumental Doric frieze whose metopes are filled with attributes of the early martyr. In general, in view of the prevalence of Corinthian/ Composite it is not unreasonable to consider the possibility of such an expression of character in any Doric church dedicated to a male saint; but when Corinthian is used for churches of the Virgin it is impossible to decide whether similar principles are at work.

Even when Doric was unquestionably used in churches for reasons of morality or character, it was still often thought desirable to use Corinthian for doors and façades (e.g. S. Francesco della Vigna and S. Martino, Venice) in order to articulate the building's status to the outside world, since this was far and away the most important function of the orders in ecclesiastical buildings. These expressions could, indeed, be quite nuanced. Composite, for example, was used for churches of the highest worldly status, such as Palladio's S. Giorgio Maggiore, Venice (1566), which was the scene of great occasions of state and appropriately had the same order as the Loggetta. Compared to Composite even Corinthian looked restrained, and so in his Redentore (1577) Palladio could contrast the Composite façade—the focus of the great annual procession commemorating Venice's liberation from the plague—with a Corinthian interior which reflected, however subtly, the rejection by the church's Franciscan congregation of extremes of external display.

The one field of religious architecture where the need to use Corinthian/Composite as an expression of high

press a less extreme restraint, as in Moroni's S. Giustina (1531) at Padua for the Benedictines, or Giunti's S. Angelo (1552) at Milan for the Franciscans.

If there are not many examples of churches where the choice of order was governed by moral considerations, there are perhaps even fewer where the order is chosen as an expression of character. In many cases it is impossible to tell whether this was a factor. Francesco Zorzi thought that the Doric order of Sansovino's S. Francesco della Vigna was "both proper to the saint to whom the church is dedicated and to the brethren who have to officiate in it," thus providing two dif-

185. A. da Sangallo the Younger: Palazzo
Baldassini, Rome, c.1520: portal

186. A. da Sangallo the Younger and Michelangelo:
Palazzo Farnese, Rome, 1517 onwards: court

status was rarely allowed to predominate was that of
conventual buildings and other such institutions. The
pattern of using the simpler orders for these structures,
already established in the fifteenth century, was continued in the sixteenth. Michelangelo's work for S. Lorenzo in Florence provides one demonstration of what
might be done. While the church façade (1516) was intended to have free-standing Corinthian below and
Corinthian pilasters above, and while the Medici
Chapel had an interior elevation of two storeys of Corinthian pilasters, the *ricetto* or library entrance used
free-standing columns which are of Doric simplicity
but taller and with a Corinthian abacus, and the library
interior was lined with a form of Doric pilasters. Thus
the façade of the main devotional area was in a higher
key than the interior of the minor devotional area, and
the entrance to the meditative/scholarly area was in a
higher key than its interior. By using one column form
for "façades" and another for "interiors" Michelangelo has been able to distinguish relatively "worldly"
and showy environments from relatively "spiritual"
ones. At the same time, by his choice of capital types he
has been able to distinguish between those structures
which have a devotional character and those which do
not. While his system may be particularly rational and
consistent, the principles it embodies are familiar from
other buildings. Non-devotional religious buildings are
frequently sober and typically Doric or Ionic.

By the end of the century, however, even in non-devotional religious buildings Corinthian comes back.

Thus even the otherwise austere Jesuit Collegio Romano in Rome has Ionic and Corinthian orders in its
court (1583), just as the otherwise austere interior of
the Gesù church (1568) was Composite.[8] It is almost as
if Corinthian and Composite had become essential attributes of the Catholic Church and its leading institutions, symbols of the Church's claim to overall dominance. Certainly the Catholic preference for rich forms
was only confirmed by the Protestant taste for simpler
ones. Indeed, it is scarcely an exaggeration to say that

187. Palazzo Farnese, Rome: detail of façade

188. Palazzo Doria Pamfili, Genoa, portal, c.1530

in Rome, at least, by the end of the century, the Corinthian/Composite column was rarely used except on church buildings. The most "Roman" structures in the city were those of Roman Catholics.

Palaces and villas: to be good or to be great?

For secular buildings the choice was not so easy. The reinstatement of Corinthian in religious structures did much to improve the order's image, but for houses and palaces in particular it was still liable to be interpreted as an emblem of vainglory. If even the mighty Julius II went on giving precedence to Doric in his secular buildings long after he had accepted Corinthian in churches,

then others could not easily return to the richer form. Doric remained the most prominent order on the façades of Roman palaces, as it had been in the first two decades of the century. Typical is the door of the Palazzo Baldassini, by A. da Sangallo the Younger, of c.1520, with its frieze of triglyphs and carved metopes asserting a military virtue to which its lawyer owner had no claim (Fig. 185). Even Sangallo's contemporary Palazzo Farnese, for the future Pope Paul III, still gave prominence to Doric in the magnificent colonnaded atrium and in the ground floor of the court, where the metopes were again charged with military equipment as well as with the Farnese lily (Fig. 186). Vasari describes the whole court as Doric, and it is evidently with that order and its attributes that the family wishes to be associated, more than with Ionic and Corinthian. On the façade of the palace, where the only orders are Ionic and Composite attached to the window frames, their main function is to emphasize the importance of the first and principal floor (Composite) over the top floor (Ionic) (Fig. 187). Later in the century even such a subdued use of the orders as this would become exceptional on palace exteriors.

189. Palazzo Spinola (now Banco di Chiávari), Genoa, portal, c.1565

In Rome the chief pressure encouraging architectural restraint was provided by the Church: elsewhere the pressures might be social as well. This is probably the case at Genoa, where the jealousy of competing noble families imposed a mutual restraint. Moreover, the teachings of Saint Bernardino had already made them particularly aware of the folly of architectural vainglory, as the IHS inscriptions discussed in chapter VIII make clear. Thus, when Genoa's leading citizen, the papal admiral Andrea Doria, rebuilt his palace (now the Palazzo Doria Pamfili) after 1521, he adorned its long plain façade with nothing but a magnificent marble Doric portal decorated with military trophies, figures of Peace and Abundance, and two inscriptions (Fig. 188). The biggest of these, completed after 1529, ran the whole length of the front and was composed in such a way that the record that the palace was built in order that Doria, "with his body tired after great toil, might have peace in honest leisure" flanked the door with its emblems of Doric virtue. The second inscrip-

tion on the lintel of the door itself declares FUNDAVIT EAM ALTISSIMUS ("The Highest hath founded it").[9] As in the earlier inscriptions, credit for the building is in a sense transferred to the Almighty, while at the same time the Dorias are part of a divine plan.

It is possible that Andrea Doria, like his Ligurian neighbours the della Roveres, felt that Doric was particularly appropriate as an expression of his name (Doria/Doric), but there is also evidence for a general persistence of moral pressures in Genoa in the sixteenth century. In a city where the ruling families were exceptionally alert to any attempt by one of their number to raise himself above the others, virtuous restraint was at a premium. The ambitious Strada Nuova planned by Galeazzo Alessi in 1550 seems to have been purposely designed to provide equal plots for competing palaces, which would also be limited in their height.[10] The scheme recommended itself to the city government for its enforcement of equality within the oligarchy and for its expression of order and moderation. Within this

190. Giulio Romano: *Destruction of the Giants*, Palazzo del Te, Mantua, 1530s

frame, individual builders in following decades were happy to project their own images of virtue. The Doric order, inscriptions, and figure sculpture too were all employed to this end. Of the ten palaces begun in the thirty years between 1558 and 1584, eight had large Doric portals. The largest palace of all, that of Niccolo Grimaldi, nicknamed *monarco* for his wealth (now Palazzo Municipio), had Doric pilasters on both floors and free-standing military trophies over the entrance, making it appear more the residence of a virtuous soldier than an extravagant banker. The palace of Baldassare Lomellino (now Palazzo Campanella) had no order on the façade but a well-calculated inscription on its Doric doorway, VENTURI NON IMMEMOR AEVI ("Not unmindful of the age to come") indicating that

it was built not for himself but for his heirs. The palace of Nicolosio Lomellino (now Palazzo Podestà) also had no order but had bundles of weapons hung between the *piano nobile* windows and the biblical quotation SAPIENTIA AEDIFICAVIT DOMUM ("Wisdom hath builded her house" [*Proverbs* 9, 1]) on its Doric portal. Perhaps most virtuous of all was the palace of Pantaleo Spinola (now Banco di Chiávari), with a completely plain façade adorned only with a Doric portal crowned with statues of Prudence and Vigilance (later changed), and having a frieze of metopes filled with armour and partly covered by the inscription MUNIAT QUI DEDIT ("May He who gave it protect it") directly inviting divine aid (Fig. 189). Seldom has so much opulence been reined in by so much virtue. To see how far the moral

191. Giulio Romano: Palazzo del Te, Mantua, exterior, 1525

pressures relate directly to the urban Genoese context, it is only necessary to compare these palaces with the villas built at about the same time by Galeazzo Alessi in the suburbs of the same city. Two examples are the Villa Cambiaso (1548) and the Villa Pallavicino (1560), the one with Doric and the other with Ionic on the ground floor, and both with rich Corinthian or Composite orders above. Moral inscriptions and the insignia of military virtue are absent. The same freedom from constraint once away from the centre of Genoa is apparent in Alessi's Palazzo Marino at Milan (1558), also built for a wealthy Genoese and richly encrusted with architectural detail.

There can be little doubt that the single greatest source of pressure on the Genoese nobility in the de-

velopment of the Strada Nuova was Andrea Doria, who constantly sought to bring order to the city's warring factions, and who had set a lofty tone in his own palace. Indeed, his role as suppressor of vice was directly alluded to in Perino del Vaga's great vault decoration of the main room of the palace, showing the *Destruction of the Giants* who fall under Zeus's thunderbolts.[11] Doria first found his role as punisher of evil in the service of the pope and of the emperor, and the figure of Zeus could be taken to allude to the latter as well as to himself. The defeat of the giants was a subject also associated with the emperor's instruments elsewhere, as at Mantua, where it was used by Federigo Gonzaga as the theme of the last in a series of rooms in the Palazzo del Te. Giulio Romano, who designed both

.. Ammanati: Loggia Benavides, Padua, 1540s

palace and room, had been a fellow pupil of Raphael's with Perino del Vaga, but the inspiration for the theme is likely to have come from interpretations of Charles V's military activity that were promulgated for the emperor's visit to Italy in 1530.

What makes the Mantuan *Destruction of the Giants* especially interesting is the further light it sheds on architectural ethics (Fig. 190). The annihilation of the giants at the hands of the gods, in punishment for their arrogance in seeking to scale Olympus, fills the walls and vault of the room in one dramatic scene. On entering, the visitor first of all sees the giants being crushed in a collapsing mountain of boulders as Zeus, far above

under a circular colonnade, wields his thunderbolt surrounded by the other Olympians. Once in the room, however, the visitor has the shock of turning round to find that the giants' dwelling represented in the wall he has just come through also has a magnificent portico of coloured marble columns, with gilt capitals of the most opulent Composite order, and this too is brought crashing down by divine justice. By its material, order, and decoration as well as by its unstable structure this architecture is brilliantly expressive of the overweening materialist ambitions of the giants. As such it contrasts with the white marble colonnade of the gods above, with its restrained Ionic order. They, who could have afforded the most extravagant forms, have chosen an architecture of moderation, and in the name of this same moderation they now overwhelm the giants and their palace. But the giants' portico contrasts even more strongly with the plain and economical Doric architecture of the palace itself (Fig. 191). For the Palazzo del Te had been planned from the outset as a relatively cheap structure, faced largely in stucco and with its principal entrance façades decorated only with simple Doric pilasters. Although these choices had been made before the *Destruction of the Giants* can have been conceived, they were now given a more positive meaning. Federigo Gonzaga appears in the best possible light, with tastes diametrically opposed to those of the giants, and with a modesty which also distinguishes him from the Olympians.

In the case of the Palazzo del Te it was the subsequent fresco decoration which brought out the moral meaning of its Doric architecture. Fifteen years later in Padua, an inscription and sculptural decoration made such a meaning explicit at the outset. In the 1540s the wealthy lawyer Marco Benavides, who, like Federigo Gonzaga, could easily have been charged with excessive indulgence in the fruits of material wealth, erected in the garden of his house at the rear of the Eremitani church a noble loggia (Fig. 192) and a colossal statue of Hercules. Both were designed by the Florentine Ammanati, lately assistant to Sansovino in Venice, and both were calculated to help in shaping Benavides' image. The moral message of the architecture is carried in the inscription over the central aperture: ID FACERE LAUS EST QUOD DECET NON QUOD LICET ("It is praiseworthy to do what is appropriate, not what licence permits").[12] A rich and powerful man is permitted (*licet*) to do almost anything, but he will deserve praise only if he limits himself to what is morally appropriate (*quod decet*). The text is presumably primarily intended to refer to the restraints of law and justice by which the powerful should be guided. The text on the base of the Hercules statue nearby refers to the work of the hero in the service of justice, and Zeus and Apollo (the two figures in the loggia's flanking niches) are deities celebrated for enforcing heaven's rules. The theme was particularly appropriate to Benavides, who was both a lawyer and a man of personal power. As he passed under the central arch his virtue would be crowned by the wreath-bearing Victories in the span-

193. Ammanati: Benavides tomb, Eremitani, Padua, 1540s

drels. These ladies stand contemptuously on the faces of half-animal satyrs who, like the Mantua giants, represent unrestrained appetites. Such appetites lead to disorder and excess in art as in other fields, and the text above can as easily be applied to the architecture of the arch itself. The choice of sober and correct Doric when the patron could have afforded the richest Composite is an apt illustration of his virtuous restraint. At the same time, the unparalleled precision and correctness with which the order is handled, its disciplined—almost legalistic—accuracy, make it also a suitable commemoration of his public work for law and order.

After viewing the loggia it may come as a surprise to

194. Fondaco dei Tedeschi, Venice, 1505–8

discover that Benavides' tomb erected by Ammanati at the same time only a few yards away in the Eremitani employs the very Composite order which the loggia deliberately shunned (Fig. 193).[13] Once again the change of context is critical. In his house Benavides presented the image he wished to have in life, and sought to deflect the criticism which the rich lawyer is always likely to attract. In the church, on the other hand, after his death he need no longer fear moral detractors. The re-

ligious context and the Christian virtues in the niches provided a sufficient guarantee of his reputation. He could allow the Composite architecture to provide an unashamed testimony to his wealth and power. During his life everyone knew he was great but needed to be convinced that he was good. After his death he risked being forgotten altogether unless he left some permanent memorial expressive of his status. Benavides the successful advocate well knew how to present his own case, whether to his contemporaries who knew him personally or to later generations who could not.

Benavides' loggia and tomb admirably illustrate the conflicting desires of the wealthy man to appear at once powerful and virtuous. Many palaces in the Veneto represent the same combination of aspirations in a single façade. Sansovino's grandest Venetian palace, the Palazzo Cornaro, boldly states the owner's power and opulence in its rising sequence of Doric, Ionic, and Corinthian orders but at the same time indicates his virtue by an unprecedented display of sculpted military trophies. At Verona, Sanmicheli's Palazzo Canossa has a prominent display of trophies round the door but lofty Composite pilasters on the *piano nobile*, while on his Palazzo Bevilacqua, where the *piano nobile* is extravagantly Corinthian, the family's virtues are suggested by the noble Classical busts in the keystones of the lower Doric order. All these buildings are of the 1530s, and, perhaps as a result of their first judicious presentation of opulence, later palaces tend to use the richer forms with less diffidence. Thus Sanmicheli's Palazzo Grimani on the Grand Canal in Venice uses richly fluted Corinthian on both its original floors, and at Vicenza most of Palladio's palaces use Ionic, Corinthian, and Composite forms with only the occasional introduction of emblems of military virtue.

Besides the palace, the other important dwelling type of the mid-sixteenth century was the villa. Since villas were built usually out of the public eye, the factors governing their design were different from those which affected palaces. Being rarely seen and rarely even lived in by their owners, they had no need to be ostentatious, nor was it appropriate for them to express the owner's values or character. Normally they continued to be built in sober Doric and Ionic forms like the first villas of the late fifteenth and early sixteenth centuries expressing not so much the specific virtue of their builder as the traditional simplicity of country life. Rustication and the Tuscan order are occasionally introduced, especially for service buildings which allude to the life of the simple peasant, even closer to nature. At the other end of the scale, Corinthian is sometimes introduced in true country villas but appears more often in those immediately outside towns, where it is called for by their more public role. Examples of the Doric and/or Ionic true villa are Falconetto's Villa dei Vescovi (c.1535), Sansovino's Villa Garzoni (c.1550)—both in the Ve-

195. Palazzo dei Camerlenghi, Rialto, Venice, 1525–28

neto—and Giunti's Villa Simonetta (c.1550) outside Milan, as well as the majority of Palladio's. Examples of richer suburban villas are those of Alessi outside Genoa, noted earlier. A rare example of a contrast between a genuinely palatial villa in the country and its genuinely humble working wings is Palladio's Villa Trissino at Meledo, which was intended to have a main house with four Corinthian porticoes but Tuscan loggias adjoining the working areas below. A similar

196. Vasari: Uffizi, Florence, 1560

197. Uffizi, Florence: end bay with Cosimo I, flanked by figures of Rigour and Equity

though less abrupt contrast is found in his Villa Maser, with its rich Ionic central block and plainer rusticated service wings.

Finally, it is worth pointing out that many of the greatest residential buildings after the mid-sixteenth century, whether palaces or villas, use few if any orders or decorations. This is particularly true of the façades of both urban and rural residences of the most powerful family in Italy, the Medici rulers of Florence. It is also true of the palaces and villas of Roman cardinals and popes. The Palazzo Farnese and the Villa Giulia contrast strikingly with the austere later Borghese and Lateran palaces. What makes this absence of ornament all the more noteworthy is the increasing popularity of enormously elaborate church façades using the richest columnar forms, façades often paid for by the patrons of the plain palaces and bearing large inscriptions with their names. The reason for the restraint in residential façades must be those same social and religious pressures outlined earlier: social pressures in Florence, where the Medici were at pains not to excite antagonism by disturbing the city's established architectural traditions, and religious pressures in Rome, where the Church and churchmen had been challenged to reform themselves in response to the rise of Protestantism.

Evidently the theories of the architectural expression of character and status propounded first by Serlio and repeated by Vasari have little relevance to the real world of the sixteenth century; nor was an interest in an Antique revival of much importance. The factors which chiefly decided whether and how a palace was decorated were rampant ambition when it was free to operate, and moral and social restraint where they were required—that is, the same factors which would affect the owner's behaviour in other areas. Residential architecture, at least, was always judged principally as the action of a patron.

Government and commerce: public buildings and the social order

While private buildings raised delicate problems for their owners, who had to decide carefully whether to express their status in social or in moral terms, public buildings could with less inhibition represent the social order. The structure of society, however, was not the same in all the cities of Italy, and in each community the principles applied to the design of public buildings were different.

Thus, at Venice, where trade and manufacture had an important place but one that was clearly subordinate to the wishes of the nobility, it was appropriate that Sansovino's Piazzetta should give each section of the population its proper place, while leaving no doubt as to their relative importance. In this Sansovino followed an established Venetian tradition. The city government was happy to build monumental structures to house merchants' exchanges such as the Fondaco dei Tedeschi, but the forms they approved for them were simple square piers with plain capitals, quite different from those found in more important buildings (Fig. 194). In the rebuilding of the commercial Rialto area in the 1520s, the brick walls and plain square piers of the shops were in sharp contrast to the fine masonry and elaborate Corinthian pilasters of the Palazzo dei Camerlenghi, where the revenues of the city's trade were collected (Fig. 195). When Sansovino came to build additional warehouse accommodation in this area in 1554, the Fabbriche Nuove which he erected had Doric and Ionic pilasters on the upper floors, with emphatically rough surfaces to go with the rusticated arcade below. The function of the building was as clearly inferior to that of the Palazzo dei Camerlenghi as that building was to the Loggetta which, with its marble columns and Composite capitals, was the resort of the nobility who were the ultimate authority. In the Venetian subject city of Vicenza, Palladio exploited a similiar contrast between ruler and ruled. The arcades of the Basilica c.1550, which had local governmental

and commercial functions, are sober Doric and Ionic, but the Loggia del Capitaniato, the ultimate symbol of Venetian domination put up in 1571, has giant Composite shafts and elaborate decorations, directly recalling the architecture of the Loggetta in Venice itself.

A feature of both the Loggetta and the Loggia del Capitaniato is that as well as being richer than the adjoining structures they are also much freer and less regular, as if in expression of the arbitrary power with which they are associated. A similar contrast is also effectively exploited by Vasari, a great admirer of Sansovino's Piazzetta, in the Uffizi or administrative complex designed for Duke Cosimo in Florence in 1560 (Fig. 196). Ostensibly the structure houses the collected magistracies of the Florentine state, and the regularity of its forms and the sobriety of its Doric order aptly evoke this. But a statue of the duke (once seated and now standing) presides over their activities on the first floor of the end bay over the river (Fig. 197), flanked by the same extravagant Composite order and freely arcuated forms as are found in the structures housing the ultimate authorities at Venice and Vicenza.

The distinction between the two parts of the Uffizi is not between trade and government, as at Venice and Vicenza, but between two levels of authority. Indeed, it was impossible to develop the same distinction in Florence, where there was no clearly separate aristocracy and where the ruling families such as the Medici had long been closely involved in trade. As a result the need was rather for a system of architecture which marked off the gradations of status not between commerce and government but within commerce itself. Thus, when G. B. del Tasso designed a magnificent loggia to house trade in gold and silks, the Loggia di Mercato Nuovo (1547), he was able to use grand Composite columns that would have been unthinkable in Venice (Fig. 198), though admittedly they are still combined with the simple square pier forms of Vasari's Loggia del Pesce (Fish Market) of 1567 and those of the Ponte Vecchio which then housed the shops of butchers and others. Distinctions between the classes in Florence were essentially distinctions between trades.

In Rome, where trade and commerce were of marginal importance, there was no need for an acknowledgement either of those activities or of their practitioners. The principal requirement of public buildings was that they should confirm the authority of the city's

198. G. B. del Tasso: Loggia di Mercato Nuovo,
Florence, 1547

government as sanctioned by the papacy and implicitly
associate that government with the Church. Thus Michelangelo clothed all of the Capitoline palaces with
the giant Corinthian pilasters introduced by Bramante
at St Peter's, and when Antonio da Sangallo the
Younger designed a papal mint around 1530 he made
it magnificently Composite. Papacy and city were assimilated in façades which were closest to those of contemporary churches.

Fortifications: keeping people out and keeping people in

In earlier chapters much emphasis was placed on the
tensions affecting church and palace design, especially
in the late fifteenth century, when the need to express
high morality came into conflict with the need to express high status. In one type of fortification, the city
gate, similar and perhaps even more exasperating tensions came to the surface during the sixteenth century.
The basic conflict which had always been present in
such structures was between the wish to attract and impress friends and the need to repel and deter enemies.
What sharpened the conflict around 1500 was the
strain between the need to make gates ever more strong
in the face of rapidly improving artillery and the desire
to ornament them more richly with Classical forms as
testimony to the values of those who lived behind
them: a gate could tell you either about the impene-
trability and defensiveness of the wall in which it was
placed or about the openness and cultivation of the
community behind it—and often it was required to tell
you about both.

In the fifteenth century the conflict was happily resolved in several instances by placing enormous cylindrical flanking towers on either side of a doorway opulently carved with Corinthian and/or Composite
orders. One such was the Porta Capuana at Naples, designed in 1485 by Giuliano da Majano in imitation of
the similar earlier entrance of the Castelnuovo inside
the city. But by the sixteenth century such designs came
to seem less satisfactory. Only in the Veneto were a
whole series of elaborate portals constructed. These
were probably intended by the Venetian government to
reassure wavering vassals after the disastrous wars of
the League of Cambrai in 1509–11. Cities such as
Padua and Treviso received gates which displayed rich
collections of Corinthian and Composite columns and
pilasters on their exteriors. The more important the
gate the more magnificent it was made, as in the case
of Guglielmo Bergamasco's Porta S. Tommaso in Treviso, which barred the main road from Austria (Fig.
199). The six free-standing Composite columns with as
many alert crouching lions in high relief on their pedestals and four large panels of sculpted military trophies are better calculated to impress with the benefits

199. G. Bergamasco: Porta S. Tommaso, Treviso, outer façade, 1518

of Venetian rule than to convince of their ability to resist an attack.

Elsewhere it was above all an appearance of strength that was required. What was needed was an architecture which still evoked Classical refinement but at the same time expressed a greater strength and impregnability. Not surprisingly it was in the circle of Bramante and Raphael, who more than anyone had sought to increase the expressive power of architecture, that a better solution was found. Bramante had already used both Rustication and Doric as emblems of strength; so when Giulio Romano designed a series of city gates for Mantua in the 1530s he combined the two features with appropriate sculptures to make façades which are eloquent of power and toughness as well as of wealth

and culture.[14] Similar combinations were then used with great effect by Sanmicheli on the Porta Nuova at Verona (1533–40) and on the Forte di S. Andrea at the entrance to the Venetian lagoon (begun 1543). Later still the same mixture was used by many other architects, following the recommendations of Serlio which appeared in 1537.

There was only one problem with the new rusticated portals, especially after Serlio's treatise appeared. This was the awkwardness of using bossed masonry, *opera rustica*, a form associated with the roughness of the peasantry, on the portal of a great city. It is probably for this reason that when Sanmicheli came to design the Porta Palio, again at Verona, around 1550 he carefully avoided the use of rough rustication on the exterior

200. Sanmicheli: Porta Palio, Verona, c.1550, outer façade

(Figs. 200 and 201). The new gate was arguably the most important in the circuit of walls. It led directly to the main street of the town and was used each year for the great race of the Palio. It was the main entrance to Verona almost as the Piazzetta was to Venice, and it too had to represent its city's best qualities. Accordingly, Sanmicheli reduced the rough masonry of the Porta Nuova to relatively smooth channelled blocks and set in front of it an engaged order, still of Doric but of the most refined variety. At the same time, as if to compensate for the impression of greater weakness, he placed three enormous busts of warriors on the keystones above the doors. Rustication is concentrated instead on the inside face of the gate, and it is tempting to see it there as an appropriate expression of the wilds of the countryside to which it served as the prelude. All cities had strong economic reasons for emphasizing both the civilization of their confines and the wildness

and unpredictability of the areas outside them, since it was from the people who lived inside their walls and the goods which entered them that they raised their taxes.

The principal factor which led Sanmicheli to change his approach between his two Veronese gates is likely to have been the appearance of Serlio's Book IV in 1537. He may also have been affected by Sansovino's subsequent association of rustication with the crude labourers of the Zecca, and Doric with the noble characters of the Procurators on the Piazzetta. The last straw may have been the appearance of the bizarre rusticated fantasies of Serlio's Libro Estraordinario, generated as they were in the wild forests of Fontainebleau. The idea of the two sides of the gate expressing very different "personalities" and encouraging different responses may also come from Serlio, since it finds such a clear expression in the account of the bridge in

201. Porta Palio, Verona: inner façade

his book on fortifications—though Sanmicheli's connections with the Grimani family suggest that he may have got the ideas directly from Serlio's source, Cardinal Grimani.

Ten years later a similar approach seems to have been applied to the design of two gates for *the* city, Rome itself. The more famous is Michelangelo's Porta Pia (Fig. 203). This was first planned in 1561 as the inner face of a gate in the walls of Rome at the end of a broad street, the whole scheme being the idea of the reigning pope, Pius IV. The main portal—the only part certainly by Michelangelo—has always impressed by the freedom with which it combines Tuscan/Doric with rusticated masonry, and by the savagery of the face above the keystone. Ackerman has also pointed out how it resembles in its free composition some of the "rustic" portals published in the Libro Estraordinario.[15] Since the work stands out from Michelangelo's

generally conventional treatment of the orders on major monuments, we should expect it to relate to the specific requirements of the context. The closest analogy is provided by the recent Porta Palio, and if this is followed up the conclusion must be that Michelangelo intended the gate to be an introduction to the rustic and wild countryside outside the walls. The frightening face on the keystone in particular is a powerful warning that one is leaving a safe city for untamed nature. Attempts were repeatedly made to discourage members of the papal court from spending too much money building retreats in the country and too much time living in them when built. Pius IV had good reasons to deter people from leaving the city. He had just laid out the Via Pia leading up to the gate, in order to encourage building in that area within the walls and restore to it an urban character. The portal provided a stark statement of what lay beyond the elegant new thorough-

202. Michelangelo?: Porta del Popolo, Rome,
outer façade, c.1561

fare. The Porta Pia has no exterior façade, since no major road approaches it from the countryside; but at
exactly the same time Pius IV commissioned an outer
face for the Porta del Popolo, always the main entrance
to the city (Fig. 202). This consisted of two pairs of
Doric columns with correctly finished details. In its refinement it matches the outside of the Porta Palio, just
as the Porta Pia in its wild rusticity can be said to match
the Veronese gate's inner face. Many northern visitors

to Rome must have been dismayed to find that much
of the *urbs* had been invaded by *rus*. For Pius to reaffirm this distinction anew at the ancient walls could
only improve the city's image. The Porta del Popolo
announces to the traveller that he is entering a world of
order and refinement; the Porta Pia warns the citizen
that he is departing into a world of savage licence.

What makes the contrast between the two gates particularly telling is that both were probably planned not
just by the same patron but by the same designer. Vasari explicitly states that Michelangelo made drawings
for other Roman gates besides the Porta Pia,[16] and
strong evidence that he conceived at least the basic
scheme of the Porta del Popolo is provided by its similarity to the tomb of Pius IV's warrior brother, the
Marquis of Marignano, in Milan Cathedral. This too
was ordered by the pope, and again Vasari says that
Michelangelo was responsible for the original design;
although he passed on to Leone Leoni the responsibility for its execution, he was kept well informed of its
progress. If something similar happened in the case of
the Porta del Popolo, Michelangelo could have helped
the pope by determining the character of both structures, recognizing that symmetrical pairs of Doric columns were equally appropriate to the main gate in the
fortifications of Rome and to the tomb of the great general. The qualities of discipline, strength, and refinement which Pius attributed to his brother were precisely those he wished to claim for Rome and its
government under his pontificate. The chief reason
why Michelangelo's authorship of the Porta del Popolo
has been doubted is that it has been felt not to match
his personality. But Michelangelo's personality was
best expressed in the service of his patrons. Like those
who worked on other buildings we have seen, Michelangelo was employed above all because he was so good
at sensing what was required in a particular structure
in a particular context. He undoubtedly involved himself much more deeply in the design of the Porta Pia
than in that of the Porta del Popolo. The problem of
creating a gateway which, viewed from a distance,
would be a beautiful termination to a street but which,
when approached, would become a frightening and
disturbing warning of what was beyond presented a
greater challenge than that of designing one which was
intended to calm, to reassure, and to confirm expectations of arriving in a safe environment. The way that

203. Michelangelo: Porta Pia, Rome, inner façade, c.1561

the Porta del Popolo has soothed us into neglecting it while the Porta Pia has for centuries been a disturbing focus of attention shows how well both designs satisfied Pius' needs. These two gates demonstrate once again that a principal function of architectural ornament, and of the orders in particular, is to articulate the characters and values of individuals and institutions and to express and affect states of mind. What people do for themselves using their bodies and their faces, their gestures and their voices, those who build for them do using architectural forms. Pius IV could not himself stand at the gates of his city. Michelangelo made the gates speak for him.

It is appropriate to end with these two gates opening in different directions in sixteenth-century Rome, for they are also gateways in time. If we ignore the warning of the wild forms of the Porta Pia and pass through it northwards, and into the present, we will indeed en-

counter unpredictable forces and energies which have subverted the power of many institutions—including that of the orders. If we return southwards, through the regular Doric façade of the Porta del Popolo, we meet a changing sequence of authoritative columnar forms that lead back through three millennia to the Lion Gate at Mycenae. Together they form a colonnade which runs like a hard spine through the soft flesh of European history. Those who erected it, section by section, knew, consciously or unconsciously, that fundamental instincts would lead people to pay particular attention to columns and capitals. Aware of their own needs, and understanding the desires, anxieties, and uncertainties of others, they used architecture to develop a shared knowledge and to infuence ideas and actions. Columns carried culture. Our ancestors used changes in their shape and placing to find their way through life. This book is intended to help us relive their journeys.

Notes

◆

I. Classical Greece

For illustrations of most of the buildings referred to, see Dinsmoor (1975).

1. Herodotus, VII, 94.
2. Herodotus, I, 143.
3. Pollitt (1972), p. 79.
4. Thucydides, II, 41.
5. Thucydides, II, 39.
6. Thucydides, II, 40.
7. Thucydides, I, 12.
8. Thucydides, IV, 82.
9. Aristophanes, *Peace*, 46, and *Thesmophoriazousae*, 163.
10. Thucydides, I, 6.
11. Rykwert (1966), pp. 7–10.
12. Pollitt (1965), pp. 189–90.
13. Rykwert (1966), p. 8.
14. Pollitt (1965), p. 189.

II. The Hellenistic world and the Roman Republic

For illustrations of most of the Hellenistic buildings referred to, see Dinsmoor (1975); for those of Roman ones, see Boethius & Ward-Perkins.

1. Coulton (1976), p. 100.
2. Plato, *Laches*, 188d. For the background, see Anderson and Winnington-Ingram.
3. Onians (1979), pp. 17–94.
4. Aristotle, *Politics*, IV, 11.
5. Vitruvius, V, 1, 6.
6. Athenaeus, V, 40–44.
7. Ibid., V, 38–39.
8. Pliny the Elder, *Natural History*, 45.

III. Vitruvius

The best edition is that of Fensterbusch.

1. For a commentary on the text, see Ferri (1960). For the Hellenistic background to Vitruvius, see Schlikker.

2. Cicero, *De officiis*, I, 151.
3. Ritschl.
4. Vitruvius, VII, pref.
5. Plato, *Timaeus*, 286.
6. For an extended account of Vitruvian *decor* and its background, see Horn-Oncken, which is the fundamental treatment of the subject. For the background on *decorum*, see Labowsky.
7. Cicero, *Orator*, 70.
8. Cicero, *De oratore*, 3, 199. For the classification of rhetorical styles in Antiquity, see Quadlbauer.
9. Quintilian, X, 16ff.
10. Cicero, *Brutus*, 70.
11. Plato, *Republic*, 399, and *Laws*, 670.
12. Coulton (1976), p. 108 for Doric, and p. 120 for Ionic.
13. Aristotle, *Nicomachean Ethics*, II, 22b.

IV. The Roman Empire

For illustrations of most of the buildings discussed, see Boethius & Ward-Perkins and Nash.

1. See Nash, I, p. 164.
2. Alberti, *De re aedificatoria*, VII, 6.
3. Strong.
4. Livy, XXVI, 27.
5. Vitruvius, IV, 1, 3.
6. See preliminary reconstruction in Erim.
7. Suetonius, *Lives of the Caesars*, Augustus 28.
8. For examples, see the introductory passages of Pliny the Elder, *Natural History*, XXXIII, XXXV, and XXXVI.
9. See Nash, I, p. 478.
10. Petronius, *Satyricon*, 79.
11. An account of the decoration of the Pantheon can be found in Licht.
12. Discussed by Licht, p. 111.

V. Early Christianity

Most of the buildings discussed are illustrated in Krautheimer (1975) and (1937–77), and much information on the arrangement of shafts and capitals is to be found in Deichmann (1940).

1. See below, p. 72, and chapter V note 13.
2. Krautheimer (1980), p. 114.
3. Deichmann (1940).
4. Van der Meer & Mohrmann, p. 129.
5. Krautheimer (1969), pp. 181–96.
6. Van der Meer & Mohrmann, p. 129.
7. Gelasius Cyzicenus, *Historia Concilii Nicaeni*, in Migne, *P.G.*, LXXXV, col. 1232.
8. Eusebius, *Vita Constantini*, III, 37.
9. Ibid., IV, 60.
10. Mango, p. 87.
11. Ibid., pp. 57–60.
12. Theodoretus, *Historia ecclesiastica*, III, 25.
13. Ashby, p. 491.
14. Davis-Weyer, p. 11.
15. Ibid., p. 12.
16. Goldschmidt, *Carmen* 28, lines 307–13.
17. Günter, pp. 61–62.

VI. The column in the Christian Middle Ages

Most of the buildings discussed are described and illustrated in Heitz (1980), Conant, and Frankl (1962).

1. Hrabanus Maurus, *De universo*, in Migne, *P.L.*, CXI, cols. 9–614. For his background and influence, see Böhne and Heyse.
2. For an account of Pliny and his work, see Ziegler, Kroll, et al.
3. Pliny the Elder, *Natural History*, XXXVI, 56.
4. Isidori Hispalensis Episcopi *Etymologiarum sive originum libri XX*, ed.

W. M. Lindsay, Oxford 1911. For his
background, see Fontaine.

5. *Etymologiarum*, XV, 8, 13.

6. Ibid., XV, 8, 14–15.

7. Hrabanus Maurus, cols. 403–5.

8. See the interpretation of the cathedral of Tyre in Eusebius, *Ecclesiastical
History*, X, 4, 2–71.

9. Bede, *De Templo Salomonis liber*, in
Migne, *P.L.*, XCI, cols. 779–80.

10. Buchner, pp. 27ff.

11. Bandmann (1965), p. 452.

12. Ibid.

13. Ibid.

14. Kreusch, p. 478.

15. Schlosser (1892), p. 7.

16. Bloch, pp. 255–56.

17. Angilbert, *De restauratione mona-
sterii Centulensis*, in Migne, *P.L.*, XCIV,
col. 840.

18. Hariulf's *Chronicle*, in Davis-
Weyer, pp. 95–96.

19. Angilbert, *De restauratione*, in
Migne, *P.L.*, XCIV, col. 840.

20. Heitz (1980), pl. 41.

21. Schlosser (1892), p. 206.

22. Ibid., p. 95.

23. Davis-Weyer, p. 98.

24. Ibid., pp. 94–98.

25. Ermold le Noir, lines 892ff.

26. Heitz (1980), pp. 103ff.

27. *Vita Eigili*, in Migne, *P.L.*, CV, cols.
402ff.

28. Schlosser (1892), p. 184.

29. Ibid., p. 122.

30. Ibid., p. 206.

31. Lehmann, pp. 1–27, and L'Orange,
pp. 134–37.

32. Hrabanus Maurus, col. 399.

33. Beseler & Roggenkamp, pp. 110–
12.

34. Tschan, p. 273.

35. Ibid., p. 275.

36. Ibid., p. 415.

37. Bauchhenss.

38. Clemens Romanus, *Ad Corinthios
Epistula 5*, in Hefele, pp. 59–60.

39. Hrabanus Maurus, col. 394.

40. Ibid., col. 403.

41. Lehmann-Brockhaus, pp. 397ff.

42. Panofsky (1979), pp. 1–37.

43. Ibid., p. 104.

44. Ibid., pp. 18–21, and Simson,
passim.

45. Honorius of Autun, *Gemma Ani-
mae*, in Migne, *P.L.*, CLXXII, col. 586;
also ibid., cols. 316 and 407.

46. Sauer, pp. 134–35.

47. Martindale, pp. 79–84.

48. Mortet, vol. II, p. 239.

49. Ibid., vol. I, p. 398.

50. Panofsky (1979), p. 48.

51. Mango, pp. 57–60.

52. Hrabanus Maurus, col. 399.

53. Ibid.

VII. The orders in the Christian Middle Ages

Most of the buildings discussed are described and illustrated in Krautheimer
(1937–77), Heitz (1980), Conant, and
Frankl (1962).

1. Hubert et al., pp. 35–38 and passim.

2. Einhard's letter to Vussin in Schlosser (1892), pp. 6–7.

3. Ibid., p. 16.

4. Wirth, pp. 281 and 289.

5. Krinsky (1967), p. 56.

6. Schlosser (1892), p. 99.

7. For a discussion of this aspect of the
variation of capital and shaft in Medieval
Roman basilicas, see Malmstrom; and for
a similar variation in Romanesque and
Gothic churches, see Fernie.

8. Duby, passim.

9. Humbert, *Adversus Simoniacos*, in
Migne, *P.L.*, CXLIII, col. 1153.

10. Deichmann (1981). Unfortunately,
the capitals of the transverse arch in the
right transept are, incorrectly, reversed
throughout Deichmann's text.

11. Ibid., pp. 14ff.

12. For the problematic history of Pisa
Cathedral, see Boeck; for that of the Florence Baptistery, see Jacobsen.

13. It is possible that the colonnades
leading to the baptistery and the Holy
Cross chapel are an afterthought, but
this, if true, has not prevented their being
integrated into a coherent scheme.

14. Cahn (1973), p. 51.

15. Hugh of St Victor, *De Sacramentis*,
in Migne, *P.L.*, CLXXVI, col. 417.

16. Ibid., col. 441.

17. Honorius of Autun, *Speculum Ecclesiae*, in Migne, *P.L.*, CLXXII, col. 802.

18. Glass, p. 388.

19. Kubach & Haas, plate 1483.

20. See Cahn (1969) for other examples of such pairings in painting and
sculpture.

21. Rangerius, *Vita Anselmi*, lines
855ff.

22. Ibid., line 99.

23. Ibid., lines 5863ff.

24. Ibid., lines 5769ff.

25. Ibid., lines 4503ff.

26. Ibid., lines 4427ff.

27. Ibid., lines 2809ff.

VIII. The crisis of architecture: Medieval and Renaissance

1. For the general argument, see Onians (1980).

2. Davis-Weyer, p. 38.

3. Ibid.

4. See above, pp. 85–90.

5. Davis-Weyer, pp. 168–69.

6. Panofsky (1979), pp. 19–24.

7. Frisch, p. 33.

8. Ibid., p. 31.

9. Stubblebine, p. 107.

10. Ibid.

11. Ibid., p. 117.

12. For a more detailed argument,
see Onians (1984a).

13. For the earlier churches, see
Orlandi, tav. III.

14. This connection was pointed out
to me by Richard Trexler. See Trexler,
p. 62.

15. Aristotle, *Nicomachean Ethics*,
1122b; and Thomas Aquinas, *Summa
theologica*, IIa, IIae, qu. 134a.1–4, and
In decem libros ethicorum . . . expositio,
pp. 240–49.

16. See especially Braunfels.

17. Fiamma, cols. 997ff.

18. Ibid., col. 1010.

19. Ibid., col. 1011.

20. Ibid., col. 1012.

21. Ibid., col. 1014.

22. Ibid., col. 1015.

23. Salutati, *De seculo et religione*,
cap. 27.

24. Foffano publishes the letter with an
introduction.

25. Ibid., pp. 181–82.

26. Paredi, p. 80.

27. Foffano, p. 182.

28. Ibid., p. 186.

29. Ibid., p. 170.

30. Maffei, *In magnificentiae . . .*, discussed by Gombrich (1960) and Fraser-
Jenkins.

31. Wittkower, fig. 15a.

32. Pane, plate 213.

33. Bargellini, pp. 103–8.

34. Krautheimer (1937–77), vol. III, p. 188.

IX. The Tuscan Renaissance

Brunelleschi's buildings are described and illustrated in Battisti (1981), Michelozzo's in Morisani and in Ferrara & Quinterio. A wide range of recent views on Brunelleschi is presented in *Filippo Brunelleschi. La sua opera e il suo tempo* (Papers of the Convegno Internazionale di Studi Brunelleschiani, Florence 1977), two vols., Florence 1981. The author's own position was first presented at the Brunelleschi Symposium held at the Warburg Institute in 1977 and subsequently published in Onians (1982).

1. For a general review of the evidence for a Quattrocento revival of ancient architecture, see Burns (1971).
2. Filarete, fol. 59ʳ.
3. Rucellai, p. 55.
4. Manetti, passim.
5. Vasari, *Vite* (ed. Milanesi), II, pp. 327–87.
6. Manetti, p. 63.
7. For Brunelleschi and Romanesque, see Saalman (1958), Klotz, and Burns (1971). For his avoidance of Antique sources: "there is not a single major work of Brunelleschi for which a plausible and specific post-antique source or sources cannot be suggested" (Burns [1971], p. 277), and "his work contains no specific motifs derived directly from the antique" (Saalman, quoted Ibid., p. 284).
8. For this point of view, see Gombrich (1967), p. 80, and Burns (1971), p. 271.
9. Views on the antiquity of the Baptistery are discussed by Rubinstein and Wazbinski.
10. Rubinstein and Baron, passim.
11. Domenico da Prato, *Invettiva contra cierti calunniatori di Dante, Petrarca e Boccaccio*, quoted in Baron, pp. 282 and 520.
12. Baron, pp. 287 and 521.
13. Ibid., p. 336.
14. Ibid., pp. 336 and 533.
15. Migliorini, p. 254.
16. Brunelleschi, *Sonetti*.
17. Tanturli.
18. Billi, p. 315.
19. Quoted in Gombrich (1967), pp. 78–79.
20. E.g. Cennini, p. 5.

21. E.g. "lingua tusca," quoted in Brugnolo, vol. I, p. xxx.
22. E.g. Cennini, p. 5.
23. Quoted by Frankl (1960), p. 55.
24. Filarete, fol. 100ᵛ.
25. Manetti, p. 63.
26. Baron, passim.
27. Gombrich (1967), p. 79.
28. Alberti, *Della famiglia*, p. 161.
29. Grayson (1964).
30. Billi, p. 317.
31. This connection was pointed out to me by Diane Zervas. Brunelleschi's political connections are further discussed in Zervas (1984) and (1985).
32. Baron, pp. 332ff and 382ff.
33. Grayson (1972), pp. 32–33.
34. Rajna, pp. 1027–56.
35. Baron, pp. 353 and 539.
36. For this collaboration, see Lightbown.
37. Teubner, p. 249.
38. See above, pp. 103–105.
39. Panofsky (1935).

X. Alberti

References are to the edition by Orlandi, here cited as "Alberti (1966)."

1. A facsimile of the first edition is available in Lücke, and a reprint of Leoni's English translation from the Italian edition in Alberti (1955). For Alberti's thought, see Michel, Zubov (1937) and (1958), Grayson (1972), and Gadol. Part of this chapter originally appeared in Onians (1971).
2. Grayson (1960). See also Choay.
3. Krautheimer (1963).
4. Hrabanus, *De universo*, XIV, cap. 23.
5. Ibid.
6. Wittkower, pp. 20ff.
7. Ibid., p. 34.
8. Ackerman (1949), p. 98.
9. Isidore, *Etymologiae*, XV, i, 15.
10. Frisch, p. 35.
11. Alberti (1971), p. 160.
12. Vitruvius, I, 2.
13. Cicero, *De officiis*, I, 36.
14. Ibid., I, 39.
15. Ibid.
16. Ibid.
17. Ibid., II, 1.
18. Ibid., I, 4.
19. Cicero, *De oratore*, I, 42.
20. Cicero, *Orator*, IV, 16.

21. Pontanus, *De magnificentia*, fol. 128v.

XI. Filarete

1. Filarete's text is best presented in Filarete (1972). References are to the Florence MS published in facsimile, together with English translation and introduction, in Filarete (1965) by Spencer. A full account of Filarete's theories is found in Tigler. A more general study is Lazzeroni & Muñoz.
2. For a further development of this argument, see Onians (1971).
3. Panofsky (1970a), p. 105.
4. Borsa, pp. 48–49.
5. Legrand, p. 120.
6. Vasari, *Vite*, II, p. 457.
7. Tigler, p. 6.
8. For these arguments, see Onians (1973).
9. Compagni, *Chronicle*, in D.L., 151, 4.

XII. Francesco di Giorgio Martini

1. References are to the two volumes of Maltese's edition, here cited as "Martini." For a general account of Francesco di Giorgio, see Weller.
2. See Maltese in Martini, Betts, and Scaglia.
3. Martini, I, pp. xi–lxiv.
4. Rotondi, I, p. 109.
5. Piero della Francesca, *De prospectiva pingendi*, p. 63.
6. Lotz, pp. 193–226.
7. Martini, I, plate 21.
8. Llewellyn, p. 295, and Davies & Hemsoll, p. 8.

XIII. Architects and theories in the later fifteenth century

Alberti's buildings are described and illustrated in Borsi, and the rest in Heydenreich & Lotz.

1. See above, p. 127.
2. For the problem of the Palazzo Rucellai, see Preyer.
3. Wittkower, p. 35.
4. Heydenreich & Lotz, p. 355, n. 30.
5. Alberti, *De re aedificatoria*, IX, 3.
6. Ibid.
7. Ibid., IX, 5.
8. Pius II, pp. 282–86.

9. Ibid., p. 282.

10. Baron, pp. 353 and 539.

11. See Morselli & Corti.

12. See Sanpaolesi.

13. For these villas and the life associated with them, see Coffin.

14. Millon.

15. Martini, II, p. 398.

XIV. A new Christian architecture

For descriptions and illustrations of buildings outside Rome, see Heydenreich & Lotz. For those within the city, see Magnuson, Tomei, or Golzio & Zander.

1. See Westfall, passim.

2. The architectural descriptions are transcribed in Magnuson, pp. 351–62.

3. Ibid., p 361.

4. Ibid., p. 360.

5. Ibid., p. 361.

6. Ibid., p. 362.

7. Ibid.

8. Ibid.

9. Ibid.

10. Westfall, p. 19.

11. Golzio & Zander, plate LXXXIII.

12. Urban, pp. 73ff.

13. Pius II, pp. 286–87.

14. Ibid., p. 110.

15. Ibid., p. 250.

16. Tomei, p. 22.

17. See Onians (1980).

18. Krinsky (1970), p. 17. For the relation between the Sistine Chapel and the Temple of Solomon, see Battisti (1957).

19. See Golzio & Zander, plate CL.

20. Discussed in Partridge & Starn, p. 98, and in Tassinari.

XV. Francesco Colonna

1. The fundamental study is that of Casella & Pozzi. For the literary background, see also Colonna (1981), and for the architectural descriptions, Schmidt. A partial transcription and commentary is to be found in Bruschi et al. (1978). A full edition is provided in Colonna (1964).

2. Calvesi.

3. Casella & Pozzi, II, p. 9.

4. Aristides Quintilianus, *De musica*, I, 11.

5. Vitruvius, III, 3.

XVI. Luca Pacioli

1. The *De divina proportione* is most accessible in the edition of Winterberg, where it is accompanied by a German translation; references are to this edition. A partial improved transcription is available in Bruschi et al. (1978).

2. The copy of this manuscript in the Ambrosiana, Milan, was reproduced in facsimile as *Fontes Ambrosiani*, XXXI, edited by G. M. Biggiogero, Milan 1956.

3. For Leonardo's comparison of the arts, see Kemp, pp. 209–11.

4. Leonardo, MS A, fol. 99ʳ. Leonardo's manuscripts are conveniently presented in the edition and commentaries of Richter and Pedretti (see Bibliography under "Leonardo"). The secondary compilation, the Codex Urbinas 1270, is best presented in McMahon.

5. Leonardo, Cod. Atlant. 9Ca.

6. Leonardo, Cod. Urb. 2b; McMahon, chapter 17.

7. Leonardo, Cod. Urb. 4b; McMahon, chapter 11.

8. Leonardo, Cod. Urb. 15a; McMahon, chapter 28.

9. Leonardo, Cod. Urb. 16b, 19a; McMahon, chapters 39–41.

10. Leonardo, Cod. Urb. 17a; McMahon, chapter 44.

11. Leonardo, Cod. Urb. 18a; McMahon, chapter 26.

12. Gaffurio, *De harmonia*, fol. lxxxiiiᵛ.

13. Ibid.

14. Burke, p. 132.

15. Caretta et al., p. 114.

16. Leonardo, Cod. Urb. 14a; McMahon, chapter 33.

17. Leonardo, Windsor, 19037ᵛ.

18. Leonardo, Windsor, 19019ʳ.

19. Leonardo, Cod. Urb. 157a; McMahon, chapter 437.

XVII. Bramante

Most buildings are described and illustrated in Bruschi (1969, and English ed. 1977).

1. Alberti, *De re aedificatoria*, IX, 1.

2. Bruschi (1969), p. 295.

3. Leonardo, Cod. Urb. 10a; McMahon, chapter 40.

4. Leonardo, Cod. Urb. 10b; McMahon, chapter 40.

5. Leonardo, Cod. Urb. 18a; McMahon, chapter 41.

6. Gaffurio, *Practica musicae*, III, 10. For Gaffurio and architecture, see Verga.

7. Gaffurio, *De harmonia*, I, fol. xviiiiʳ.

8. Vasari, *Vite*, IV, p. 164.

9. For the Belvedere Court, see Ackerman (1954).

10. Serlio (1619), VII, p. 168.

11. Ibid., III, fol. 67ʳ.

12. Gombrich (1951), pp. 119–25.

13. Cesariano, fols. ivᵛ, lᵛ, lxxxviᵛ, lxxviiʳ, and lxxviiiʳ. For Cesariano in general, see Krinsky (1965).

14. Cesariano, fols. viiiʳ ff.

15. Ibid., fol. viiiᵛ.

16. Ibid., fol. ixʳ.

17. Ibid., fol. lxxxixʳ.

18. Ibid., fol. liiiᵛ.

19. Pacioli (ed. Winterberg), p. 41.

20. Kemp, pp. 196–98.

21. Cesariano, fol. lxxviiᵛ.

22. Förster, pp. 139–42.

23. Gaffurio, *De harmonia*, fol. lxxxiiiᵛ.

24. Ibid., fol. lxxxivᵛ.

25. Ibid., fols. lxxxiiiᵛ and lxxxivʳ.

26. See, already, Ignatius, *Letter to the Ephesians*, 4, Hefele, pp. 155–56; and Clement of Alexandria, *Protrepticus*, 9, 72.

27. Bruschi (1969), p. 1037.

28. For a discussion of rustication, see Heydenreich (1960).

29. For an extended treatment of this subject, see Onians (1985).

30. Frommel, p. 126.

31. Vasari, *Vite*, IV, p. 162.

32. Shearman (1972b), pp. 77–79.

33. Ibid., p. 80.

34. Buscaroli, pp. 155–56.

35. Ibid.

36. Panofsky (1935).

37. See above, pp. 143–45.

38. Villari & Casanova, Sermon XXIII.

39. Doni, p. 55.

XVIII. Raphael

For a general account of Raphael as an architect, see Ray.

1. Shearman (1967).

2. Reprinted with Raphael's other writings in Golzio (1971). A shortened English version is available in Holt.

3. Golzio (1971), p. 92.

4. Gaffurio, *De harmonia*, fol. lxxxviiʳ.

5. See, most recently, Najemy.

6. Golzio (1971), p. 92.

7. Shearman (1972b), p. 58, n. 149.

8. Shearman (1961), p. 143, n. 64.

9. Shearman (1972a), p. 22.

10. Cortese, passim.

11. Fulvius, *Antiquitates*, fol. 96ᵛ.

12. Golzio (1971), p. 91.

13. See, most recently, Shearman (1972b), p. 125.

XIX. Serlio

1. The fundamental account of Serlio's activity is Dinsmoor (1942). The first attempt to take him seriously was Argan. The most recent studies are the introductions to Serlio by Rosci and Rosenfeld, in the editions here cited as "Serlio (1966)" and "Serlio (1979)" respectively. References here to the printed books are to Serlio (1619).

2. For Serlio's copyrights, see Howard (1973).

3. For the history of these plates, see Zerner.

4. See Serlio (1966) and (1979).

5. Munich, Staatsbibliothek, Cod. Icon. 190. Discussed in Marconi, and recently the subject of a Ph.D. dissertation by June Johnson, University of California at Los Angeles, 1984.

6. Cellini, p. 798.

7. Burns (1987).

8. Günther (1988).

9. Olivato (1971) and (1979). See also Günther (1981).

10. Ackerman (1983).

11. Gombrich (1934) and (1935).

12. Cesariano, fol. lxxxiiiᵛ.

13. The importance of Serlio's use of architectural style in those blocks was first pointed out by Panofsky (1970b), p. 234, n. 60.

XX. Serlio's Venice: Sansovino, Aretino, Titian, and Vasari

1. The fundamental accounts of Sansovino's buildings on the Piazzetta are in Howard (1975) and Tafuri.

2. An attempt to do this occupies the first part of the author's Ph.D. dissertation, Onians (1968).

3. Sansovino (1556) and (1581).

4. Aretino, *Lettere*, I, pp. 82–83. For English versions of selected letters, see Bull.

5. Vasari, *Vite*, VII, pp. 502–4.

6. Aretino, *Lettere*, I, pp. 82–83 (see note 4 above).

7. Howard (1975), p. 163, n. 34.

8. Aretino: see note 6 above.

9. Sansovino (1565), fols. 25ᵛ and 26ʳ.

10. Sansovino (1581), fols. 115ʳ⁻ᵛ.

11. Serlio (1619), IV, fol. 126ᵛ.

12. Ibid., IV, fol. 133ᵛ.

13. Aretino, I, pp. 67–69, also reprinted at the front of the first edition of Serlio's Book IV (1537).

14. Aretino: see note 6 above.

15. Sansovino (1581), fol. 113ʳ.

16. Ibid.

17. Aretino: see note 6 above.

18. Sansovino (1565), fols. 21ᵛ and 23ᵛ.

19. Serlio (1619), IV, fol. 175ʳ.

20. Ibid., V, fol. 203ʳ.

21. Vasari, *Vite*, VII, p. 501.

22. Uffizi A 5282.

23. See above, p. 119.

24. Aretino, I, p. 71. For the house itself, see Schulz.

25. Aretino, I, p. 125.

26. Ibid., II, p. 127.

27. Ibid., I, p. 97.

28. Ibid., I, p. 213.

29. Ibid., I, pp. 49–50.

30. Ibid., I, pp. 101–5.

31. For the general interest in *giudicio*, see Summers, pp. 368ff.

32. Dolce, *L'Aretino . . .* , p. 44.

33. Michiel, p. 84.

34. Jacobus de Voragine, *The Golden Legend*, p. 523. For an alternative commentary on the painting, see Rosand (1976).

35. Ridolfi, I, p. 172.

36. Vasari, *Vite*, VII, p. 503.

37. For an alternative view of this material, see Summers, pp. 158–59.

38. Panofsky (1970a), pp. 262–65.

39. Vasari, *Vite*, I, p. 146.

40. See Summers, pp. 332ff.

XXI. Sixteenth-century choices

1. Burns (1975), p. 144.

2. Pirri (1955), p. 162.

3. Ibid., tav. IV.

4. Ibid., tav. XVIII a.

5. Wittkower, p. 157.

6. Burns (1975), p. 149.

7. Algeri, tav. IX.

8. Pirri (1955), tav. XXXIV.

9. Gorse provides the most recent account of the palace and its decoration.

10. Poleggi describes and illustrates the palaces.

11. Gorse.

12. Kinney, pp. 150–72.

13. Ibid., pp. 134–49.

14. Hartt, plates 415–17.

15. Ackerman (1970), p. 226.

16. Vasari, *Vite*, VII, p. 260.

Bibliography

◆

Ackerman, J. S. (1949). "Ars sine scientia nihil est: Gothic Theory of Architecture at the Cathedral of Milan," *Art Bulletin*, 31 (1949), pp. 84–111.

———— (1954). *The Cortile del Belvedere*, Vatican City 1954.

———— (1966). *Palladio*, Harmondsworth 1966.

———— (1970). *The Architecture of Michelangelo*, revised ed., London 1970 (originally two vols., London 1964 and 1966).

———— (1983). "The Tuscan/Rustic Order: A Study in the Metaphorical Language of Architecture," *Journal of the Society of Architectural Historians*, 42 (1983), pp. 25–34.

Alberti, L. B. (1955). *Ten Books of Architecture*, translated by James Leoni from the Italian translation of Cosimo Bartoli, reprinted with notes by J. Rykwert, London 1955.

———— (1966). *L'architettura*, Latin text of *De re aedificatoria* with Italian translation and notes by G. Orlandi and introduction by P. Portoghesi, two vols., Milan 1966.

———— (1971). *The Albertis of Florence: Leon Battista Alberti's Della famiglia*, trans. with intro. and notes by G. A. Guarino, Lewisburg, Pa., 1971.

Algeri, G. "Alessi in Umbria," in *Galeazzo Alessi e l'architettura del Cinquecento*, Genoa 1975, pp. 193–201.

Anderson, W. D. *Ethics and Education in Greek Music*, Cambridge, Mass., 1966.

Aquinas, Saint Thomas. *Summa theologica*, Turin 1922.

————. *In decem libros ethicorum Aristotelis ad Nicomachum expositio*, Turin 1934.

Aretino, P. *Lettere sull'arte di Pietro Aretino*, ed. F. Pertile and C. Cordie, two vols. Milan 1957 and 1958.

Argan, G. C. "Sebastiano Serlio," *L'Arte*, 35 (1932), pp. 183–99.

Aristides Quintilianus. *De musica libri tres*, ed. R. P. Winnington-Ingram, Leipzig 1963.

Ashby, T. *A Topographical Dictionary of Ancient Rome*, London 1929.

Bandmann, G. (1951). *Mittelalteriche Architektur als Bedeutungsträger*, Berlin 1951.

———— (1965). "Die Vorbilder der Aachener Pfalzkapelle," *Karl der Grosse*, III, 1965, pp. 424–62.

Bargellini, P. *San Bernardino da Siena*, Brescia 1959.

Baron, H. *The Crisis of the Early Italian Renaissance*, Princeton 1966.

Battisti, E. (1957). "Il significato simbolico della Cappella Sistina," *Commentari*, 1957, pp. 96–104.

———— (1981). *Brunelleschi: The Complete Work*, London 1981.

Bauchhenss, G. *Jupitergigantsäulen*, Stuttgart 1977.

Baxandall, M. *Painting and Experience in Fifteenth Century Italy*, Oxford 1972.

Beseler, H., & H. Roggenkamp. *Die Michaelskirche in Hildesheim*, Berlin 1954.

Betts, R. "On the Chronology of Francesco di Giorgio's Treatises: New Evidence from an Unpublished Manuscript," *Journal of the Society of Architectural Historians*, 36 (1977), pp. 3–4.

Białostocki, J. "Das Modusproblem in den bildenden Künsten," in J. Białostocki, *Stil und Ikonographie: Studien zur Kunstwissenschaft*, Dresden 1960, pp. 9–35.

Billi, A. *Il libro di Antonio Billi*, ed. E. von Fabriczy, Florence 1981 (reprinted Farnborough 1969).

Bloch, P. "Das Apsismosaik von Germigny des Près," *Karl der Grosse*, III, 1965, pp. 234–61.

Blunt, A. F. *Artistic Theory in Italy 1450–1600*, Oxford 1964.

Boeck, U. "Der Pisaner Dom zwischen 1089 und 1120," *Architectura*, 1981, pp. 1–30.

Boethius, A., & J. B. Ward-Perkins. *Etruscan and Roman Architecture*, Harmondsworth 1970.

Böhne, W. *Hrabanus Maurus und seine Schule*, Fulda 1980.

Borsa, M. "Pier Candido Decembrio e l'umanesimo in Lombardia," *Archivio Storico Lombardo*, 20 (1893), pp. 5–75.

Borsi, F. *Leon Battista Alberti*, London 1971.

Braunfels, W. *Mittelalterliche Stadtbaukunst in der Toskana*, Berlin 1953.

Brugnolo, F. "Il canzoniere di Nicolo de' Rossi," *Medioevo e umanesimo*, 16, Padua 1974, vols. I and II.

Brunelleschi, F. *Sonetti . . .*, intro. G. Tanturli, Florence 1977.

Bruschi, A. (1969). *Bramante Architetto*, Bari 1969 (condensed English version, London 1977).

Bruschi, A., et al. (1978). *Scritti rinascimentali di architettura*, Milan 1978.

Buchner, M. *Einhard als Künstler*, Strassburg 1919.

Bull, G. *Select Letters of Aretino*, Harmondsworth 1976.

Burke, P. *Culture and Society in Renaissance Italy 1420–1560*, London 1972; revised ed., *The Italian Renaissance: Culture and Society in Italy*, London and Princeton 1987.

Burns, H. (1971). "Quattrocento Architecture and the Antique: Some Problems," in *Classical Influences on European Culture A.D. 500–1500*, ed. R. R. Bolgar, Cambridge 1971, pp. 269–87.

———— (1975). "Le idee di Galeazzo Alessi sull'architettura e gli ordini," in *Galeazzo Alessi e l'architettura del Cinquecento*, Genoa 1975, pp. 147–66.

———— (1987). "Peruzzi," in Guillaume.

Buscaroli, R., *Melozzo e il Melozzismo*, Bologna 1955.

Cahn, W. (1969). "The Tympanum of the Portal of Saint Anne at

Notre Dame de Paris and the Iconography of the Division of Powers in the Middle Ages," *Journal of the Warburg and Courtauld Institutes*, 32 (1969), pp. 55–77.

———— (1973). "Solomonic Elements in Romanesque Art," in J. Gutmann, *The Temple of Solomon*, Ann Arbor 1973.

Calvesi, M. *Il Sogno del Polifilo prenestino*, Rome 1980.

Caretta, A., L. Cremascoli, & L. Salamina. *Franchino Gaffurio*, Lodi 1951.

Casella, M. T., & G. Pozzi. *Francesco Colonna. Biographia e opere*, two vols., Padua 1959.

Cellini, B. *La Vita di Benvenuto Cellini sequita dai trattati dell'oreficeria e della scultura e dagli scritti sull'arte*, ed. A. J. Rusconi and A. Valeri, Rome 1901.

Cennini, C. *Il libro dell'arte*, Vicenza 1971.

Cesariano, C. *Vitruvius De architectura*, Italian trans. with commentary, Como 1521 (facsimile ed., London 1968).

Charlemagne: see below, *Karl der Grosse*.

Choay, F. "Alberti and Vitruvius," *Architectural Design*, 1979, pp. 26–35.

Ciapponi, L. A. "Il 'De architectura' di Vitruvio nel primo umanesimo," *Italia Medioevale e Umanistica*, 3 (1960), pp. 59–99.

Coffin, D. *The Villa in the Life of Renaissance Rome*, Princeton 1979.

Colonna, F. (1499). *Hypnerotomachia Poliphili*, Venice 1499.

———— (1964). *Hypnerotomachia Poliphili*, ed. G. Pozzi and L. Ciapponi, two vols., Padua 1964.

———— (1981). *Hypnerotomachia Poliphili*, intro. by Peter Dronke, Zaragoza 1981.

Conant, K. J. *Carolingian and Romanesque Architecture 800–1200*, Harmondsworth 1959.

Cortesius, P. *Libri tres de cardinalatu*, Castro Cortesio 1510.

Coulton, J. J. (1976). *The Architectural Development of the Greek Stoa*, Oxford 1976.

———— (1977). *Ancient Greek Architects at Work. Problems of Structure and Design*, Ithaca, N.Y., 1977.

Crinito, P. *De honesta disciplina* (1504), reprinted and ed. C. Angeleri, Rome 1955.

Davis-Weyer, C. *Early Medieval Art. Sources and Documents*, Englewood Cliffs, N.J., 1971.

De Fusco, R. *Il Codice dell'architettura*, Antologia di Trattatisti, Naples 1968.

Deichmann, F. W. (1940). "Säule und Ordnung in der frühchristlichen Architektur," *Mitteilungen des Deutschen Archäologischen Institute Rom*, 55 (1940), pp. 114ff.

———— (1981). *Corpus der Kapitellen in San Marco zu Venedig*, Wiesbaden 1981.

Dinsmoor, W. B. (1942). "The Literary Remains of Sebastiano Serlio," *Art Bulletin*, 24 (1942), pp. 55–91, 115–54.

———— (1975). *The Architecture of Ancient Greece*, New York 1975.

Dolce, L. *L'Aretino: Dialogo della pittura . . .* , Venice 1557.

Doni, A. F. *La seconda libraria*, Venice 1555.

Duby, G. *Les trois ordres ou l'imaginaire du féodalisme*, Paris 1978.

Erim, K. "Ancient Aphrodisias Lives through Its Art," *National Geographic*, October 1981, pp. 526–51.

Ermold le Noir, *Poème sur Louis le Pieux et épître au Roi Pepin*, ed. and trans. E. Faral, Paris 1932.

Ettlinger, L. D. *The Sistine Chapel before Michelangelo*, Oxford 1965.

Fensterbusch, C. *Vitruv, Zehn Bücher über Architektur*, Darmstadt 1964.

Fernie, E. C. "The Use of Varied Nave Supports in Romanesque and Early Gothic Churches," *Gesta*, 23 (1984), pp. 107–17.

Ferrara, M., & F. Quinterio. *Michelozzo di Bartolomeo*, Florence 1984.

Ferri, S. (1946). *Plinio il Vecchio, Storia delle arti antiche*, text, translation, and notes, Rome 1946.

———— (1960). *Vitruvi De Architectura quae pertinent ad disciplinas archaeologicas selegit recensuit vertit adnotationibus instruxit*, Rome 1960.

Fiamma, G. *Opusculum de rebus gestis ab Azone, Luchino et Johanne Vicecomitibus*, in *Rerum Italicarum Scriptores*, ed. L. Muratori, XII, part 4, pp. 1ff.

Filarete (1965). *Treatise on Architecture*, facsimile of Florence, Bibl. Naz. MS Magl. II, IV, 140, transl. and intro. by J. Spencer, New Haven and London 1965.

———— (1972). *Trattato di architettura*, ed. A. M. Finoli and L. Grassi, two vols., Milan 1972.

Foffano, T. "Castiglione Olona in un opuscolo di F. Pizzolpasso," *Italia Medioevale e Umanistica*, 3 (1960), pp. 173–87.

Fontaine, J. *Isidore de Seville et la culture classique dans l'Espagne Visigothique*, Paris 1959.

Forssman, E. (1956). *Säule und Ornament*, Stockholm 1956.

———— (1961). *Dorisch Ionisch Korintisch. Studien über das Gebrauch der Säulenordnungen in der Architektur des 16.–18. Jahrhunderts*, Stockholm 1961.

Förster, C. H. *Bramante*, Munich and Vienna 1956.

Francesco di Giorgio: see below, Martini.

Frankl, P. (1960). *The Gothic*, Princeton 1960.

———— (1962). *Gothic Architecture*, Harmondsworth 1962.

Fraser-Jenkins, A. D. "Cosimo de' Medici's Patronage of Architecture and the Theory of Magnificence," *Journal of the Warburg and Courtauld Institutes*, 33 (1970), pp. 162–70.

Frisch, T. *Gothic Art. Sources and Documents*, Englewood Cliffs, N.J., 1974.

Frommel, C. L. "Die Peterskirche unter Papst Julius II in Licht neuer Dokumente," *Römisches Jahrbuch für Kunstgeschichte*, 16 (1976), pp. 58–136.

Fulvius, A. *Antiquitates urbis*, Rome 1527.

Gadol, J. *Leon Battista Alberti: Universal Man of the Early Renaissance*, Chicago and London 1973.

Gaffurio, F. (1496). *Practica musicae*, Milan 1496.

———— (1518). *De harmonia musicorum instrumentorum*, Milan 1518.

Gelasius Cyzicenus, *Historia Concilii Nicaeni*, in Migne, *P.G.*, LXXXV.

Germann, G. *Einführung in die Geschichte der Architekturtheorie*, Darmstadt 1980.

Glass, D. "Papal Patronage in the Early Twelfth Century: Notes on the Iconography of Cosmatesque Pavements," *Journal of the Warburg and Courtauld Institutes*, 32 (1969), pp. 386–90.

Goldschmidt, R. C. *Paulinus' Churches at Nola*, Amsterdam 1940.

Golzio, V. (1971). *Raffaello nei documenti nelle testimonianze dei contemporanei e nella letteratura del suo secolo*, Vatican City 1971.

Golzio, V., & G. Zander. *L'arte in Roma nel secolo XV*, Bologna 1968.

Gombrich, E. H. (1934, 1935). "Zum Werke Giulio Romano's," *Jahrbuch der Kunsthistorischen Sammlungen in Wien*, N.S., 8 (1934), pp. 70–104, and 9 (1935), pp. 121–50.

—— (1951). "Hypnerotomachiana," *Journal of the Warburg and Courtauld Institutes*, 14 (1951), pp. 122–25.

—— (1960). "The Early Medici as Patrons of Art: A Survey of Primary Sources," in *Italian Renaissance Studies*, ed. E. F. Jacob, London 1960, pp. 279–311.

—— (1967). "From the Revival of Letters to the Reform of the Arts," *Essays in the History of Art presented to Rudolf Wittkower*, London 1967, pp. 71–82.

—— (1979). *The Sense of Order*, Oxford 1979.

Gorse, G. L. "The Villa Doria in Fassolo, Genoa," Ph.D. diss., Brown University 1980; University Microfilms 1981.

Gould, C. "Sebastiano Serlio and Venetian Painting," *Journal of the Warburg and Courtauld Institutes*, 25 (1962), pp. 56–64.

Grayson, C. (1960). "The Composition of L. B. Alberti's Decem libri de re aedificatoria," *Münchner Jahrbuch der Bildenden Kunst*, 11 (1960), pp. 152–61.

—— (1964). *Leon Battista Alberti: la prima grammatica*, Bologna 1964.

—— (1972). *L. B. Alberti, on Painting and Sculpture*, ed. with introduction, translations, and notes, London 1972.

Guillaume, J. (ed.). *Les traités d'architecture de la Renaissance*, Paris 1988.

Günter, R. *Wand, Fenster und Licht in der Trierer Palastaula und in spätantiken Bauten*, Herford 1968.

Günther, H. (1981). "Studien zum venezianischen Aufenthalt des Sebastiano Serlio," *Münchner Jahrbuch für Kunstgeschichte*, 32 (1981), pp. 42–94.

—— (1988). "Il terzo libro del Serlio," in Guillaume.

Hartt, F. *Giulio Romano*, two vols., New Haven 1958.

Hefele, C. *Patrum Apostolicum opera*, Tübingen 1855.

Heitz, C. (1963). *Recherches sur les rapports entre architecture et liturgie è l'époque Carolingienne*, Paris 1963.

—— (1980). *L'architecture religieuse Carolingienne*, Paris 1980.

Hersey, G. *Pythagorean Palaces, Magic and Architecture in the Italian Renaissance*, Ithaca, N.Y., 1976.

Heydenreich, L. H. (1960). "Il Bugnato rustico nel Quattro- e nel Cinquecento," *Bolletino del Centro Internazionale di Studi di Architettura Andrea Palladio*, 2 (1960), pp. 40ff.

Heydenreich, L. H., & W. Lotz. *Architecture in Italy 1400 to 1600*, Harmondsworth 1974.

Heyse, E. *Hrabanus Maurus' Enzyclopädie "De rerum naturis": Untersuchungen zu den Quellen und zur Methode der Kompilation*, Munich 1969.

Holt, E. G. *A Documentary History of Art*, vol. I, Garden City, N.Y., 1957 (reprinted Princeton 1981).

Honorius of Autun, *Speculum Ecclesiae*, in Migne, *P.L.*, CLXXII.

Horn-Oncken, A. *Ueber das Schickliche. Studien zur Geschichte der Architekturtheorie*, Göttingen 1967.

Howard D. (1973). "Sebastiano Serlio's Venetian Copyrights," *Burlington Magazine*, 115 (1973), pp. 512–16.

—— (1975). *Jacopo Sansovino. Architecture and Patronage in Renaissance Venice*, New Haven 1975.

Hrabanus Maurus. *De universo*, in Migne, *P.L.*, CXI, cols. 9–614.

Hubert, J., J. Porcher, & W. F. Volbach. *Carolingian Art*, London 1970.

Hugh of St Victor. *De sacramentis*, in Migne, *P.L.*, CLXXVI.

Isidore of Seville. *Isidori Hispalensis Episcopi Etymologiarum sive originum libri XX*, ed. W. M. Lindsay, Oxford 1911.

Jacobsen, W. "Zur Datierung des Florentiner Baptisterium's S. Giovanni," *Zeitschrift für Kunstgeschichte*, 43 (1980), pp. 225–43.

Jacobus de Voragine. *The Golden Legend*, trans. G. Ryan and H. Ripperger, London and Toronto 1941.

Karl der Grosse. Lebenswerk und Nachleben, ed. W. Braunfels, three vols., Düsseldorf 1965.

Kemp, M. *Leonardo da Vinci, the Marvellous Works of Nature and Man*, London 1981.

Kinney, P. *The Early Sculpture of Bartolomeo Ammanati*, New York 1976.

Klotz, H. *Die Frühwerke Brunelleschi's und die mittelalterliche Tradition*, Berlin 1970.

Krautheimer, R. (1937–77). *Corpus Basilicarum Christianarum Romae*, with W. Frankl and S. Corbett, vols. I–V, 1937–77.

—— (1963). "Alberti and Vitruvius," *Studies in Western Art: Acts of the Twentieth International Congress of the History of Art*, II: *The Renaissance and Mannerism*, Princeton 1963, pp. 42–52.

—— (1969). "Alberti's Templum Etruscum," in *Studies in Early Christian Medieval and Renaissance Art*, New York and London 1969, pp. 65–72.

—— (1975). *Early Christian and Byzantine Architecture*, Harmondsworth 1975.

—— (1980). *Rome: Profile of a City 312–1308*, Princeton 1980.

Kreusch, R. "Kirche, Atrium und Portikus der Aachener Pfalz," *Karl der Grosse*, III, 1965, pp. 463–533.

Krinsky, C. H. (1965). "Cesare Cesariano and the Como Vitruvius Edition of 1521," Ph.D. diss., New York University 1965.

—— (1967). "Seventy-eight Vitruvian Manuscripts," *Journal of the Warburg and Courtauld Institutes*, 30 (1967), pp. 36–70.

—— (1970). "Representations of the Temple of Jerusalem before 1500," *Journal of the Warburg and Courtauld Institutes*, 33 (1970), pp. 1–19.

Kubach, H., & W. Haas. *Der Dom zu Speyer*, two vols., Darmstadt 1972.

Labowsky, L. *Die Ethik des Panaitos. Untersuchungen zur Geschichte des Decorum bei Cicero und Horaz*, Leipzig 1937.

Lazzeroni, M., & A. Muñoz. *Filarete scultore e architetto del secolo XV*, Rome 1980.

Legrand, E. (ed.). *Cent-dix lettres grecques de François Filelfe . . .*, Paris 1892.

Lehmann, K. "The Dome of Heaven," *Art Bulletin*, 27 (1945), pp. 1–27.

Lehmann-Brockhaus, O. *Schriftquellen zur Kunstgeschichte des 11. und 12. Jahrhunderts für Deutschland, Lothringen und Italien*, Berlin 1938 (reprinted Hildesheim and New York 1971).

Leonardo da Vinci. *The Literary Works of Leonardo da Vinci*, ed. J. P. Richter, two vols., London and New York 1970; with *Commentary* by C. Pedretti, two vols., Oxford 1977.

Licht, K. de F. *The Rotunda in Rome*, Copenhagen 1968.

Lightbown, R. *Donatello and Michelozzo*, two vols., London 1980.

Llewellyn, N. "Two Notes on Diego da Sagredo," *Journal of the Warburg and Courtauld Institutes*, 40 (1977), pp. 292–300.

L'Orange, H. P. *Studies in the Iconography of Cosmic Kingship*, New Rochelle, N.Y., 1982.

Lotz, W. "Das Raumbild in der Italienischen Architekturzeichnung der Renaissance," *Mitteilungen des Kunsthistorischen Instituts Florenz*, 7 (1956), pp. 193–226.

Lücke, H. K. *Alberti Index*, four vols., Munich 1975–76.

Maffei, T. *In magnificentiae Cosmi Medicei Florentini detractores*, in C. Lami, *Deliciae Eruditorum*, XII, Florence 1745.

Magnuson, T. *Studies in Roman Quattrocento Architecture*, Rome 1958.

Malmstrom, R. "The Colonnades of High Medieval Churches in Rome," *Gesta*, 14 (1975), pp. 37–45.

Manetti, A. di Tuccio. *The Life of Brunelleschi*, ed. H. Saalman, trans. C. Enggass, University Park, Pa., and London 1970.

Mango, C. A. *The Art of the Byzantine Empire 312–1453: Sources and Documents*, Englewood Cliffs, N.J., 1972.

McMahon, A. P. (trans. and ed.). *Treatise on Painting by Leonardo da Vinci*, two vols., Princeton 1956.

Marconi, P. "Un progetto di città militare, l'VIIIº libro inedito di Sebastiano Serlio," *Controspazio*, 1 (1969), part I, no. 1, pp. 51–59, and part II, no. 3, pp. 53–59.

Martindale, A. *The Rise of the Artist*, London 1972.

Martini, Francesco di Giorgio. *Trattati di architettura, ingegneria e arte militare*, ed. C. Maltese, two vols., Milan 1967.

Michel, P. H. *Un idéal humain au XVᵉ siècle: la pensée de L. B. Alberti 1404–72*, Paris 1930.

Michiel, M. *Der Anonimo Morelliano*, Vienna 1888 (reprinted Hildesheim and New York 1974), pp. 2–118.

Migliorini, B. *Storia della lingua italiana*, Florence 1960.

Migne, J. P. (*P.G.*). *Patrologia Graeca . . .*, Paris 1857ff.

——— (*P.L.*). *Patrologia Latina . . .*, Paris 1842ff.

Millon, H. "The Architectural Theory of F. di Giorgio," *Art Bulletin*, 40 (1958), pp. 257–61.

Morselli, P., & G. Corti. *La chiesa di Santa Maria delle Carceri in Prato*, Florence 1982.

Mortet, V. *Recueil des textes relatifs à l'histoire de l'architecture et à la condition des architectes en France au moyen âge*, XIᵉ–XIIᵉ siècles, two vols., Paris 1911 and 1929.

Najemy, J. M. " 'Arti' and 'Ordini' in Machiavelli's *Istorie*, " in *Essays presented to Myron P. Gilmore*, vol. I, Florence 1978, pp. 161–91.

Nash, E. *Pictorial Dictionary of Ancient Rome*, two vols., London 1968.

Olivato, L. (1971). "Per il Serlio a Venezia, documenti nuovi e documenti rivisitati," *Arte Veneta*, 25 (1971), pp. 284–91.

——— (1979). "Dal teatro della memoria al grande teatro dell'architettura: Giulio Camillo Delminio e Sebastiano Serlio," *Bolletino del Centro Internazionale di Studi di Architettura Andrea Palladio*, (1979), pp. 223–52.

Onians, J. B. (1968). "Style and Decorum in Sixteenth-Century Italian Architecture," Ph.D. diss., London University 1968.

——— (1971). "L. B. Alberti and Φιλαρετη," *Journal of the Warburg and Courtauld Institutes*, 34 (1971), pp. 96–114.

——— (1973). "Filarete and the 'qualità': Architectural and Social," *Arte Lombarda*, 38–39 (1973), pp. 116–28.

——— (1979). *Art and Thought in the Hellenistic Age*, London 1979.

——— (1980). "The Last Judgement of Renaissance Architecture," *Journal of the Royal Society of Arts*, 128 (1980), pp. 701–720.

——— (1982). "Brunelleschi: Humanist or Nationalist," *Art History*, 5 (1982), pp. 259–72.

——— (1984a). "S. Maria Novella and the Meaning of Gothic," in *Studi in onore di Roberto Salvini*, Florence 1984, pp. 143–47.

——— (1984b). "On How to Listen to High Renaissance Art," *Art History*, 7 (1984), pp. 411–37.

——— (1985). "Storia dell'architettura e storia della religione: Bramante, Raffaello e Baldassare Peruzzi," in *Rome e l'antico nell'arte e nella cultura del Cinquecento*, Rome 1985, pp. 131–48.

——— (1988). "The System of the Orders in Renaissance Architectural Thought," in Guillaume, pp. 162–67.

Orlandi, S. *Necrologio di S. Maria Novella*, vol. I, Florence 1955.

Pacioli, L. *Divina proportione* (from Venetian edition of 1509), ed. and trans. C. Winterberg, Vienna 1889.

Pane, R. *Il Rinascimento nell'Italia meridionale*, I, Milan 1975.

Panofsky, E. (1935). "The Friedsam Annunciation," *Art Bulletin*, 17 (1935), pp. 449ff.

——— (1953). *Early Netherlandish Painting*, two vols., Cambridge, Mass., 1953.

——— (1970a). "The History of the Theory of Human Proportions as a Reflection of the History of Styles," in *Meaning in the Visual Arts*, Harmondsworth 1970, pp. 82–138.

——— (1970b). "The First Page of Giorgio Vasari's 'Libro,' " in *Meaning in the Visual Arts*, Harmondsworth 1970, pp. 206–265.

——— (1979). *Abbot Suger on the Abbey Church of St. Denis and Its Art Treasures*, Princeton 1979.

Paredi, A. *La biblioteca del Pizzolpasso*, Milan 1961.

Partridge, L., & R. Starn. *A Renaissance Likeness: Art and Culture in Raphael's Julius II*, Berkeley, Calif., 1980.

Pedretti, C. "Note sulla cronologia del 'Trattato della pittura' di Leonardo," *L'Arte*, 1960, pp. 3–91.

Pellati, F. "Vitruvio nel Medio Evo e nel Rinascimento," *Bolletino del Reale Istituto di Archeologia e Storia dell'Arte*, 5 (1932), pp. 15–36.

Pellegrin, E. *La bibliothèque des Visconti et des Sforza ducs de Milan au XVᵉ siècle*, Paris 1955.

Piero della Francesca. *De prospectiva pingendi*, ed. G. Nicco Fasola, Florence 1942.

Pirri, P. (1955). *Giovanni Tristano e i primordi della architettura gesuitica*, Rome 1955.

————— (1970). *Giuseppe Valeriano S.I. architetto e pittore 1542–1596*, Rome 1970.

Pius II (Aeneas Sylvius Piccolomini). *Memoirs of a Renaissance Pope. The Commentaries of Pius II*, trans. F. A. Gragg, London 1960.

Pliny the Elder: see above, Ferri (1946).

Poleggi, E. *Strada Nuova*, Genoa 1972.

Pollitt, J. J. (1965). *The Art of Greece: Sources and Documents*, Englewood Cliffs, N.J., 1965.

————— (1972). *Art and Experience in Classical Greece*, Cambridge 1972.

Pontanus, J. *De magnificentia*, in *Opera*, vol. I, Venice 1518, fols. 123ff.

Prater, A. *Michelangelo's Medici-Kapelle: ordine composto als Gestaltungsprinzip von Architektur und Ornament*, Waldsassen-Bayern 1979.

Preyer, B. "The Rucellai Palace," *A Florentine Patrician and His Palace*, Studies of the Warburg Institute, 24, II, London 1981, pp. 155–228.

Quadlbauer, R. F. *Die Genera dicendi bis Plinius den Jüngeren*, Vienna 1958.

Rajna, P. "Le origini del certame coronario," in *Scritti in onore di R. Renier*, Turin 1912, pp. 1027–56.

Rangerius. *Vita Anselmi Lucensis Episcopi auctore Rangerio*, in *Monumenta Germaniae Historica. Scriptores XXX*, 2, Leipzig 1934, pp. 1152–1307.

Ray, S. *Raffaello architetto*, Bari 1974.

Ridolfi, C. *Le meraviglie dell'arte* (Venice 1648), ed. D. von Hadeln, two vols., Berlin 1914 and 1924.

Ritschl, F. G. *De M. Terentii Varronis Disciplinarum libris commentarius*, Bonn 1845.

Robertson, D. *A Handbook of Greek and Roman Architecture*, Cambridge 1945.

Rosand, D. (1976). "Titian's *Presentation of the Virgin in the Temple* and the Scuola della Carità," *Art Bulletin*, 58 (1976), pp. 55–84.

————— (ed.)(1982). *Titian, His World and His Legacy*, New York 1982.

Rotondi, P. *Il Palazzo Ducale di Urbino*, two vols., Urbino 1950.

Rubinstein, N. "Vasari's Painting of *The Foundation of Florence* in the Palazzo Vecchio," in *Essays in the History of Architecture presented to Rudolf Wittkower*, London 1967, pp. 64–73.

Rucellai, G. *Giovanni Rucellai ed il suo Zibaldone*, vol. I, London 1960.

Rykwert, J. (1966). "The Corinthian Order," *Arena*, 1966, pp. 7–10.

————— (1982). "On the Oral Transmission of Architectural Theory," *Res*, 3 (1982), pp. 68–81.

Saalman, H. (1958). "Filippo Brunelleschi: Capital Studies," *Art Bulletin*, 40 (1958), pp. 115ff.

————— (1959). "Early Renaissance Architectural Theory and Practice in Antonio Filarete's *Trattato di architettura*," *Art Bulletin*, 41 (1959), pp. 89–106.

Salutati, C. *De seculo et religione*, ed. B. L. Ullman, Florence 1957.

Sanpaolesi, P. "Il Palazzo di Bartolommeo della Scala," in *Toskanische Studien. Festschrift für Ludwig H. Heydenreich*, Munich 1963.

Sansovino, F. (1556, 1565). *Dialogo di tutte le cose notabili che sono in Venetia . . .* , pseudonymous first ed., Venice 1556; edition used here, F. Sansovino, *Delle cose notabili che sono in Venetia*, Venice 1565.

————— (1581). *Venetia città nobilissima et singolare*, Venice 1581.

Sauer, J. *Symbolik des Kirchengebäudes und seiner Ausstattung in der Auffassung des Mittelalters. Mit Berücksichtigung von Honorius Agostudensis, Sicardus und Durandus*, Freiburg im Breisgau 1924.

Scaglia, G. "Autour de Francesco di Giorgio Martini, ingénieur et dessinateur," *Revue de l'Art*, 48 (1980), pp. 7–25.

Schlikker, F. W. *Hellenistische Vorstellungen von der Schönheit des Bauwerks*, Münster 1940.

Schlosser, J. von (1892). *Schriftquellen zur Geschichte der Karolingischen Kunst*, Vienna 1892 (reprinted Hildesheim and New York 1974).

————— (1964). *Le Letteratura Artistica*, ed. O. Kurz, Florence and Vienna 1964.

Schmidt, D. *Untersuchungen zu den Architekturekphrasen in der Hypnerotomachia poliphili*, Frankfurt am Main 1978.

Schulz, J. "The Houses of Titian, Aretino and Sansovino," in Rosand (1982), pp. 73–118.

Serlio, S. (1619). *Tutte l'opere d'architettura et prospettiva di Sebastiano*, Venice 1619 (reprinted 1964).

————— (1966). *Sesto libro delle abitationi di tutti li gradi degli huomini*, vol. I (facsimile of Munich MS), vol. II (*Il trattato*), ed. M. Rosci, Milan 1966.

————— (1979). *Serlio's Sixth Book: On Domestic Architecture* (facsimile of Columbia University MS), with introduction and commentary by W. N. Rosenfeld, Boston 1979.

Shearman, J. G. (1961). "The Chigi Chapel in S. Maria del Popolo," *Journal of the Warburg and Courtauld Institutes*, 24 (1961), pp. 129–60.

————— (1967). "Raphael . . . 'fa il Bramante,' " in *Studies in Renaissance and Baroque Art presented to Anthony Blunt*, London and New York 1967, pp. 12ff.

————— (1968). "Raphael as Architect," *Journal of the Royal Society of Arts*, 116 (1968), pp. 338ff.

Shearman, J. G. (1972a). "The Vatican Stanze. Functions and Decorations," British Academy Italian Lecture, London 1972 (also in *Proceedings of the British Academy*, 67 [1971], pp. 369–424).

———— (1972b). *Raphael's Cartoons in the Collection of Her Majesty the Queen*, London 1972.

Simson, O. von. *The Gothic Cathedral*, New York and London 1956 (reprinted Princeton 1983).

Strong, D. "Some Observations on Early Roman Corinthian," *Journal of Roman Studies*, 53 (1963), pp. 73–84.

Stubblebine, J. H. *Giotto: The Arena Chapel Frescoes*, London 1969.

Summers, D. *Michelangelo and the Language of Art*, Princeton 1981.

Summerson, J. *The Classical Language of Architecture*, London 1964.

Tafuri, M. *Jacopo Sansovino e l'architetettura del '500 a Venezia*, Padua 1969.

Tanturli, G. "Rapporti del Brunelleschi con gli ambienti letterari Fiorentini," in *Filippo Brunelleschi. La sua opera e il suo tempo*, two vols., Florence 1980, pp. 125–44.

Tassinari, M. "Osservationi su Giovanni Mazone," *Argomenti di storia dell'arte*, ed. Corrado Maltese, Genoa 1980.

Teubner, H. "San Marco in Florenz: Umbauten vor 1500. Ein Beitrag zum Werk des Michelozzo," *Mitteilungen des Kunsthistorischen Instituts in Florenz*, 23 (1979), pp. 239–72.

Thoenes, C. " 'Spezie' e 'ordine' di colonne nell'architettura del Brunelleschi," in *Filippo Brunelleschi. La sua opera e il suo tempo*, two vols., Florence 1980, pp. 459–69.

Tigler, P. *Die Architekturtheorie des Filarete*, Berlin 1963.

Tomei, P. *L'architettura a Roma nel Quattrocento*, Rome 1942.

Trexler, R. *Public Life in Renaissance Florence*, New York and London 1980.

Tschan, F. *Saint Bernward of Hildesheim*, vol. III, *His Works of Art*, South Bend, Indiana, 1951.

Urban, G. "Die Kirchenbaukunst des Quattrocento in Rome," *Römisches Jahrbuch für Kunstgeschichte*, 9–10 (1961–62), pp. 73-287.

Van der Meer, F., & C. Mohrmann. *Atlas of the Early Christian World*, London 1959.

Vasari, G. *Le Vite de' più eccellenti pittori, scultori ed architettori scritte da Giorgio Vasari pittore Aretino*, ed. G. Milanesi, nine vols., Florence 1906 (reprinted Florence 1981).

Verga, G. "Francesco Gaffurio e Giambattista Caporali: due umanisti tra musica e architettura," *Archivio Storico Lodigiano*, 1964, pp. 18–26.

Vignola, G. Barozzi da. *Regola delle cinque ordini*, Rome 1562.

Villari, P., & E. Casanova. *Scelta di prediche e scritti di Fra Girolamo Savonarola*, Florence 1898.

Vitruvius: see above, Cesariano, Fensterbusch, and Ferri (1960).

Wazbinsky, Z. "Le polemiche intorno al Battistero Fiorentino nel Cinquecento: le loro premesse e il loro significato," in *Filippo Brunelleschi. La sua opera e il suo tempo*, two vols., Florence 1980, pp. 16–22.

Weller, A. *Francesco di Giorgio*, Chicago 1943.

Westfall, C. W. *In this most perfect Paradise*, University Park, Pa., and London 1974.

Wiebenson, D. (ed.). Architectural Theory and Practice from Alberti to Ledoux, Charlottesville, Va., 1982.

Winnington-Ingram, R. P. *Mode in Ancient Greek Music*, Cambridge 1936.

Winternitz, E. *Leonardo da Vinci as a Muscian*, New Haven and London 1982.

Wirth, P. "Bemerkungen zum Nachleben Vitruvs im 9. und 10. Jahrhundert und zu dem Schlettstädter Vitruv-codex," *Kunstchronik*, 20 (1967), pp. 281–91.

Wittkower, R. *Architectural Principles in the Age of Humanism*, London 1962.

Zerner, H. "Les illustrations des traités," in Guillaume.

Zervas, D. (1984). "The Parte Guelfa Palace, Brunelleschi and Antonio Manetti," *Burlington Magazine*, 126 (1984), pp. 494–99.

———— (1985). *The Parte Guelfa, Donatello and Brunelleschi*, Locust Valley, N.Y., 1985.

Ziegler, K., W. Kroll et al. "C. Plinius Secundus der Ältere," *Paulys-Wissowa, Realencykopädie*, vol. XXI, 1951, cols. 271–439.

Zubov, V. P. (1935, 1937). *Leon Battista Alberti, De re aedificatoria*, two vols. (I: *Tekst*; II: *Materialy i commentarii*), Moscow 1935 and 1937.

———— (1958). "Leon Battista Alberti et les auteurs du moyen âge," *Mediaeval and Renaissance Studies*, 4 (1958), pp. 245–66.

Index

◆